Revolution on the Hudson

Revolution

ON THE

HUDSON

★

NEW YORK CITY AND THE HUDSON RIVER VALLEY IN THE AMERICAN WAR OF INDEPENDENCE

George C. Daughan

W. W. Norton & Company
Independent Publishers Since 1923
New York   London

For information about permission to reproduce selections from this book,
write to Permissions, W. W. Norton & Company, Inc.,
500 Fifth Avenue, New York, NY 10110

For information about special discounts for bulk purchases, please contact
W. W. Norton Special Sales at specialsales@wwnorton.com or 800-233-4830

Manufacturing by Quad Graphics Fairfield
Book design by Daniel Lagin Design
Production manager: Julia Druskin

Library of Congress Cataloging-in-Publication Data

Names: Daughan, George C., author.
Title: Revolution on the Hudson : New York City and the Hudson River Valley
   in the American War of Independence / George C. Daughan.
Description: First edition. | New York : W. W. Norton & Company, 2016. |
   Includes bibliographical references and index.
Identifiers: LCCN 2016007017 | ISBN 9780393245721 (hardcover)
Subjects: LCSH: New York (State)—History—Revolution, 1775-1783. | Hudson
   River Valley (N.Y. and N.J.)—History, Military—18th century. | New York
   (N.Y.)—History—Revolution, 1775-1783.
Classification: LCC E230.5.N4 D38 2016 | DDC 974.7/3—dc23 LC record available at
http://lccn.loc.gov/2016007017

W. W. Norton & Company, Inc.
500 Fifth Avenue, New York, N.Y. 10110
www.wwnorton.com

W. W. Norton & Company Ltd.
Castle House, 75/76 Wells Street, London W1T 3QT

1 2 3 4 5 6 7 8 9 0

To Kay, with love

Contents

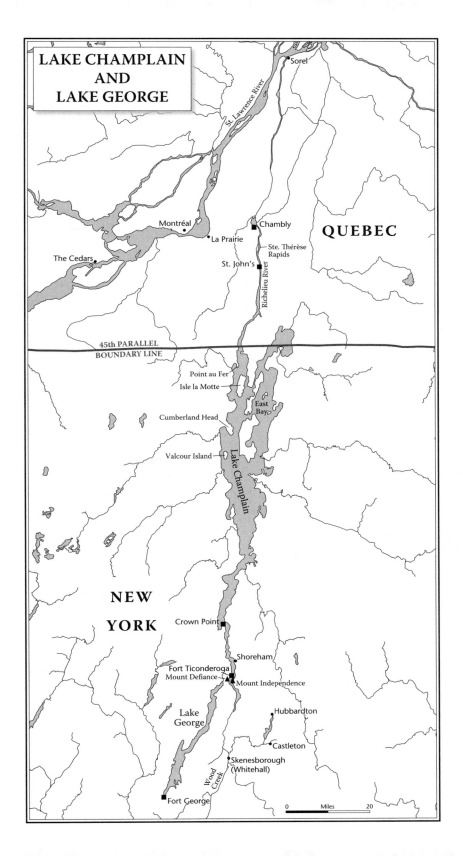

LAKE CHAMPLAIN
AND
LAKE GEORGE

Sorel

St. Lawrence River

Montréal

La Prairie

Chambly

Ste. Thérèse
Rapids

St. John's

The Cedars

QUEBEC

Richelieu River

45th PARALLEL
BOUNDARY LINE

Point au Fer

Isle la Motte

East
Bay

Cumberland Head

Valcour Island

Lake Champlain

NEW

YORK

Crown Point

Shoreham

Fort Ticonderoga
Mount Defiance

Mount Independence

Hubbardton

Lake
George

Castleton

Skenesborough
(Whitehall)

Wood Creek

Fort George

0   Miles   20

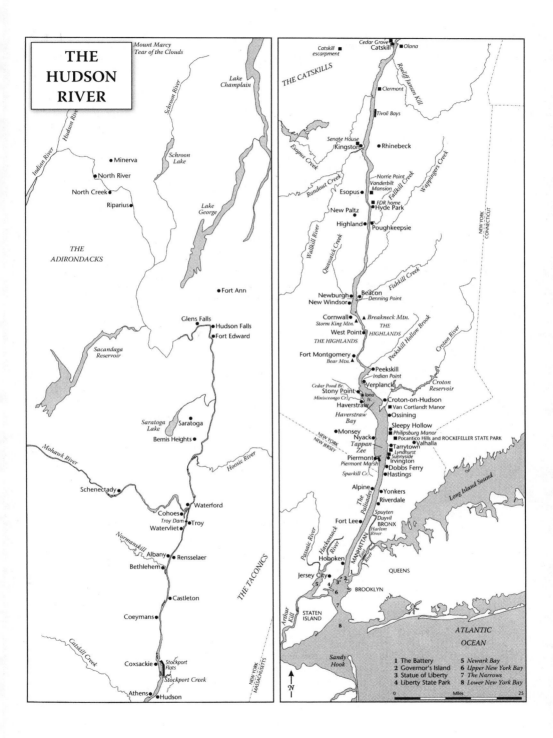

THE
HUDSON
RIVER

THE ADIRONDACKS

Mount Marcy
Tear of the Clouds

Hudson River

Schroon River

Lake Champlain

Indian River

• Minerva

• North River

Schroon Lake

North Creek •

Riparius •

Lake George

THE ADIRONDACKS

• Fort Ann

Glens Falls •
• Hudson Falls
• Fort Edward

Sacandaga Reservoir

Saratoga Lake
Saratoga •
Bemis Heights •

Mohawk River

Hoosic River

Schenectady •

Cohoes •   • Waterford
Troy Dam
Watervliet •   • Troy

Normanskill

Albany •   • Rensselaer
Bethlehem •

THE TACONICS

• Castleton

Coeymans •

Catskill Creek

Coxsackie •   Stockport Flats
Stockport Creek

Athens •   • Hudson

NEW YORK
MASSACHUSETTS

THE CATSKILLS

Catskill escarpment
Cedar Grove   Olana
Catskill

Clermont •

Roeliff Jansen Kill

Tivoli Bays

Esopus Creek

Senate House
Kingston •   • Rhinebeck

Rondout Creek   Norrie Point
Vanderbilt Mansion
Esopus •

Wappingers Creek

Falkill Creek

FDR home
New Paltz •   Hyde Park

Highland •   • Poughkeepsie

Wallkill River   Quassick Creek

NEW YORK
CONNECTICUT

Fishkill Creek

Newburgh •   Beacon
New Windsor   Denning Point

Cornwall •   ▲ Breakneck Mtn.
Storm King Mtn.   THE HIGHLANDS
West Point •
THE HIGHLANDS   Peekskill Hollow Brook

Croton River

Fort Montgomery •
Bear Mtn. ▲

• Peekskill
Indian Point   Croton Reservoir
Verplanck
Cedar Pond Br.
Stony Point •   • Iona Is.
Minisceongo Cr.   Croton-on-Hudson
Haverstraw •   Van Cortlandt Manor

Haverstraw Bay   Ossining •

Monsey •   Sleepy Hollow
Nyack •   Philipsburg Manor
Tappan   Pocantico Hills and ROCKEFELLER STATE PARK
Zee   Valhalla
Piermont •   Tarrytown
Piermont Marsh   Lyndhurst
Sunnyside
Sparkill Cr.   Irvington
• Dobbs Ferry
• Hastings

NEW YORK
NEW JERSEY

Long Island Sound

Alpine •   • Yonkers
• Riverdale

The Palisades

Spuyten Duyvil
Fort Lee •   BRONX
Harlem River

Passaic River   Hackensack River   MANHATTAN

Hoboken •

Jersey City •   QUEENS

1 · 3 · 2
5   4
6   BROOKLYN
7

STATEN ISLAND

Arthur Kill

8

ATLANTIC OCEAN

Sandy Hook

1 The Battery   5 Newark Bay
2 Governor's Island   6 Upper New York Bay
3 Statue of Liberty   7 The Narrows
4 Liberty State Park   8 Lower New York Bay

N

0   Miles   25

Magnanimity in politics is not seldom the truest wisdom.

—EDMUND BURKE

Mankind will at length, as they call themselves reasonable creatures, have reason and sense enough to settle their differences without cutting throats.

—BENJAMIN FRANKLIN

Revolution on the Hudson

Introduction

S ize, location, an extensive harbor, sophisticated port facilities, and a large population put Manhattan and the Hudson River at the center of the War of Independence. Not only was New York City and its environs one of the most vibrant urban centers in America, it was also the beginning of a unique watery highway that extended deep into the interior of the continent, linking Manhattan with Quebec. Navigable water ran nearly the entire way from New York Harbor to the mouth of the St. Lawrence River. The only significant interruptions were the few miles of land connecting the Hudson with Lake George: the boisterous three-and-a-half-mile La Chute River that emptied Lake George into Lake Champlain—what Native Americans called "the place between the waters"—and the ten miles of rapids on the Richelieu River between Saint-Jean and Chambly.

To anyone looking at a map in London, this striking sea-land corridor appeared to form a natural boundary between New England, the epicenter of the revolt, and the less militant colonies to the south. Since the Royal Navy was the unquestioned mistress of the sea, and Britain already possessed Canada, it looked to George III and his advisors that by seizing the passageway connecting Manhattan with Canada they could isolate New England's radicals, destroy them, and end the rebellion in a single campaign season.

That season was to be 1776. After failing in 1775 to crush the revolt in Massachusetts with a tiny army, His Majesty decided to go all out in 1776 and send the largest amphibious force ever assembled to seize Manhattan. His armada would then use it as a base from which to push north up the Hudson River Valley for a grand rendezvous at Albany with an impressive army driving down from Canada under General Guy Carleton via the St. Lawrence, the Richelieu, Lake Champlain, Lake George, and the Hudson.

As the king imagined it, the junction of the two armies would isolate New England and leave it vulnerable. From Albany the combined forces—over twenty thousand strong—would invade Massachusetts, Connecticut, New Hampshire, and Rhode Island, radically altering the political landscape. Once New England Loyalists saw Britain's awesome power, His Majesty was convinced they would flock to his banner, as would political fence-sitters, while rebels would be cowed. He expected that radicals in the Mid-Atlantic and the South would then lose heart and return to their allegiance.

Without being fully aware of it, the king was making three critical assumptions. The first was the capacity of the Royal Navy to impose a tight blockade along the entire New England coast, while at the same time supporting an amphibious force pushing up the Hudson River Valley and the one marching from Canada. He also assumed that the navy could maintain a continuous presence all along the Hudson, as well as provide support for permanent posts that the army would be establishing at key points along the route linking New York and Canada. Belief in the prowess of the navy was such that its ability to perform this outsized task was never questioned.

The second assumption concerned colonial politics, which His Majesty studied carefully, albeit with little understanding. He had long since concluded that the armies he was sending up the Hudson and down from Canada would meet with enthusiastic support along the way. He felt that most Americans—including New Englanders—understood the unique benefits a great empire provided, and were generally loyal to him. They only needed a strong military presence to regain power in their provinces from the tiny coterie of radicals who had usurped them.

The third assumption was that Britain could accomplish her objectives through military means alone. Since the king believed that Loyalists were already the majority, there was no need, in his view, to offer any concessions to win over the rest of the colonists. All His Majesty had to do was crush a vocal, self-aggrandizing minority. Brandishing the sword appeared to be the quick way to victory.

Although isolating New England from the rest of the colonies seemed to be the perfect strategy, it unaccountably failed in 1776. Blame was placed on poor execution, however, not on the concept. Convinced that he was right, the stubborn monarch employed the same approach, with modifications, in 1777. When his plan failed again, the culprit was deemed to be, once more, poor implementation, not the strategy. In fact, since the king's armies never actually met at Albany in either year, the theory continued to fascinate and attract because it was never really tested.

The entrance of France into the war in 1778 forced George III to drastically revise his overall strategy. Instead of focusing on New York, he shifted emphasis to the West Indies and the South. New York City would still be the principal base of operations, but British efforts would now be directed mainly at the southern provinces, which were thought to be easier to conquer and control.

In spite of this change, fascination with seizing the Hudson River Valley as a fast way to end the conflict persisted and had a profound effect on the rest of the war, becoming, in the end, one of the principal reasons Britain's military effort failed. Indeed, the idea was so powerful it did not die when the war ended. It became one of the enduring myths embedded in all accounts of the Revolution. Students of the war, without exception, took it for granted that British control of the Hudson–

Lake Champlain corridor was possible, and that it would have severed New England from the rest of the colonies, with fatal results for the rebellion. The fact that no armies ever met at Albany, that the idea was only a hypothesis, helped give it a long life.

The great naval historian Admiral Alfred Thayer Mahan was as attached to the theory as every other scholar. He argued that the strategy would have worked had it been executed properly. "The difficulties in the way of moving up and down such a stream [the Hudson]," he wrote, "were doubtless much greater to sailing vessels than they now are to steamers; yet it seems impossible to doubt that active and capable men wielding the great sea power of England could so have held that river and Lake Champlain with ships-of-war at intervals and accompanying galleys as to have supported a sufficient army moving between the headwaters of the Hudson and the lake, while themselves preventing any intercourse by water between New England and the states west of the river."

Probably the most important reason historians accepted the viability of the king's strategy was that George Washington and every other patriot leader shared His Majesty's fixation with the Hudson. They were just as certain as he was that Britain was capable of seizing the Hudson–Champlain corridor and that, if she did, New England would be cut off and the rebellion ended.

On December 2, 1777, Washington sent a letter to Major General Israel Putnam ("Old Put") explaining the strategic significance of the Hudson as if it were obvious. "The importance of the North [Hudson] River in the present contest," he wrote, "and the necessity of defending it, are subjects which have been so frequently and so fully discussed, and are so well understood, that it is unnecessary to enlarge upon them. These facts at once appear, when it is considered that it runs through a whole state; that it is the only passage by which the enemy from New York, or any part of our coast, can ever hope to cooperate with an army from Canada; that the possession of it is indispensably essential to preserve the communication between the eastern, middle, and southern states; and further, that upon its security, in a great measure, depend our chief supplies of flour for the subsistence of such forces, as we may have occasion for, in the course of the war, either in the eastern or northern departments, or in the country lying high up on the west side of it."

Thomas Jefferson agreed. He wrote that the loss of the province of New York would "cut off all communication between the northern and southern colonies and which effected would ruin America." John Adams was equally strong in his opinion. He famously wrote to Washington explaining that "the North [Hudson] River is the nexus of the northern and southern colonies, as a kind of key to the whole continent, as it is a passage to Canada, to the Great Lakes, and to all the Indian Nations. No effort to secure it ought to be omitted." Washington's biographer Douglas Southall Freeman, reflecting the views of other historians, called the Hudson "the jugular of America, the severance of which meant death."

Although scholars and practitioners generally shared Mahan's opinion that only the absence of "active and capable" men accounted for the failure of the king's grand plan, a careful examination of the part that the strategy actually played in the War of Independence reveals something quite different. It shows that the king's theory was unsuccessful, not because it wasn't implemented properly but because it was seriously flawed. None of its underlying assumptions were true. It was never possible to cut off New England from the rest of the colonies. The Royal Navy never had the capacity to dominate—at the same time and in all weather—the waterways between Manhattan and Canada, while simultaneously maintaining a tight blockade of the New England coast. Nor could the navy protect, on a continuing basis, the outposts Britain intended to build in order to maintain control of the corridor. Moreover, the notion that most of the American people were with His Majesty was a fantasy, as was the idea that military power alone could secure and preserve British rule without strong political support.

Even though the notion that Britain could control the Hudson–Champlain corridor was an illusion, the fact that both sides believed she could, and that it would lead to a quick victory, continued to have a powerful influence throughout the war. A close study of events and personalities shows that from the invasion of New York in 1776 to the final defeat of the British at Yorktown, the Hudson–Champlain fantasy made a major contribution to frustrating His Majesty's quest to keep the American colonies within the empire.

Chapter 1

GEORGE III DECLARES
WAR ON AMERICA

During the final week of June 1776 the long-awaited British invasion of New York began. Lookouts on the high ground at Navesink, New Jersey, and at Todt Hill, on Staten Island, signaled Washington's headquarters in Manhattan that dozens of transports, victuallers, storeships, and men-of-war were approaching Sandy Hook, the narrow, six-mile-long barrier peninsula guarding the entrance to New York's Lower Bay—the gateway to the city. One hundred ten enemy vessels had arrived by June 30, and hundreds more were on the way.

The twenty-eight-gun frigate HMS *Greyhound* led the parade of hostile ships, arriving on June 25 with forty-six-year-old General William Howe, the commander in chief, and his suite aboard. The general's mistress, twenty-four-year-old Elizabeth Loring, and her husband, Joshua, were not far behind, sailing with Vice Admiral Molyneux Shuldham, the naval chief, aboard his 50-gun flagship, HMS *Chatham*. Even though the invasion was the most important undertaking of

General Howe's career, he saw no need to forgo his personal pleasure while carrying it out.

Mr. Loring's reward for not creating a fuss about his wife's notorious liaison with the commander in chief was appointment to the lucrative post of commissary general of military prisoners. Assisting him as provost marshal would be his former colleague in Boston, the raging sadist William Cunningham. They were well known as the heartless duo in charge of the thirty-one prisoners taken at Bunker Hill the previous year. Within a few weeks, twenty of the prisoners died of starvation or diseases caused by malnutrition. Their jailers sold most of the prisoners' food before it ever got to them, and pocketed the money. No one expected their behavior to be any different in New York.

The dark record of his jailers held scant interest for General Howe. He was preoccupied with the daunting task of defeating the American army on its own turf and suppressing the rebellion before Christmas. The colonial troubles that had bedeviled the kingdom since the end of the Seven Years' War in 1763 had reached a crisis point. Ever since the spring of 1775, when provincial militiamen had administered stunning defeats to British arms at Lexington and Concord (April), Fort Ticonderoga (May), Crown Point (May), Fort George (May), Lake Champlain (May), Machias, in the Maine District of Massachusetts (June), and Bunker Hill (June), the king and his first (prime) minister, Frederick North, 2nd Earl of Guilford, had felt an urgent need to develop a new strategy or risk losing the colonies altogether.

On July 26, 1775, twenty-four hours after receiving the shocking news of General Howe's Pyrrhic victory at Bunker Hill, an exasperated Lord North told the king that enough was enough; the fighting had grown to a point where "it must be treated as a foreign war, and . . . every expedient which would be used in the latter case should be applied in the former."

The king needed no prodding. Using the full force of the empire to crush the American malcontents seemed to him the only feasible course left. For the past decade and more, other palliatives had been tried and had failed; now was the time for sterner measures. He was convinced that if left unchecked, the colonial revolt would unravel an empire that was not only larger than Rome at its height but the most progressive in history. He was not going to let that happen. The constitutional subordination of the parts to the center in London was essential, he believed, to the well-being of the whole. The maintenance of order and harmony required the empire's diverse elements to accept Parliament's supremacy unconditionally, particularly with respect to taxation.

Most of the tiny coterie of aristocrats—fewer than four hundred—who ruled Great Britain agreed with the king. Ever since the Boston Tea Party on December 16, 1773, a strong current of anti-American feeling had been running in their rarefied circles. They had no intention of sharing power with lower-class colonial radicals. If the king attempted to chart a different course than massive repression, he would have met serious parliamentary opposition, even though he had long since obtained control of the legislature on most matters through an elaborate system of favors and bribes.

In the months following Bunker Hill, His Majesty approved measures that, taken together, amounted to a declaration of war on the thirteen original colonies. Lord North, who in theory possessed great power as first lord of the Treasury, titular head of the ministry, and leader of the House of Commons, might have charted a different course had a real opportunity presented itself. Although North consistently used his impressive parliamentary skills to pass every harsh piece of legislation that His Majesty and the ministry directed at the colonies, he appeared at times to be open to a negotiation. But given the political sentiments of Britain's elite, who seemed to actually welcome a war, he found it impossible to shape any conciliatory measures that could obtain the assent both of recalcitrant colonists and their English masters.

While the king and his supporters were preparing for all-out war, patriots were trying to avoid one. On July 5, 1775, the Continental Congress approved the Olive Branch Petition, pleading for a dialogue to restore "harmony" in the king's dominions. The petition affirmed the colonial attachment to "His Majesty's person, family, and government, with all the devotion that principle and affection can inspire."

Many members did not agree with these sentiments, of course. The time for humbly asking the king to listen, they believed, had passed. John Adams urged defiance, and so did his cousin Samuel Adams, who warned, "It is folly to supplicate a tyrant." Nonetheless, when the time came, they signed the petition in the interest of solidarity.

Neither of them felt it mattered. They were confident the petition would fall on deaf ears, which it did. His Majesty was not interested in a parley; he had made up his mind a long time ago to fight. He even refused to officially receive the petition. Entering into talks with an illegal, unrepresentative body like the Continental Congress, he thought, was exactly the wrong thing to do. Colonies should always be dealt with separately, never as part of an association. If an unrepresentative group of radicals was ever allowed to negotiate with the august British monarch, the entire empire would be at risk. There was no need to treat with them; they were just noisy demagogues with thin support in the population.

The king issued a royal proclamation on August 23, 1775, formally committing Britain to "suppress" with massive force the revolt spreading in America. He insisted that since "many of his subjects" were engaged in "open and avowed rebellion," it was his duty "to bring the traitors to justice." Two months later, on October 26, 1775, in a speech opening Parliament, he reaffirmed his bellicose stance. "The rebellious war now levied is become more general," he declared, "and is manifestly carried on for the purpose of establishing an independent empire." He assured members he would never let that happen.

The king's wrath was on full display on October 18, 1775, at Falmouth (now Portland), in the Maine District of Massachusetts, where four warships set fire to the entire town. Under orders from Vice Admiral Samuel Graves, Shuldham's predecessor as the commander of the North American squadron in Boston, a four-ship task force under Lieutenant Henry Mowat fired incendiaries into the defenseless city, turning it into a gigantic ball of flame. Terrified townspeople fled into the cold countryside to escape the holocaust.

Admiral Graves was the same officer who, with the approval of

Major General Howe, burned Charlestown (a town older than Boston) during the fighting at Bunker (actually Breed's) Hill on June 17. The king and his supporters viewed both brutal acts as effective ways to bring dissident colonists to heel.

A short time after the destruction of Falmouth, Congress received word of the king's refusal to receive the Olive Branch Petition, and, even more outrageous, of his plans to hire thousands of German mercenaries to help put down the rebellion. His Majesty obviously preferred repression to dialogue.

The far-reaching Prohibitory Act soon followed, on December 22. It aimed at nothing less than shutting down America's economy. The Royal Navy was instructed to seize any colonial vessel found engaged in commerce and to impress its sailors. In addition, the navy was ordered to attack any foreign vessel attempting to trade with the colonies, "as if the same were the ships and effects of open enemies." The act also empowered the crown to send commissioners to receive submissions and grant pardons. Benjamin Franklin considered the noxious law His Majesty's reply to the Olive Branch Petition. Lord North easily guided the powerful legislation through Parliament. When word of its contents reached New York on February 27, 1776, John Adams characterized it as "a complete dismemberment of the British Empire."

On May 23, 1776, as the time for the invasion of New York approached, the king reiterated his belligerent stance, as well as his unquestioned confidence in British arms. He told Parliament that subduing the colonial revolution was "a great national cause. . . . The essential rights and interests of the whole empire are deeply concerned in the issue. I am convinced that you will not think any price too high for the preservation of such objects." He assured members that he would "effectuate [the subordination of his subjects] by a full exertion of the great force with which you have entrusted me."

The hopes of Britain's rulers now rested with General William Howe and his older brother, fifty-year-old Vice Admiral Lord Richard Howe. With resumes as impressive as their armada, they were unquestionably the most qualified men to lead the expedition against New

York. They were also close to the king personally. It was widely believed that their mother, who was still a force in London society, was the illegitimate daughter of King George I.

Both her sons had enviable military records, particularly against France during the Seven Years' War. General Howe's bravery and skill were legendary. Six feet tall, taciturn, and self-assured, Howe had been a close friend and comrade in arms of the sainted General James Wolfe, who considered him the finest field officer in the army.

Wolfe lost his life defeating the formidable French general Louis-Joseph de Montcalm at Quebec on September 13, 1759. The stunning victory led to the unraveling of French power in North America. Lieutenant Colonel Howe played a key role in the historic battle, fearlessly leading the army in a seemingly impossible climb up two-hundred-meter cliffs to surprise Montcalm. Had Wolfe survived the fighting on the Plains of Abraham that day he would have been lavish in his praise of his brave subordinate.

Howe's performance during the rest of the war was just as impressive. In 1760 he led a regiment that played an important part in securing a British victory at Montreal, which completed Britain's conquest of Canada. After returning to Europe, he won laurels for his valiant performance at Belle-Île-en-mer, near La Rochelle, and later in the Caribbean, when the Earl of Albemarle led the British in an amphibious attack on Havana, capturing the port on August 13, 1762. By the end of the war in 1763, William Howe was one of Britain's military stars.

Admiral Howe, who would replace Shuldham, came to America with an immense reputation as well. Even more taciturn than his brother, he was fearless in combat, and much admired by colleagues and subordinates. A gifted tactician, he was always seeking ways to improve the navy's methods and equipment. Admiral Horatio Nelson considered him "the greatest sea officer the world has ever produced."

With a large, prominent nose and sad eyes, Lord Howe's visage bore a slight resemblance to the king's. It wasn't hard to imagine that they were related. The admiral had a serious way about him; he rarely smiled, and never joined in the gambling, womanizing, and drinking that attracted his brother. He stuck to business. His thirty-five-year naval career was marked by uninterrupted success. Beginning as a midshipman in 1740 at the age of fourteen, he was promoted at an exceptionally fast rate, making lieutenant in four years and post captain only two years after that. During the Seven Years' War he was heralded for leading amphibious raids along the French coast at Rochefort, St. Malo, Cherbourg, and other places. Some of the raids were successful, some not, but taken together they compelled the French to fight on two fronts—their coasts and the European mainland—which is what Secretary of State William Pitt, who ran the war, wanted.

To add to Captain Howe's luster, on November 20, 1759, his ship, the 74-gun *Magnanime*, played a key role in helping Admiral Edward Hawke win the war's decisive naval battle in Quiberon Bay, near St. Nazaire. The French fleet was broken that day and never recovered.

Without King George's fully appreciating it, Lord Howe's views on the American war differed markedly from his own and from those of Howe's immediate superior, the first lord of the Admiralty, John Montague, the Earl of Sandwich. Unlike them, Howe believed that Britain's long-term interests could be served best by bringing about a reconciliation with the colonies rather than conquering them. He believed that for the war to end permanently, for the colonies to be brought back happily into the empire, there had to be a political settlement with Congress, not just an abject defeat on the battlefield. The admiral's attitude was bound to create friction with the first lord, who was convinced that a quick, decisive military victory was the only sure way to regain permanent control of the colonies.

Sandwich, who had no experience in America, had never been there, and never wanted to go, was convinced that suppressing the rebels militarily would be easy. He famously declared on March 16, 1775, in the House of Lords, that colonials were cowards who would soon submit. "Suppose the colonies do abound in men," he declared, "what does that signify? They are raw, undisciplined, cowardly men. I wish that instead of 40 or 50,000 of these brave fellows, they would produce in the field at lease 200,000, the more the better, the easier would be the conquest; if they did not run away, they would starve themselves into compliance."

Sandwich remained in power throughout the war, and it was said that he later regretted these remarks, but his actions indicated otherwise. His belief in the efficacy of raw military power remained and was plain to see. The king found the first lord's views compatible with his own and never saw any reason to replace him.

General Howe's superior and Lord Dartmouth's successor, Lord George Germain, secretary of state for the American Department, was also sanguine about the ability of military power to end the rebellion in a single campaign season. The king liked his views as well, appointing him to direct the land war on November 10, 1775. Without His Majesty's fully appreciating it, Germain's opinions differed markedly from both Lord Howe's and his brother's.

General Howe's views were closer to his brother's than to Germain's. He differed with his brother to the extent that he thought a decisive victory over the rebel army was necessary before a negotiation with Congress could succeed. The difference between the brothers was that Admiral Howe hoped a negotiation could be arranged first, without more blood being shed—thereby reducing the rancor on both sides and putting a long-term reconciliation on more solid ground. Germain, Sandwich, and the king, on the other hand, wanted a military victory that would allow them to dictate to the losers. Reconciliation was not in their vocabulary.

Absent negotiations, the Howes intended to defeat the rebel army quickly in 1776. With the resources at their command, few doubted that they would. Not only were they outstanding fighters, they got along well together, avoiding the destructive bickering, posturing, and competition that so often prevented cooperation between the services and stood in the way of success. The king was confident that, working in harness, the brothers would be masters of New York City before the end of September 1776, if not before. He then expected them to waste no time pushing north up the Hudson River Valley to form a junction at Albany with General Carleton's army driving down from Canada. Once joined, the armies, supported by a tight naval blockade, would hand him the victory he sought by year's end.

Although General Howe believed that he could produce what the king wanted, there was an important difference between the way he viewed the military capacity of the rebels and the way Britain's rulers did. He had spent almost a year battling the colonials in Massachusetts and had developed a modicum of respect for their army and its leaders. Since coming to Boston, on May 25, 1775, he had learned the hard way not to take the rebels too lightly. The condescending attitude he had arrived with soon disappeared when he suffered a major setback at Bunker Hill, losing 1,054 men, either killed or wounded—out of 2,200 engaged—while the patriots lost 441 out of 3,200.

And Bunker Hill was not the only hard lesson he learned. George Washington, a provincial with considerable experience in the French and Indian War but with a poorly trained and badly equipped army of sixteen thousand militiamen—mostly farmers and artisans—had contained nine thousand of His Majesty's finest in Boston during the entire winter of 1775–76. It was humiliating and, worse, unnecessary. His Majesty had long since concluded that Boston was not the proper base for operations. He planned to move the army to Halifax in the fall of 1775, reinforce it substantially, and then turn it on New York.

Howe did not receive his orders until the onset of winter in November, however. He was forced to remain in Boston until spring. During that time he was on high alert for a rebel attack across the water or ice, something Washington dearly wanted to do. Boston was a tiny peninsula, tenuously hitched to the mainland by a causeway that was submerged from time to time, making the city an actual island. Washington had strong support from Congress, especially from Samuel Adams and the Massachusetts delegation, for attacking the city, but Washington's senior generals, especially Artemas Ward and William Heath, thought it would be foolhardy to assault the strongly fortified British positions in Boston. Given their opposition, Washington decided on a different approach.

Nothing happened until the night of March 2, when patriot artillery batteries unexpectedly opened fire from Lechmere's Point, Roxbury, and Cobble Hill. The British responded, and a loud but inconsequential duel developed, continuing on and off for the next two days. Then, on the night of March 4, with the barrage of gunfire acting as a distraction, Brigadier General John Thomas and two thousand men quietly dragged enough artillery onto Dorchester Heights to threaten Howe's army in Boston and even Shuldham's fleet in the harbor. Dorchester Heights commanded the city from the southeast, just as Bunker Hill did from the northwest. Thomas's movements went undetected by British sentries, thanks to an elaborate wall of hay that Washington had built along Thomas's route.

Stunned, and furious at being completely fooled, Howe gave way to his anger and prepared to attack the Heights, as he had Bunker Hill. A savage storm intervened, however, forcing him to pause and reflect. By the time the gale subsided, he had calmed down and recognized that his situation was untenable. If he attacked, he'd be confronting not only Henry Knox's formidable artillery on the Heights but an amphibious assault across the water by Generals Israel Putnam, John Sullivan, and Nathanael Greene. Even if by some miracle Howe won, he would inevitably suffer high casualties, which he could not afford. And what would victory bring him? Washington could withdraw and not much would have changed, except that Howe would have fewer troops. Much as he hated to, he chose to retreat. He wrote to Lord Dartmouth (William Legge, 2nd Earl of Dartmouth), who was still American secretary at the time: "The importance of preserving this force when it could no longer act to advantage did not leave any room to doubt of the propriety of its removal." Although Howe was convinced that his move was the correct one, and he was planning to leave Boston anyway, it was galling to have it appear that Washington was forcing him out.

Since neither commander wanted to demolish Boston, Washington was content to let the British leave peacefully, provided Howe agreed not to destroy the city as he evacuated, which he did, although he looked the other way when wholesale looting took place. It took several long days for the British to get organized, and during that time Washington just watched, ready to react if Howe changed his mind and decided to fight it out. Finally, on March 17, the entire British army, including animals and equipment, was packed aboard Shuldham's transports and warships, along with eleven hundred Loyalists and their treasured possessions. Before nightfall the unlikely convoy began crawling away from Boston, stopping below Castle Island for a few days before anchoring at Nantasket Roads outside the harbor.

On March 21 the *New York Journal* reported the exodus and added that "there is no doubt but their destination is for New York. General Washington has already detached six regiments for this place, who are already advanced one hundred miles." The report was accurate. Washington wasn't taking any chances. He thought there was a strong possibility that Howe would head straight for New York. But on March 27, when a crestfallen Howe finally left Nantasket Roads, Shuldham shaped a course for Halifax, Nova Scotia.

In spite of Howe's humiliation in Boston, when his grand armada finally began arriving off New York at the end of June 1776, prospects for an early victory looked bright. Substantial reinforcements gave him enough power to deal Washington and the revolution a mortal blow. The disgrace of March seemed about to be wiped out. As Howe stood on the quarterdeck of HMS *Greyhound* surveying the coast, his confidence must have grown when he saw that Sandy Hook was undefended. No artillery or troops were in place to dispute his entrance into the Lower Bay.

If the rebels had had the wherewithal, they would have exacted a heavy toll for passing the Hook. Washington certainly wanted to; it was not something he had overlooked. Ever since the revolution began, New York had been uppermost in his mind. He believed, as every leader on both sides of the Atlantic did, that whoever controlled Manhattan and the Hudson River Valley would dominate the North American continent. All during the long winter of 1775–76 in Boston, he worried about New York's vulnerability. When Major General Henry Clinton, Howe's second in command, departed Boston unexpectedly on December 20, 1775, and sailed south with a small force, Washington suspected his destination was New York and immediately dispatched Major General Charles Lee, his second in command, to strengthen the city.

Washington explained why to Governor Jonathan Trumbull of Connecticut, a strong ally, "As it is of the utmost importance to prevent the enemy from possessing themselves of the City of New York and the North [Hudson] River, which would give them command of the country and the communication with Canada; I shall dispatch Major General Lee with orders to repair thither . . . to put the city and fortifications on the North River, in the best posture of defense . . . as expeditiously as possible."

Lee reached Manhattan on February 5 with more than seventeen hundred men (mostly from Connecticut) and went right to work. He was hard at it until March 7, when Congress, fearing a simultaneous British move on the Carolinas and Georgia, appointed him commander of the newly created Southern Department and sent him to Charleston. John Adams and his colleagues were so taken with Lee that they wanted him to also have command of the struggling patriot army in Canada. Since he could not be in two places at the same time, they decided the South needed him more.

When Lee and his men arrived in New York they found a surprising number of homes already abandoned. A mass exodus had already begun. In the coming months the original population of twenty-five thousand would shrink to less than four thousand, leaving a partially empty city for the military to organize, rip apart, and aesthetically ruin.

Since the Royal Navy would have command of the water, Lee assumed that the British would inevitably possess the city, but he also believed that they should be made to pay a high price for it. He planned to fortify key points, particularly the high ground on Long Island known as Brooklyn Heights, directly across the East River from Manhattan. It was generally believed that whoever controlled the Heights would command the city. Lee hoped to create a crossfire between batteries on the Heights and in the town, making the East River difficult for the British to control. He also planned to fortify the high ground on the northwestern side of Manhattan near present-day 183rd Street, close to the George Washington Bridge, and another strongpoint directly across from it on the New Jersey side of the Hudson, to deny the Royal Navy control of the river. In addition, he planned to seal the East River by placing artillery at the southern end of Manhattan. And he intended to deny the enemy access to Hell Gate, the narrow tidal strait connecting the East River with Long Island Sound, by constructing forts on either side of the East River, close to the entrance.

After Lee left for Charleston, his work continued under fifty-eight-year-old Brigadier General William Alexander, better known as Lord Stirling. The title derived from his claim to a Scottish earldom through his father, which London did not recognize. A hard-driving, hard-drinking fighter from New Jersey, he was a leader Washington relied on. When Major General Israel Putnam arrived from Boston on April 4, he and Stirling continued work on the city's defenses. Both were concerned about Staten Island, where support for the king was strong. Stirling requested help from Brigadier General William Livingston, head of the patriot militia in New Jersey. Livingston did his best, but the lack of political support on the island frustrated his efforts.

Putnam was more successful in other places. Building on Lee's plan to seal off the East River, on April 8 Old Put led a thousand men and occupied Governors Island off the tip of Manhattan. At the same time, he erected a strong fort on Red Hook, a tiny arm of land jutting out from Brooklyn into the East River, directly across from Governors Island. He then sank obstructions in the water between the two posts, hoping to at least slow down warships trying to get by so that gunners on land could get a good shot at them.

Washington himself rode into New York on April 13, invigorated by his victory in Boston. He had a good idea of what London was planning in the Hudson River Valley and got to work further strengthening the city. He expected the British to conduct amphibious landings around Manhattan, initiating street-to-street and house-to-house fighting. To counter them he expanded Lee's plan to fortify key points around and within the town, throwing up more barricades, traverses (obstructions), trenches, redoubts, and forts seemingly everywhere, making Manhattan look as if it had been torn apart. The beautiful city was no longer recognizable. The tree-lined streets, beautiful parks and gardens, the lovely homes, churches, and schools—all had been sacrificed.

Washington also built Fort Independence just above Spuyten Duyvil Creek, near Kings Bridge, to guard the only substantial link connecting Manhattan with the mainland. And he began constructing the two big forts on either side of the Hudson that Charles Lee had envisioned to prevent the enemy from penetrating upriver.

Washington was unable to accomplish all he had hoped before the British arrived. With a woefully inadequate army and no assistance from the hapless Continental navy, he wasn't at all prepared when General Howe's armada appeared. Washington was forced to watch, helpless, as one vulnerable British transport after another crawled unmolested around Sandy Hook's tricky sandbar into the Lower Bay.

The situation at the Narrows, a strategically important tidal strait connecting the Upper and Lower bays, was even more troublesome. Running between Staten Island and Long Island, the Narrows was the channel through which the Hudson River flowed into the Atlantic. If Washington had had sufficient artillery and men, as well as political support on the two islands, he would have exacted a heavy toll of enemy ships as they threaded their way through the narrow passage. The most he could do, however, was place a pathetically small detail on the tip of Long Island, armed with muskets. If they had had artillery they might have done some damage. Without it, all they could do was fire a few shots and run.

Washington was frustrated. He wanted to attack Howe right then, before the entire British armada arrived, but he was too weak. "Our situation at present, both in regard to men and other matters," he wrote to his brother John Augustine Washington, "is such as not to make it advisable to attempt anything against them, surrounded as they are by water and covered with ships, lest a miscarriage should be productive of unhappy and fatal consequences."

Over the next few weeks an amazing number of British ships, amounting to more than four hundred, appeared off Sandy Hook. After taking on pilots, they made their way unopposed over the shifting sandbar just to the east of the Hook and sailed into the Lower Bay. From there, they continued through the Narrows into the Upper Bay and dropped anchor off Staten Island, where Tories were in firm political control.

Twenty substantial men-of-war were among the arrivals, including the 64-gun *Eagle*, flagship of Admiral Lord Richard Howe. During the afternoon of July 12—a gorgeous summer day—the *Eagle* slipped past Sandy Hook, and at six o'clock she let go her anchor off the eastern side of Staten Island. The assembled fleet gave the admiral a rousing welcome. Every warship thundered a salute, while sailors and marines waved and cheered.

The invaders were understandably exuberant. Not until the world wars of the twentieth century would a larger amphibious force be deployed. King George was confident that by Christmas the Howes would have delivered the mighty blow that would force the colonial radicals to submit. The resolve of American patriots was about to be tested as never before. The next few weeks would determine whether a revolution against the world's mightiest power had any chance of success.

Chapter 2

THE IMPORTANCE
OF NEW YORK

No part of America was better suited as a base for carrying out the king's plans than New York City. Centrally located along the Atlantic seaboard, its magnificent harbor, superb port, and marine specialists, skilled in building and servicing every type of vessel, made it ideal. And just as important, if not more so, it was the perfect staging area for the Howes' grand amphibious thrust up the Hudson to form a junction at Albany with General Carleton's army invading from Canada.

The great majority of Britain's leaders found the king's strategy of splitting the colonies convincing, and none more so than forty-six-year-old Major General Henry Clinton, General Howe's second in command and future replacement. Clinton's fixation with the Hudson would play a large part in determining the outcome of the war. "The Hudson naturally presented itself as a very important object," he wrote in his memoirs. "If Britain could capture the Highlands and secure them, communication between the colonies to the north and those to the south would be effectively severed, making it impossible for them to join forces, or even for the northern colonies to feed their troops." Clinton knew the ground well. His father, Admiral George Clinton, had been the colonial governor of New York for over a decade, from 1741 to 1753. Henry, who could trace his noble lineage back to the thirteenth century, had joined the army when he was fifteen, living with his father until 1749.

When General Clinton came back to America in 1775, he was a distinguished professional. He had served in the Seven Years' War, fighting briefly in Canada and then in Germany, in the battles of Corbach and Kloster Kampen, and in Freiberg, where he was badly wounded. Earlier in the war, he had served as an aide to Field Marshal Sir John Ligonier, commander in chief of British forces and a key figure in winning the conflict.

Although a lifelong warrior like General Howe, Clinton and his boss could not have been more different. Touchy, sensitive, quick to take offense, Clinton had great difficulty getting along with colleagues, superiors, and subordinates. Major James Wemyss, who had observed him closely while serving in various capacities in New York and South Carolina, and who was not unsympathetic, described him as "an honorable and respected officer of the German school; having served under Prince Ferdinand of Prussia and the Duke of Brunswick. Vain, open to flattery, and from a great aversion to all things not military, too often misled by aides de camp and favorites." Clinton's biographer, William B. Willcox, was far more critical, describing him as a classic neurotic with an inability to handle authority, a commander in chief who was difficult to understand, much less warm up to. Clinton's relations with General Howe were, not surprisingly, strained the entire time they worked together.

The king had no inkling of Clinton's personal quirks. As far as His Majesty was concerned, Clinton's outstanding military record and close ties to the Duke of Newcastle more than qualified him to be Howe's deputy. The king expected Clinton to be a source of sound, experienced advice for Howe, as well as an outstanding field commander. His personal acquaintance with New York was also a help. The king was comfortable, indeed enthusiastic, about his entire leadership team.

He was also sanguine about the political sympathies of New Yorkers in and around Manhattan. In fact, a friendly political environment was an additional reason why the king found New York City and the surrounding counties so attractive as a base of operations. Richmond County (Staten Island), for instance, was one of the most loyal in America. Closer to New Jersey than to New York, it had a population of less than three thousand, led by a few families, the most prominent of whom were Billopps, Seamans, Micheaus, and Dongans. Former governor William Tryon and other Tory leaders confirmed the island's loyalty when they met with General Howe aboard the *Greyhound* immediately after he arrived.

Tryon painted a picture of extensive Loyalist support throughout the region. He predicted that the king's faithful would supply Howe with whatever he needed, particularly men. "I have the satisfaction to inform your Lordship," Howe wrote to Germain, "that there is great reason to expect a numerous body of inhabitants to join the army from the provinces of New York, New Jersey, and Connecticut, who in this time of universal apprehension only wait for opportunities to give proofs of their loyalty and zeal for government."

Tryon urged Howe to attack Washington immediately. The governor was already doing all he could to organize clandestine resistance in the city and surrounding counties. Working with prominent Loyalists like Oliver De Lancey, Tryon was planning an uprising within the city to coordinate with Howe's invasion. He even hoped to capture or assassinate General Washington. One of Tryon's men, Thomas Hickey (posing as a British deserter), succeeded in joining Washington's bodyguards and was about to capture or kill him when he was discovered on June 20. Hickey was tried and hanged eight days later in front of a crowd of soldiers and irate New Yorkers.

Washington moved fast to counter Tryon's efforts. He urged the New York Provincial Convention (the patriot governing body) to remove from Manhattan "all persons of known disaffection and enmity to the cause of America." The convention responded forcefully, rounding up prominent Tories, including former mayor David Matthews, and imprisoning them in Litchfield, Connecticut, and other places. Oliver De Lancey narrowly escaped capture by jumping into a rowboat in the dead of night and pulling for the battleship *Asia*, conveniently anchored in the Upper Bay on high alert.

The aggressive Tryon was not discouraged; he continued calling for immediate action, arguing that the rebels would offer little resistance. Howe's splendid army mesmerized him and warmed his heart. He had been hoping for a stupendous display of British power ever since he lost control of the city and province the previous year. By the fall of 1775 his political power had deteriorated to the point where he almost landed in jail. On October 19 an aide warned him that Congress had ordered his arrest. Tryon reacted quickly, fleeing in the middle of the night with his family to the packet *Halifax* and then to the larger British transport *Duchess of Gordon*.

The 64-gun *Asia*, under Captain George Vandeput, and the 44-gun *Phoenix* (Hyde Parker Jr.) protected Tryon. The *Asia* had been in New York since May 26, 1775, and the *Phoenix* since the middle of December. Vice Admiral Samuel Graves had dispatched the *Asia* from Boston in response to an urgent request from then royal lieutenant governor Cadwallader Colden, who desperately needed protection from New York's rebels. Growing in numbers and confidence, inspired by victories at Lexington and Concord and at Fort Ticonderoga, the patriots were in effective control of the city.

The *Asia*'s guns had a calming effect. Captain Vandeput worked out a modus vivendi with the rebels. Fearing the battleship's guns, they supplied him with provisions and even allowed him to peacefully evacuate the tiny contingent of redcoats left in Fort George, at the southern tip of Manhattan. Vandeput wanted to put a stop to the garrison's growing number of desertions.

When Washington arrived in the city in April he put a quick stop to trafficking with the warships, but they remained in the harbor, a constant threat, and a reminder of how weak the patriots were on the water. Vandeput had no trouble obtaining supplies from the surrounding countryside, where he was quietly supplying arms to Loyalists engaged in a vicious civil war for control of their counties.

Governor Tryon's description of New York's political sympathies was nothing new to General Howe. The dramatic difference between politics in New York and in New England, particularly Massachusetts, was well known to Howe. But he wasn't counting on anything like the level of support that Tryon was predicting, although serious help from Loyalists in Staten Island, Long Island, New Jersey, and even Connecticut would be welcome. The general hoped for the best.

On July 2, when Howe's redcoats began debarking on Staten Island, they received the kind of welcome Governor Tryon had predicted. The landing was a peaceful, indeed joyous, occasion. The soldiers were greeted as liberators. Before long, nine thousand regulars were comfortably camped ashore, with more coming. Water, wood, and food were available in abundance, and so were Loyalist troops. Christopher Billopp, commander of the island's militia, immediately offered his services. Over five hundred islanders—nearly every adult male—took the oath of allegiance to the king. Governor Tryon administered it. Even more encouraging, militiamen from New Jersey and Long Island were joining their ranks.

General Howe received strong support from other counties close to Manhattan. In Kings County, where strategically vital Brooklyn Heights dominated the landscape, Loyalists were in firm control. Prominent figures from Manhattan like former mayor David Matthews, Governor Tryon, Chief Justice Daniel Horsmanden, and William Axtell had estates there and had been active in organizing local Tories. With a population close to four thousand, the county could provide Howe with men who knew the countryside and were willing to assist as guides and fighters. At the same time, the county's rich farmland could supply him with food. Well-to-do farmers of Dutch descent owned the land, while slaves, who were over 20 percent of the population, worked it. The farmers did not want the British commander in New York to free their slaves, as John Murray, 4th Earl of Dunmore—the deposed royal governor of Virginia—was attempting to do. Siding with General Howe was a way to forestall a similar attempt on Long Island.

Queens County also supported Howe. It adjoined Kings and was three times its size, with borders on the East River, Hell Gate, Long Island Sound, and the Atlantic. With a population of eleven thousand, 20 percent of whom were slaves, and substantial towns like Hempstead, Jamaica, Oyster Bay, Flushing, and Newtown, it was predominantly Loyalist, particularly in the western part. Tories were not as dominant as they were in Richmond and Kings counties, but they were in control and could supply important support for Howe. Manhattan Loyalists who maintained country homes there provided leadership. Cadwallader Colden and his son David, Loyalist judge Thomas Jones, and their friends led the way.

As one traveled farther away from the city, Loyalist support decreased. Westchester County, which bordered on Long Island Sound, Connecticut, and the Hudson, had a population of twenty-one thousand, including thirty-five hundred slaves, and was more or less evenly divided among Loyalists, patriots, and fence-sitters. Its prominent families—Van Cortlandt, Philipse, Pell, De Lancey, and Morris—were split politically, as were smaller landowners and others who owned little or no land. Political divisions in Westchester made the county of little use to Howe and led to a vicious civil war that was more intense than in any other part of New York.

Sentiment in eastern New Jersey was also mixed. Although no exact estimate is possible, probably 37 percent were Loyalists, 40 percent patriots, and the rest neutral. The royal governor of New Jersey, William Franklin (Benjamin's illegitimate son), led the Tories. Anxious to prove that he did not share his father's political views, he was a potent antagonist. When the British armada began appearing off Sandy Hook, the New Jersey convention (the patriot assembly) captured Franklin and imprisoned him in Connecticut. He was unable to escape to a British ship, as Governor Tryon and every other royal governor had.

William Livingston, the able commander of New Jersey's patriot militia (and soon to be the governor), led the rebels. After William Franklin's removal, Livingston rounded up Loyalists in Perth Amboy and sent them to the interior of the province. The town needed protection. It was a possible landing place for General Howe, and also a location where an American force (the Flying Camp) under Brigadier General Hugh Mercer would likely be stationed.

For one reason or another, a significant number of Loyalists remained in Manhattan. When Washington's army arrived in April their ranks decreased, but some stayed. Those who could not or would not leave kept a low profile.

The king anticipated that once the Howes secured Manhattan and the surrounding counties, Loyalists would come forward in large numbers, as they had on Staten Island and as he anticipated they would in other parts of the country—particularly the South. He expected them to form their own units and fight alongside regulars, as well as replace deserters. The British army and navy would be in constant need of recruits. Any time His Majesty's fighting men got close to America they deserted in droves.

Loyalists would also be indispensable after victory was secured. To guarantee long-term colonial submission, the king would be forced to undertake a wholesale recasting of American society. Tories would play a prominent role in instituting that makeover.

★

FOR THE KING'S GRAND SCHEME TO WORK, SPEED WAS ESSENtial. The revolt had to be crushed in 1776, before France became more deeply involved. She was already active. On August 7, 1775, Adrien-Louis de Bonnières, Comte de Guines, the French ambassador to Britain, received approval from Charles Gravier, Comte de Vergennes, the powerful minister of foreign affairs in Paris, to dispatch retired naval officer Julien-Alexandre Achard de Bonvouloir from London to Philadelphia. The extent of patriot victories in the spring and summer of 1775 surprised Vergennes, who watched closely, and excited his interest, as it had the Comte de Guines'.

Bonvouloir was to make contact with the Continental Congress and let it be known that France had a strong interest in supporting their independence movement and would have her ports open to American ships. He was also to stress that France had no interest in regaining Canada. Whatever information he acquired was to be funneled to Paris through the Comte de Guines. None of this activity surprised George III. His secret agents were just as busy as Vergennes'. In fact, British spies were working in the French embassy in London. They gave the king an accurate picture of what Paris was up to.

Bonvouloir sailed from London on September 8, 1775. By December he was in Philadelphia, where he approached Benjamin Franklin, the leading member of the newly created congressional Committee of Secret Correspondence, which handled foreign affairs. Bonvouloir carried a message from Vergennes promising that French aid could be expected on a small scale but that the open involvement of France, which would mean war with Britain, was impossible if the colonies remained part of the empire, either willingly or unwillingly. For France to become a full partner, the patriots had to both declare independence and survive the mighty blow coming at them in New York from the Howes.

As long as the Anglophobe Vergennes remained the dominant political figure in Paris, France posed a real danger to Britain. Louis XVI, the inexperienced, not overly bright, but well-intentioned twenty-two-year-old monarch, looked increasingly to his foreign minister for advice. At the same time, he listened to the ominous forecasts of Anne-Robert-Jacques Turgot, his finance minister, who warned that the wretched state of the kingdom's finances precluded any thought of revenge against Britain. Turgot predicted that a war would be catastrophic.

Vergennes had a different view, which the young king found more appealing. If prospects for America's success rose, Vergennes advised using the revolt to avenge France's defeat in the Seven Years' War. He was not overly concerned about the country's finances. Since France had a population of twenty-four million (compared to Britain's eleven million) and a large expanse of Europe's most fertile and strategically located territory, he thought she was a formidable power, with a unique opportunity to weaken what he liked to call her "natural enemy."

On March 12, 1776, he wrote to the king, "Providence has marked this moment for the humiliation of England. That it has struck her with blindness is the most certain precursor of destruction. It is time to avenge upon that nation the evils which she has done since the beginning of the century against those who have had the misfortune to be her neighbors or her rivals."

The young monarch did not desire a war. He listened carefully to Turgot's warnings, but, in the end, given France's humiliating defeat in the Seven Years' War, he sided with Vergennes. The moment seemed propitious. Britain was diplomatically isolated—largely by her own choice. If France entered the American conflict, and possibly Spain and Holland as well, Britain would face them alone. Prussia, Russia, Austria, and the smaller states could not be used to balance French power as they had in the past.

From London's point of view, a speedy dispatch of Washington's army while Britain gained control of the Hudson River–Lake Champlain corridor to Canada would forestall French intervention. King George was confident that his mighty armada would achieve its objective in the required time and keep French participation in the war at a low level. Unquestioned faith in the Royal Navy strengthened his resolve. He assumed that Admiral Howe would have no trouble erecting an effective blockade of the Atlantic coast while supporting the amphibious force moving up the Hudson to cut off New England.

To secure a complete victory over all the colonies simultaneously, the king planned to send a strong fleet south with two thousand men to act against rebels in the Carolinas and Georgia. The royal governors of North Carolina (Josiah Martin) and South Carolina (Lord William Campbell) had been reporting that once the British army and navy appeared in force, Loyalists would flock to the royal banner—exactly what George III wanted to hear. Governor Campbell predicted that with Loyalist sentiment so strong in South Carolina, only two battalions, two frigates, and a detachment of artillery would be required to hold Charleston, the South's most important city. Governor Martin sent even more glowing reports about the chances of suppressing the rebellion in North Carolina.

The king had long believed that the southern provinces were the soft underbelly of the revolution and could easily be restored to the crown. Lord Dartmouth, the secretary of state for the American Department prior to Germain's appointment, wrote to Josiah Martin, informing him that a substantial force was being sent in the winter of 1775–76 "upon assurances given by yourself and the rest of His Majesty's governors in the southern provinces, that, even upon the appearance of a force much inferior to what is now sent, the friends of government would show themselves, and the rebellion crushed and subdued." London assumed that by early summer Loyalists in all the southern colonies would be in control once again and not require further assistance.

The southern strike force was expected to complete its work at least by the first of July, in time to return to New York and join General Howe for his assault on the city. Major General Clinton was in charge of the southern task force, with Earl Cornwallis his second, and Admiral Peter Parker assisting with a potent fleet. Cornwallis and Parker expected to sail from Ireland on December 1, 1775, with five regiments. They hoped to arrive the first week of February off the Cape Fear River in North Carolina, where they planned to meet Clinton, who was sailing from Boston on January 20 with two companies of light infantry. On his way south he intended to stop in New York for advice from Governor Tryon, who had served as royal governor of North Carolina from 1765 to 1771.

Clinton's sudden appearance off Sandy Hook on February 4 caused a panic in the city until people realized that his force was tiny, and he only wanted to talk with Governor Tryon. Clinton also conferred unexpectedly with the rebel commander, his old friend General Charles Lee, a former British army officer. Clinton told him quite frankly what he expected to accomplish in the South. He wasn't aware that he was chatting with the general who would oppose him in Charleston.

The king was also rapidly bolstering his sparse army in Canada, where General Carleton was holding his own against an American invasion that had begun during the fall of 1775. The king was sending mammoth reinforcements for Carleton. Major General John Burgoyne was bringing them. An army of ten thousand began arriving at Quebec in May 1776, just as the ice softened on the St. Lawrence River. Once adequately reinforced, Carleton was expected to drive the American invaders out of Canada and establish supremacy on Lake Champlain, which the British had thoughtlessly lost to the enterprising Benedict Arnold in the spring of 1775. Carleton was then to push south and retake Crown Point and Fort Ticonderoga, before moving on to the upper Hudson and Albany, where the Howes would meet him and provide a secure lifeline to the sea. The combined armies would end all intercourse between New England and the rest of the colonies, as well as conduct large-scale raids into Connecticut and Massachusetts that would end the rebellion.

To put his drive to Albany on a solid foundation, General Carleton had to prevent the French Canadian *habitants* (peasants) from joining the American revolt against the hated English. It was a diplomatic assignment requiring considerable skill, which, fortunately for George III, Carleton, with long experience in Canada, possessed.

A combination of patriot ineptitude and Carleton's deft political touch kept the French, who themselves were divided, neutral. Many of the eighty thousand *habitants* were unhappy with Parliament's Quebec Act (1774) because it reinforced the power of the Catholic hierarchy and the *seigneurs*, the great French landowners.

The *habitants*, who were by far the largest group in Canada (the English settlers numbered only a few hundred), might have supported the Americans had they received proper treatment, but they did not, which gave Carleton his opportunity. He understood that for British rule to succeed he had to respect the distinctive character of the non-English people and treat them honestly. The patriots, on the other hand, were in the habit of taking whatever they pleased from French farmers, whose religion and culture they found repulsive. Carleton could never make the *habitants* enthusiastic about English rule, but at least he could keep them from supporting the American rebels.

By the spring of 1776 it looked as if the king's goal of forcing colonial submission before the end of the year would be easily attained. Although conceived by men who knew next to nothing about America, His Majesty's strategy appeared perfectly suited to secure victory in only a few months and, with it, an end to years of colonial upheaval.

Chapter 3

THE GREAT
HUDSON RIVER ILLUSION

Despite the apparent logic of the king's strategy, it had serious flaws. The most glaring was its reliance on raw military power alone. There was no political dimension. The war's supporters in England imagined that they already had the political support they needed from the multitudes of Loyalists they thought existed in every colony. As it turned out, however, support from the Loyalists was far weaker than imagined, which made the military's task much more difficult. The Hudson River Valley and the corridor to Canada were so extensive they could never be controlled without a high level of political collaboration along its entire length. Absent that support, the Royal Navy and the British army, as mighty as they appeared, were inadequate.

The king and his advisors never grasped this fundamental flaw in their approach to the war. They continued thinking that the rebellion could be crushed without the need to hold out a vision for a better future. Instead of offering a more agreeable tomorrow, they were demanding unequivocal submission now; the future was left to the imagination. It hardly seemed likely that they meant to give more respect and autonomy to their subjects, however. Far more likely would be a recasting of colonial society to make it more closely resemble England's. The leveling tendencies British aristocrats found so unpalatable, especially in New England, would be reversed. The ability of ordinary people to affect governance would cease, and power would reside, as in Britain, with a small landed elite who could be relied on to never question Parliament's supremacy, no matter how unrepresentative and corrupt that body might be. The order and peace that supposedly existed in Britain (despite endemic urban and rural unrest, including large-scale riots) would replace the anarchy and confusion of civil war.

According to the prevailing dogma in London, Parliament was the foundation of British liberty, and had been since the Glorious Revolution of 1688. Parliamentary supremacy guaranteed the very liberties the rebels were crowing about. Questioning Parliament's authority, especially with regard to taxation, was by definition undermining Britain's cherished constitution, which restrained the power of the throne. That Parliament was in the hands of only a few hundred privileged gentlemen who approved laws for their own benefit was beside the point.

Britain's leaders imagined that even if they wanted to negotiate with the rebels it would be impossible. They were convinced that colonial malcontents would never accept parliamentary supremacy, never understand that it was the basis of their own liberty. All the rebels ever wanted, they believed, was independence, so that they could solidify their own power. Britain's aristocrats fancied that the emotional ties binding radicals like the brace of Adamses to the empire had long since dried up—if they had ever existed. Lord North, articulating a widely held belief, declared in October 1775 that "the leaders of the rebellion . . . manifestly aim at a total independence."

This was a gross misreading of the actual state of opinion. Despite the harsh legislation Parliament had approved by large margins in the two and a half years since the Tea Party; despite the bloodletting at Lexington and Concord and at Bunker Hill; despite the flaming carcasses thrown into defenseless Charlestown by the Royal Navy during the Battle of Bunker Hill; despite the mindless burning of Falmouth (now Portland), in the Maine District of Massachusetts; despite the destruction of Norfolk, Virginia; despite the clash of arms in Canada; despite the king's declaring war on the colonies; despite his refusal to even receive the Olive Branch Petition; despite the hiring of thousands of German mercenaries—there was still a vocal minority in Congress who did not want to break with Britain. They clung to the hope that the leaders of the approaching armada were, as rumors had it, empowered to negotiate a settlement.

The truth was that Americans were deeply divided over the wisdom of separating from England. By insisting that they wanted independence all along, Britain's leaders were pushing them toward something many colonists were not ready to accept. A substantial number wanted to avoid a civil war. Had King George and the ministry chosen to talk instead of fight, they would have found many willing to listen. Any credible move to open serious negotiations would have slowed the movement toward independence, if not stopped it altogether. John Jay, a conservative New Yorker and one of the authors of the Olive Branch Petition, had it right when he said that America "was prompted and impelled to independence by necessity and not by choice."

Since London was offering patriots only submission, refusing all political compromise, and relying on massive repression, the Continental Congress had no alternative but to declare independence. By the time General Howe arrived off Sandy Hook, the movement toward self-government, which had been gathering momentum for months, was irresistible. Since January, Congress had authorized armed privateers, opened America's ports to the world, except Great Britain, and embargoed all trade with the British and their West Indian colonies.

Those in Congress who still hoped for a bloodless reconciliation, like John Dickinson of Pennsylvania, were marginalized. With Howe's attack now imminent, most members realized that a vote on independence was imperative. Beyond the inspiration a declaration of independence would provide, it was essential to make a complete break with Britain in order to bring France into the war as a full partner.

When the historic vote was taken in Philadelphia on July 2 not a single colony was opposed. Achieving unanimity amid such diversity was nothing short of miraculous. Overcoming the doubts and anguish, the continuous haggling and clashing of interests and personalities, could never have been achieved without the mindless animus of the British government. On July 3, a joyful John Adams, who did as much as anyone to secure passage of the Declaration of Independence, wrote to his wife, Abigail, "Yesterday the greatest question was decided which ever was debated in America, and a greater perhaps, never was or will be decided among men."

Paris looked on with growing enthusiasm, admiring the courage it took to unanimously declare independence as the United States of America while a British armada of historic size lay just offshore. On August 18, 1776, Vergennes' agent, Pierre-Augustin Caron de Beaumarchais, wrote to the Committee of Secret Correspondence, promising "to supply you with necessaries of every sort, to furnish you expeditiously and certainly with all articles—clothing, linens, powder, ammunition, muskets, cannon, or even gold for the payment of your troops, and in general everything that can be useful for the honorable war in which you are engaged."

For the patriots, there would be no turning back. An uncertain future and a bloody war were preferable to what the king and his supporters were offering—unconditional submission to a tiny group of self-interested aristocrats who believed that government was there to serve them, not the governed. John Jay, who had hoped for a compromise as much as anyone, declared, "We will never submit to be hewers of wood or drawers of water for any ministry or nation in the world."

The great majority of the country gentlemen in Parliament saw things differently. They had long been convinced that colonists would submit rather easily—if compelled to. All that was needed was the will to make them. Confidence in the empire's military capacity ran so high, its limitations were never seriously examined. The ability of the Royal Navy to project English power three thousand miles away over an uncertain ocean was never questioned. It was simply taken for granted. Belief in the Royal Navy was so strong that some officials, most notably William Barrington, the secretary at war, wanted to rely on sea power alone to deal with the rebellion.

Accomplishing the multiple tasks necessary to achieve the king's goals in America, however, was beyond the capacity of even the Royal Navy, unquestionably the finest in the world. As powerful as Admiral Howe's squadron was, it could not possibly do all that was required. The load on the navy would have been significantly diminished had political compromise been added to Howe's arsenal of weapons, but London specifically ruled that out.

To support the invasion of New York and carry out Howe's other assignments, Lord Sandwich, with the king's approval, gave him seventy warships of various kinds and twelve thousand seamen. The entire British navy had one hundred fifty ships and twenty-four thousand seamen. On the assumption that the war would be over quickly, Admiral Howe was given nearly half of the king's sea force. At no time during the Revolutionary War did he or his successors have more than ninety warships, yet as large as that figure was as a percentage of the entire British navy, Howe still did not consider it enough.

And raw numbers alone did not tell the story. These were wooden ships that were continuously decaying and in need of repair. The actual number at sea was always fewer than the overall numbers would indicate. Dockyards equipped to make substantial repairs on a number of large men-of-war did not exist in North America. Even Halifax, Nova Scotia, did not have the facilities to accommodate the needs of the fleet. It did not even have a dry dock. Any repairs that could not be done by heaving down (putting a ship on its side) were sent to England. On numerous occasions London urged Howe to construct port facilities in the colonies that could handle his ships, but he never seemed to have the time or the inclination. New York, by default, became the place where quick repairs were made. But this was never sufficient. A certain portion of the admiral's squadron was always returning to England to refit.

The distribution of British warships in the summer of 1776 showed how impossible Lord Howe's assignment really was. Thirty-one were at

New York (including Parker's squadron from Charleston and the 50-gun *Renown*). They were supporting the invasion of New York, which was the admiral's first priority. In order to do that, he had to keep tight control over all the waterways in the area, including around Staten Island and Manhattan, Hell Gate, and Long Island Sound, as well as the lower Hudson from its mouth to the beginning of the Highlands at Peekskill. He also had to supply large numbers of seamen to conduct General Howe's amphibious operations around Manhattan. There were times when the admiral's ships were so undermanned they could not be brought into action against enemy warships, although, given the absence of any threat from the Continental navy, that was not a problem around New York.

The rest of Lord Howe's fleet was distributed over a wide area. One man-of-war was stationed off Delaware Bay. Two were patrolling off Boston, two off Block Island, four off the Cape Fear River, three off Savannah, and three at St. Augustine. Five were at Halifax (including the hospital ship *Jersey*), two were in the Bay of Fundy, three in Chesapeake Bay, one at Prince Edward Island, one at Bermuda, and ten in the St. Lawrence River.

If all the admiral had to do was support the invasion of New York, his fleet would have been adequate. But his duties extended far beyond that. He was ordered to blockade the entire New England coast. Hostile vessels were to be prevented from getting to sea, and vital war matériel stopped before they got in. It was well known that foreign suppliers were sustaining the rebellion. The rebels could not begin to provision their army from domestic sources alone. In the first three years of the war over 90 percent of their gunpowder was imported.

Interdicting all this traffic with the number of ships Howe had was manifestly impossible. The two men-of-war patrolling off Boston could not seal that busy port. And there were no warships at all off the other important Massachusetts ports like Salem, Beverly, Marblehead, Newburyport, Gloucester, Cape Ann, Scituate, Plymouth, and New Bedford. The other New England states could not be successfully blockaded, either, and for the same reason—not enough warships.

And the men-of-war themselves were not as invulnerable as London assumed. They were subject to surprise attacks from squadrons of small boats and even from the tiny Continental navy.

In addition to controlling the Hudson around New York, Howe was also required to dominate the river from Sandy Hook all the way to Albany—one hundred fifty miles. The notion that he could do this through a hostile countryside and prevent all crossings regardless of ice or fog or wind, sleet or rain, was a fantasy. And, in fact, throughout the long six and a half years of fighting, the British, even with a sizable fleet at New York City, never, on any important occasion, prevented the troops or provisions of the Continental army, in spite of its vulnerability, from crossing.

In order for Admiral Howe to seal off the Hudson, he would have had to commit a large number of his scarce warships to that task alone. Even then, his men-of-war could never actually prevent all crossings. While they were attempting it, they would be subject to continuous attack from patriots hiding in the Hudson's countless creeks and rivers, sneaking out at night and in foul weather with fireships, or swarming aboard patrolling warships with overwhelming numbers and capturing them. During the winter, Howe's warships would be particularly vulnerable.

Even if by some miracle the Royal Navy did establish control of the Hudson from Manhattan to Albany, it was still 222 miles from Albany to Montreal. To secure control over that vast area, the political support of the inhabitants was essential, but the king's unwillingness to make any political compromises made that impossible. Had the countryside been filled with Tories, as Staten Island was, establishing control might have been feasible, but that was not the case. In fact, patriots were in command in too many areas for the British to establish control of the Hudson for any length of time. Neither the Howes nor any of their successors ever came close to dominating the great river. They didn't even try.

In addition to maintaining a tight grip on the Hudson, Howe was expected to somehow contain the entire American privateer fleet. Hundreds had already set out before he arrived on the North American station, and hundreds more would follow. In November 1775 Massachusetts commissioned privateers and set up courts of admiralty. Other provinces soon followed. On March 18, 1776, Congress approved the commissioning of privateers. In the course of the war over two thousand set out (the actual number has never been determined). Howe never had enough ships to contain more than a small percentage of them. From countless creeks, rivers, and ports they put out to seek their fortune. The profits to be made were potentially so big, and the American coastline so vast, that keeping them in port was a hopeless task. In one brief eight-month period, from May 1777 to January 1778, Lloyd's reported that American privateers took 733 British merchantmen.

To combat the ubiquitous privateers, hardliners like Sandwich and Germain urged Lord Howe to attack coastal towns, as Lieutenant Henry Mowat did Falmouth on October 18, 1775. Germain assumed the attacks would keep seamen at home defending their harbors. Lord Howe's North American fleet was stretched so thin, however, that he did not begin to have the capacity to carry out these raids while performing his other duties; nor did he have the inclination. In fact, he found the whole idea so repugnant and politically counterproductive that he dismissed it out of hand.

Lord Germain had a great belief in the efficacy of terror. Destroying towns and slaughtering innocent people was, in his view, a sure way to cow the king's American subjects. Far from trying to win over disaffected colonists, he believed that abject submission could best be achieved through fear. Not only did he advocate burning coastal towns, he urged his commanders to make use of Britain's Native American allies to terrorize colonists. "The dread the people of New England etc. have of a war with the savages proves the expediency of our holding that scourge over them," he insisted. Indiscriminate scalping, he thought, was an excellent way to change minds. Throughout the war, he assumed that he could frighten the rebels into submitting.

In addition to Lord Howe's other assignments, he had to contend with the minuscule Continental navy. Despite its weakness, two or three Continental warships could successfully attack Britain's isolated men-of-war on blockade duty. Howe was particularly concerned with Continental navy captain John Manley, who had the skill and daring to threaten any of his blockading ships. If Manley led a squadron, which he was capable of doing, he could capture any number of isolated British blockaders, going after one ship at a time.

The Admiralty also expected Lord Howe to supply warships to guard convoys and to carry important dispatches and personnel. At times, these seemingly mundane tasks could be of great importance. Trying to find the ships to do them, however, was often difficult.

The admiral could not be easily reinforced, either, for fear of weakening the home fleet. The ever-present threat from the Bourbon powers, France and Spain, limited the number of warships that could be sent to North America.

Lord Howe's obvious need for more men-of-war inevitably led him to ask for more, and Sandwich regularly turned down his requests. There simply weren't enough ships or seamen. That did not lead the Admiralty to demand less of Howe. Their lordships expected him to perform miracles with what he had. When that did not happen, he was blamed, not his superiors' unrealistic expectations.

There were also distinct limitations on the British army. Exactly how many troops it would take to subdue the colonies over a long period of time was unknown. Although General Howe would eventually have an army of thirty-two thousand to carry out his invasion of New York, it still might not be enough. Even more worrisome, raising thirty-two thousand soldiers had proven so difficult that the king had had to look to the German states, particularly Hesse-Cassel, to find them. If Howe needed more troops, where would they come from? The answer wasn't obvious.

Patriots, on the other hand, had access to large numbers. The colonial population, excluding slaves, was over two million. New England alone was capable of producing a much larger force than Howe's. The raw numbers did not favor His Majesty. Only if one had an exceptionally low opinion of the rebels' fighting ability did the king's calculations make sense.

———————

The convenient assumptions that George III and his supporters were making about the prowess of British arms created expectations that put enormous pressure on the Howes, who were forced to deal with a reality that was quite different from the fantasies of their superiors. Although the king's armada was the largest the world had ever seen, it contained inherent weaknesses that made it unlikely the Howes would achieve the quick victory His Majesty was expecting. Whether they could ever accomplish what he wanted remained to be seen.

Chapter 4

HMS *PHOENIX*
AND HMS *ROSE*
PROVIDE A LESSON

On July 12, 1776, only hours before Lord Howe's grand entrance into New York Harbor, Admiral Shuldham, who had no idea when Howe would arrive, ordered two of his best captains to make a run up the Hudson to Haverstraw Bay, thirty-five miles north of Manhattan, to test rebel defenses along the way. Shuldham wasn't anxious to do it. He didn't like risking men-of-war and their crews in this way. They could not be replaced and would be needed shortly in the invasion that was about to take place, but General Howe was insisting. Since control of the Hudson was such a vital part of the king's overall strategy, he wanted some idea of how strong the defenses were as soon as possible.

A run to Haverstraw Bay seemed a good way to find out. Five miles long and three and a half wide, the bay, near present-day Croton Point Park, was the widest part of the Hudson. Howe thought warships could anchor there, reasonably safe from attacks by land or water. He wanted to block the movement of supplies and men from the northern colonies to Washington in Manhattan, and prepare the way for an amphibious assault on the Highlands. He never anticipated that he would also be demonstrating why gaining command of the Hudson, never mind the entire corridor to Canada, was illusory.

Ever since Washington had arrived in New York in April he had been working on the Hudson's defenses, lining the New Jersey and New York shores with fortified batteries, and erecting two forts facing each other across the river—Fort Constitution (later renamed Fort Lee in honor of the general) and Fort Washington. Large obstructions were sunk between the two forts to slow any vessel attempting to run by so that gunners could get a good shot at them.

Colonel Rufus Putnam, acting chief engineer of the Continental army, was in charge of constructing the forts and placing obstructions in the river. He built Fort Washington on Manhattan's highest point, a rocky, 230-foot-high cliff north and west of Harlem Heights, and placed Fort Constitution opposite it on the New Jersey side, 3,300 feet from Jeffrey's Hook, a tiny point of land jutting out into the river below Fort Washington. By the first week in July, Colonel Putnam had Fort Washington up and running, and he had begun Fort Constitution, but neither the fort nor the obstructions were far advanced when Shuldham tested them.

At 3:00 p.m. on the twelfth, the 44-gun *Phoenix* (Captain Hyde Parker Jr.), the 20-gun *Rose* (Captain James Wallace), and three tenders, *Tryal*, *Shuldham*, and *Charlotta*, pulled their hooks, left their anchorage off Staten Island, and raced north toward the Hudson with a favorable southerly wind and a strong incoming tidal current. Their sudden movement created panic in the city. People assumed that this was the start of a major assault. Their hysteria subsided only when it became clear that just two warships and their tenders were on the move. When they sped by, batteries on Red Hook, Governors Island, Paulus Hook, and the city peppered them. Smoke and the smell of gunpowder filled the air, but the warships kept moving.

As they swept upriver, returning fire as they went, they soon approached Fort Washington, and raced by it with no problem. The fort's fire cut them up some, but not enough to even slow them down. Total casualties aboard from all the cannonading were three men wounded. The American gunners suffered far more. Several inexperienced artillerists were killed or wounded when their cannon burst due to insufficient swabbing.

As the men-of-war sailed beyond Fort Washington, batteries on the woody heights of Westchester County fired on them for eleven miles with no effect. Nothing stopped their progress upriver. Eventually they anchored in Tappan Bay and then moved farther north to Haverstraw Bay with no opposition.

When Washington heard that men-of-war had broken through his defenses as if they were cobwebs, he became determined to improve them. He told his brother John Augustine that the ships exhibited "proof of what I had long religiously believed; and that is, that a vessel, with a brisk wind and strong tide, cannot, unless by a chance shot, be stopped by a battery, unless you can place some obstruction in the water to impede her motion within reach of her guns. . . . They now, with their three tenders . . . lie up . . . Hudson's River, about forty miles above this place, and have totally cut off all communication, by water, between this city and Albany, and between this army and ours upon the lakes. . . . Their ships . . . are . . . safely moored in a broad part of the river, out of reach of shot from either shore."

Preventing passage of enemy ships upriver was a high priority for Washington. No one believed more firmly in the importance of denying Britain control of the Hudson than he did. Time and again, he described the river as "of infinite importance." "Almost all our surplus of flour and no inconsiderable part of our meat are drawn from the states westward of Hudson's River," he explained. "This renders a secure communication across that river indispensably necessary. . . . The enemy, being masters of that navigation, would interrupt this essential intercourse between the states."

Washington never doubted that if left unchecked, the British would dominate the Hudson and cut off New England from the rest of the country. He held this view while demonstrating, over and over, that they had not done so as yet, by continuously crossing with troops and supplies. In fact, throughout the long war, he and his subordinates were never prevented from crossing, and only on rare occasions were they even inconvenienced.

In order for the British to actually command the river, the political support of the countryside was essential, and if they had had that, there would have been no need for a revolution in the first place. Lack of political support along important stretches of the Hudson meant that warships would be subject to guerrilla-style attacks, as would the guard boats they would be forced to run alongside their big ships, not just to protect against the patriots but to impede desertion.

Rebel fireships would be a constant problem, as would row galleys and other small vessels darting out from tiny creeks, inlets, harbors, and rivers—places ships of the Royal Navy could not reach, even with their smaller vessels. Going after patriot guerrillas in unfamiliar creeks using ship's boats and galleys would be asking for trouble. Transports bringing food and other vital supplies to sustain the warships would be subject to attack as well. Food and water, not to mention liquor, would be impossible to obtain from a hostile countryside.

In spite of the gloomy report to his brother, Washington did not sit idly by; he attacked. With help from the New York Provincial Convention, he rushed to complete Fort Constitution and the obstructions in the river. He was counting on the obstructions to slow down the *Phoenix* and the *Rose* on their return downriver, as well as handicap any other men-of-war or transports attempting trips upriver. While General Mercer worked on Fort Constitution, Colonel Putnam sank more old ship hulks and *chevaux-de-frise* between the forts. Washington had high hopes for the *chevaux-de-frise*—huge, sharp, wooden stakes with iron tips. Putnam built them in Brooklyn and floated them over to the Hudson.

While Washington was making these preparations, he was also trying to figure out what the *Phoenix* and the *Rose* were up to. They might be carrying weapons to Loyalists for an attack on the Highland forts, Montgomery and Clinton, which were incomplete and weakly manned. They might also intend to destroy the two Continental frigates being built at Poughkeepsie, the *Montgomery* and the *Congress*. They would certainly be making detailed charts of the river, and laying down guides to navigation up to the Highlands and beyond for a future amphibious thrust to Albany.

Whatever they were doing, Washington was determined to give them plenty of trouble. He urged the New York Convention to improve the incomplete Highland forts, and he placed his troops at Fort Washington on Manhattan and at Kings Bridge on alert. He also sent an urgent message to Brigadier General George Clinton in New Windsor. Clinton had just returned from Philadelphia for the vote on the Declaration of Independence. In addition to being a member of Congress, he was a brigadier general of militia and a leader in Ulster and Orange counties—both staunchly patriot.

Washington told Clinton to be prepared for an "insurrection of your own Tories," aided by the warships and their tenders. He urged him to seek aid from Connecticut governor Jonathan Trumbull if he had to.

The politically astute Clinton was a step ahead of Washington. He already knew about the warships and was busy gathering as large a force as possible to counter them. And he was watching for Loyalists in his counties cooperating with them. He even had men guarding against a possible Indian attack.

Clinton's brother, Colonel James Clinton, had sounded alarm guns the minute he heard about the warships. He also put Forts Montgomery and Clinton on alert. They were located just north of Bear Mountain on the west side of the Hudson on either side of Popolopen Creek.

The whole countryside had swung into action. Hundreds of militiamen turned out. General Clinton assigned one regiment to Fort Constitution, another to Fort Montgomery, and a third to Newburgh, just north of the Highlands. Every other regiment was placed on high alert. General Clinton urged boat owners on the west side of the Hudson to be ready to move troops, and those on the east side to form a barrier of boats, stretching across the Hudson at Fort Constitution. If necessary, he planned to set the boats on fire to stop the warships from sailing north through the winding, fifteen-mile-long Highland passage running between Peekskill and Newburgh. Clinton gave orders to destroy any boat liable to fall into British hands. He also ordered the carpenters building the Continental frigates at Poughkeepsie to make fire rafts out of vessels seized from Tories and stored at Esopus and Kingston.

The fast response of New York's yeomanry acted as a tonic for Washington, who had been dealing for weeks with citizens of a much different political stripe. It was nice to see that the revolution had plenty of adherents in the counties up north. It demonstrated better than anything else that attempting to control the Hudson without the political support of the countryside was a hopeless endeavor.

William Smith, the prominent Tory lawyer, could not understand why the warships did not have plenty of marines on board to harass the patriots, as if they could possibly do anything other than get themselves and their Loyalist allies slaughtered. Smith had no idea how many men General Clinton had at his command.

The enemy frigates kept in touch with Lord Howe's fleet anchored off the east side of Staten Island by sending a whaleboat with a petty officer and six men running downriver. Shore batteries fired on them and sometimes hit them but did not stop them. Food and supplies were another matter. New York patriots made it impossible for the warships to get them from the countryside. One of the first things Captain Hyde Parker Jr. did was dispatch a squad from the *Phoenix* to take cattle from nearby fields, but the patriots were ready and drove them off. The cattle were then moved inland beyond the reach of the ships.

In their clumsy attempts to seize food and other provisions, the British created more enemies. On July 16, Captain Wallace sent men from the *Rose* to raid the farm of Jacob Halstead, a half-blind farmer whose land ran down to the water. Wallace's men burned Halstead's meager barn and house and stole his few pigs. News of the incident soon spread, creating a strong backlash. Vicious attacks were typical of Wallace, who had the same mind-set as Lords Sandwich and Germain. He had been harassing Rhode Island for months before moving to New York. His behavior was applauded in London, as he knew it would be.

Washington wanted to attack the warships, but his resources were pathetically few. The Continental navy, which might have played an important part in protecting the Hudson, was nowhere to be found. Even though a decisive battle that might determine the outcome of the war was about to be fought in places where naval support was critical, no ships of the American navy were taking part. Washington certainly needed them, and so did Benedict Arnold and Generals Schuyler and Gates on Lake Champlain.

The absence of the patriot navy was the fault of the amateur warriors in Congress who established the Continental navy in the fall of 1775. They created the wrong kind. They opted for building a poor, indeed laughable (if it hadn't been so serious), imitation of the Royal Navy, when they could have looked to the fleet of row galleys that Benjamin Franklin and his colleagues built in the summer of 1775 to defend Philadelphia and the Delaware River. Franklin's galleys were far from the glamorous frigates Congress found so appealing. The galleys were fifty feet long and eighteen feet wide, with flat bottoms, and carried a single cannon of between twelve and thirty-two pounds in the prow. Powered by twenty oars and two lateen sails, they were ideal for maneuvering in shallow river waters, strong currents, and bad weather. A flotilla of these boats could be a formidable force against His Majesty's frigates on the Hudson and in the East River, Hell Gate, and Spuyten Duyvil Creek, as well as on Lake Champlain.

The Congress had no interest in this type of craft, however. Members wanted to build frigates and sail of the line. They put their money and energy into constructing a small squadron of frigates that could do very little against the Royal Navy. If Continental frigates had been available in New York, Admiral Howe would easily have captured them and used them against the patriots.

Not only did Congress build the wrong type of fleet, it appointed the wrong individual to lead it—Esek Hopkins, of Providence, Rhode

Island. When he was appointed, in December 1775, Congress expected him to be Washington's naval counterpart. Members envisioned him working closely with Washington, especially in the defense of New York. Instead, Hopkins, who was soon censured by Congress, remained idle in Providence the entire time Washington was fighting to defend Manhattan. Even if Hopkins had been a seagoing Washington, however, he still would not have been of much use. He would not have had the right type of warships.

The Continental navy had a number of outstanding fighters, among them John Paul Jones, John Barry, John Manley, Lambert Wickes, Nicholas Biddle, Joshua Barney, Samuel Tucker, Hoysted Hacker, Silas Talbot, Seth Harding, and Charles Alexander. They could have been of signal importance in defending New York, but they were employed elsewhere on inconsequential missions like commerce raiding, which hundreds of privateers were doing far more effectively.

The burden of fighting on the water around New York fell to an army lieutenant colonel, Benjamin Tupper. He had impressed Washington the previous year with his guerrilla-style attacks in Boston Harbor. Tupper's activity in Boston, small though it was, actually rattled Vice Admiral Samuel Graves. Graves knew that if Tupper had been given sufficient resources he would have threatened the largest British warships anchored in the harbor. Unfortunately, Congress did not appreciate Tupper or even seem to know about him. But Washington did. He liked Tupper's aggressive small boat tactics and appointed him head of his small naval force in New York.

Washington also employed David Bushnell's submarine against Lord Howe's flagship *Eagle*, but the attempt failed. Had it succeeded, which it almost did, Congress might have paid some attention and rethought the composition of the navy. But since it failed, its possibilities were ignored. Bushnell was a gifted Connecticut inventor from Saybrook. He had constructed a single-man submarine that actually worked and caught the attention of Benjamin Franklin, who was racking his brain in 1775 trying to figure out how to defend the Delaware River. Franklin recommended Bushnell to Washington, who saw him in Boston and was impressed. He would have used the submarine then, but it was too late in the season.

Bushnell brought his invention to New York, and on September 6, 1776, Washington allowed him to try it out. The *Turtle,* as it was called because of its peculiar shape, performed well that day and got close enough submerged to almost plant an underwater bomb, which Bushnell had also invented, on the *Eagle*'s hull. At the last minute it struck metal and would not attach, ruining the attempt. Bushnell came very close, however. He made a second attempt on a frigate, but for a variety of reasons that did not work either, and the whole project was given up.

Colonel Tupper, meanwhile, used the few resources at his command to courageously attack the *Phoenix,* the *Rose,* and their three tenders. He had only five small row galleys with a single cannon in their prows. His flagship, *Washington,* had a 32-pounder; the rest had similar armament. With only five guns Tupper could not possibly do much harm to the big warships. Nonetheless, on August 2 he bravely tried, running close enough to inflict minor damage, shooting for a remarkable hour and a half before being forced to retreat.

He tried again on August 16 with six row galleys and had the same results. He roughed up the warships but did not actually threaten them. Tupper also attacked the frigates and their tenders with fireships, but again, the attacks were on too small a scale to have a great effect. They did succeed in burning the tender *Charlotta* on August 16. A six-pound cannon, three smaller ones, and ten swivels were salvaged from her charred remains.

Tupper's effort was a heroic but futile gesture. At the same time, it was instructive. If he had had a large fleet of galleys and far more fireships, which he might have had if Congress had allotted its resources differently, he would have been a real problem for the British.

Three days before the Howes launched their long-awaited attack on New York, the *Phoenix* and the *Rose* returned with their surviving tenders to Staten Island—recalled to participate in the invasion of Long Island. After the last of the fireship attacks, on the seventeenth they moved down to Tappan Bay. On the eighteenth, in the dead of night, they pulled their anchors and, taking advantage of wind and tide, sped downriver, bracing for underwater obstacles and concentrated fire from Forts Constitution and Washington.

The wind was blowing hard and a heavy rain falling. When they came to the line of river obstructions, they breezed through them once more. Cannon in the two big forts and near the city fired away without effect. By ten o'clock in the morning the warships and their tenders dropped their hooks off Staten Island, having sustained little damage. The *Rose* had two wounded and the *Phoenix* none. It was a complete defeat for Washington's river defense, although he refused to recognize it.

Washington explained what had happened to Governor Trumbull of Connecticut. "On the night of the 16th, two of our fire vessels attempted to burn the ships of war up the river. . . . The only damage the enemy sustained was the destruction of one tender. It is agreed on all hands, that our people . . . behaved with great resolution and intrepidity. One of the captains, Thomas, it is to be feared, perished in the attempt or in making his escape by swimming, as he has not been heard of. . . . Though this enterprise did not succeed to our wishes, I incline to think it alarmed the enemy greatly."

Although the *Phoenix* and the *Rose* made a mockery of Washington's river defense, they did not prove that the British could control the river. The continuous attacks on them in Haverstraw Bay and the Tappan Zee showed that control of the Hudson wasn't possible when rebels dominated an aroused countryside. Admiral Shuldham reported to the Admiralty that the expedition had actually been "fruitless."

Chapter 5

ATTACK DELAYED

Long before the invasion of New York began on August 22, Admiral Howe raced from England to New York to get peace negotiations started. It was more than a little odd for this fighting admiral, acknowledged to be the best in the Royal Navy, and one of the two men King George was counting on to smash the rebellion, to be so determined to get negotiations started before doing any fighting. In fact, negotiations were his first priority. They were not the king's, or the ministry's, or Parliament's, but they certainly were Admiral Howe's.

When the decision was being made in London about who was going to lead the invasion of New York, Howe had not kept his priorities a secret. In fact, his views on negotiations made his appointment controversial. Confidence in his diplomatic skill was nonexistent. Lord Sandwich opposed making him one of the two peace commissioners authorized by the Prohibitory Act. He even opposed making Howe commander of the North American squadron, arguing that Shuldham was perfectly capable of handling the job and should remain in place.

Lord Germain also opposed making the admiral one of the two

peace commissioners (the other being his brother). Even the king had misgivings. But His Majesty had confidence in Howe's fighting ability, as did Germain. Their backing overrode Sandwich's objections, and Howe was appointed both supreme naval commander in America and a peace commissioner.

Lord Howe was in the anomalous position of having strong support for crushing the rebels militarily but almost none for conducting peace negotiations. The ministry and a large majority in Parliament were not in the least interested in compromising with the rebels. Even opposition leaders like Edmund Burke had no confidence in Howe's ability to reach a settlement with the rebels. General Howe also had doubts. He was lukewarm about attempting talks until he had won a convincing military victory over Washington.

In order to secure appointment as a peace commissioner Admiral Howe was forced to accept strict guidelines. Germain, with the king's approval, placed severe restrictions on his powers, requiring him to obtain consent from London for literally everything he agreed to, which meant that he had no actual capacity to make peace.

Howe refused to desist. He continued believing that there was a way to satisfy the colonists' desire to participate meaningfully in decisions about their own affairs without undermining Parliament's authority. Finding that way, however, appeared politically impossible. Parliament had already proclaimed itself to be supreme "in all matters whatsoever," which the patriots found unacceptable. They were convinced that the institution had degenerated into a group of corrupt aristocrats masquerading as a representative body. The reality was that George III dominated Parliament. Over the years, through the deft handling of favors, bribes, and appointments, he had obtained inordinate influence over the legislature.

As American patriots viewed Parliament, it appeared as a body dominated by people who represented only their greedy selves. It was impossible not to see that its members enjoyed lives of unimaginable luxury, while the mass of "represented" British people worked very hard just to maintain themselves during short, difficult lives.

Finding a way to keep the colonies comfortably within the empire, despite these huge differences, had occupied Lord Howe's thoughts for a long time. During the winter of 1774–75, the months following the Tea Party, he did his utmost to stop the momentum for war building in England, holding secret discussions with Benjamin Franklin that Lord North and North's brother-in-law Lord Dartmouth quietly sanctioned.

The talks failed, but Howe continued his quest, believing that the civil war he was about to dramatically escalate might guarantee a permanent rupture between Britain and her most important provinces. His thoughts were on the future. He still hoped to pull off a miracle and keep the colonies in the empire without a bloody war. If he could prevent that, he would be serving the real long-term interests of the kingdom. He seemed to believe that if he could just get the two sides talking, it could lead to an arrangement that London might consider as a basis for negotiation. He hoped that the hard-liners in Parliament and in the ministry, and even the king himself, might at last realize that finding common ground was far better than the path they were on.

Even before he reached New York, Howe was working hard to get discussions going. While the *Eagle* was en route from Halifax, where he stopped, expecting his brother to still be there, he began advertising his role as peacemaker. To make colonists aware that there was an alternative to fighting, he issued a proclamation on June 7 (while the *Eagle* was off Massachusetts), announcing his power as peace commissioner to grant pardons.

On June 20 he followed his proclamation with a letter to each colonial governor in the middle and southern colonies (all of whom the rebels had driven out of office), asking them to give the widest possible publicity to his peace mission. He announced that he had broad powers, which, of course, he did not.

The patriots made no attempt to frustrate his designs. On the contrary, they wanted his views widely disseminated, believing it would reveal that he did not have the power he claimed. It was perfectly obvious that he had no specifics to offer, only vague generalities. Even the Continental Congress publicized his proclamation.

Nothing deterred the admiral, however. Even when he reached New York and discovered that Congress had already declared independence—which shocked him—he tried to initiate a negotiation before the shooting started, hoping that Congress would change its mind. At no time did he countenance independence. All his efforts were directed at keeping the colonies within the empire. Unfortunately, thanks to the restrictions placed on him by the king, he had nothing to offer that would interest Congress.

Nonetheless, he persisted. Events in Canada encouraged him. It appeared that Generals Carleton and Burgoyne were having great success against the American army. He hoped that this would impress the rebels with the hopelessness of their cause. On July 13, the day after Howe arrived in New York, he continued his quest for talks, dispatching Lieutenant Samuel Reeve of the *Eagle* to Perth Amboy with copies of his dispatches of June 20 to the royal governors. He also sent private letters, which he left unsealed, hoping they would receive the widest possible distribution. In them, he was essentially offering pardons to those who surrendered and returned to their allegiance (except for certain notorious patriot leaders).

Howe was eminently successful in having his peace mission publicized. Patriots continued to help him. Two packets of letters came into the hands of General Mercer at Perth Amboy; he forwarded them to Washington in New York. In this roundabout way the commander in chief received direct information about the admiral's hopes for a negotiation.

Washington alerted John Hancock, the president of Congress, of his receipt of Admiral Howe's communications. "This will be handed to you by Mr. Griffin," he explained, "who has taken upon him the charge and delivery of two packets containing sundry letters, which were sent to Amboy yesterday by a flag, and forwarded to me to-day by General Mercer. The letter addressed to Governor Franklin came open to my hands."

Washington took the occasion to write to Generals Howe and Burgoyne about the uncivilized conduct toward American prisoners in

Canada. He could not believe the atrocious treatment being routinely inflicted on helpless American captives, although he had seen some of it on a small scale in Boston. His protests, which continued throughout the war, went unheeded, which made the kind of discussions Admiral Howe hoped for impossible.

"The inhuman treatment of the whole, and murder of part, of our people, after their surrender and capitulation," Washington warned both generals, "was . . . a flagrant violation of that faith, which ought to be held sacred by all civilized nations, and was founded in the most savage barbarity. It highly deserved the severest reprobation."

On July 14 Lord Howe, oblivious to the general disrespect, indeed hatred, exhibited by His Majesty's troops toward America soldiers, sent a letter directly to Washington in Manhattan under a flag of truce, requesting a meeting. Lieutenant Philip Brown of the *Eagle* carried it personally, but Colonel Joseph Reed, Washington's closest aide, turned him back because the letter was deliberately addressed improperly to a "George Washington, Esq."

The admiral could not recognize Washington in his official capacity as commander in chief of the army of the United States of America, because London not only did not recognize the United States but intended to destroy it.

Washington, on the other hand, insisted that Howe recognize him in his official capacity—among other reasons, because it might induce the British to treat captured American soldiers and sailors with respect as prisoners of war rather than as criminals with no protection.

Howe tried again, sending an experienced officer, Lieutenant Colonel James Patterson, the adjutant general of the British army in New York. On July 20 Washington talked with him personally, but Patterson got nowhere. He pleaded with Washington to meet with Howe, claiming that the admiral had large powers to negotiate. Washington again refused, insisting that any negotiation had to be done through Congress. He used the occasion to speak directly with Patterson about the gross mistreatment of American prisoners in Canada. Patterson assured him that the Howes, although they did not have jurisdiction in

Canada, agreed about the necessity for the humane treatment of prisoners. Future events would show that these were empty words.

Howe considered Washington's rebuff a serious setback. Nonetheless, he kept trying, even writing a letter to Benjamin Franklin, which drew a thoughtful but severely negative response. On July 30, Franklin told the admiral publicly what he did not want to hear. Franklin's words were the most cogent of all the patriot replies to Howe's peace feelers. "Were it possible for *us* to forgive and forget," Franklin wrote, "it is not possible for you (I mean the British nation) to forgive the people you have so heavily injured. You can never confide again in those as fellow-subjects, and permit them to enjoy equal freedom, to whom you know you have given such just cause of lasting enmity. And this must impel, were we again under your government, to endeavor the breaking of our spirit by the severest tyranny, and obstructing, by every means in your power, our growing strength and prosperity."

★

WHILE ADMIRAL HOWE WAS PURSUING HIS PEACE INITIATIVE and General Howe was waiting for the rest of his army to arrive, the results of General Clinton's initiative in the South and General Carleton's push toward Albany became known and were shocking—the exact opposite of what Lord Howe had been hoping. Their lack of success was bound to adversely affect not only Howe's peace initiative but the king's goal of isolating New England and ending the war before year's end.

Clinton's mission turned out to be a fiasco from beginning to end. The planned rendezvous with Lord Cornwallis and Admiral Parker off the Cape Fear River in February 1776 did not occur until May 3. And the hoped-for rising of southern Loyalists turned out to be a caricature of what London had imagined. When Loyalists tried to challenge the rebels, they were soundly beaten. Long before Clinton reached the Cape Fear River, southern Loyalists suffered important defeats at Great Bridge, Virginia, in December 1775—and in February 1776 at Moore's Creek Bridge, North Carolina. As was the case in New York, most

Loyalists wanted the British to do the fighting for them. Cornwallis and Parker looked more than a little ridiculous bringing ten thousand stand of arms for a mythical army of supporters that never materialized.

Given the changed circumstances, Clinton might have given up and turned back to New York, as Germain's orders allowed him to do. Instead, he and Parker decided to attack Charleston. They did not begin their assault until June 28, however, and when they did, patriots, led by Colonels William Moultrie, John Thompson, and John Peter Muhlenberg, administered a humiliating defeat, although Clinton and Parker were not forced to surrender. General Lee, who was on the scene, played a negligible part. In fact, he urged Moultrie to abandon Fort Sullivan at a particularly inopportune moment, which might have led to a patriot defeat. Fortunately, Moultrie, showing the courage he exhibited on the battlefield, ignored him.

Uncertain what to do next, Clinton kept his troops sweltering aboard transports in the waters just offshore for three ghastly weeks, subject to the fatal diseases of a lowland summer. Admiral Parker, with whom Clinton had poor relations, used the time to repair his battered fleet for the long trip to New York, his tars suffering in the same sickly climate.

An even bigger surprise for the Howes was General Carleton's march to Albany stalling. At first it looked as if Carleton and Burgoyne were going to reach Albany rather handily. The king assumed that his reinforcement of ten thousand men would guarantee success. Captain Charles Douglas led the fleet that brought the first of them. From his flagship, the 50-gun *Isis*, he directed the lead ships up the ice-bound St. Lawrence River, pushing through what turned out to be soft ice that gave way when the ships ran at 5 knots or more. The *Surprise*, the lead ship, reached Quebec on May 6.

General Carleton, who had been holed up for the winter in the great fortress at Quebec, did not even wait for the first regiments to land before bursting out of the castle and driving the ailing, dispirited American army down the St. Lawrence and Richelieu rivers out of Canada by the first of June. Carleton won a great victory, which he would have been content with, had not Burgoyne caught up with him and presented the king's grand design to push south, beyond the Canadian border to Albany, and form a junction with General Howe.

To move farther south Carleton first had to gain control of Lake Champlain, which had been thoughtlessly conceded to Benedict Arnold the previous year and remained in American hands. The patriots still had the armed schooner *Liberty*, the large armed sloop *Enterprise*, and the armed schooner *Royal Savage* guarding the lake. Although the American army had been routed, the patriot navy, such as it was, continued to thwart the king's ambition.

Carleton could have easily dealt with the American fleet, but he could not sail directly down the Richelieu onto the lake. Ten miles of rapids between Chambly and St. Jean made that impossible. He could not move his big warships overland on rollers, either. The ground was too soft. He was forced to dismantle the ships he needed to take command of the lake and reassemble them—all of which would take weeks.

He became involved in an arms race with Benedict Arnold. On June 25, the day General Howe appeared in the *Greyhound* off Sandy Hook, Arnold was in Albany with General Philip Schuyler explaining in detail the true situation of the American army fleeing Canada, and the need to build a fleet on Lake Champlain to halt Carleton, whose army could only be transported by water. Schuyler was in complete agreement. Arnold had been in Canada since December 1775 and knew the situation better than anyone else.

On the same day, June 25, Arnold wrote to Washington about the urgent need for a much stronger navy on Lake Champlain to stop Carleton's thrust south. Washington, Schuyler, and General Horatio Gates were in full agreement with Arnold. Gates had just been appointed by Congress on June 24 to take command of the wretched American army fleeing Canada before Carleton's onslaught. The three generals were anxious for Arnold to build a fleet to stop him, and lead it into battle, which Arnold was keen to do.

Washington told John Hancock that it was "a matter of infinite importance to have a considerable number of gondolas [flat-bottomed gunboats able to carry over two hundred men and five cannon] on the lakes to prevent the enemy from passing." He thought that the men and materials being used to build the two Continental frigates at Pough-keepsie should be sent immediately to help Arnold construct these war-ships. Washington could not spare any men from his army, but he thought some might perhaps be sent from Philadelphia. Whatever was done, he wanted it done right away. He agreed with Gates when the lat-ter wrote, "The command of the water is of the last importance."

When Carleton stopped to build his fleet, it gave the disease-ridden American army, which had been in a disastrous headlong retreat, time to begin healing its wounds. Gates estimated that since the beginning of May and Carleton's spring offensive, the American northern army had lost more than five thousand men through death, capture, and desertion. Most of the deaths were from disease. Gates was able to gather what was left of the army at Fort Ticonderoga and begin recon-stituting it.

Carleton's movement toward Albany was thus stalled while he built a fleet large enough to command the lake. When General Howe finally began the invasion of Long Island on August 22, Carleton was still working on his warships. Howe began to seriously doubt that the hoped-for junction at Albany would actually take place. The rebels were doing far better than London had imagined, which did not surprise him. He started operating on the assumption that the king's grand strategy would not succeed in 1776. All of this was evident before he attacked Washington on Long Island. Howe's tactics were now dictated by the need to marshal his resources in the expectation that the cam-paign would last into another season.

Chapter 6

THE BATTLE OF BROOKLYN

In spite of unexpected reversals in the South and the North, His Majesty had no intention of adjusting his goals. As disappointed as he was, he intended to go forward with his original plan. The burden of rescuing his grand strategy now rested entirely with the Howes. William Knox, Germain's influential undersecretary, wrote to Lord Dartmouth, "All our hopes are now fixed on General Howe."

Indeed they were. London still expected the Howe brothers to destroy the rebellion before the end of the year. General Howe, on the other hand, did not have the luxury of ignoring realities on the ground. Before he arrived off Sandy Hook in June, he had had every intention of following the king's plan to capture New York and meet Carleton at Albany. But now, with defeats in the South and Carleton's problems in the North, Howe was forced to consider that a second campaign in the spring of 1777 might be necessary, in which case he had to think about where his army was going to spend the winter, and what would be a suitable port for his brother's fleet. He decided that, in view of the new situation, the immediate objectives of his forces would be securing

Manhattan Island, the New York and New Jersey counties surrounding it, and Narragansett Bay—a much reduced vision.

He did not immediately communicate this huge change of plans to Lord Germain. He waited to see what the outcome of the battle for New York would bring. If he decisively crushed the rebel army and forced Washington to surrender, the king's objective might still be achieved in 1776, albeit not quite in the way he anticipated.

Germain's insistence that Howe wait until his entire force arrived before launching the invasion of New York made the general's new, reduced plan more difficult. He would have liked to strike Washington as soon as possible. Germain's requirement inevitably produced a long delay, which took the edge off fighting units already on Staten Island, wasted precious days with winter coming on, and gave Washington more time to prepare.

A substantial portion of Howe's force did not reach New York until after July. General Clinton, Lord Cornwallis, and Admiral Parker did not return from Charleston until August 1. Several of their warships were banged up, and their demoralized soldiers needed time to recuperate—not only from a long voyage but from their unexpected repulse.

The final body of troops did not reach New York until August 12, when Commodore William Hotham arrived with eighty-five ships and eight thousand Hessians. His passage from England had been long and difficult, taking a gut-wrenching fourteen weeks. The German mercenaries—none of whom had been to sea before—stood the passage well until the last fourteen days, when scurvy broke out. A dozen were dead before they reached Staten Island. Their superiors were relieved the number was so small. Nevertheless, all recently arrived German troops, as well as those from Scotland, Ireland, and England, needed time to recover from their long voyages. General Howe could not put them into action until ten days later.

★

AT 7:30 ON THE MORNING OF AUGUST 22, ADMIRAL HOWE hoisted his flag aboard HMS *Phoenix*. A gun sounded, and a blue-and-white striped flag rose at the mizzen topmast flagstaff, signaling to the vast number of assembled troop transports, barges, and flat-bottomed boats to begin ferrying fifteen thousand regulars and a train of artillery to the beach at Gravesend Bay on Long Island. Baggage and horses were to follow later. There was no opposition. Generals Clinton and Cornwallis, along with Generals Hugh Percy, James Grant, and William Erskine, landed all the troops by noon and marched to Flatbush, where they camped around the small town.

The fact that the British were ready to go on the morning of the twenty-second was itself something of an achievement. The day before, the worst summer storm in memory had deluged New York. It might have delayed them for days, but nothing was going to stop the Howes now. They had waited so long for this day that even a tempest of historic proportions was not enough to deter them.

Admiral Howe directed the gigantic operation from the *Phoenix*. It was superbly orchestrated by a renowned virtuoso. The landing craft were the best in the world—unique, in fact. He had designed them, perfecting the art of large-scale amphibious assaults through trial and error while fighting along the French coast during the Seven Years' War.

Washington watched carefully, wondering what the Howes' real plans were. He estimated that perhaps eight or nine thousand troops landed—far fewer than actually did. Since he misjudged the number so badly, he had trouble deciding if the troops he saw were going to attack Brooklyn Heights, or if they were only a large detachment intended to draw his attention while the Howes directed their principal attack against Manhattan.

He moved eighteen hundred more men over to Brooklyn Heights just in case, bringing the total to a little less than six thousand. Two-thirds of them were untried militiamen. He kept the bulk of the army in Manhattan. Content to let Washington divide his force, Admiral Howe never attempted to prevent any patriot troop crossings, which he easily could have.

In the ensuing hours, the British remained where they were on Long Island, while Washington sent two thousand more troops to Brooklyn

Heights, increasing the total to around eight thousand, about half his effectives. Perhaps as many as four or five thousand more of his men were unavailable, suffering from various diseases. General Howe's troops, in contrast, were noticeably healthy. It should have been the other way round. The patriot soldiers on their own home ground should have been faring much better than the enemy, who came from overseas. The cause of this anomaly was the marked professionalism of Howe's men and their camps as compared to the rank amateurishness of the army they were facing. Washington simply had not had enough time to inject the discipline necessary to shape up his men and improve their camps.

An inferior army and inadequate equipment were not the only handicaps Washington was operating under. He was also without the leadership of Major General Nathanael Greene, who had been in charge of the defenses on Brooklyn Heights but was now, at this critical moment, sick in his tent with a raging fever. Greene had done a superb job preparing to defend the Heights, erecting a three-mile defense barrier of forts, redoubts, pickets, ditches, and entrenchments stretching from Gowanus Bay to Wallabout Bay. He knew the ground better than anyone else, and he was an intelligent, albeit inexperienced, fighter. To be without his services at this moment was an enormous disadvantage.

Confusion reigned in the American camp as no good substitute for Greene was found. At the last minute, Washington replaced him first with John Sullivan, who had just returned from presiding over the defeat in Canada. Sullivan perhaps didn't cause the disaster, but he certainly contributed to it by sometimes rash, ill-considered movements. Israel Putnam soon replaced him, but neither he nor Sullivan was Greene's equal, and neither knew the ground as he did or had the experience to successfully fight a battle on this scale.

Washington was in overall command, of course, but he had the entire area, including Manhattan and the surrounding waterways, to think about. His problems grew on August 25, when Howe landed an additional corps of five thousand Hessians—fully recovered from their voyage—bringing the total of the invading army up to twenty thousand.

The behavior of the Hessians on Staten Island, although they were there only a few days, was noteworthy for its savagery. Raping, pillaging, and murdering friend and foe alike with abandon, they continued their loathsome behavior on Long Island. Ambrose Serle, Lord Howe's conservative, anti-American secretary, noted in his journal that the Germans "had committed already several depredations, and even upon the friends of government. . . . I should have rejoiced if the rebellion could have been reduced without foreign troops at all, for I fear our employment of these upon this service will tend to irritate and inflame the Americans."

The problem of keeping the Germans from abusing anyone they pleased was something that would bedevil General Howe and his successor throughout the war. Their numbers exacerbated the problem. In the course of the war the king employed over thirty thousand German mercenaries.

Four days of unnerving inaction followed the Howes' spectacular landing at Gravesend Bay on the twenty-second. Washington was understandably anxious. He was committed to defending Brooklyn Heights with only eight thousand inexperienced, poorly equipped amateurs, while the enemy had twenty thousand well-trained, splendidly outfitted professionals. Washington didn't know how many he faced. His principal source of information was deserters, who themselves were only guessing.

In fact, Washington's position, especially with General Greene disabled, was untenable. Yet retreating from the Heights meant giving up Manhattan, and neither Congress nor the commander in chief had made the momentous decision to do that. Washington considered the city of vital importance, yet impossible to defend against an enemy with overwhelming naval power. He felt he had to fight for Manhattan, but he didn't quite know how. He was without a viable strategy, his army dangerously divided between Manhattan and Brooklyn, waiting for the Howes' next move.

As each day went slowly by, the mystery of what General Howe was planning deepened. The only thing of note occurred on the twenty-sixth, when Clinton and Cornwallis shifted their headquarters east to the village of Flatlands. Neither Washington nor his generals read anything into the move.

Meanwhile, General Howe was carefully studying the disposition of the American troops. The strong defensive perimeter that General Greene had constructed on Brooklyn Heights did not invite a frontal attack. But situated between Greene's defense and Howe's army were the Heights of Guan, a thickly wooded ridge, one-hundred fifty feet high, that ran west to east and formed a natural outer barrier for Greene's defenses. Four passes ran through the dense forest: Martense Lane, Flatbush, Bedford, and Jamaica.

Without considering the problem of whether to defend the passes fully, Washington, who was still without a strategy, permitted General Sullivan, a strong advocate of making a stand at the Heights of Guan, to move over three thousand defenders from Greene's fortress and distribute them at the first three passes, while inexplicably leaving the fourth, the Jamaica Pass, undefended except for five meaningless scouts.

General Howe expected all four passes to be heavily guarded, but as his scouts, most notably General Clinton, searched the terrain, they discovered that this was not the case. Clinton urged Howe to exploit this major oversight, and he laid out a cogent plan for doing it. Howe was not receptive at first. After Clinton's humiliation at Charleston, he had a hard job convincing Howe to follow any of his proposals. The two men did not like each other and had a hard job working together. Howe found Clinton irksome, particularly his continually badgering him with advice.

Determined to redeem himself for Charleston, Clinton persisted, urging Howe to make a flanking movement through the undefended pass. He argued that a secret night march could bring half the British troops through the Jamaica Pass undetected. They could then roll up the Jamaica Road, which connected Brooklyn's East River wharves with Long Island's farmers. At the same time, diversionary attacks could be made at the other passes, holding the American defenders in place, while the redcoats got in back of them before they knew it, creating a panic that would allow the British to overwhelm them and force a surrender of the Heights.

The decision Howe had to make was not without risk of a flank attack when he divided his army. But the risk was so small he decided to take it. As it turned out, Washington, Sullivan, and Putnam were not contemplating a flank attack with their weak army; they were waiting on the defensive, hoping for another Bunker Hill. Washington couldn't be sure there wouldn't be a simultaneous attack on Manhattan. Even though the patriot leadership was focused on their defenses, they were totally unaware of their all too obvious weak spot to the east. A surprise envelopment movement through the Jamaica Pass never crossed their minds.

On August 26, in the dead of night, Howe went into action. Aided by Loyalist Oliver De Lancey and three local farmers who knew the ground well, Clinton and Cornwallis began quietly marching ten thousand troops and their artillery toward the Jamaica Pass to outflank and envelop the patriots. A few stray reports came to Sullivan and Putnam warning of the movement of a large British column, but they dismissed them. General Howe traveled along with the column; he was not leaving any key decisions to either Clinton or Cornwallis. He placed little trust in either of them.

At the same time that Howe's column was in motion on the twenty-seventh during the wee hours of the morning, Admiral Howe was sailing forward in a menacing fashion toward Manhattan with nine big warships, including the *Eagle,* the *Asia*, the *Renown*, the *Preston*, and the *Repulse*. Their guns were run out, giving the impression that the main attack would be on the city, not on Brooklyn. The warships also made a show of attacking Fort Defiance on Red Hook, but only a few harmless shots were exchanged.

Meanwhile, General Howe's column, traveling in miraculous silence, slipped through the Jamaica cut in the thick woods without incident, taking Washington completely by surprise. Howe continued on with no opposition, moving west down the Jamaica Road toward

Bedford, easily getting in the American rear as planned. While he did, General Grant, who had already begun his diversionary attack on the American far right, pushed forward on the Gowanus Road toward the Martense Lane Pass. He met strong opposition from Lord Stirling, who believed that this was the main British thrust. Stirling and the American leaders at the other passes and at the fortifications on Brooklyn Heights—indeed, Washington himself—had no idea what was taking place at the unguarded Jamaica Pass.

By 9:00 a.m. Howe had managed to move ten thousand troops through the pass undetected and on down the Jamaica Road west to the crossroads village of Bedford. His scheme had worked to perfection. As his army continued to push west toward Brooklyn Heights, Grant kept pressing the attack on the patriots' far right, while the Hessians, under General Philip von Heister, attacked the Flatbush and Bedford passes with superior numbers and artillery. Cornwallis, meanwhile, drove his men from Bedford village directly at the Americans fleeing from the passes.

As Howe's main body pushed toward Brooklyn Heights, frightened, bewildered patriots on the Heights of Guan, reacting to the tremendous British force in back of them, broke and ran, fleeing in a wild retreat, trying desperately to get back to the fortress on the Heights. Incredibly, around 80 percent of them did. The rest were either killed or captured. Many were bayoneted by Germans after they surrendered.

General Grant ran into the stiffest opposition from Lord Stirling's men, who included crack troops from Delaware and Maryland—perhaps Washington's best. Grant had an initial force of five thousand, which he bolstered with marines from the ships, and although Stirling fought well, the numbers inevitably overwhelmed him. When Cornwallis eventually came down on his rear with perhaps four thousand additional troops, Stirling did not have a chance. At the same time, over at the Flatbush and Bedford passes, the Hessians had an easy time of it with General Sullivan, who was personally in command. In the ensuing chaos, both Sullivan and Stirling were captured.

The major part of the battle was over around noon. In just a few superbly planned hours, General Howe won an immense victory, a triumph that could well have spelled doom for the American cause. Around two hundred patriots were killed or wounded and close to nine hundred taken prisoner. The British had about 63 killed and 314 wounded or missing. The numbers were not precise; they were never accurately determined.

Clinton wanted to keep pursuing the Americans into their fortifications on the Heights. He thought their panic was so great Howe could easily overpower them, take the fort, and have all Long Island under control by the end of the day. From Clinton's point of view, all they had to do was keep the panicky rebels on the run and chase them clear to the East River. As Clinton and General John Vaughan approached the Heights, they received serious fire from Putnam's men at the fort, but they thought it wouldn't matter.

General Howe saw it differently. There was no need to hurry, in his view. Brooklyn was theirs, in any event, and so was Washington's surrender. Regular approaches to the Heights might mean having to wait a day or two for the rebels to give up, but that was a small price to pay for minimizing losses. Unlike Washington, Howe had no quick way to reinforce his army. "I well knew," he insisted, "that any considerable loss sustained by the army could not speedily, nor easily be repaired." "[E]ven a victory," he wrote, "attended by a heavy loss of men on our part, would have given a fatal check to the progress of the war, and might have proved irreparable."

Washington's surrender would probably have meant that the Revolution was over, at least temporarily and perhaps forever. On the other hand, if he retreated successfully and kept his army intact, the Revolution was only dealt a body blow—severe but not necessarily fatal. Howe saw no chance that the rebels could escape. Their only avenue of retreat was across the East River, and the Royal Navy was in command there, or so it seemed.

Washington and Putnam, meanwhile, were preparing for a bloody showdown. They were surprised, and more than a little relieved, when Howe decided to pause. While he did, Washington brought three more regiments over from Manhattan. Admiral Howe did nothing to stop him.

The Howes were not ready for the large number of prisoners they acquired. No plans had been made to house them. They had to improvise. Every facility within New York City was used, as well as ships anchored in the harbor. The Americans were not considered prisoners of war, since Britain was not officially at war with the United States of America, an entity London did not recognize. The prisoners were simply rebels who could be treated any way the British pleased. And that turned out to be unimaginably cruel, under the dominion of past masters of the bizarre and gruesome, Joshua Loring Jr. and William Cunningham.

Their main instrument of torture was starvation. Rations allotted for prisoners were under their direct control. Instead of feeding their captives, they starved them to death and sold their food for large sums. Emaciated captives contracted diseases of every kind and often died of them before they succumbed to actual hunger. Those that remained alive were crowded into confined spaces that were so small, there was often no place to lie down. When they had space, they slept on hard wood or stone without straw. The prisoners were deprived of clothing and heat during the winter and fresh air in the summer. The little water they were given was foul, and they got no medical care.

The wanton, officially condoned murder of hundreds and then thousands of patriots was the direct responsibility of the Howes. Joshua Loring had traded his wife with General Howe for the money he could line his pockets with by starving prisoners to death. There was no way Howe and Mrs. Loring could not have known what was going on. And the same goes for Admiral Howe when ships were being used to kill prisoners.

When unsuspecting young patriots were captured during the Battle of Brooklyn, they were bewildered by the cursing and abuse they were subjected to, and utterly unprepared for being starved and allowed to die wretched deaths. Their treatment was even worse than that inflicted on American captives in Canada—as bad as that was—and it began a tale of woe that lasted throughout the long war. What happened to the prisoners was so horrendous it easily ranks as the worst war crime of the eighteenth century.

Chapter 7

A MASTERFUL RETREAT

When news of the American rout reached Admiral Howe late on August 27, he must have thought that his chance to be the peacemaker who saved the colonies for the empire finally had arrived, and he moved quickly. He took it for granted that Washington was trapped on Brooklyn Heights and would surrender in a day or two. His brother was so confident of victory, he was not requesting any additional support from the navy. Lord Howe wrote to Commodore Hotham, "I have the satisfaction to hear from General Howe, that he has every reason to be contented with the prospects before him."

Indeed he was. Both Howes believed that they had achieved their primary objective—defeating Washington's army. Lord Howe expected the war to end and a new era in relations between colonies and mother country to begin. Instead of concentrating on keeping Washington penned up in Brooklyn Heights, Howe focused on getting negotiations started right away and ignored the obvious need to patrol the East River. He could easily have sealed it off and made certain Washington was trapped. No matter what the weather was, Howe had the resources to keep the river clear of rebel boats.

Instead, he forgot about the East River and turned his mind to the Continental Congress and the effect the defeat would have on the delegates. He hoped it would change enough minds to set in motion a new dialogue. Preoccupied with the peace initiative, he never considered that the rebel army might survive. Even though there were unmistakable signs that Washington might try to retreat across the river, Lord Howe ignored them. He overlooked the unusual amount of rebel activity on the water, as large numbers of boats were collected to bring the defeated army back to Manhattan.

On August 28, while the fighting was still going on in Brooklyn, Howe invited two prominent prisoners, Generals Stirling and Sullivan, aboard the *Eagle* for dinner and a long conversation about the possibilities of peace. Sullivan was captivated by the talk and agreed to go to Philadelphia to convince Congress of the importance of at least listening to what the admiral had to say.

Meanwhile, on the same day, Washington reinforced his army on Brooklyn Heights, bringing the total to 9,500. Among them were Colonel John Glover and his regiment of mariners from Marblehead, Massachusetts. Washington was committed to fighting it out. He was not going to surrender, even though the odds against him were daunting. His men, as may be imagined, were tired, downcast, many sick or wounded, and, for the most part, without shelter. The enemy was close, less than a mile away. Their artillery was firing, and General Howe was beginning a formal siege by digging trenches five hundred yards away that would bring troops and guns within easy striking distance without unduly exposing them. But a heavy rain developed that day, mercifully bringing the activity to a halt, as the British moved into their tents.

During the evening of the twenty-eighth the rain let up, and while Lord Howe was having dinner with Stirling and Sullivan, General Howe, assuming that Washington had no place to go, continued his formal siege. Engineers started digging trenches again.

As nervous patriot militiamen listened to the sound of shovels moving dirt and stone, they dreaded what lay ahead. At the same time, Washington was having second thoughts about his strategy. When he rode over the ground early on the morning of the twenty-ninth, he realized there was no hope if he stayed where he was. He had made a terrible mistake, splitting his amateur army and trying to defend Brooklyn Heights against a force more than twice the size of his. His close confidant Adjutant General Joseph Reed confirmed this dismal view of their situation. Washington quickly decided to attempt the impossible and retreat, even though Lord Howe controlled the East River. As Congress required him to do, he called a council of senior officers, and they agreed that the entire army should leave that night.

Before the dramatic council meeting, Washington had already sent orders to General William Heath to round up all available boats and assemble them on the New York side of the East River, across from the encampment at Brooklyn Heights. If Admiral Howe was paying attention, Washington wanted him to think he was bringing more troops from Manhattan over to Brooklyn.

Heath ordered Colonel Hugh Hughes, assistant quartermaster general in New York, to round up every boat he could lay his hands on. Once Washington had the boats in place, he could use Colonels John Glover and Israel Hutchinson and their regiments of mariners from the Massachusetts towns of Salem, Beverly, Gloucester, Cape Ann, Danvers, and Marblehead to man them. Tough fighters and excellent seamen, they would be tasked with the seemingly impossible job of bringing all of Washington's troops, horses, and equipment across the East River during the night under the noses of the Royal Navy and its renowned fighting admiral.

As the sun set, strong winds were blowing from the northeast, keeping Lord Howe's big warships out of the East River, but his smaller craft with swivel guns in their prows could easily have worked up the river and disrupted Washington's entire operation. Fortunately, Admiral Howe was preoccupied with organizing peace. His boats were nowhere to be seen.

Washington was planning to bring off all 9,500 men, their horses, equipment, and supplies. It was a gamble of a high order. As Glover and Hutchinson raced to get every small boat ready and crews assigned, Washington kept watching for the Royal Navy. He naturally worried that Lord Howe's small boats might sound the alarm, triggering a frontal assault from his brother. The navy could then have wreaked havoc on Glover's small boats while they were in the middle of the mile-wide East River loaded with men.

But Admiral Howe, who had a well-deserved reputation for paying close attention to detail, hadn't the least suspicion what was up. He was confident that Washington wasn't going anywhere. The vicious storm that blew in on the twenty-ninth made him doubly certain. It brought heavy rain pelting down, making it even less likely the rebels would attempt to withdraw over the water.

Actually, the storm made it easier for them to cloak their movements. The operation began at 8:00 p.m. Washington was everywhere, directing and encouraging. Wind was blowing from the northeast, increasing to the point where the small craft were in danger of being swept downriver into the arms of Lord Howe's fleet. Despite the conditions, the Massachusetts mariners rowed men and equipment across the East River all during the night. Back and forth they went, fighting off every obstacle.

The strong wind abated around 11:00 p.m., making the going far easier but also making the flotilla more visible and vulnerable. Glover and his men kept at it. At daybreak a providential fog covered the final stages of the retreat. Incredibly, General Howe's men did not discover what was going on until the evacuation was almost finished. They managed to fire at the last of the retreating patriots but succeeded in wounding only four. None were killed. Three looters, who stayed behind, were captured. The operation was as perfectly executed as it could possibly have been. The failure of Admiral Howe to either prevent or detect the retreat was a colossal oversight that would cost him and his cause dearly.

With Washington's departure, General Howe gained control of Brooklyn Heights with a minimal loss of men. New York City lay at his feet.

The rebel army was in retreat and in disarray. It was a surpassing achievement. The only thing marring it was the wanton and indiscriminate cruelty of the Germans and some redcoats as they pillaged and raped in Queens and Kings counties. Word of their depravity spread fast and hurt the Howes' cause, as would the sadistic behavior of their jailers, which was just beginning and was not yet known.

News of the victory reached London on October 10. Britain was ecstatic. King George assumed that Washington's army would soon be suppressed, followed by the joining of British forces at Albany and, soon after, the submission of Congress. His vision of the way to preserve the empire had been vindicated. The ambitions of France were frustrated. It was a great triumph. The king made General Howe a Knight of the Bath and wrote him a personal letter promising a lucrative sinecure when he returned.

★

WHILE THE KING CELEBRATED, THE NEGOTIATIONS THAT Lord Howe had set in motion on August 28 proceeded apace, with the critical difference that Washington's army, although defeated and humiliated, had survived. Nevertheless, the admiral was so dazzled by the prospect of being the great peacemaker that he hoped the easy victory on Long Island would be enough to make Congress reconsider independence.

He persuaded Sullivan, but not Stirling, to help arrange a conference on Staten Island with a congressional delegation. Howe wanted to inform Congress of the terms that might follow if the patriots surrendered. Germain and the king had insisted, as a key part of Howe's instructions, that until the rebels gave up, no discussion of the terms of reconciliation could take place. And even then, anything Howe agreed to had to be approved in London.

On August 30, Sullivan, who was on parole, visited Washington and requested permission to go to Philadelphia and present Howe's request for a conference. Washington thought that Sullivan was naïve to think Howe had anything real to offer, but he agreed that the matter was for Congress to decide. The following day, Sullivan set out for Philadelphia. By September 2 he was hard at work trying to convince delegates that no harm could come from listening to what Howe had to say. After considerable discussion and argument, Congress agreed.

Three delegates were selected—one from the North, another from the middle states, and a third from the South: John Adams of Massachusetts, Benjamin Franklin of Pennsylvania, and Edward Rutledge of South Carolina. They left Philadelphia on September 9 and reached Perth Amboy two days later. The admiral's barge was waiting to take them to Captain Christopher Billopp's landing at his estate on Staten Island, where Lord Howe welcomed them cordially. The ancestral home was a two-story gray stone mansion, and "dirty as a stable," according to John Adams. It was being used to house military guards. Lord Howe had two rooms cleaned up for the occasion.

Franklin knew Howe fairly well; the others had never met him. The discussion took place over dinner, and, not surprisingly, they found no common ground. It was clear from the start that none existed. Howe was frank in telling his guests that only after the colonies surrendered could real negotiations about the future take place. That was a nonstarter—as it was meant to be. Germain and the king imposed the requirement in order to keep total control of any talks. In spite of this, Howe insisted that acceptable terms could be worked out after surrender, but he wasn't convincing.

Franklin told Howe that it was too late to return to the empire. Too much had been inflicted on Americans for them to reverse course. "Forces have been sent out and towns have been burned," he said. ". . . We cannot now expect happiness under the dominion of Great Britain. All former attachments have been obliterated."

Adams and Rutledge felt the same. The discussion did not stop there, however. Franklin wanted to suggest a real alternative to Howe, although he wasn't expecting him to agree. He wanted to open Howe's mind to the possibility of a different approach that might avoid more needless slaughter. To begin with, he argued that independence was inevitable. Even if, in some sense, Britain won the existing war, it would only usher in an indefinite period of unrest requiring a large army of occupation. Perpetual resistance would inevitably move London to try to remake colonial society, which could never work. It was a recipe for continual strife. British troops would become a permanent fixture, as in Ireland, keeping down a hostile population, impoverishing both countries.

Franklin argued that instead of compounding Britain's errors and fighting a long, expensive war that could never be won, it would be far better for London to accept American independence. It would cost nothing. Trade between the two countries could flourish, enriching both, as it had in the past. Britain and America had been each other's principal trading partners. They could be again. Why not bring that lucrative business back to life, as an alternative to endless bloodshed? In time, even an alliance was possible. Why would that future not be better than constant, costly strife?

Even though Franklin knew they had no chance of persuading Howe's superiors, he did not feel the exercise was a waste of time. He wanted the admiral to be aware that an attractive alternative to civil war existed. He did not expect to change Howe's mind about independence, but he did want to give him something to think about.

What Howe actually thought was that the war would continue. He wrote a joint letter with his brother to Germain, telling him, "We do not yet perceive any symptom of that disposition to allegiance and submission to legal government, which would justify us in expecting to see public tranquility soon restored."

In the same letter, Howe felt obliged to record that "[t]he three gentlemen were very explicit in their opinions, that the associated colonies would not accede to any peace or alliance, but as free and independent states; and they endeavoured to prove that Great Britain would derive more extensive and more durable advantages from such an alliance, than from the connection it was the object of the commission to restore."

Franklin could not even convince Lord Howe, never mind George III, that independence was a realistic way out of the bloody mess they were in. The king could never accept an independent America. Even though a war would be averted, a huge sum of money saved, along with thousands of lives, independence would diminish England's power and prestige, diminish her place in the world, and that was intolerable. Friendly relations might be restored, and beneficial trade resumed, even an alliance formed, but the thought of destroying Britain's dominion over North America was abhorrent.

Germain and Sandwich, of course, felt the same. After the spectacular victory on Long Island they expected submission, not a negotiated settlement, and certainly not independence. Their fixation with military power was too strong to consider any alternative, particularly when it appeared they were winning.

John Adams shared his impressions of the meeting with Abigail:

> Yesterday morning I returned with Dr. Franklin and Mr. Rutledge from Staten Island, where we met Lord Howe and had about three hours conversation with him. The results of this interview will do no disservice to us. It is now plain, that his lordship has no power but what is given him in the act of Parliament [the Prohibitive Act]. His commission authorizes him to grant pardons upon submission, and to converse, consult, and advise with such persons as he may think proper, upon American grievances, upon the instructions to governors and the acts of Parliament, and if any errors should be found to have crept in, His Majesty and the ministry were willing they should be rectified. . . . His lordship is about fifty years of age. He is a well-bred man, but . . . his head is rather confused.

The talks on Staten Island did not serve Lord Howe well. They made him appear a novice out of his depth, but they were of great importance to the patriots, giving them critical time to recover somewhat from the terrible beating they had taken on Long Island. Had General Howe, instead of pausing to allow his brother time to negotiate, immediately followed up his victory with an attack on Washington's depressed army in Manhattan, it probably would have been fatal.

———

If London was happy with the victory on Long Island, Paris was not. The easy defeat of the American army was discouraging, and the negotiations that took place immediately afterward unsettling. There were second thoughts. The possibilities generated by patriot successes in 1775 now seemed further and further away, if not beyond reach. A worried Silas Deane, the sole American agent in Paris at the time, wrote to the Committee of Secret Correspondence from Paris, warning, "The ministry had become [unnerved by] . . . the bold assertion of the British ambassador that you were accommodating matters. . . . [This] had brought them to apprehend not only a settlement between the two countries, but the most serious consequences to their West India islands, should we unite again with Great Britain. . . . So strong were their apprehensions, that an order [was] issued to suspend furnishing me with stores." Deane went on to note that Beaumarchais had intervened and that the suspension was removed, but the French remained uneasy.

Chapter 8

THE HOWES TAKE
NEW YORK CITY

Despite the helpful pause that Lord Howe's talks provided, the amount of work needed for Washington to restore his shattered army remained prodigious. "Our situation is truly distressing," he wrote to Hancock on September 2. "The check our detachment sustained on the 27th ultimo has dispirited too great a proportion of our troops and filled their minds with apprehension and despair."

The defeat on Brooklyn Heights had a profound impact on the inexperienced patriot militiamen. Depression set in; desertion was rampant, recriminations widespread. Three-quarters of the disillusioned Connecticut militia—over four thousand men—simply went home. Washington did nothing to stop them; there were just too many. In spite of his brilliant retreat, confidence in his leadership plummeted. The need to replace him with someone like General Charles Lee, who was mistakenly given credit for the victory at Charleston, was a common refrain among officers and men, as well as many in Congress.

Washington was as dissatisfied with his troops as they were with him. In the same heartfelt letter of September 2, he complained to

Hancock about the army: "No dependence could be put in a militia, or other troops than those enlisted for a longer period than our regulations heretofore have prescribed. . . . our liberties must of necessity be greatly hazarded if not entirely lost, if their defense is left to any but a permanent standing army; I mean one to exist during the war."

Washington had been urging these views on Congress for a long time but had gotten nowhere. Given the experience of the last few weeks, however, Congress was finally willing to listen, although Washington did not know it yet. And even if Congress was willing to consider remaking the army, actually doing it would prove enormously difficult.

With Washington lacking confidence in his militiamen and they doubting him, the atmosphere was toxic. And not just in the army. Throughout the country, and in France, Howe's easy triumph raised serious questions. Having come close to losing everything, there was plenty of soul-searching. One thing stood out—Washington's army had to survive. Under no circumstances should it be put at risk again. Already the army had shrunk to around sixteen thousand dejected men, and at least four thousand more were sick. General Howe had over twenty-five thousand healthy, well-equipped regulars.

Not only was Washington in need of a different kind of army, he desperately needed a new strategy. As always, he sought advice from his senior officers and Congress. In spite of the horrific conditions he was working under, he always kept Congress well informed and sought its guidance. In the same letter of September 2, he asked Hancock this critical question: "If we should be obliged to abandon the town, ought it to stand as winter quarters for the enemy? . . . I dare say the enemy mean to preserve it, if they can. If Congress, therefore, should resolve upon the destruction of it, the resolution should be a profound secret, as the knowledge of it will make a capital change in their plans."

The response from Philadelphia was uncharacteristically swift. Congress was already considering the question and on September 3 resolved that special care should be taken that no damage be done to the city, on the assumption that even if the enemy possessed it, in time it would be recovered.

Washington hadn't made up his mind yet to abandon Manhattan Island. Congress hoped it could be held, but left the decision up to the commander in chief and his senior officers. The New York Provincial Convention also left the decision up to them. Washington had long believed in the unique importance—real and symbolic—of the city, but he also feared that the patriots could lose the army trying to defend it. He had a tendency—uncommon in military leaders—to see all sides of difficult issues, which in some cases led to wise decisions and in others to a dangerous indecision.

He told Hancock that he was making preparations to leave the island just in case. "Judging it expedient to guard against every contingency, as far as our peculiar situation will admit and that we may have resources left if obliged to abandon this place," he wrote, "I have sent away and am removing . . . all of our stores that are unnecessary, and that will not be immediately wanted."

Although Washington had not made up his mind what to do, General Greene, the officer he most respected, had. Greene, who had recovered enough to write his opinion but not to resume his duties, had no doubt about what should be done. On September 5 he urged immediate evacuation to save the army, and burning the city to deprive the British of a comfortable winter base. He told Washington that once Long Island was lost New York could not be held, what with the land and sea forces available to the enemy. Greene pointed out that Tories owned two-thirds of the town anyway. "A general and speedy retreat is absolutely necessary," he said, and then added, "burn the city and suburbs."

Deciding what to do about Manhattan would have been easier if Washington had had good intelligence about the enemy's plans, but he did not. "Their designs we cannot learn," he told Hancock on September 6, "nor have we been able to procure the least information of late, of any of their plans or intended operations." Nevertheless, Washington thought it likely that the Howes would attempt to trap him on Manhattan, stopping intercourse between the island and New Jersey with their warships, while at the same time "crossing the Sound above us" with their army and cutting off all "intercourse with the country [Connecticut and the rest of New York]."

The next day, Washington held a crucial meeting with his senior officers to discuss strategy, and on September 8 he reported the results to Hancock. "On our side the war should be defensive," he wrote, ". . . we should on all occasions avoid a general action, nor put anything to risk, unless compelled by a necessity into which we ought never to be drawn." He added, "It would be presumption to draw out our young troops into open ground against their superiors both in numbers and discipline. I have never spared the spade and pickaxe."

Even while conceding the probable need to abandon Manhattan, Washington and the majority of his officers proposed delaying their departure for as long as possible. The result of their meeting, thus, was actually to remain exposed on Manhattan, and to inexplicitly divide their force, leaving them even more vulnerable.

The already outnumbered American army was separated into three divisions. General Putnam was to receive an additional fifteen hundred men to add to the thirty-five hundred he already had in the city at the southern tip of the island. General Heath was given command of nine thousand to guard Harlem Heights and Kings Bridge—Washington's only way off the island—while General Greene and General Joseph Spencer of Connecticut were given the rest to defend the middle of the island around Kip's Bay (a large cove near present-day Thirty-fourth Street) and Turtle Bay. The already strong patriot fortifications at Harlem Heights were to be strengthened, along with Fort Washington and the Hudson River defenses. Washington ordered General Mercer in Perth Amboy to put more men and supplies into Fort Lee, while the obstructions in the river were improved. Despite Washington's experience with the *Phoenix* and the *Rose*, he continued to believe that the two forts and obstructions could deny Admiral Howe access to the Hudson above Manhattan.

The minds of Washington and his officers soon changed, however. On September 12, at another council meeting, they agreed (Mercer was an exception) that the city had to be abandoned as soon as possible. Washington told Hancock that General Howe's strategy was "to get in our rear" and added, "We are now taking every method in our power to remove stores. . . . I fear we shall not effect the whole before we meet with some interruption."

The interruption came the very next day, when General Howe conducted a huge amphibious assault on Manhattan from the East River, landing 12,500 men at Kip's Bay. His movements during the preceding two weeks plainly indicated that a major attack was in the works, but Washington was still unprepared.

As far back as September 3, Captain Wallace and the *Rose* had led three dozen flatboats up the East River to Wallabout Bay on Brooklyn's northwest shore, where the Brooklyn Navy Yard once stood. After being fired on from Manhattan, he had moved to Newtown Creek, the tidal estuary dividing Brooklyn from Queens. On September 9, General Howe moved troops up the river and occupied the three big islands, Blackwell's (Roosevelt), Buchanan's (Wards), and Montresor's (Randalls).

On September 13 the *Phoenix* (44 guns), the *Roebuck* (44), the *Orpheus* (32), and the *Carysfort* (32) ran through the channel to the east of Governors Island and up the East River under topsails alone. Patriot gunners fired on them from batteries on Manhattan, cutting up sails and rigging and killing a seaman on the *Roebuck*. British artillery on Long Island returned fire but with little effect. The four warships—exhibiting contempt for patriot gunners—did not fire a single shot as they ran up the river to Kip's Bay, where they found the *Rose* already anchored.

The following day, six big transports under Lieutenants John Knowles and David Laird brought up more men and artillery. They ran close to the shore of Long Island, unnoticed by the patriot batteries on Manhattan. Later, flatboats, bateaux, and galleys made their way to Kip's Bay the same sheltered way. By this time Washington knew that the long-expected landing on Manhattan Island was imminent, but he still did not know exactly where it would be.

Early on the morning of September 15 Lord Howe tried to divert his attention. The warships *Pearl* (32), *Repulse* (32), *Renown* (50) and the armed schooner *Tryal* pulled their anchors and ran north toward the Hudson, making a great deal of noise as they opened fire on patriot batteries on and around Manhattan. After running by them with no difficulty, the ships anchored near Bloomingdale, between present-day Ninety-sixth Street and 110th Street. They were there to distract the Americans from the invasion about to start in the East River, and also to stop the movement of men and baggage from the city by water to the strong patriot fortifications on the northern part of the island at Harlem Heights.

Later that morning, a little before eleven o'clock, five big warships, *Phoenix*, *Roebuck*, *Orpheus*, *Carlsfors*, and *Rose*, began bombarding Kip's Bay and Turtle Bay. They positioned their broadsides parallel to the shore and unleashed a horrendous fire on the divided, ill-prepared American defenders manning breastworks. Ambrose Serle wrote that few in the army or navy had ever witnessed "so terrible and so incessant a roar." It lasted for an hour, clearing the landing area on the beach.

When the cannon ceased firing, General Clinton and Hessian colonel Carl von Donop led two divisions from Long Island in flatboats—about four thousand men—and landed on the beach without opposition. Not wasting any time, they pushed inland about a mile to the high ground at Inclenberg, near present-day Thirty-fifth Street and Park Avenue, again without incident.

Stunned, vastly outgunned and outnumbered, the American defenders, who had not yet recovered from the disasters on Long Island, had already fled north toward the safety of Harlem Heights, throwing away their guns as they ran pell-mell for their lives. Not all of them got away; some were captured.

Washington was surprised that the landing was where it was; he expected it to be at Harlem or Morrisania (now the South Bronx). Fearing the worst, he leaped on his horse and galloped down to stop the wild, disorganized retreat himself, risking death or capture. Eventually he restored order, and the patriots retired to the protection of the strong entrenchments on Harlem Heights.

Meanwhile, General Putnam, responding to a quick message from

Washington, worked with inspiring speed to get his remaining thirty-five hundred troops, including Colonel Henry Knox's indispensable corps of artillery, out of the city and up north to the defense perimeter at Harlem Heights before Howe cut them off. With the help of Major Aaron Burr, his aide, Putnam fled north without encountering any of Howe's troops, reaching Harlem Heights safely. The only enemy fire he received was from Lord Howe's warships anchored near Bloomingdale. Their shooting was wide of the mark, however, and did no damage. Not all of Putnam's men could travel with him. Many escaped across the Hudson to New Jersey, while others remained hidden in town.

Fortunately for Putnam and Knox, Howe's landing went slowly. His small, flat-bottomed boats and galleys could not ferry troops across the river as fast as he wished. After General Clinton led the first contingent onto the beach, Howe followed at 2:00 p.m. By five o'clock, 12,500 men were at Inclenberg. Howe had been expecting strong resistance; a major battle developing on the beach, or close to it, would not have surprised him. He was not anticipating that the landing place would be a mystery to the patriots; he had done little to conceal it.

Since hours had gone by before all the British troops were ashore, it was impractical for them to cut across Manhattan and trap Putnam. Howe's main concern was getting his men safely on shore with their artillery and supplies. His attention was on Washington, not Putnam. Gathering enough force to withstand a possible counterattack was his first priority. The patriots theoretically had a strong army close by.

Under different circumstances, Washington might have been planning to strike from the north while Putnam worked up from the city with Knox and his artillery to challenge Howe from the south. Given the state of the Continental army, however, such a scenario was extremely unlikely. Striking Howe was the last thing on Washington's mind. He was in a defensive mode, creating as strong a position as possible on Harlem Heights. Still, Howe had to be cautious; he had no way of knowing what Washington was planning. He could not afford a single defeat. The aura of invincibility he was so carefully cultivating had to be protected.

As if to underscore the need for caution, at three in the morning on September 16 four American fireships attacked the *Renown*, the *Repulse*, and the *Pearl*, still anchored at Bloomingdale. Lookouts on the *Eagle* spotted the blazing fireships from five miles away. Guard boats on routine patrol around the big men-of-war reacted quickly, as did the warships themselves. The *Renown* and the *Pearl* got under way and easily maneuvered out of harm's way, while the fireships drifted harmlessly to the beach, ran aground, and burned themselves out. The *Repulse* did not have to move. Only one fireship got close, and it was easily dealt with. Washington was showing again that he meant to contest every inch of the river.

★

THE ACTUAL FALL OF NEW YORK CITY WAS ANTICLIMACTIC. Late in the afternoon of September 15, General Howe dispatched a brigade south to take possession of the town. There was no resistance. The populace gathered in the street to greet the victors as if they were liberators. Admiral Howe sent a party of marines to Fort George at the tip of the city to take formal possession and hoist the Union Jack. He also stationed the *Mercury* (24) and the *Fowey* (20) close to town as a precaution against wholesale looting by men from the transports. Ambrose Serle reported, "A great concourse of people assembled round the marines . . . with loud acclamations, and every possible demonstration of joy." Hundreds would later sign a "Declaration of Dependence" to affirm their loyalty to King George III.

Serle also noted ominously, "Sad complaints are made of the Hessians, who plunder all men, friends of government as well as foes, indiscriminately."

Four days later, Serle took a morning stroll around the city and was surprised by what he saw. "The fortifications of the rebels particularly excited my astonishment," he wrote. "They have formed breastworks and embrasures at the end of every street or avenue leading to the town; redoubts, forts, and lines of communication everywhere round about it. The infinite pains and labor, which they must have bestowed, one would have thought, from regret alone, would have inclined them to make some kind of stand. But their fears overpowered their resolution, and they evacuated the object of their toil in one short hour, without making the least defense or anything like a handsome retreat."

★

WHILE THE UNION JACK WAS BEING RAISED OVER THE CITY, General Howe marched the bulk of his army north and established himself a little over two miles south of Washington's heavily fortified lines on Harlem Heights. The two armies now faced each other across the width of the island, which at this point was only a mile wide. Washington's entrenchments, breastworks, and abatis extended between the Hudson and Harlem rivers; Howe's stretched from Horn's Hook to Bloomingdale.

Although Washington's army was reduced to about sixteen thousand effectives, it was still strongly positioned on Harlem Heights. Heavily fortified Fort Washington was a short distance north and west. General Howe did not want to get into a fight over Harlem Heights. He had no intention of risking large casualties in a frontal assault. He wanted to get Washington off Manhattan Island, which was his principal objective now, by inducing him to evacuate voluntarily. Threatening to get in back of him and cutting him off from the mainland seemed a good way to do it.

By now, the king's original strategy of sending an army up the Hudson and joining Carleton at Albany had been set aside. Howe's focus was entirely on Washington. Carleton was still bogged down building a fleet to regain control of Lake Champlain. It must have crossed Howe's mind that if he had had the thousands of troops that Carleton had received in May, he could have accomplished far more around New York than Carleton was doing up north. Howe must also have considered that New England could be attacked more easily from Narragansett Bay than by attempting to send an army through the uncertain northern wilderness to Albany.

———

With little or no good intelligence about what Howe intended, Washington was alert to every enemy movement. On September 16, the day after the Kip's Bay fiasco, he was concerned enough about the movement of large numbers of British troops to ride down to his advanced posts and make sure everyone was ready. When he approached the front line, he suddenly heard firing between an advance party of the enemy—about three hundred, it turned out—and a patriot scouting party of one hundred and fifty, under Lieutenant Colonel Thomas Knowlton and Major Andrew Leitch. Knowlton was a hero of Bunker Hill and one of Washington's most respected officers.

Anxious to hit back after the humiliation of the previous day, Washington decided to attack the three hundred redcoats in earnest. He added to his force, and in the fighting that followed, the patriots gave the enemy more than they could handle, forcing them to retreat in a hurry. In the melee, Leitch was wounded (dying two weeks later), and Knowlton was killed.

Not wanting a larger engagement to develop outside the protective barrier on the Heights, Washington ordered a withdrawal when he sensed that Howe was sending a large reinforcement. "Fearing the enemy, as I have since found was really the case, were sending a large body to support their party," Washington explained, he wisely withdrew.

The action, small though it was, restored Washington's spirits. His troops, unlike at Kip's Bay, gave a good account of themselves. He thought that they had won an important point against the British. Word of the victory spread fast, sparking a renewal of confidence. A remarkable change of attitude surged through the ranks. "This affair," Washington wrote to Hancock, "I am in hopes will be attended with many salutary consequences, as it seems to have greatly inspirited the whole of our troops."

After the skirmish, the two armies faced each other for several days while Howe considered his next move. A frontal attack on Harlem Heights was out of the question. Using the fleet for a flanking movement to threaten to get in Washington's rear and frightening him into a hurried evacuation became Howe's preferred strategy.

While the Howes prepared, they issued yet another proclamation on September 19, urging Americans to end their futile resistance and embrace their benevolent ruler. Once again, they claimed powers they did not have and distorted the king's views, claiming that His Majesty was prepared to change his previous royal proclamations and acts of Parliament, which, of course, he was not in the least prepared to do— especially with his army doing so well.

As if to demonstrate how far away peace was, just after midnight on September 21, a giant fire engulfed New York City. Mysterious incendiaries touched it off in multiple places, trying, it appeared, to burn the entire town. A strong wind aided them. The murderous flames swept over the west side of the city, consuming hundreds of buildings. Over a quarter of the town was destroyed. General Howe believed that the entire city would have been in ashes had it not been for the heroic efforts of Major General James Robertson and the British troops in town.

Some of Putnam's men who had stayed behind probably had disguised themselves and run through the streets setting one fire after another. It looked to Howe as if the fires had been carefully planned. He and Governor Tryon immediately claimed that the rebels were responsible. In the view both of the British and of later historians, too many men had been discovered setting fires for the events to be considered accidental. Once the fires started, they spread on wood shingles from roof to roof. Washington would never admit any involvement, but he was certainly pleased with the results. He only wished that the entire city had been destroyed.

General Howe was furious, and as luck would have it, an American spy fell into his hands, someone he could vent his spleen on. Nathan Hale, a Connecticut schoolteacher, operating undercover for Colonel Knowlton, was captured on the night of September 21, summarily dragged to the execution post, and hanged the next morning without a trial on orders from an enraged Howe. It was said that Hale's last words were, "I regret that I have but one life to give for my country." His devotion could not help but inspire not only patriots but those putting the noose around his neck.

Washington's problems kept piling up. Among his worries was the approaching dissolution of his army. Enlistments would begin expiring on December 1. He desperately needed to raise militia from the eastern states before January 1, when the enlistments of nearly his entire army would be over. He wrote to his brother, expressing dismay. "The dependence which the Congress have placed upon the militia has already greatly injured, and I fear will totally ruin our cause. . . . In short, it is not in the power of words to describe the task I have to perform. Fifty thousand pounds would not induce me again to undergo what I have done."

Two days later he wrote to Hancock, arguing again for a professional army with real compensation. Patriotism alone, he insisted, cannot sustain an army. "The jealousy of a standing army, and the evils to be apprehended are remote," he said, "and, in my judgment, situated and circumstanced as we are, not at all to be dreaded; but the consequence of wanting one, according to my ideas formed from the present view of things, is certain and inevitable ruin." He went on to insist that, based on experience, continuing to rely principally on militia was a sure road to disaster.

Washington had not been informed that in the previous two weeks Congress, after intense debate, had finally come around and accepted his view, resolving to form eighty-eight battalions "to be enlisted as soon as possible, and to serve during the war." Furthermore, Congress had voted appropriate compensation for all ranks and outlined the role each state was expected to play in raising battalions, making individual promotions, and providing arms and clothing. It helped allay Washington's fears, but as he knew only too well, passing resolutions was one thing, while producing battalions and their equipment was another.

Chapter 9

WASHINGTON EVACUATES MANHATTAN

On October 9, the heavy frigates *Phoenix* and *Roebuck*, the sloop of war *Tartar*, and three tenders raced up the Hudson from Bloomingdale toward Forts Washington and Lee and the enhanced river obstructions. The ships were well barricaded on their sides against small-arms fire. Captain Hyde Parker Jr. led the way in the *Phoenix*, remaining close to the east side of the river, its deepest part.

The forts were alerted and ready, firing as the men-of-war sped by, damaging sails, rigging, masts, spars, and ship's boats while killing nine and wounding eighteen. Several shots pierced the ships' hulls, but nothing stopped them. They continued north, attacking Colonel Tupper's small fleet of row galleys and other vessels in Spuyten Duyvil Creek, capturing some, and sinking others. Tupper's men beached their boats when they could and ran. When they could not, they leaped overboard and swam for shore. After the one-sided melee was over, the men-of-war settled in Tappan Bay for repairs and to bury their dead. Hyde Parker Jr. had once again demonstrated the inadequacy of the river defenses, and also the Howes' ability to easily land troops in Washington's rear.

Although Washington's defenses inflicted more damage this time, they failed in the main task of blocking the river. Nonetheless, Washington continued to have confidence in the forts and obstructions and kept adding to them.

Three days later, with all possible opposition on the water removed, General Howe began his long-delayed push to induce Washington to evacuate Manhattan. Nearly thirty critical days had elapsed since the landing at Kip's Bay, and winter was fast approaching. It looked as if the king's objective of crushing the American rebels in a single season was now completely beyond reach. Howe had already written to Germain on September 25 telling him that achieving victory by the end of the year was impossible. "I have not the slightest prospect of finishing the contest this campaign," he wrote, "nor until the rebels see preparations in the spring that may preclude all thoughts of further resistance."

Although Howe's armada had been extraordinarily large, it had not been enough, in his opinion. He needed another season and more troops. He also needed ten more sail of the line, so that, among other things, he would have enough seamen to conduct amphibious operations. He was having great difficulty with the number he had. The promised help from Loyalists never materialized.

Adding to Howe's conviction that gaining control of the corridor to Canada could not be accomplished in 1776 was word that Carleton and Burgoyne were still on Lake Champlain jousting with Benedict Arnold, Horatio Gates, and Philip Schuyler. The chances of a British army reaching Albany before the snow flew appeared nonexistent.

Since Howe had ruled out a direct attack on Harlem Heights long ago, he decided that the best way to force Washington into a precipitous withdrawal was to threaten his line of communication with Connecticut and the Hudson River Valley by an amphibious operation in Westchester County. Howe planned to lead his main army on another grand envelopment movement, as he had on Long Island, get in back of Washington, and perhaps lure him into a major battle on grounds far more advantageous than Harlem Heights. Admiral Howe's recent activity on the Hudson would serve as an important distraction. Lord Percy would be left behind with three brigades stationed in front of patriot lines at Harlem Heights to hold Washington's attention, while the main British army got in his rear.

During the discussions on strategy, General Clinton urged Howe to conduct the amphibious landing at New Rochelle, but Lord Howe did not like that area because of poor anchorage. General Howe decided to land on Throg's Neck. On October 12 an advance party of four thousand set out from Kip's Bay in flatboats, galleys, and bateaux—eighty in all— manned by hundreds of seamen from the fleet. They made their way in a dense fog through treacherous Hell Gate and landed at Throg's Neck. The fog made the tricky passage even more dangerous than it already was, but it also concealed the exact landing area.

It looked as though Howe could not possibly have chosen a worse place. At high tide Throg's Neck, a tiny peninsula two miles long, was actually an island attached to the mainland by a causeway running through a marsh and a small bridge over Westchester Creek. Despite the fog, patriots were soon aware of Howe's movements. General Heath, who had previously reconnoitered the area, sent Colonel Edward Hand with thirty riflemen to remove the planks from the bridge and defend the causeway. He also sent Colonel William Prescott, a hero of Bunker Hill, with a regiment, and Lieutenant John Bryant, with a 3-pounder, to help Colonel Hand. At the same time, Heath alerted Washington at his head- quarters in Morris House, near present-day West 160th Street. Washing- ton responded immediately, reinforcing Hand, Prescott, and Bryant.

By late afternoon, most of Howe's army was ashore. He wrote to Germain, "The very strong positions the enemy had taken on the island and fortified with incredible labor, determined me to get on their prin- cipal communication with Connecticut, with a view to forcing them to quit the strongholds in the neighborhood of Kings Bridge, and if pos- sible to bring them to action."

While the American army was preparing to move, Howe waited patiently on Throg's Neck for six days, during which time supplies and

German reinforcements arrived. He then moved, not to Dobbs Ferry on the Hudson, but to Pell's Point (in present-day Pelham), three miles away.

Washington, in the meantime, was certain that Howe was trying to get in back of him and cut him off from the north, but he was still moving slowly to escape the trap. As long as Howe was stuck at Throg's Neck, which was only four short miles from Kings Bridge, Washington for some reason felt safe. He did not call a meeting of senior officers until October 16. General Charles Lee, who had acquired enormous, entirely unwarranted prestige in and out of the army, had returned from South Carolina two days earlier, eager to take part in the proceedings. He quickly sensed the disappointment many officers felt about Washington's leadership. Ambitious to take his place, Lee watched for opportunities to undermine him. He lost no time urging Washington to abandon Manhattan immediately—implying that it should have been done much sooner—and march to defensible positions in the hills at White Plains before it was too late. There was plenty of protection there, Lee argued, and the army could keep in close contact with Governor Trumbull of Connecticut, who could be relied on to provide strong support, as he always had.

The council decided on the sixteenth to abandon Manhattan right away, except for Fort Washington, which the participants considered not only impregnable but critical for the defense of the Hudson, even though Lord Howe had repeatedly demonstrated that the forts and river obstructions did not work. The main army began moving out of Manhattan on October 18, crossing Kings Bridge, marching north toward White Plains, twenty miles away, keeping on the west side of the Bronx River.

Howe cooperated. He appeared in no hurry to attack. On October 18, Washington's long column, handicapped by a lack of wagons and horses, was marching slowly only a few miles away from the much stronger British army. But Howe ignored his opportunity for a flank attack. He concentrated on moving his men to Pell's Point and nothing else. He had already achieved his primary objective of getting Washington out of Manhattan without sacrificing a man. He was content with that for the moment.

When Washington saw the redcoats moving to Pell's Point, he naturally feared an attack on his flank, and dispatched Colonel John Glover—the same intrepid officer who had led the army's retreat across the East River on August 29—with 750 men to keep Howe from threatening the American column, although it's doubtful that Howe intended to. Glover opposed Howe with such skill and bravery that it looked as if he had altered Howe's plans for a flank attack, but it's unlikely that he did. In any case, Howe, who appeared in no hurry, remained on Pell's Point for another three days, giving Washington critical time to reach White Plains safely. On the night of October 20, Washington sent Lord Stirling, who had been exchanged with Sullivan, ahead to hold White Plains with a brigade and to prepare the ground. The main army arrived on the twenty-second. Washington had fourteen thousand men fit to fight. Another thirty-five hundred were with General Greene at Fort Lee, and two thousand were left with Colonel Robert Magaw to defend isolated Fort Washington on Manhattan.

Earlier on the twentieth, General Howe had moved a short distance to an area between Eastchester and New Rochelle. Still in no hurry, he had remained there until the twenty-first, when he moved another short distance to a place slightly north of New Rochelle and then, on the twenty-fifth, to ground that was four miles from Washington's lines at White Plains.

By this time Washington's defensive positions at White Plains extended three miles, from the Bronx River on the right to a swamp on his left. It was not altogether satisfactory, and he planned, if necessary, to fall back to more defensible ground on the heights of North Castle, between White Plains and the Croton River.

Howe, having been reinforced by Percy, now had around twenty thousand men. On the twenty-eighth he attacked, and although he won the first skirmish against Washington's exposed right wing at Chatterton Hill, he did not follow up. Three days passed. Washington spent the time organizing a short retreat to the higher ground at North Castle, which gave him the ability, if necessary, to withdraw to safety across the Croton River Bridge. He moved to the heights of North Castle during the night of October 31, surprising Howe. Washington was now in so strong a position that Howe had no incentive to attack him. In fact, Washington was where Howe wanted him—out of Manhattan.

Instead of attacking, Howe waited another day, and on November 2 he ordered Hessian Lieutenant General Wilhelm von Knyphausen to march back toward Manhattan with his corps and seize Fort Independence, near Kings Bridge. When Knyphausen arrived, he found the fort already in ruins. Washington had destroyed it. General Greene reported Howe's troops in substantial numbers around the ruins, guarding Kings Bridge.

More time passed while Washington waited anxiously for the enemy's next move. During the night of November 4, his sentinels heard odd sounds coming from the British lines. He ordered a full alert, but nothing happened. The following morning, November 5, he found, to his utter amazement—and relief—that Howe had disappeared. He had withdrawn his entire army from White Plains in the middle of the night and marched directly west to the Hudson.

Washington later explained to his brother John Augustine, "At White Plains, the enemy advanced a second time upon us as if they meant a general attack; but finding us ready to receive them, and upon such ground as they could not approach without loss, they filed off and returned towards New York."

It's likely that Howe left White Plains without attacking because he saw no point in losing men in a bloody battle where Washington had the advantage of fighting behind strong entrenchments. Howe wanted to fight only when he had an overwhelming advantage. Since he had achieved his limited objective of getting Washington out of Manhattan—except for Fort Washington, which he intended to attack shortly—it was time to prepare for the winter months and the spring campaign ahead. Any hope of achieving the king's grand objective of isolating New England had long since passed.

Howe intended to request massive reinforcements for the spring campaign. If Britain's forces were large enough at that time, he thought, it might even be possible to induce the rebels to seek peace rather than face the tidal wave that was coming at them. They could see how wretched Washington's army had become. They might conclude that more fighting was useless and just give up. That was his hope. If Congress chose, against all reason, to continue fighting, Howe would be prepared for that as well. Given this line of reasoning, he saw no sense in attacking Washington at North Castle and depleting his army. Why risk anything? The most important thing for Howe was protecting his aura of invincibility.

On the same day that General Howe withdrew unexpectedly from White Plains, Admiral Howe, in preparation for an attack on their next objective, Fort Washington, sent HMS *Pearl* and two tenders, *Joseph* and *British Queen*, racing by Forts Lee and Washington. They easily sailed through the improved obstructions. The forts fired on them, and the ships sustained casualties and damages, but they ran by with no trouble. This finally changed Washington's mind about the usefulness of both forts. It was obvious now that they should immediately be evacuated, particularly Fort Washington, but he did not order it. Instead, he allowed Greene to make the final decision.

In the meantime, Washington had to decide what to do with his army on the heights at North Castle. Uncertain where Howe was going after leaving White Plains, he divided his army again. He left Lee in charge at White Plains with the bulk of the army in case Howe turned and drove into New England, which was the last thing Howe had in mind. Leaving Lee with a large independent command was a serious error that would come back to haunt Washington again and again in the ensuing days. It was yet another of his tactical errors, in this case a large one. On paper Lee had perhaps nine thousand men, but only five thousand were fit for duty.

The rest of the army was also divided. General Heath was to guard the Highlands with 5,400, of whom perhaps 3,500 were fit for duty. Washington planned to take 2,500 and cross over to New Jersey, where he expected to combine with Greene's 2,500. He was anticipating that an additional two to three thousand New Jersey militiamen would join him as well.

Washington thought Howe would most likely move into New Jersey and threaten Philadelphia—something Howe, at the moment, wasn't planning to do. Washington expected Lee to cross the Hudson and reinforce him if it became clear that Howe was indeed moving into New Jersey in force. The safety of Fort Washington, which obviously was Howe's next objective, was, strangely, not a concern. Washington thought that Greene could quickly withdraw the garrison across the Hudson if he had to. He did not feel that Lord Howe's command of the waters around Manhattan would prevent them from ferrying more than two thousand men across in a hurry.

While all of this was being decided, an incident occurred that Washington reacted to with special fury. He was taken completely by surprise when a small contingent of Massachusetts militiamen looted the tiny village of White Plains, setting fire to homes as well as the courthouse. He was immediately alerted and the perpetrators apprehended. He had done everything he could to prevent this kind of thing, and he was understandably shaken by it. A Major Jonathan Austin led the criminals, and they were all punished, albeit lightly. A court-martial determined that Austin was guilty of conduct "not only unworthy [of] the character of an officer but of a human creature," and he was thrown out of the service.

Washington was certain that Howe's next objective would be Fort Washington, and he thought it should be abandoned, but Greene was convinced the fort could be held, or evacuated if necessary, but he did not believe it would be. This was the same General Greene who, only a short time before, had advocated abandoning Manhattan completely. Colonel Robert Magaw, in command at the fort, agreed with Greene.

Washington did not want to countermand them until he saw the situation firsthand. He wrote to Greene on November 8 from White Plains, "I am . . . inclined to think, that it will not be prudent to hazard the men and stores at Mount Washington; but, as you are on the spot, I leave it to you to give such orders, as to evacuating . . . as you may judge best." Washington was obviously comfortable leaving the decision to Greene, but if he were wrong, he would suffer another blow to his reputation. How many more he could take before Congress was forced to think seriously about replacing him was unknown, but it would not be forever.

Washington left White Plains for New Jersey on November 10 with twenty-five hundred troops. The presence of the British navy at the lower ferries forced him to march north to Peekskill, where he crossed the Hudson with his men on the morning of the twelfth. Before doing so, he reconnoitered the mountain passes on both sides of the river and inspected Forts Constitution and Montgomery on the west bank. He then brought his men across the river and in company with Lord Stirling, who had been scouting the area, and Colonel Reed, he led the troops through a gap in the mountains that Stirling knew and wound his way to the Hackensack River, where he established camp, ten miles from Fort Lee.

On November 14 Washington was conferring with Greene at Fort Lee and discovered that Greene was still determined to hold both Fort Washington and Fort Lee, and that he had reinforced Fort Washington. At this critical juncture there was barely time to override Greene and evacuate the troops, but Washington hesitated, unsure if Howe intended to bring his whole force against Fort Washington or invest it with only part of his men and send the rest elsewhere.

Unfortunately, Washington misjudged his opponent again. Howe intended to use his entire army against Fort Washington, and he moved quickly, determined to clear Manhattan of every rebel soldier before winter. He had a distinct advantage that the patriots were unaware of—complete details of the fort's defenses. Magaw's adjutant, William Demont, turned out to be a spy, and he had given the information to Lord Percy, who had passed it on to Howe.

The attack actually began the evening of November 14—much sooner than any of the patriots expected—when Lord Howe's seamen navigated thirty flatboats from the Hudson over Spuyten Duyvil Creek to the Harlem River unobserved. They would later move General Howe's army across the river to Manhattan for the assault on the fort.

There was still time for Washington to evacuate the fort during the night of the fourteenth. Instead of ordering Greene to do so as fast as possible, however, he let matters stand as they were and went off to his camp on the Hackensack River. None of the American leaders believed for an instant that the fort was so vulnerable it would fall in a matter of hours and leave them with no options.

Early on the morning of November 15, Colonel Magaw was asked to surrender, but, still thinking his defenses were strong, he refused. By then, Magaw had 2,837 men. Greene and Mercer had sent over eight hundred reinforcements. Greene notified Washington that day of the British demand for the surrender and of Colonel Magaw's refusal. Instead of acting right then, Washington waited until the sixteenth and crossed the Hudson with Greene, Mercer, and Putnam to see for himself what should be done. All of them believed there was still time. They soon found out differently. Even before they landed, they heard the opening shots of the battle, and they were forced to return to the other side of the river as the fighting heated up.

The assault on the fort was ferocious—unlike anything Magaw, or anyone else on the patriot side, had anticipated. The British and Hessians seemed to come from everywhere. Even batteries on the eastern side of the Harlem River, and from the frigate *Pearl* in the Hudson and three warships in the Harlem River, were firing. Magaw, who had never dreamed of being overwhelmed in this way, was forced to capitulate at 4:00 that afternoon. The fortress he thought was impregnable fell in a matter of hours.

Washington, meanwhile, assuming that Magaw could hold out for some time, finally had decided on the sixteenth to evacuate Fort Washington. He was arranging for the entire garrison to be withdrawn across the Hudson that night, and sent a young officer with the order to Magaw. Miraculously, the young officer got through, and, even more miraculously, he returned with a message from Magaw—telling the commander in chief that he was already in the process of surrendering.

It was a crushing blow. Obviously, the fort should have been evacuated long before. Washington and Greene were to blame. The loss devastated morale, which was already low, and Washington's credibility, which was also sinking fast.

Fifty-nine patriots were killed and one hundred wounded. The healthy and the injured—2,778 men—increased the number of prisoners in New York to more than 5,000. Their incarceration turned the already hellish nightmare devised by Loring and Cunningham into something even more foul. One of the American soldiers wrote, "As soon as the enemy took possession of the fort the abuse and plunder commenced . . . even the clothes on our backs were wrested from us. . . . We were marched to New York, where . . . the soldiers were thrust into Bridwell's sugar houses, &c., where they suffered almost every privation, and soon became diseased and died off . . . fast. . . . A great number enlisted with the enemy to save life, while suffering in close confinement and from starvation."

Hard as it was to believe, by the end of 1776, the willful starvation and brutal treatment of the prisoners would lead directly to the excruciating deaths of half their number. The Howe brothers could not possibly have been unaware of this catastrophe. Nor could they keep it hidden. For the patriots, it was one more indication of what awaited them if they submitted to His Majesty.

Once Fort Washington had been taken, it looked as if Washington would order the immediate evacuation of Fort Lee, but he did not. Instead, he returned to his camp on the Hackensack River and left the fort as it was. He intended to withdraw only when it was threatened. In the meantime, he was doing everything he could to increase the size of his army, assuming that Howe intended to cross the Hudson and make a major move on Philadelphia before the end of the campaign season. If Philadelphia fell, adding to the other disasters that had befallen the patriots, Washington assumed that the revolution would be pretty well done for, at least in the near term.

Chapter 10

RACE FOR THE DELAWARE

With the capture of Fort Washington, the British base in Manhattan was secure. To protect it through the winter, Howe prepared to establish strong outposts in eastern New Jersey at Perth Amboy and Brunswick (now New Brunswick) on the Raritan River. He also began organizing a strike on Rhode Island to provide winter anchorage for the fleet in Narragansett Bay as well as a base from which to attack New England in the spring.

He was not thinking about seizing Philadelphia at the moment. Attempting to take the rebel capital, although certainly appealing, would force Lord Howe into a fight for the Delaware River. It was too late in the year for that; the Delaware's defenses, unlike the Hudson's, were formidable. Lord Howe already had plenty of evidence of that. On May 8, 1776, his close friend Captain Andrew (Snape) Hamond sailed up the Delaware in the *Roebuck* (44), accompanied by Henry Bellew, in the 20-gun *Liverpool*, to test the river's defenses—much as Admiral Shuldham had done on the Hudson in July, only with far different results.

Thirteen row galleys of the Pennsylvania State Navy, led by Captain Henry Dougherty, engaged the two British warships in a two-and-a-half-hour running gun battle and came close to capturing both of them. Hamond ran aground just as Dougherty ran out of powder and shot. The *Liverpool* and a thick fog protected Hamond while he got unstuck during a tense night. He said later, "If the commanders of the galleys had acted with as much judgment as they did courage, they would have taken or destroyed [the *Roebuck*]." He might have added that if Pennsylvania patriots had had far more galleys, or Dougherty more powder and shot, the *Roebuck* would have been in much greater trouble.

The idea of taking Philadelphia remained attractive to General Howe. Since it was the capital of the revolutionary government and the largest city in the colonies, attacking it was a way to draw Washington into a general battle in which the British would have significant advantages. Howe was convinced that Washington would feel obliged to defend the city. Not only was Philadelphia of prime importance politically, it was a major commercial center only ninety miles from New York. The two cities combined were the economic heart of the colonies. Capturing both would go a long way toward crushing the revolt.

Howe never considered moving up the Hudson in force and capturing the Highland forts at this point, much less traveling all the way to Albany. Carleton had already returned to Canada, wisely putting off a drive on Albany until spring. He had finally completed building his fleet, and on October 11 defeated Benedict Arnold at the Battle of Valcour Island, near the western shore of Lake Champlain southeast of Plattsburgh. Carleton then chased the remnants of Arnold's navy south to Crown Point, which he occupied after Arnold fled. Nothing was left but ruins. Gates had already evacuated and destroyed it, so Carleton didn't gain much. Immediately afterward, he brought part of his army down the lake to Crown Point, which he was restoring, in preparation for an attack on Ticonderoga. The Americans, meanwhile, were busy preparing for a massive British assault on the fort. General Arnold was among the defenders.

The reality of the northern climate soon intruded on Carleton's preparations. On October 20, when the first snow began falling, it made a drive on Albany look quixotic to him. Before making up his mind what to do, he reconnoitered Ticonderoga. Even if he did not attempt to get to Albany, he could take the fort and leave a substantial garrison to hold it for the winter. It would be a good jumping-off point for the spring campaign.

Carleton, accompanied by Burgoyne and some of their officers, took boats south to look over the situation at Ticonderoga, appearing off the fort on October 28. Carleton didn't like what he saw. The defenders were ready for him. General Gates had taken the broken American army and restored it enough to make Ticonderoga difficult to capture with winter so close.

That was the final straw; Carleton decided to go back to Quebec, much to the annoyance of General Burgoyne, who wanted to show London that something important had come from their foray into New York. He urged Carleton to at least take the fort and hold it for the winter. But Carleton refused; he was not going to be pressured into doing something he knew made no sense. Supplying the fort all through a northern winter would be a major, and largely unnecessary, undertaking. Ticonderoga could wait until spring. He wrote to General Howe, explaining that the season was so advanced, attacking Ticonderoga and having to garrison it for the winter was a bad idea, and that he was retreating to Canada.

Carleton's decision made eminently good sense to Howe, who had become absorbed with planning for the spring campaign himself. Presumably, Carleton would resume his offensive then. Howe intended to do the same. In the meantime, he looked forward to settling down in Manhattan for the winter, resting his army, and waiting for the reinforcements he intended to request.

Before doing so, he moved with uncharacteristic speed to secure Brunswick and Perth Amboy. During the night of November 19 Admiral Howe sent two hundred boats and barges across the Hudson with Cornwallis and five thousand troops aboard, landing them near Closter

Dock, at the base of the Palisades, five miles north of Fort Lee. General Greene, unaccountably, was still in the fort with his men. Washington was at Hackensack village, with a diminishing, exhausted, demoralized army. Cornwallis hoped to catch both Greene and Washington by surprise.

He almost did. Fortunately, one of Greene's officers riding patrol early in morning of the twentieth discovered Cornwallis's landing and raced to Fort Lee. Greene immediately informed Washington, who leaped on his horse and galloped from the Hackensack to Fort Lee to urge on Greene, who was evacuating as fast as he could, leaving everything except gunpowder, which Washington had ordered removed earlier. Cannon, muskets, cartridges, shot, and shell were left, as well as flour, tents, and entrenching tools.

Cornwallis was so close and moved so fast that, when he reached the fort, fires beneath the kettles were still burning. He caught a few stragglers, but Greene managed to get away with most of the garrison to Hackensack.

The operation had gone so well for the British that General Howe came over from New York to have a look at Fort Lee and assess where to go from there. His immediate objective was securing Brunswick and Perth Amboy, but since Cornwallis was having such an easy time of it, he decided to reinforce him, go after Washington in earnest, and see what might come of it. In the succeeding days he brought Cornwallis's force up to ten thousand.

On November 22 Cornwallis left Fort Lee and went after Washington. But the American army, such as it was, had already left Hackensack the previous day and marched toward Newark. Washington reached the Acquackanonk Bridge over the Passaic River late in the day on the twenty-first, crossed it, and burned it before entering the village of Acquackanonk Landing, on the west bank of the river, close to Newark.

He departed Acquackanonk on the twenty-second and arrived in Newark late that afternoon, where he remained for six days, making his headquarters at the Blanchard House. On the twenty-eighth, when he finally left, the British vanguard was in sight. Why they had not appeared sooner was a mystery. Bad weather had slowed Cornwallis down, as well as the sheer size of his force. Obstructions thrown in his path also delayed him. But he could have reached Washington much sooner than he did.

During his time in Newark, Washington aggressively sought help. He sent Colonel Reed to Burlington to advise Governor Livingston of his desperate need for troops. General Thomas Mifflin was dispatched to Philadelphia for the same purpose, and Washington asked Schuyler to send Gates and Arnold with as many men as he could spare from the northern army. The 2,837 men lost at Fort Washington were sorely missed.

Even more of a problem was the unexplained absence of General Charles Lee and his army. They were desperately needed. Lee had become an enormous headache for Washington. Ever since Cornwallis's appearance, Washington had been urging—not ordering—Lee to bring his troops across the Hudson and join him. On November 21 he told him, "the public interest requires you coming over. . . I would have you move . . . by the easiest and best passage."

Technically this was not an order, but its import was unmistakable. Lee wouldn't budge, however. He had his own agenda. He wanted to supplant Washington as commander in chief. In spite of Washington's explicit requests, Lee remained in White Plains. He was immensely popular in the army and in Congress. Washington, on the other hand, having suffered an uninterrupted series of defeats since the Howes had landed in New York, was fast losing support. The horror of Fort Washington was an immense blow to his prestige, and now it looked as if he might be forced to surrender his army in New Jersey. Lee, it seemed, hoped that he would, and that he would then emerge as the savior of the revolution.

There was no doubt that many officers in the Continental army had lost confidence in the commander in chief, including General Gates and others closer to Washington, like thirty-five-year-old Colonel Joseph Reed, the adjutant general, one of Washington's most trusted advisors. Gates was simply an opportunist with ambitions of his own, but Reed was genuinely disillusioned. The capture of Fort Washington had been the last straw for him, as he confided to Lee, whom he had, unaccountably, come to admire. In Reed's eyes, Washington's indecision, which allowed Greene to lead the army to disaster at Fort Washington, fatally undermined the commander in chief's credibility.

Instead of immediately coming to Washington's aid, Lee was keeping his army apart, sending one excuse after another, explaining why he was remaining at White Plains. Neither he nor Washington had the slightest doubt that his army could be brought across the Hudson expeditiously, even when, in theory, Admiral Howe's fleet controlled all the waters around New York. In fact, Cornwallis was worried that Lee would suddenly appear in his rear. The British had a high regard for Lee's ability since, in a sense, he was one of their own, a respected former British officer—however misguided his political views had become. Cornwallis thought his whole operation could be put in jeopardy if Lee and Washington attacked him simultaneously.

Cornwallis had nothing to fear. Lee wasn't coming. He had already begun setting up an independent command, even requesting men from Massachusetts to bolster his army. Instead of responding to Washington's appeals, he ordered General Heath in the Highlands to send two thousand men across the Hudson to help in New Jersey. Heath refused, and Washington backed him, telling Lee that he wanted his troops, not Heath's. The Highlands, he said, were too important for them to consider withdrawing any units from the area. General George Clinton was with Heath at the time, urging him to defy Lee.

★

WHILE WASHINGTON WAS IN NEWARK, HE SERIOUSLY thought about giving up the idea of defending Philadelphia and taking what was left of his army to nearby Morristown in the Watchung Mountains for the winter. Morristown was only twenty-five miles west of Newark. Many of his officers thought that this was the best alternative. There was a much better chance, they thought, of preserving and expanding the army by establishing a strong defensive position in the mountains than by continuing to retreat to Brunswick and being over-whelmed by Cornwallis. It was a difficult decision for Washington, but, in the end, he felt that the loss of Philadelphia would be cata-strophic. He was determined to do everything in his power to prevent it. He continued south to Brunswick, intending to make a stand on the Raritan, if sufficient reinforcements arrived—particularly from Gen-eral Lee.

Washington left Newark on November 28, just before Cornwallis arrived. Once again, the patriot rear could see the British vanguard approaching. Washington reached Brunswick the next day at noon and, after crossing the Raritan, made the bridge impassable. During his impromptu retreat his continuous pleas for more men had borne some fruit, swelling his army to around 5,400, but on December 1 the enlist-ments of 2,000 would expire. He did not expect many to remain. He thought Cornwallis's army was now at least twice the size of his—as many as ten thousand or more, and growing.

In view of Cornwallis's strength, Washington gave up the idea of making a stand at Brunswick and decided to march as fast as he could south to the Delaware River, cross it, and set up defensive positions, hoping the river would act as a protective barrier.

With Cornwallis coming on fast from Newark, Washington pulled out of Brunswick on December 1, his army now reduced to around 3,400. He headed for Trenton, intending to cross the Delaware River into Pennsylvania as fast as possible. Cornwallis was right behind him, arriving in Brunswick just as the Americans were leaving.

Fortunately for Washington, Cornwallis stopped there for several days. General Howe was coming over from New York to confer, and Howe was apparently in no hurry. With the British giving him breath-ing room, Washington sped south to Princeton, then to Trenton (twenty-six miles from Brunswick), and finally crossed the Delaware on December 7 and 8.

Howe did not arrive in Brunswick from nearby New York City until December 6. After conferring with Cornwallis, he decided that going to Philadelphia this campaign was now a possibility. The weather was unseasonably mild; perhaps taking Philadelphia would make sense. It might even end the war. But he was not committing himself to doing it just yet.

In the meantime, he raced after Washington in hopes of catching him before he crossed the Delaware. Even if he missed him, he could at least bring his army up to the river and be in a better position to attack Philadelphia in the spring. The capital was only thirty-two miles from Trenton. On December 7, with Cornwallis in the lead, Howe took off after Washington, reaching nearby Princeton that afternoon. The following day, he arrived at Trenton just as the last of Washington's bedraggled army reached the Pennsylvania side of the Delaware. Howe's vanguard was approaching the riverbank as Washington's rear guard was climbing up the opposite side.

Howe could not follow immediately. No boats were available. Washington had commandeered all of them within miles. Days before, he had sent Captain Richard Humpton, a former British officer, to organize enough boats at Trenton to bring the army across the Delaware. After that, Humpton had seized every other boat along a seventy-mile stretch of river and moved them to the Pennsylvania side. If Howe had wanted to, he could have found the means to cross. There was plenty of wood in and about Trenton. But he decided not to.

There were other problems beside boats. Henry Knox's artillery was already firing from the other side of the river, indicating that a crossing would be contested. And Howe was uncomfortable not having naval supremacy on the Delaware. Robert Morris, who was functioning at this moment of supreme crisis almost as a head of government, since Congress had fled to Baltimore, was rushing row galleys and supplies upriver from Philadelphia to support Washington. In view of all this and the lateness of the season, on December 14 Howe decided that an attack on Philadelphia and Washington could wait. The British chief declared that the campaign of 1776 was over.

Without giving the matter much thought, he amended his original strategy of securing eastern New Jersey with strong garrisons only at Perth Amboy and Brunswick and added cantonments located roughly ten miles apart at Hackensack, Kingston, Princeton, Trenton, Borden-town, and Burlington. He thought that this new arrangement would afford him perfect starting points from which to take Philadelphia in the spring. The rebel capital was only twenty miles from Burlington.

Adding to his confidence was the reaction he was getting in New Jersey from another, more generous peace proposal that he and his brother proclaimed on November 30. The response was so strong it looked for all the world that New Jersey might be the first colony to return to the British fold. The Howes offered pardons and, more impor-tantly, protection against forfeiture of any property or suffering any other penalty, to anyone who appeared before a British official and swore allegiance to the king within sixty days. Past behavior did not matter. The offer was extended to everyone, even, and perhaps espe-cially, to those actively participating in the rebellion. Three thousand men accepted the terms immediately—a breathtaking number.

Satisfied with the arrangements in New Jersey, on December 16 Howe returned to New York for the winter. Cornwallis, who was going to England, went with him. Howe appointed General James Grant to take Cornwallis's place while he was away. Grant had orders to stay in Princeton for the winter. As far as Howe was concerned, there was no point pursuing any further action until spring. He had already achieved his basic objectives—control of Manhattan and the sur-rounding area, establishing a strong position in eastern New Jersey, and taking control of Narragansett Bay.

Just days before, on December 8, General Clinton and a large task force had taken Newport. Clinton left New York on November 29 with seven thousand men. Commodore William Hotham had taken the troop transports and three supporting warships by way of Hell Gate, while Admiral Sir Peter Parker had sailed by way of Sandy Hook with twelve additional warships.

While Clinton had dutifully carried out his orders, he thought that sending him to Rhode Island at that critical moment was a huge mis-take. He had urged Howe to let him combine with Cornwallis and go after Washington, but Howe thought that Cornwallis had enough men to do the job. Clinton wasn't needed. Relations between Howe and his second in command were such that he never explained to Clinton how important Rhode Island would be in the spring, never told him that he was establishing a base there for a large ground operation against New England in 1777. In fact, the two men continued to have little rapport. Clinton never ceased irritating Howe. His second-guessing made him appear perpetually disgruntled.

Clinton's task force had arrived off Newport in bitter cold on December 8. Lord Percy, who was arguably the best British general in America, accompanied him as second in command. They encountered no opposition in Narragansett Bay or on Rhode Island and quickly occupied Newport. Not only did they secure the best anchorage on the East Coast for half of Admiral Howe's fleet, they also, without realizing it, shut down a major base for American privateers. And if the weather had not been so severe, Clinton and Percy might have made a move on Providence, but the cold, wind, and ice made that impossible.

With Clinton's victory in Rhode Island, General Howe could rest easy in New York City for the winter. He had not achieved the king's goals for 1776, but he had created a solid foundation for reaching them in 1777.

Adding to the general optimism in British ranks was the unexpected capture of General Charles Lee. Cornwallis knew that Lee had finally begun moving his army across the Hudson on December 2, and he was anxious to find out more about his intentions. On December 11 he dispatched Lieutenant Colonel William Harcourt with twenty-five dragoons to scout. Harcourt soon received a tip from a Tory that Lee was at a tavern in Basking Ridge, New Jersey, three miles away from his army with only a few guards. Harcourt sent Lieutenant Banastre Tarleton with six men to investigate. It turned out that Lee, for some unknown reason, was spending the night in the tavern, a dangerous distance from his camp. Tarleton, who would later become famous for his audacity, had no trouble capturing him on December 13.

Cornwallis believed that seizing Lee was a major event. Like everyone in the British high command, he had a high opinion of Lee's ability, believing that he was an important rebel asset and that his capture would have an impact on the war. Howe was just as sanguine.

Washington had been urging Lee to cross over to New Jersey for what seemed an eternity. When he actually did, it was unclear exactly how many men were with him. Washington had directed him to cross the Delaware well north of Trenton in order to avoid British strongpoints to the south. Lee had resisted, however. He wanted to remain in New Jersey and attack the enemy at Brunswick or Princeton, but Washington insisted that he cross the Delaware and help defend Philadelphia.

Lee gave no indication that he was personally going to join Washington. He might send some men under Major General Sullivan, his second in command, but he did not want to be associated with a possible defeat. All of this high-level infighting became moot when Lee surrendered.

Only one glaring failure marred the Howes' great success in the closing weeks of 1776, and that was their consistent inability to control the ravenous appetites of their troops, especially the Hessians. When their crimes continued, even intensified, in New Jersey, an otherwise open-minded population eventually turned against them and gave Washington critical support. The unwillingness of the Howes to curb the miscreants cost them dearly.

Chapter 11

REDEMPTION AT TRENTON

lthough Washington managed to prevent Howe from crossing the Delaware, the American army's situation on the south side of the river was precarious. Washington wrote to his brother, explaining his dreadful predicament and how he got there. "Our affairs have taken an adverse turn," he told him, "but not more than was to be expected from the unfortunate measures, which had been adopted for the establishment of our army."

The retreat of the enemy from White Plains led me to think that they would turn their thoughts to the Jerseys [New Jersey], if not further [to Philadelphia], and induced me to cross the North [Hudson] River with some of the troops, in order, if possible, to oppose them. I expected to meet at least five thousand men of the Flying Camp and militia, instead of which I found less than half that number and no disposition in the inhabitants to afford the least aid. This being perfectly well known to the enemy, they threw over a large body of troops, which pushed us from place to place, till we were obliged to cross the Delaware with less than three thousand men fit for duty, owing to the dissolution of our force by short enlistments; the enemy's numbers, from the best accounts, exceeding ten to twelve thousand men.

Before I removed to the south side of the river I had all the boats and other vessels brought over or destroyed from Philadelphia upwards for seventy miles.

But we are in a very disaffected part of the province; and, between you and me, I think our affairs are in a very bad condition; not so much from the apprehension of General Howe's army, as from the defection of New York, the Jerseys, and Pennsylvania. In short, the conduct of the Jerseys has been infamous. Instead of turning out to defend their country, and affording aid to our army, they are making their submissions as fast as they can.

If the Jerseys had given us any support, we might have made a stand at Hackensack, and after that at Brunswick; but the few militia that were in arms, disbanded themselves and left the poor remains of our army to make the best of it.

I have no doubt but General Howe will still make an attempt upon Philadelphia this winter. I see nothing to oppose him a fortnight hence, as the time of all the troops, except those of Virginia, now reduced almost to nothing, and Smallwood's regiment of Marylanders, equally as low, will expire before the end of that time. . . . if every nerve is not strained to recruit the new army with all possible expedition, I think the game is pretty nearly up, owing, in a great measure, to the insidious arts of the enemy, and disaffection of the colonies before mentioned, but principally to the ruinous policy of short enlistments, and placing too great a dependence upon the militia, the evil consequences of which were foretold fifteen months ago, with a spirit almost prophetic.

To add to Washington's burden, Congress had hurriedly departed Philadelphia for Baltimore in a panic in the first part of December, adding to the general impression that the revolution was collapsing. Before leaving, they gave Washington power to raise fifteen additional battalions, to appoint the officers, and to take necessaries for his army from civilians at an appraised value.

Some months later, John Adams vehemently denied that Congress had made Washington a dictator, which many were claiming. "Congress never thought of making him a dictator or of giving him a sovereignty," Adams wrote.

Whatever powers Congress did or did not confer, there was no doubt that members looked to Washington to save the revolution and gave him whatever authority he needed. They were in no position to quibble about what he did. Washington and his men in their tattered clothes were all that stood between them and disaster.

While Congress was retreating, Washington was thinking not of standing down for the winter and concentrating on building the eighty-eight-battalion army Congress had voted for earlier but of making a surprise attack on Trenton. It was one of Howe's smaller posts; the town was held by only fourteen hundred Hessians. And they were exhausted from continually fighting without a rest for weeks.

Howe knew little of their condition or of Washington's. He assumed that the Americans were done for the winter, as he was. In the unlikely event of an attack, he was confident that General Grant could defend the posts. Hessian colonel Johann Gottlieb Rall, an experienced combat leader who had performed signal service at White Plains and at Fort Washington, was in command in Trenton. Although a fighter of some distinction, he was also a heavy drinker, with little respect for Washington or his makeshift army.

General Sullivan strengthened Washington by finally bringing General Lee's troops across the Delaware and joining him. Their number turned out to be two thousand. Washington could never get an accurate count from Lee. Gates and Benedict Arnold brought another six hundred from the northern army. As soon as Gates reached Washington's camp, he used a flimsy excuse to leave. Like Lee, Gates did not want to be associated with a losing enterprise.

With Gates and Lee unavailable, Washington sent Generals Arnold and Spencer (both from Connecticut) to Rhode Island to counter Generals Clinton and Percy, although the British generals had no intention of moving beyond Newport. Clinton was going home on leave and Percy would soon follow, after unexpectedly resigning when Howe, for no good reason, went out of his way to offend him.

Neither Lee nor Gates dreamed that Howe would present Washington with a perfect opportunity to reverse his fortunes by setting up lightly defended outposts to attack. Howe was focused on luxuriating in New York for the winter and once again badly misjudged his opponent. Instead of settling down for a long respite, Washington was planning a lightning strike on Trenton when Colonel Rall least expected it— Christmas night. The attack was to come from three directions. To the south, Brigadier General John Cadwalader, the wealthy Philadelphia merchant turned soldier, was to cross the Delaware at Bordentown with one thousand Philadelphia volunteers (called Associators) and attack Hessian colonel Donop's fifteen hundred men at Bordentown, to prevent them from reinforcing Colonel Rall. Donop was in overall command of the two posts at Trenton and Bordentown.

Brigadier General James Ewing was to make the second attack just south of Trenton with seven hundred Pennsylvania and New Jersey militia. He was to prevent Rall from retreating south over the Assunpink Creek bridge to join Donop.

The main attack would come from the north, with Washington in the lead. His force would be divided into two columns. Greene would command one and Sullivan the other. Colonel Henry Knox would accompany them with eighteen pieces of artillery, which were to play a major role.

If all went well, Washington hoped to attack Princeton and Brunswick afterward, taking the British by surprise, administering a triple blow before they realized what was happening.

Early in the afternoon on December 25, twenty-four hundred very cold soldiers began to form up into their units and march down to

McKonkey's Ferry on the Delaware, nine miles above Trenton. The river was only a thousand feet wide at this point.

The weather grew worse by the hour. Large blocks of ice floated in the rapid current. The wind was blowing snow, sleet, and hail into the soldiers' faces. The shivering troops boarded large Durham riverboats, used for transporting goods. The odd-looking craft were forty to sixty feet long, with eight-foot beams and shallow drafts. A steering oar that could be used at either end guided them, while pole men on both sides pushed them along. A few had sails, but they were of no use that night. As awkward as they looked, the big boats were ideal for moving troops and artillery. Glover's mariners had never seen anything like them before, but they managed to get them across the water without losing a single boat. Henry Knox was even able to get his eighteen pieces of heavy artillery across safely.

The inspired patriots, although dreadfully clothed, trudged through snow, many with rags wrapped around bare feet, determined to strike a blow at their tormentors. They didn't know it at the time, but neither Cadwalader nor Ewing made it across the river. The going was too difficult where they were.

Led by Washington, Greene, Sullivan, Knox, Mercer, Stirling, Adam Stephen, Matthias Alexis Roche de Fermoy, Arthur St. Clair, Glover, and Sargent, the American fighters succeeded beyond their wildest dreams, defeating Johann Rall and capturing or killing over a thousand Hessians, while only one patriot officer and one soldier were killed. It was a Christmas miracle.

When the fight was over, Washington crossed back to the south side of the Delaware with nine hundred prisoners. He did not try to make a move on Princeton, but the idea was still in the back of his mind. The German captives were understandably fearful. They worried that the Americans would afford them the same brutal treatment Hessians had inflicted on patriot prisoners after the battle on Long Island and at Fort Washington, bayoneting many after they had surrendered. Colonel Rall, who had been mortally wounded, pleaded with Washington before he died not to take revenge on his men, as he would have done had their situations been reversed. Washington promised Rall that he would treat his men decently, and he did. In fact, throughout the war, he refused to abuse helpless prisoners as his opponents were doing.

Washington's victory caught the world by surprise. Patriots, particularly in Congress, were ecstatic. So were the French. The British were shocked. Many Loyalists were angry with General Howe for letting Washington off the hook so many times. Wealthy New York Tories were the most savage in their criticism. Governor Tryon was particularly incensed, as were Colonel Stephen Kemble and Judge Thomas Jones. None was as angry as General Howe himself, however. His entire strategy was in jeopardy. The dream he had—that in the spring, just the appearance of a massively reinforced army and navy would be enough to bring Congress begging to the negotiating table—was now open to question.

Washington wasn't finished. On December 29–30 he recrossed the Delaware and dug in south of Assunpink Creek below Trenton, intending to establish a base from which to attack Howe's other posts, particularly Princeton and Brunswick. He was joined finally by Brigadier General John Cadwalader, with twelve hundred Philadelphia patriots, and Brigadier General James Ewing, with five hundred men. Washington now had an army of around five thousand troops plus Knox's artillery. He had succeeded in convincing many men to stay beyond the expiration of their enlistments. He appealed to their patriotism but also got Robert Morris to produce money for bounties.

Meanwhile, Howe was in a fury, ordering Cornwallis, who was about to board a ship for England, to return to New Jersey and go after the American army. Believing that Washington had made a monumental mistake in recrossing the Delaware, Howe hoped to limit the damage to his prestige by quickly destroying him.

Cornwallis assumed command from the hapless Grant and marched toward Trenton with eight thousand men. Washington knew he was coming and sent Colonel Edward Hand with his Pennsylvania riflemen to harass the British column and slow it down, which Hand did masterfully. Cornwallis did not reach Trenton until late in the day on January 2, with his men fatigued from wrangling with Colonel Hand's deadly riflemen.

Cornwallis found Washington looking hopelessly trapped. Since it was late in the day and Washington had a substantial force, Cornwallis decided to wait until daylight to administer the coup de grâce. His men were exhausted, and so was he.

The following morning, after a good night's sleep, he awoke to find that the American army had disappeared. He couldn't believe it. Washington had again eluded him, making another masterful escape. He was now in back of Cornwallis, marching for Princeton. On the way, part of the patriot army, under General Hugh Mercer, ran into British Lieutenant Colonel Charles Mawhood, leader of Cornwallis's rear guard. Mawhood was rushing with around seven hundred men to Trenton to bolster Cornwallis. A fierce battle ensued. General Mercer was killed in the melee, and Washington was forced to rally Mercer's troops to prevent a disaster, nearly getting killed himself. Afterward, he went on to defeat the small British contingent holding Princeton. Cornwallis, of course, was coming after him as fast as he could, desperate to catch his elusive prey, who was making a fool of him. But Washington wasn't easy to catch. He got out of Princeton just ahead of Cornwallis.

When he did, he thought about attacking Brunswick. That had been part of his plan all along, and there was now an added incentive. A sizable cache of gold was stored there—perhaps as much as seventy thousand pounds. And General Lee was being held there temporarily, looked after by two hundred fifty guards. Washington thought briefly about marching his whole army to Brunswick, but when he saw how dead tired his men were, and was informed that Cornwallis was now racing to protect Brunswick, he thought better of it and headed for Morristown and the protection of the Watchung Mountains.

He moved fast along the west bank of the Millstone River to Somerset Court House (now Millstone) and then to Middle Brook. From there he skirted the western edge of the mountains, traveling through

Pluckemin to what is now Bernardsville, then to Basking Ridge and Morristown. His army straggled into town on January 5 and 6 near total collapse. Expiring enlistments and disease, particularly smallpox, had reduced the ranks to less than a thousand Continentals and two thousand short-term militia.

Since the mountains were accessible primarily through passes at Springfield and Chatham, or by skirting their western edge at Middle Brook and Pluckemin, they offered some protection, but Washington worried that the British would discover how weak he really was and mount a quick strike that he simply would not have been able to withstand.

He tried to deal with the problem by diverting Howe's attention. On January 5, two days after the battle of Princeton, he wrote from Pluckemin to General Heath at Peekskill, ordering him to "move down towards New York . . . as if you had a design on the city," which Washington hoped would force the enemy to withdraw "a considerable part of their force from the Jerseys, if not the whole, to secure the city." He told Heath to employ the four thousand militiamen he anticipated would be "coming on from the New England governments."

Two days later he wrote to Heath again. "I beg you will keep up every appearance of falling down upon New York, as that will be the surest method of obliging the enemy to withdraw their whole force from this side [New Jersey] to protect the city. . . . If they throw part of their force into New York, they will leave themselves in such a situation, that we may in all probability fall upon them with success." Washington even went so far as to suggest that "if there is a fair opening, I would have you [actually] make the attempt [on the city]."

These orders and musings were based on pure fantasy. There was no possibility of either Washington or Heath making a successful attack against Howe right then. Nonetheless, Washington persisted. On January 9 he wrote to Heath again, this time from Morristown: "as many valuable purposes may, I think, be answered by your moving towards New York, I wish no time be lost in doing it. I have good reasons to believe, that there are very few men left in the city of New York, or upon the Island; consequently a body of troops marched that way may possess themselves of the city, or occasion a reinforcement to be thrown in there, and in either case cannot fail of advancing our cause."

Washington seemed to be convinced that his recent successes had thrown the veteran Howe into a complete panic. To General Lincoln, who was to be part of Heath's drive toward New York, he wrote, "the sooner a panic-struck enemy is followed, the better. If we can oblige them to evacuate Jersey, we must drive them to the utmost distress."

General Heath dutifully followed Washington's bizarre order to move on New York with around thirty-five hundred newly arrived militiamen. He got to Kings Bridge on January 18 and engaged the enemy outposts briefly. Shots were exchanged and a few prisoners taken, but, given the weakness of Heath's force, nothing more could be attempted. The skirmish took on the aura of a farce, especially given the grand objectives Washington had in mind. When Heath demanded the surrender of Fort Independence, the two thousand regular troops guarding it—half British, half Hessian—responded with derision and even laughter. Soon Heath pulled back, having accomplished the exact opposite of what Washington had predicted.

Understandably, Heath was not anxious to report to Washington, but the commander in chief was very keen to hear from him. On January 27 he wrote asking for a report, still expecting a result that Heath could not possibly have delivered. "Although the original design of your movement may not be fully answered in all its parts," he said, "yet, if you can take possession of the country round about the city, or the city itself, I do not desire you to desist."

On January 30, 1777, when Washington received the news of what actually had happened, he was upset that his wildly unrealistic expectations had not been fulfilled and unfairly blamed Heath, accusing him of exposing "us to the ridicule of the enemy." Indeed he had, but the fault rested with the commander in chief, not with Heath.

Washington's treatment of Heath was in marked contrast to his handling of General Greene after the much larger disasters at Fort Washington and Fort Lee. He did not rebuke Greene but took responsibility entirely on himself, which is where it belonged. In many ways he grew closer to Greene, for whom he still had the utmost admiration. And Greene responded, making a major contribution to the successes at Trenton and Princeton. Greene even became Washington's close personal confidant, after Reed left and returned to Philadelphia.

Reed and Washington had had a sad falling out. When Washington inadvertently discovered that Reed had become an admirer of Charles Lee and was corresponding with him behind Washington's back and criticizing him to Lee, their intimate relationship ended. Greene, in a sense, took Reed's place.

With the American army in the state it was in, Morristown was not a safe haven. It was less than forty miles from New York City. Howe could have easily marched there in January, and that would have been the end of the Continental army, and perhaps the revolution. Washington did everything he could to disguise his weakness and obtain more troops, but he remained vulnerable. On January 19 he wrote, "The army is much reduced since we left Trenton; and the many that will be discharged in a few days will so weaken our force that it will be impossible to oppose the enemy with success, should they advance toward us; or do any essential service, if they should move toward Philadelphia. As I cannot expect our situation can long be a secret to the enemy, there is no doubt, but they will avail themselves of it, and take advantage of our weakness."

But Howe did not "take advantage." He could have marched into Philadelphia with no opposition, as well as attacked Morristown, but he never considered doing either. Instead, beginning on January 10, he consolidated his troops in New Jersey, withdrawing them from five of the cantonments and gathering them at Brunswick under Lord Cornwallis and at Perth Amboy under General Vaughan. The numbers were substantial, amounting to around ten thousand—five thousand in each location. They were more than enough, if combined with the seventeen thousand Howe had in Manhattan and Staten Island, to destroy Washington and take Philadelphia.

Howe ignored his opportunity, however, and remained comfortably ensconced in Manhattan for the entire winter. His inaction infuriated New York's Tories. Judge Thomas Jones accused him of wasting a perfect opportunity to finish off Washington, spending his time instead on "feasting, gunning, banqueting, and in the arms of Mrs. Loring."

Not only was Howe refusing to attack Morristown, he was allowing New Jersey militiamen to harass his bases at Brunswick and Perth Amboy. Washington was receiving far more support from New Jersey than expected. Governor Livingston was working hard to help, as he always did, and he was aided by a rejuvenated militia, incensed by the behavior of Hessian and British soldiers.

Just acquiring food became a major problem for Cornwallis and Vaughan. Judge Jones pointed out, "Not a stick of wood, a spear of grass, or a kernel of corn could the troops in New Jersey procure without fighting for it, unless sent from New York. Every foraging party was attacked in some way or another. The losses upon these occasions were nearly equal, they could be called nothing more than skirmishes, but hundreds of them happened in the course of the winter." No matter, Howe continued to look the other way, allowing the carnage to go on.

Even worse, he abandoned New Jersey Loyalists, who included the thousands of people who had signed the loyalty oath to the king after the Howes' November 30 proclamation. They were left to the mercy of the patriots who sought revenge. Loyalists were forced out of their homes, becoming exiles in the filth of Manhattan, running to escape reprisals that often meant death.

Howe was criticized by his own officers for his inactivity, and to counteract this corrosive mood, he authorized a raid on Peekskill on the twenty-third of March and on Danbury, Connecticut, in April. Both succeeded and improved morale a bit but were a waste of time and resources, as far as Howe's overall objectives were concerned. The winter of 1776–77 thus passed with Howe anticipating a great victory in the coming summer while his officers waited uneasily for some action against what they considered to be a very weak rebel army.

A good part of the reason Howe never mounted a serious assault on Washington was that he had already made extensive plans for the spring campaign, and he apparently thought that there was no need to rush things. Resting his army for the coming struggle seemed more important. He had a much higher appreciation of the risks involved in attacking Washington's mountain stronghold than Judge Jones did, or some of his officers. It was the kind of battle that he had avoided since Bunker Hill. He wanted to fight Washington where he had all the advantages— on an open plain. So, incredibly, he left Washington alone, and by the time he was ready to mount another campaign, Washington's army had been restored. By the first of May he had around nine thousand men.

Putting together the new army in Morristown was not easy. One of the problems Washington had to deal with was endemic to the military enterprise—namely, the contretemps raised by promotions for officers. One of the worst began on February 19, 1777, when Congress passed over Brigadier General Benedict Arnold for promotion to major general and he threatened to resign. Washington was dismayed. He not did want to lose Arnold, who had performed so magnificently against Carleton on Lake Champlain.

Washington had had no way of knowing what Carleton's orders were; he did not know that he was trying to reach Albany. But he did know that thanks to Arnold's heroics on Lake Champlain, Carleton returned to Quebec with his entire army, and the Americans were still in control of Fort Ticonderoga.

Washington felt that the five men who were promoted to major general were not Arnold's equal. They were good men, but far from being his superiors. Oddly, Washington was not consulted about a matter so vital to the army. He did not even know what criteria Congress was using for promotions, but when he was told, he found them to be "a strange mode of reasoning."

In a few weeks, after more of Arnold's stunning heroics while fighting Tryon's raid on Danbury, Congress changed its mind and voted to promote him. But, again, for obscure reasons, they adamantly refused to adjust his seniority, which rankled Arnold as much as, if not more than, the original unwillingness to promote him.

News of Trenton and Princeton arrived in Paris on February 25, 1777. Relief mixed with joy as the French celebrated. The three American commissioners, Silas Deane, Benjamin Franklin, and Arthur Lee, described the political reaction to Congress: "The hearts of the French people are universally for us and the opinion for an immediate war with Great Britain is very strong, but the court has its reasons for postponing a little longer." The principal reason was that the French navy wasn't quite ready yet; it would not be until the winter of 1778.

Of course, the French army—170,000 strong—was vastly superior to Britain's, and eager to fight their traditional rival. Vergennes allowed Beaumarchais to dramatically increase the war matériel flowing to America. And in January Louis XVI presented the patriots with a loan of two million livres, with indefinite terms of repayment.

Chapter 12

DEPRAVED INDIFFERENCE

The city that General Howe presided over was unrecognizable. It resembled a charnel house more than the vibrant metropolis it had once been, and Howe's indifference to the squalor was hard to understand. Since he had taken over, Manhattan had been transformed into an ugly, dangerous garrison town. The old New York had been obliterated, as if it had never existed. Some of the gruesome makeover had been done by Washington's army, but the British went far beyond anything the Americans had done.

The transformation was so rapid it had the look and feel of something gross but transient. Even Loyalists, who were aghast at the changes, believed that at least it was temporary. But it wasn't. New York remained an eyesore for seven more years.

Prominent Tories like former Governor Tryon, Judge Thomas Jones, and William Smith urged the Howes to end military rule as quickly as possible and restore civilian government, so that civil magistrates, a representative assembly, courts of law, trial by jury, habeas corpus, and all the other historic rights Englishmen expected could be reestablished. But the Howes refused, preferring a military dictatorship. They had a war to fight, and they didn't want well-meaning citizens getting in the way.

The continual pleas of Loyalists for relief from martial law were ignored. Civilian government was never restored. An exasperated William Smith wrote, "[N]othing can be more injurious to the king's interest than this negligent and untender conduct of the army." On another occasion he wrote to William Eden, a member of Parliament, an undersecretary of state, and an accomplished spymaster, warning, "If the military are to govern us as well as conquer, govern the loyal who have assisted to dethrone the usurpers, prepare to employ your island to garrison this entire continent." No one was listening.

Most of the old inhabitants were gone. Ninety percent had fled to keep out of harm's way. At the end of 1776, when General Howe had settled down for the winter, fewer than three thousand of the original twenty-five thousand remained. The city wasn't empty, of course; new people rapidly replaced the old, swelling the population until eventually it was much larger than before, although no one knew by how much.

The new residents were a mix of returning Loyalists; Tories from other colonies; runaway slaves; free men, women, and children of color; bold entrepreneurs of every stripe; camp followers; thousands of prisoners; and, of course, British and Hessian soldiers. Around five thousand of Howe's troops were housed in the city, but most were stationed outside on Staten Island and in Kings, Queens, and Suffolk counties.

Trade resumed. The famed waterfront was alive again. Alongside an impressive array of merchantmen were dozens of British privateers and their captures. Luxury goods from Europe were available once more, finding their way into the rebel-held interior for those with money and connections. Newspapers reappeared as well, Gaine's *Weekly Mercury;* Rivington's *New York Gazetteer,* which became the *Royal Gazette,* and Robertson's *Royal American Gazette* among them.

They were His Majesty's propaganda organs, read by Tories through-out the colonies when they could get them.

The city was far more crowded than before. The great fire of September 21, 1776, had destroyed over a quarter of the housing, and a dangerous tent city, known as "canvas-town," sprang up in its place. Poor people needing cheap shelter now lived there almost exclusively. It became a lawless cesspool, some of it for entertaining troops. Sanitation was dreadful. Sickness, especially smallpox, was rampant. Nicholas Cresswell, a visitor from England, found the odor sickening. "Unwholesome smells occasioned by such a number of people being crowded together in so small a compass almost like herrings in a barrel," he wrote, "most of them very dirty and not a small number sick of some disease, the itch, pox, fever, or flux, so that altogether there is a complication of stinks enough to drive a person whose sense of smelling was very delicate . . . into a consumption in the space of twenty-four hours."

In other parts of town, competition for housing was fierce. Buildings such as churches and houses were subject to seizure for military use. Even the individual homes of rich Tories were taken, their inhabitants thrown out so that high-ranking officers could have them. Others used what influence they had to find accommodations, but no matter where they settled they had to cope with a city that was dangerous for ordinary people, particularly at night, when drunken soldiers and sailors were about. Wholesale thievery was endemic. Lawless redcoats and Hessians robbed and raped and were never held to account for their misdeeds. General Howe looked the other way. Major General James Robertson, in charge of running the city day to day, followed Howe's example. So did the other generals who were his successors as commandants of the city—Major Generals Robert Pigot and Valentine Jones and Brigadier General Samuel Birch.

General Robertson would later tell Lord Jeffrey Amherst, commander in chief of the British army, "Those who formerly wished our approach, and would with joy have seen us triumph over the rebels, will now arm to defend their all from undistinguished plunder."

———

For rich civilians, life was reasonably comfortable unless, in one unguarded moment, they ran afoul of soldiers out having a good time. Martial law supposedly governed the city, but the authorities were not interested in prosecuting military personnel. On the rare occasions they did, judgments were usually set aside. One of the more egregious examples was the murder of a miller named Derrick Amberman in Hempstead by Major Richard V. Stockman and a Major Crew. When Amberman tried to collect a debt from the officers, Stockman drew his sword and drove it through him, killing him instantly. He was tried and convicted of murder before a military court and then simply set free, along with Crew. This was typical of military justice in every area the British controlled.

Obtaining enough food was a continual problem for most people, except the military and civilian elite. Inflation soared. Supplies were always tight because of the immense size of the army and navy, and because of the large amount of mismanagement. The surrounding countryside, which could have supplied the city's needs, became so alienated it was not growing the food it had in the past. A continuous parade of transports were needed to bring provisions from Britain.

As bad as the lot of ordinary civilians was, it was nothing compared to the treatment accorded prisoners of war, especially those confined to prison ships in the harbor. Under the regime of Loring and Cunningham, prisoners starved and froze to death in large numbers.

After the great battle on Long Island in 1776, far more prisons were needed. The city's existing supply could not possibly hold all the wretched captives. Old transports were hastily pressed into service, converted into prison ships, and stuffed with men. Churches of every kind, except for the Anglican Church, were used as well. Hundreds and then thousands of young patriots died horrifying deaths in makeshift prisons in the city and prison ships in the harbor, among them the infamous *Jersey* and the *Joy*. Each morning on the *Jersey* the cry "turn out your dead" was heard, and each morning as many as a dozen bodies of patriot fighters were rolled out on deck and unceremoniously thrown overboard. In the course of the war, 60 percent of the over thirty thousand prisoners in British custody died at the hands of their jailers. Fewer than seven thousand patriots died in combat.

William Cunningham, the provost marshal, not content with simply starving and freezing his prisoners, like to play sadistic tricks on them. During hot summer days, when the overcrowded prisons were unbearable, he would have tubs of water brought to the prisoners that guards and their superiors had been using in their rooms. To avoid perishing from thirst, the prisoners, to Cunningham's delight, were forced to drink the stinking water.

The "atrocious cruelties," as John Adams called them, permitted and indeed encouraged by the willful neglect of the Howe brothers, was known not only to them but to the general public, both Loyalist and patriot. "If Mr. Howe's heart is not callous," Adams railed, "what must be his feelings when he recollects the starving, the freezings, the pestilential diseases, with which he coolly and deliberately destroyed the lives of so many unhappy men! If his conscience is not seared, how will he bear its lashes when he remembers his breach of honor, his breach of faith, his offense against humanity and divinity, his neighbor and his God (if he thinks there is any such Supreme Being), impairing the health that he ought to have cherished, and in putting an end to lives that he ought to have preserved, and in choosing the most slow, lingering, and tutoring death that he could have devised."

The jailers were not the only ones engaged in wholesale graft. It seemed that any official who could get away with it did so. One of the more notorious examples was the quartermaster who had to supply horses and wagons for the army, which was a huge undertaking. Loyalist Judge Thomas Jones, who watched closely, estimated that the four quartermasters who served the British army in New York during the war stole tens of thousands of pounds. One of them went back to England £150,000 richer by not paying farmers for their horses or wagons, billing the Treasury for them, and pocketing the money.

Not everyone suffered during the occupation, of course. Somehow, in the midst of the moral and physical depths the city had sunk to, the British high command and their wealthy admirers managed to enjoy themselves through the long winter. Taverns like Hull's Head, King's Head, Cannon's, and City's did a brisk business. A continuous round of dinners and balls occupied the privileged. Cards, horse racing, foxhunting, golf, cockfights, plays, and concerts provided continuous entertainment. General Howe set the tone, indulging himself openly in his favorite pastimes—gambling and Mrs. Loring. Lord Howe participated very little in the amusements and general debauchery that his brother found so appealing.

Mrs. Loring was the general's constant companion. Formerly Elizabeth Lloyd of New York, she was fabulously wealthy by American standards, with a huge family estate on Lloyd's Neck, Long Island. Its three thousand acres contained a stunning peninsula and miles of beautiful shoreline where Tory privateers could find refuge. Young and beautiful, Mrs. Loring enjoyed living the high life with the general. Indolence and luxury marked their days. His ability to forget that there was a war on and that his weak enemy was not far away was remarkable.

Almost forgotten in Manhattan were the fourteen thousand regulars General Howe had left in New Jersey at Perth Amboy and Brunswick, who were not living in luxury. On the contrary, they were suffering through a low-level war with New Jersey militiamen. Ignoring the trials of their soldiers was typical of many British officers who had as little regard for ordinary redcoats as they did for lower-class provincials. The high desertion rate among redcoats was in part due to the ill-treatment they received from their own superiors. This was nothing new to patriots who had witnessed how some British officers dealt with ordinary soldiers during the French and Indian War.

British rule in other places they occupied—Staten Island and Queens, Kings, and Suffolk counties—was no different than in Manhattan. Many of the Loyalists who welcomed them with open arms in the beginning were soon disenchanted. From the time the first redcoats set foot on Staten Island, things did not go quite as the sanguine natives had expected. The observations of Lord Rawdon tell the story. To his friend Lord Huntington, he wrote:

> The fair nymphs of this isle [Staten Island] are in wonderful tribulation, as the fresh meat our men have got here has made them riotous as satyrs. A girl cannot step into the bushes to pluck a rose without running the most immanent risk of being ravished, and they are so little accustomed to these vigorous methods that they don't bear them with the proper resignation, and of consequence we have most entertaining courts-martial every day.
>
> To the southward they behave much better in these cases, if I may judge from a woman who having been forced by seven of our men, [came] to make a complaint to me, "not of their usage," she said; "No, thank God, she despised that," but of their having taken an old prayer book for which she had a particular affection.
>
> A girl on this island made a complaint the other day to Lord Percy of her being deflowered, as she said by some grenadiers. Lord Percy asked her how she knew them to be grenadiers, as it happened in the dark. "Oh, good God," cried she, "they could be nothing else."

While occupied New York had undergone an extreme transformation, there were also great changes in the rest of the state, where the patriots were in control. The six counties (Orange, Ulster, Tryon, Albany, Dutchess, and Charlotte) that were not under direct British occupation were part of the new state government. On July 9, 1776, the Fourth New York Provincial Congress, elected in June 1776, met at the courthouse in White Plains and declared that as of April 20, 1775, New York was a state and no longer a colony. On the same day the Provincial Congress approved the Declaration of Independence.

When the British captured Manhattan, the Provincial Congress moved, in the space of less than a year, from New York City to White

Plains, to Fishkill, to Kingston—a small, heavily patriot town on the Hudson, midway between Manhattan and Albany—and then to Pough-keepsie, after the British burned Kingston in 1777.

Led by John Jay, Gouverneur Morris, Robert R. Livingston, and George Clinton, the delegates to the Provincial Congress approved a republican constitution in April 1777 that was written largely by Jay during the winter while Washington was in Morristown building a new army. At the end of June 1777, militia general Clinton was elected gov-ernor, in a close contest, over Philip Schuyler, John Jay, and John Morin Scott. The voting was by secret ballot, something novel in New York politics. It was but one of many progressive measures Jay wrote into the new constitution that, taken together, amounted to a revolution in New York's political life, making it far more democratic. Drastically lowered voting qualifications brought new men into the legislature who would never have been able to serve before. They were strong supporters of the new governor, who, like them, wasn't one of the great landed aristocrats who had previously dominated New York. Of course, Clinton had mar-ried one, Cornelia Tappan, which was a great help to his career, but he never lost touch with his roots.

The new government presided over counties that had their own governments and local committees. All were, to one degree or another, supporting the patriot cause. Ulster and Orange counties were strongly patriot; the others were to a lesser degree. A low-key civil war went on in all of them, with the patriots maintaining the upper hand. One of their most difficult problems was dealing with the slaves who were run-ning away in large numbers to British lines seeking their freedom. New York had more slaves than any other state outside the South—as much as 20 percent of the population. Militiamen had to be used at times to hunt down escaped slaves. It was an ugly, uncomfortable business for people whose rallying cry was liberty.

Westchester County was a special case. Its people remained evenly divided politically, as they had been before the war. They fell into a destructive civil war that they could not extricate themselves from. On and on it went, the circle of violence increasing year after bloody year. Running through the county from Long Island to the Hudson was a thirty-mile-wide strip of land called the "Neutral Ground," situated between the American army to the north and the British to the south. Its boundaries extended roughly from north of Morrisania to the mouth of the Croton River. Fighting between irregulars raged in this godforsaken territory, neighbor against neighbor, throughout the wider war and beyond. James De Lancey's "refugees" were infamous for their brutal treatment of patriots, or anyone they chose to label a rebel. Often they used the word "Skinners" to identify their victims. Other so-called Loyalists, known as "Cowboys," were also active, robbing, raping, and pillaging. Organized groups of rebels fought back as the carnage continued, year after year.

Chapter 13

NEW WAR PLANS

On November 30, 1776, the day General Howe issued his peace proclamation, he had also sent Germain a proposed plan for the spring 1777 campaign. He considered it the most realistic approach to winning the war that the British had yet come up with, provided it could be coupled with an attractive political program. Unfortunately, Howe was seeking approval from men who had no understanding of America and no hesitation about substituting their opinion for the judgment of the commander in the field.

To begin with, Howe proposed basing ten thousand troops in Rhode Island. Eight thousand would drive north with Boston as their ultimate objective; the remaining two thousand would terrorize the Connecticut and Massachusetts coast—something dear to Germain's heart. Another ten thousand would move up the Hudson and form a junction at Albany with an army coming down from Canada—a mandatory provision, given the king's predilections. This joint task force would then drive into western Massachusetts and Connecticut. New York City would retain five thousand to protect Manhattan and the surrounding area. Another eight thousand would be stationed in New Jersey and march on Philadelphia. The south would be invaded later, when colder weather slowed operations in the North. Howe estimated that only fifteen thousand additional troops and ten more sail of the line would be needed to accomplish all of these objectives. He anticipated that at some point in the summer or early fall of 1777 Washington would be forced to risk everything and fight a general battle that would destroy him and the rebellion. Unstated was the assumption that when the time came, reasonable political terms would be offered to the colonies—a very big assumption, considering that London had demonstrated no appetite for compromise.

If everything were to go well, Howe continued to hope—despite overwhelming evidence to the contrary—that just the appearance of the mighty force he was proposing would so overawe the rebels that they would finally enter into serious negotiations to end the war and embrace the king. He wrote to Germain, "[If] the force I have mentioned [were] sent out, it would strike such terror through the country that little resistance would be made to the progress of H.M. arms in the provinces of New England, New York, New Jersey, and Pennsylvania after the junction of the northern and southern armies." Howe had expressed similar views to Germain as far back as September 25, but not in as comprehensive a manner.

The peace proclamation that Howe issued on November 30, 1776, was made on the same day that he sent his new strategic proposal to Germain. The war plan and the peace proposal were meant to go together. Howe hoped that when the rebels saw the huge army coming to crush them in 1777, and saw how reasonable the peace proposal was, there would be a good chance they would simply put down their arms and negotiate a settlement. He had already seen what a dramatic effect his peace proposal had had on the people of New Jersey. If nothing else, it showed that his approach had a chance, not just in New Jersey but in other parts of the country, such as Pennsylvania, Maryland, and Delaware.

The reception that Howe's plans received in London was less than enthusiastic. Even if success on the battlefield forced Congress to renounce independence, the king and his supporters had no intention of simply welcoming the rebels back. Extensive remodeling of colonial society was thought to be necessary. When Germain received a copy of Howe's peace proposal on December 31, he rejected it out of hand. A policy of forgive and forget was not what he, or the king, or the great majority in Parliament had in mind. In their view, a lenient policy was bound to create the same problems that had led to the rebellion in the first place.

Germain was also unhappy with Howe's proposed military strategy. At first glance, it meant raising far more troops, which would be a big problem. His request seemed far in excess of what London deemed either necessary or prudent. Germain had already made a maximum effort to assemble the forces Howe and Carleton had received in 1776. He expected that they would be enough, as did the king. Sending another fifteen thousand and ten sail of the line seemed excessive. Every general wanted more troops, especially if he failed with the ones he had. It was easy for Germain and the king to imagine that this was the case here. On January 14 Germain sent a noncommittal reply. The final decision on strategy and troop levels was left hanging.

Germain's negative reaction was mild compared to Sandwich's. The first lord of the Admiralty was an inveterate foe of Admiral Howe. Releasing ten more sail of the line for the American theater struck him as irresponsible. The home fleet needed more ships; it should have priority. Lord Howe had five sail of the line and five-fifty gunships; that was enough. Giving him another ten, Sandwich maintained, would dangerously shrink the home fleet, especially with the building program the French had embarked on and the possibility that, if war broke out, France might combine fleets with Spain and possibly other countries, creating enough of a force in the English Channel to mount a serious invasion of the home island.

Before receiving Germain's response, Howe sent him, on December 20, a different proposal. It reflected the success he was having in New Jersey against Washington, and the positive response he was getting from the people of New Jersey to his recent peace proposal. If Washington's army somehow survived, and the war continued into the spring of 1777, Howe thought that, given his current success, he would need fewer troops than first proposed. His new plan put more emphasis on taking Philadelphia. Given the attitude of Pennsylvania's people, he thought it likely they would come over to the king's side if he took their capital. He proposed using ten thousand men to attack it.

The rest of his new proposal was quite different from his November 30 plan as well. He suggested only two thousand men for Rhode Island and deferred the attack north against Boston; another four thousand would be needed "to act defensively upon the lower part of Hudson's River, to cover New Jersey on that side, as well as to facilitate to some degree, the approach of the army from Canada." At the same time, three thousand would secure the Hudson.

The new plan, which Howe thought later was much too optimistic about the numbers of reinforcements needed, reached London on February 23, 1777, and since it called for far fewer troops, Germain liked it much better. He replied on March 3, approving the whole strategy, including its emphasis on Philadelphia. In focusing on the capital and Pennsylvania, Howe was not minimizing the importance of an invasion from Canada. He thought it was important to force the rebels to divide their army.

Howe wrote to Germain a third time, on January 20, 1777, as he told the House of Commons two years later. "I pressed for more troops," he declared. "I observed that if the reinforcements were small the operations would, of course, be curtailed."

The battles at Trenton and Princeton, fought at the end of 1776 and the start of 1777, had obviously changed Howe's mind about how many additional men he needed. His December 20 proposal reflected an optimism he had lost by late January. Thereafter, his correspondence with Germain made it clear that his plans would be guided by how many troops he had. If the reinforcements he requested did not materialize, he insisted that he could not accomplish what London wanted.

As Howe's thinking evolved in response to Germain's replies and the situation on the ground, he wrote, on April 2, yet another proposal, in which he gave up any thought of striking north from Rhode Island. He would limit himself to holding Narragansett Bay. Eleven thousand men would be needed for the invasion of Pennsylvania; in New York City, 4,700 regulars and 3,000 provincials; and 2,400 for Rhode Island. Also new was a proposal to travel to Philadelphia by sea.

Germain received the letter on May 8 and replied on the eighteenth, giving full approval and adding that the king expected Howe to finish with Philadelphia in time to cooperate with Burgoyne's army coming down from Canada. Howe received Germain's reply on August 16, while he was in Chesapeake Bay about to commence operations against Philadelphia. Delays in mail deliveries from London were common in the age of sail. Deliveries were even more difficult when the recipient was at sea.

Throughout the exchange of messages with Germain, the limitations on Admiral Howe were never taken into account. That he might not be able to quickly secure command of the Delaware River below Philadelphia, for instance, was not mentioned. It was simply assumed that he would. Confidence in the Royal Navy and in Lord Howe's ability was so high that no one thought to question it. Even if weather and sea cooperated, gaining control of the heavily fortified Delaware once Philadelphia had been taken might be exceptionally difficult, even for Admiral Howe. And any delay could make it impossible to cooperate with the army coming down from Canada. Germain never considered the inherent difficulties of his overly optimistic strategy. He was supremely confident in his own judgment and expected miracles from the Howes.

London also never considered how a contrary sea might interfere with movements over the water between New York and either the Delaware River or Chesapeake Bay. Any significant delay could again make it impossible to aid the Canadian army.

If Germain's directives to Howe for 1777 were, at best, tentative, with no clear understanding of how many men or ships he would have and exactly what he was expected to do, directions for the army in Canada could not have been clearer. General Burgoyne was put in command, and he was to fight his way to Albany, where Howe would join him, supposedly, with a strong fleet and army—after he took Philadelphia. The junction of the two armies would, at long last, fulfill the king's long-standing strategic dream.

If this was Germain's strategy, it clearly was not the Howes'. After their experiences in 1776, they had come to the conclusion that the key to winning the war was defeating Washington's army while he was attempting to defend Philadelphia, and then capturing the city afterward. They were not opposed to Burgoyne's marching to Albany—in fact, it was an essential part of their plan. They wanted the American army divided, defending both the Hudson and Philadelphia. The shock of losing Philadelphia and Albany simultaneously, after the devastating losses Washington had suffered in 1776, would be enough, they believed, to bring Congress to the negotiating table.

Once Burgoyne was in Albany, the Howes intended to support him by sending supplies up the Hudson, but they were relying on him to take Albany on his own. Only if, in the unlikely event Washington concentrated on Burgoyne and not on them, did they plan to join Burgoyne and fight on the Hudson.

None of this was clear to Germain or to the king. They were laboring under the impression that the Howes could miraculously defeat Washington, take Philadelphia and the Delaware River, and then march to Albany for a junction with Burgoyne. His Majesty stubbornly clung to his old strategy of 1776. The capture of Philadelphia was simply an added bonus.

General Carleton, for his part, was left in place to run Canada and facilitate Burgoyne's move south. London had been noticeably unhappy with Carleton's performance the previous year, but he was nonetheless left in charge in Canada, with instructions to support Burgoyne. On March 26, Germain sent explicit orders to Carleton that left him no discretion: Carleton was to give Burgoyne orders to "pass Lake Champlain and from thence, by the most vigorous exertion of the force under his command, to proceed with all expedition to Albany, and put himself under the command of Sir William Howe. . . . I shall write to Sir William Howe by the first packet, but you will nevertheless endeavour to give him the earliest intelligence of this measure."

Carleton, who was the senior officer in North America, was being deliberately snubbed. An officer junior to him was being given command of the army marching to Albany, and once there, he was to place himself under General Howe's orders, not Carleton's. Germain and the king were convinced that Burgoyne's army could stand on its own— that it could reach Albany unassisted and hold it until Howe arrived.

The person most outraged by Howe's proposals, or as much of them as he was privy to, was General Henry Clinton. He believed that the first order of business for the army in Manhattan should be to proceed up the Hudson and meet Burgoyne at Albany. It was ludicrous, he thought, to expect General Howe to complete the capture of Philadelphia and then turn and form a junction with Burgoyne in the same campaign season. Clinton vehemently opposed attacking Philadelphia at all in the summer of 1777. He thought that Howe should put his entire effort into coordinating with Burgoyne. Taking Philadelphia, in Clinton's view, would prove disastrous. Once conquered, it would have to be held, which would immobilize the army and make it impossible to cooperate with Burgoyne.

Germain liked the idea of taking Philadelphia, however. He assumed that Washington would defend the capital and risk his inferior army. Clinton disagreed strongly and argued his case in London that winter. After taking Rhode Island in December, he left Newport on January 13, and reached London on February 24, determined not to go back or, if he did, to take over in Canada from Carleton, whom he knew Germain hated and the king was unhappy with.

Burgoyne was a step ahead of Clinton. He had returned to London before Christmas and wasted no time elaborating on Carleton's faults to Germain and the king, who welcomed his message. By the time Clinton reached London, His Majesty had put Burgoyne in command of the new invasion from Canada, and he was already preparing for the campaign.

Burgoyne's plan, which met with the approval of Germain and the king, was to complete the previous year's project. He assumed that General Howe's first priority would be the Hudson. Howe's first proposal, written in November, was reassuring on this point. A substantial force was allocated to operate on the Hudson. But as Howe's thinking evolved and it became obvious that London was not going to give him the reinforcements he needed to carry out his original plan, he made it clear to Germain that, although the Hudson was important, it would not be the focus of his attention; Philadelphia would be.

Howe wrote to Carleton on April 2 from New York, explaining precisely what his strategy would be. "Having little expectation that I shall be able in the beginning of the campaign to act upon Hudson's River consistent with the operations already determined upon," he said, "the force your Excellency may deem expedient to advance beyond your frontiers after taking Ticonderoga will, I fear, have little assistance from hence to facilitate their approach, and as I shall probably be in Pennsylvania when that corps is ready to advance into this province, it will not be in my power to communicate with the officer commanding it so soon as I should wish."

Howe went on to explain to Carleton that after Burgoyne secured Albany, which he had no doubt would happen, he would have a supply line opened on the Hudson for him. He promised that after securing Philadelphia, "I shall endeavour to have a corps upon the lower part of Hudson's River sufficient to open the communication for shipping through the Highlands, at present obstructed by several forts erected by the rebels for that purpose, which corps may afterwards act in favor of the northern army."

Howe's strategy made no sense whatever to Clinton, and he was not reluctant to say so. While he was still in London he held discussions with Germain, who obviously had approved of Howe's plan to capture Philadelphia. Germain insisted that he would have time to help Burgoyne if needed. Clinton was not going to change his mind.

In spite of Clinton's deep misgivings about strategy, the king persuaded him to return to America as Howe's second again. His Majesty awarded him the Order of the Bath to help smooth things over. He was now Sir Henry.

Although Clinton left England the first week of May, he did not reach New York until July 5. What he found shocked him. Howe was still there. Clinton lost no time pleading with him not to make Philadelphia the principal object of the current campaign. Seizing the capital would never end the rebellion, he insisted; in fact, it would more than likely lead to a British defeat. Secure the Hudson and meet Burgoyne, Clinton advised; seize the Highland forts and gain control of the Hudson—the king's original plan.

Under Howe's current strategy, Clinton would be left in New York with a small contingent of troops, and he naturally worried that Washington might attack him, or Burgoyne, while Howe was occupied with Philadelphia. If Washington threw the whole patriot army at Manhattan, Clinton feared that he would be in serious trouble. Even if Washington did what Howe expected him to do, which was to follow him, Clinton still thought Howe's focus wrongheaded. Clinton remained convinced that control of the Hudson was the key to winning the war, and he never doubted for an instant that British arms could do it. Furthermore, Clinton thought that if Howe's objective was to lure Washington into a major battle, he could do it just as well by moving up the Hudson as he could by going to Philadelphia. Fighting Washington and the rebel army in New York's Highlands, however, was not something that ever appealed to Howe.

Chapter 14

DUEL FOR A CONTINENT

Washington's preparations for the coming spring campaign were done in a fog of uncertainty about the Howes' intentions. Were they going up the Hudson or to Philadelphia? Washington's first impulse was to think that they would drive up the Hudson for a rendezvous at Albany with an army coming down from Canada, just as they had planned to do the previous year. Since they already controlled Long Island, Manhattan, and the surrounding area, they would have a springboard, which they did not have in 1776, for moving upriver fast. And Carleton, since he now controlled both Canada and Lake Champlain, would have a much easier time reaching Albany.

Washington assumed that once the British armies joined together, New England would be isolated and the war lost. He intended to fight them in every way he could. He never considered standing aside and letting Carleton and Howe race to Albany, and then focusing his efforts on isolating them, seizing weakly defended New York City, and harassing their supply lines from both Canada and Manhattan. He never thought that Albany might be a trap for the British—that having their entire North American army gathered there was something he should promote rather than resist.

Lord Howe's fleet would have a hard job supporting two armies in Albany and doing all the other tasks assigned to it. Could the admiral's warships, strung out along the Hudson, defend the entire length of the river and move transports continuously to supply the armies in hostile territory? Would Howe be able to blockade New England and at the same time protect Manhattan, Staten Island, and Long Island?

When the armies joined at Albany, would they descend on Massachusetts, forgetting that in April of 1775 over twenty thousand militiamen had turned out to dispute a British march to Lexington and Concord? How many would turn out now? The questions and unknowns were far too numerous for it to be safely assumed that a joining of armies at Albany would defeat the rebellion instead of boomerang into a total disaster.

Nonetheless, Washington clung to the idea that it would be logical, from General Howe's point of view, to pursue the old strategy of driving up the Hudson and meeting an army coming down from Canada. It was obvious from what had happened in 1776, however, that Howe had his eye on Philadelphia. Washington felt he had to be ready to defend the capital as well as Albany.

The long-awaited campaign of 1777 finally began on May 28. Washington made the opening move. During the evening he began shifting the main body of his rejuvenated, ten-thousand-man army twenty miles south from Morristown to Middle Brook, settling in a protected valley of the Watchung Mountains on the west bank of the Raritan River, seven miles from Brunswick. At the same time, Congress, with Washington's enthusiastic approval, appointed Major General Benedict Arnold to command the defense of Philadelphia. Arnold took charge of the militia guarding the Delaware, with headquarters at Trenton.

Congress made this important appointment even though it had not restored Arnold's seniority, which he very much wanted. It would not be restored until November 29, 1777. For the moment, Arnold put aside his grievances and concentrated on resisting any attempt by Howe to cross the Delaware. General Sullivan's division was close by in Flemington. Washington was happy to find that significant numbers of New Jersey militiamen were joining him and Sullivan. Sentiment in the state had change dramatically during the last few months.

The high ground at Middle Brook was an excellent place from which to observe Howe's movements and at the same time provide protection for the patriot army. From there, Washington could respond to a move on either Philadelphia or the New York Highlands. He had been worried earlier that Howe might surprise him and quick march to Brunswick and then race south to Philadelphia via Princeton and Trenton, while the Continental army was ensconced in Morristown. Now, he was ready for whatever the British might do.

As it turned out, Howe had his sights on Philadelphia, hoping to precipitate a general battle. He assumed that Washington would be forced to defend the city. When he saw Washington moving to Middle Brook, however, he thought that he might trick him into a showdown right there in New Jersey. During the evening of June 13, he marched eighteen thousand men along the banks of the Raritan from Perth Amboy to Brunswick and then made a feint toward the Delaware River and Philadelphia, trying to lure Washington out into the open for a major engagement.

Washington wasn't taking the bait. It was obvious that Howe was not making a move on Philadelphia; he had left too much baggage in Brunswick. Washington's aggressive streak was aroused; he dearly wanted to take on Howe, but he overcame the impulse and remained in Middle Brook.

Seeing that Washington was not coming out, Howe made a big show of retreating to Brunswick, hoping that Washington might be tempted to hang on his rear. He guessed right. After a long, frustrating winter cooped up in Morristown, Washington was ready to bloody the British if he could do it without risking his army. On June 24, apparently thinking he might surprise Howe and at least inflict some damage, he sent Greene to explore the possibility, while he left the mountains and came down with the main body of the army to Quibbletown (now part of Piscataway), five miles north of Brunswick.

Two days later Howe reacted, racing toward the high ground at Middle Brook, hoping to seize it and prevent Washington from retreating back to defensible ground. Howe was a bit too late, however. Washington realized the danger in time and sped back to Middle Brook. Howe did not want to engage him there and pulled back.

Convinced now that Washington was not going to be easily manipulated, Howe gave up and withdrew all his troops from New Jersey. By June 30 his entire army was on Staten Island, preparing to leave for Philadelphia by sea. Howe was confident that Washington would follow him. Congress would expect him to, whether it made strategic sense or not. The great battle that Howe wanted would then follow. He had no doubt about the outcome.

Washington, unaware of Howe's plans, withdrew to Morristown on July 3. He thought it likely now that Howe would race up the Hudson, attempt to seize the Highlands, and cooperate with Burgoyne. Washington positioned his army near the dramatic bend in the river known as West Point and ordered George Clinton and General Israel Putnam, who had taken over from General Heath, to brace for an all-out attack on the Highland forts. At the same time, Washington remained alert for a lightning move on Philadelphia.

During this time of uncertainty, Washington's basic policy of shadowing the main British army remained in place. Howe might be heading up the Hudson or going to Philadelphia; whichever it was, Washington was determined to follow. If Howe put to sea, however, his destination would be nearly impossible to predict. It would also be impossible for Howe to find out what Washington was doing. He might ignore Howe and move against Burgoyne, following which he could attack weakly defended New York with both his army and the northern army combined. It would be some time before Howe found out what Washington was up to, and by then it probably would be too late. If Washington were successful, the war would be over.

Howe was fortunate that Washington remained committed to defending Philadelphia. It was primarily a political decision. Washington was defending the capital because that's what Congress wanted, even though it did not make strategic sense.

No matter where Howe went, Washington intended to oppose him. How he could do that without risking a general encounter wasn't clear. With Howe continually looking for ways to provoke a showdown, it was hard to see how Washington was going to defend Philadelphia and remain on the defensive. He would have to fight at some point and hazard his army. It seemed that he had made up his mind to do so, if he thought he had a good chance of winning.

Meanwhile, seventeen thousand troops under Howe began embarking for the voyage to Philadelphia. By July 9, only a few days after returning from New Jersey, they were all loaded and ready to sail. The fleet was enormous: 267 transports, plus Lord Howe's men-of-war—300 ships in all.

Washington expected them to weigh anchor the next day, but they remained in the harbor for two more weeks in sweltering heat. They did not leave until the twenty-third. Adverse weather accounted for some of the delay, but the main reason was that General Howe wanted to hear how Burgoyne was doing before he departed. That intelligence did not arrive until the fifteenth. The news was encouraging. Burgoyne had already taken Fort Ticonderoga—his first objective—on July 6.

Since Burgoyne had returned to Canada on May 6, everything had gone smoothly. With Carleton's unstinting cooperation, Burgoyne had assembled an army of 4,000 regulars, 3,000 Germans, 650 Canadians, 500 Indians, a corps of watermen, and a train of artillery. Once under way from Quebec, he moved swiftly down the St. Lawrence and Richelieu rivers to Lake Champlain, where the fleet of warships and bateaux that Carleton had built the previous year were ready to ferry him down the lake.

By June 20 Burgoyne was moving rapidly south down Lake Champlain with no opposition toward Fort Ticonderoga, which was defended by a shrinking garrison of less than 2,700 under Major General Arthur St. Clair. The northern army had been badly depleted by sickness, desertion, and troop withdrawals that Washington made to bolster his army on the Delaware River in December.

St. Clair knew he did not have enough men to defend Ticonderoga or the hills that overlooked it—Mount Independence and Mount Defiance. Nor did he have adequate intelligence about the size of Burgoyne's army or its whereabouts. Unfortunately, he did not have to wait long to find out. On July 2 the British arrived in force to lay siege to the fort. During the next few days they quietly brought their big guns up to undefended Mount Defiance. When St. Clair discovered them on the morning of the fifth, he had to act fast. The artillery commanded both Fort Ticonderoga and Mount Independence. He had to retreat immediately or surrender. By this time, his army had shrunk to fewer than 2,100 men.

During the night of the fifth, he quietly evacuated his entire army, retreating south. Most of his troops struggled overland toward Hubbardton. The rest left in boats and bateaux for Skenesborough (now Whitehall, Vermont) at the southern end of Lake Champlain—its headwaters. Burgoyne was right after them, sending Brigadier Generals Simon Fraser and Friedrich von Riedesel to catch St. Clair, who was leading the column moving to Hubbardton. They had no trouble catching him, but St. Clair managed to survive an intense fight—losing, but also inflicting heavy casualties on an overconfident enemy. Before his pursuers could recover, he slipped away and, after a grueling trek south, arrived exhausted on July 12 at Fort Edward on the Hudson, thirty miles south of Skenesborough, and fifty-five miles above Albany. His ranks, needless to say, were seriously depleted.

While St. Clair was marching to Hubbardton, Colonel Pierce Long struggled south on the water, paddling for Skenesborough. Burgoyne went after him, but Long remained just beyond his grasp until he reached Skenesborough, where Burgoyne almost caught him. He was less than three miles behind when Long and his party pulled out—after burning all they could in the area. Long raced for Fort Anne, and got there with the help of four hundred New York militiamen under Colonel Henry Van Rensselaer, whom General Philip Schuyler, commander of the Northern Department, had sent. After reaching the fort, the intrepid Long then fended off attacks as he struggled to reach Fort Edward. He arrived there with one hundred fifty men on July 12. It was a remarkable performance.

At this point, Burgoyne, instead of pushing right on to Fort Edward before the Americans could recover, chose to remain several critical days with the body of his army at Skenesborough, twenty-three difficult miles away. He greatly underestimated his foe, forty-three-year-old Schuyler, a native who knew the territory intimately and was moving fast to take advantage of Burgoyne's lethargy.

★

AFTER HEARING THAT THE INVASION WAS GOING WELL IN the north, General Howe felt he could get on with the campaign against Philadelphia, provided, of course, that Washington did what he expected and followed him. If not—if Washington turned north and sped up the Hudson River Valley to attack Burgoyne—Howe planned to abandon the Philadelphia campaign and come to Burgoyne's aid. He did not intend to leave Burgoyne to face the entire American army alone. Howe wanted Washington's forces divided, fighting for Albany and Philadelphia at the same time.

Once the main British army was at sea, however, Washington could move north rapidly, without Howe's knowledge, and join Schuyler to defeat Burgoyne rather easily, and then turn south and attack weakly defended Manhattan and Long Island. General Clinton, whom Howe left to defend New York with a woefully inadequate force, was understandably worried that Washington might ignore Howe for the moment and attack him with his whole army. By advancing to Philadelphia by sea and assuming that Washington would follow him, Howe was taking a big chance. If he lost his gamble, Clinton and Burgoyne would pay the price. Fortunately for Howe, Washington was preoccupied with following him.

———

As Howe prepared to leave New York Harbor, he wrote to Burgoyne on July 17, explaining what to expect from him. He told him exactly what he had told General Carleton back in April—namely, that he was going to Philadelphia but would open a supply line on the Hudson for him when he reached Albany. Just how he was going to do that when he had the army and navy in Philadelphia wasn't explained. In fact, this was all empty rhetoric. Howe had no real plan for carrying out such an immense project.

Since things were going particularly well for Burgoyne at the moment, he was not looking for aid from Howe; in fact, he probably wanted to be on his own. Things were shaping up precisely as he had hoped. He thought he would reach Albany easily and dreamed of subduing all of New England before winter—winning the war on his own. What a glorious achievement that would be. On July 12 he told Germain there was a real chance of reducing New England to subservience in a few weeks. He expected his army to grow as continuous success drew more Loyalists to his ranks—even from Massachusetts and Connecticut.

Lieutenant Colonel Barry St. Leger's diversion in the west added to Burgoyne's confidence. St. Leger was advancing down Lake Ontario with eighteen hundred regulars, Loyalists, and Indians to Oswego, New York, with orders to meet Burgoyne at the confluence of the Mohawk and Hudson rivers, just above Albany. He appeared to be encountering no opposition.

From Oswego he traveled along the Oswego River to Lake Oneida, Wood Creek, and the Oneida Carrying Place to Fort Stanwix (Rome), at the headwaters of the Mohawk—only 110 miles west of Albany. He reached the fort on August 2, planning to capture it and move down the Mohawk to the Hudson for the rendezvous with Burgoyne.

On July 11 Washington received the disheartening news of Ticonderoga falling without a fight. Although surprised and chagrined, he responded fast, sending all the help he could to General Schuyler. He dispatched

General John Nixon from Peekskill with six hundred men and Colonel Glover with thirteen hundred. St. Clair's battered survivors, numbering around fifteen hundred, added to Schuyler's ranks, as did Colonel Pierce Long's one hundred fifty.

Generals Benedict Arnold and Benjamin Lincoln were also sent to assist with the New England troops, who by this time were shaken and looking for scapegoats. Many were calling Schuyler and St. Clair traitors. They blamed them for Ticonderoga and Hubbardton.

Despite all his problems, Schuyler fought on, putting his troops to work creating obstacles along the difficult road Burgoyne would have to travel from Skenesborough to Fort Edward. Moving with surprising speed, Schuyler threw innumerable impediments in Burgoyne's path—tearing up forty bridges, felling countess trees, and rolling boulders across the primitive forest trail that wound its way from Skenesborough to Fort Edward. Schuyler's quick action slowed Burgoyne's progress. He did not reach Fort Edward, which Schuyler had evacuated, until July 30, twenty-three days after arriving at Skenesborough.

Burgoyne's big guns, which were transported on Lake George, arrived two days earlier at the southern end of the lake. Although they were difficult to move, Burgoyne thought that the forty-three pieces of artillery were essential. He anticipated that at some point he would face enemy numbers larger than his own—how large he didn't know, but he was convinced that the heavy guns would be effective against inexperienced troops, and indispensable for assaulting Fort Edward, as well as countering any rebel gunboats on the Hudson.

Burgoyne had not yet received news of how St. Leger was faring. He assumed he was doing well. Still full of confidence, he continued moving forward. On August 6 he wrote to General Clinton that he expected to be in Albany by the twenty-third. To do so, he needed more supplies and horses. Once he crossed to the west side of the Hudson, which he would have to do, his supply line to Montreal would be severed. He needed enough provisions to last an additional month to get to Albany. He was told that they were available at Bennington, only thirty miles away. Tory Philip Skene assured him that Loyalists outnumbered rebels in that area five to one.

Burgoyne dispatched German Lieutenant Colonel Friedrich Baum with eight hundred men to Bennington and a few hours later sent Lieutenant Colonel Heinrich von Breymann with six hundred more to reinforce him. Their movements were soon detected. Veteran New Hampshire brigadier general John Stark gathered two thousand militiamen to counter them and ordered Colonel Seth Warner, who had six hundred men at Manchester, in the Hampshire Grants (Vermont), to join him. They met the German detachments on August 16 and badly mauled Baum first, and then Breymann. Burgoyne himself was marching toward the battlefield with a large reinforcement, but turned back—luckily for Stark—when he was misinformed that the fight was over.

The defeat was a turning point. Burgoyne lost nine hundred men he could not replace. The sensible course now was to retreat, but for Burgoyne that was unthinkable. The victor of Ticonderoga, the man who talked of subduing New England and winning the war on his own, could not admit that a few militiamen had checked him. And so, the prisoner of his image, he pressed on, still pretending that victory, even without Howe, was possible.

While Schuyler, John Stark, and Seth Warner were countering Burgoyne, Washington was still pondering what the Howes were up to. When their giant fleet finally lumbered out of New York Harbor on July 23, its destination was still unclear. Philadelphia was the most likely target, but the Howes could also be conducting an elaborate feint to lure Washington away from the Hudson while they doubled back to New York and pushed upriver to unite with Burgoyne.

Alternatively, they might sail directly for the New England coast and cooperate with Burgoyne from there. They might even go south to Charleston, but the most likely places remained either the Hudson or Philadelphia. On July 27 a large part of the British fleet was seen off Egg Harbor, New Jersey, and two days later, Henry Fisher, a lookout at

Lewes, Delaware, spotted even more of their ships off the Delaware capes. Admiral Howe had noticeably slowed down, remaining offshore for hours. Fisher assumed he intended to enter Delaware Bay and run up the river for an attack on Philadelphia.

Actually, the Howes spent the day conferring with Captain Snape Hamond, commander of the British squadron on Delaware Bay, and by the end of the day they decided—against Hamond's advice—to avoid the Delaware entirely and approach Philadelphia from Chesapeake Bay. A puzzled Henry Fisher reported the next morning that the great fleet had disappeared out to sea again.

Washington was left to speculate about where it was going. The Howes might have turned around and, having gotten Washington to move his army closer to Philadelphia, raced back to the Hudson. They might also be sailing for Charleston, attempting to draw him far to the south during the unhealthy summer, and then abruptly turning about and making a dash for the Hudson.

As late as August 21 Washington had no good intelligence on the fleet's whereabouts.

So much time had passed since the Howes had left New York that he thought they indeed must be sailing for Charleston. He became so convinced of it that after conferring with his senior officers (who now included nineteen-year-old Major General the Marquis de Lafayette) and obtaining the approval of Congress, he made a firm decision to march his army to the North (Hudson) River and prepare an attack on Burgoyne, or on General Clinton in Manhattan, depending on the circumstances when he got there.

Washington had already initiated small, coordinated attacks against eastern Long Island, Kings Bridge, and Staten Island to keep Clinton off balance. General Sullivan was in command of the operations. He led the strike on Staten Island personally, with three thousand men, on August 22. It was the largest of the strikes. Sullivan had information indicating that about one thousand Loyalist militia were regularly separated from the main fortified camp on the island, and he focused on them. His attack was blunted, however, when regulars came more quickly to the rescue than Sullivan had anticipated, and he was forced to retreat fast. Unfortunately, there weren't enough boats to carry his men off the island all at once, and he needlessly lost much of his rear guard.

Although Sullivan failed on Staten Island, he succeeded with General Clinton, who became even more anxious about his position on Manhattan. It kept him from seriously considering helping Burgoyne.

Things changed dramatically on August 22, however, when Washington received good intelligence that the British fleet was deep in Chesapeake Bay, so deep that turning back was out of the question. An attack on Philadelphia was now certain. He immediately dropped plans for traveling to New York and concentrated on defending the capital.

Assuming that Howe was sailing for the Head of Elk (Elkton) in Maryland (the head of navigation on the Elk River), Washington moved his army in that direction. On the way, he paraded fourteen thousand men through Philadelphia with Major General Lafayette riding at his side. They camped that night at Wilmington on Brandywine Creek.

The following day, August 25, Washington received good news from the North of a major American victory over a large foraging party that Burgoyne had sent to Bennington. Reports were also coming in of a surprising British defeat at still unfinished Fort Stanwix (also known as Fort Schuyler).

When Lieutenant Colonel St. Leger arrived at the fort and began his siege the first week of August, he met surprisingly strong opposition from Tryon County patriots led by twenty-eight-year-old Colonel Peter Gansevoort, who had only 750 men. The head of Tryon County's militia, Brigadier General Nicholas Herkimer, had tried to reinforce Gansevoort but failed.

Herkimer had been marching toward the fort with eight hundred men when St. Leger had gotten wind of it and alerted his ally, Mohawk war chief Joseph Brant, who ambushed Herkimer at Oriskany, near the Mohawk River, ten miles southeast of Fort Stanwix. A fierce fight developed on August 6 in which Herkimer was killed and his army decimated, but Brant's men suffered severely as well. Despite the loss of Herkimer's column, Gansevoort continued his stubborn resistance.

St. Leger's siege dragged on for days until Schuyler sent a relief column under resourceful Benedict Arnold, who tricked St. Leger into abandoning the attack on August 22 and fleeing back to Canada. The unexpected news showed that Schuyler's northern army, after a poor start, was holding its own, giving Washington and his men a tremendous boost.

General Burgoyne's problems continued to mount when he was obliged to dispatch more men back to garrison Fort Ticonderoga and protect his supply line. General Carleton was cynically sticking to the letter of his instructions from Germain and refusing to send any men outside Canada for garrison duty. If Burgoyne needed to guard his supply line to Canada he would have to do it himself. Ironically, Germain made it impossible for Burgoyne to receive help from Carleton by giving Carleton detailed orders as to which regiments would be under Burgoyne and which were to stay in Canada. Tying the hands of local commanders was a costly habit of Germain's.

Burgoyne's difficulties were exacerbated when Washington dispatched Benjamin Lincoln to aid Schuyler by threatening Burgoyne's rear. Lincoln arrived at Manchester on August 2 and began the tedious job of pulling together a diverse force that could threaten Ticonderoga and the whole supply line to Canada. It took time to coordinate with John Stark, who was angry with Congress. Stark had been mindlessly passed over for promotion from colonel in the Continental army to brigadier general (the title he held in New Hampshire), which made Lincoln's task even more difficult, but he stayed with it and was making progress after Stark's brilliant victory at Bennington. There was no interruption in Lincoln's work when General Horatio Gates replaced Schuyler during the third week of August. Gates saw the advantage of Lincoln's work just as Schuyler had. Lincoln was eventually able to close off any hope that Burgoyne had of retreating, forcing him to look for succor only from Henry Clinton coming up from New York.

Washington urged Governor Clinton to do everything possible to get New York's patriot militias to fight Burgoyne. Clinton did not need to be told. He was already working hard to get as many militiamen to the northern army as he could. He also had to think about the defense of the Highland forts, which needed men as well.

Meanwhile, Burgoyne was on the move, marching south from Fort Edward to Fort Miller, still on the eastern side of the Hudson, forty-seven miles from Albany. He was no longer talking about subduing New England on his own; he was complaining about lack of support from Howe and Clinton. On August 20 he reported to Germain, "The prospect of the campaign . . . is far less prosperous than when I wrote last." He was particularly incensed that Loyalists were not supporting him. "I find daily reason to doubt the sincerity of the resolution of the professing Loyalists," he wrote. "I have about 400 (but not half of them armed) who may be depended upon; the rest are trimmers, merely actuated by interest." It galled him to find that at the same time that the Tories were letting him down, the countryside was swarming with rebels, particularly on his left flank in the Hampshire Grants. "The great bulk of the country is undoubtedly with the Congress, in principle and in zeal . . . ," he complained. "Wherever the king's forces point, militia to the amount of three or four thousand, assemble in twenty-four hours."

In spite of his problems, Burgoyne was not considering giving up. He was doggedly pressing forward. "I yet do not despond," he told Germain. "Should I succeed in forcing my way to Albany, and find that country in a state to subsist my army, I shall think no more of a retreat, but at the worst fortify there and await Sir W. Howe's operations." It was not a cheery forecast for the American secretary. In a few days Burgoyne would be further troubled when he received word of St. Leger's flight back to Canada. The news did not bother him enough, though, to cause him to think seriously about retreating.

Chapter 15

NEW YORK AND
PHILADELPHIA

On August 19 General Horatio Gates arrived in Albany to take command of the northern army. Just when General Schuyler had the situation in hand, Congress decided to replace him with the ever ambitious Gates. The New England delegation, led by Massachusetts, had lost confidence in Schuyler. Washington continued to support him, based on the excellent job he was doing in tough circumstances. Congress, on the other hand, had scant appreciation of what he had accomplished.

Despite Schuyler's strengths, his weaknesses were impossible to overlook. No matter how skilled he was as an administrator, he was not a battlefield general, which the northern army required. More importantly, New England militiamen, who were desperately needed, were not going to respond to Schuyler's call, whereas they would undoubtedly follow Gates. During the time Gates served in Boston as Washington's adjutant general, he became a favorite of political leaders, especially Samuel Adams. Gates's role in stopping Carleton the previous year had been much appreciated as well.

Gates had received his appointment on August 4 and had immediately sent out a call to the New England states for militia, and they had responded. Not long after he arrived in Albany on the nineteenth, the northern army nearly doubled, going from about 5,300 effectives to around 9,000. These included 1,200 troops under Arnold arriving back from Fort Stanwix and Daniel Morgan's 500 riflemen, sent by Washington from his army. Morgan's was the most effective fighting unit in the American army.

While Gates found it easy to work with New England politicians who could be useful to him, he did his best to destroy Schuyler. Instead of using Schuyler's incomparable knowledge of northern New York, Gates snubbed him—not even inviting him to the first conference of senior officers. Schuyler found it difficult to fight back. Governor Clinton—not one of Schuyler's enemies—wrote, "Our friend Phil has good qualities, but he has contrived to make himself disagreeable and suspected by the Yankees—prejudices not easily got over. His cursed attachment to the comforts of Albany and doing the fighting business by proxy for two campaigns has destroyed him."

Gates was fortunate to be inheriting a remarkable group of talented, experienced officers, among them Benedict Arnold, Henry Dearborn, John Glover, Benjamin Lincoln, John Dixon, John Patterson, Enoch Poor, Ebenezer Learned, Seth Warner, and, of course, Daniel Morgan. In addition, Gates had a gifted group of militia officers from counties in New York, Massachusetts, New Hampshire, and Connecticut.

★

WHILE EVENTS IN THE NORTH WERE MOVING INEXORABLY toward a showdown, so too were Generals Howe and Washington. On August 25 Howe began debarking his army at Head of Elk, at the northern headwaters of Chesapeake Bay, fifty-seven miles from Philadelphia. As the troops were unloading, Howe received news of the defeat at Bennington, and he was stunned. It had the potential to ruin all of his plans. He had no hope of helping Burgoyne. He never had much of a chance to begin with, and now, with the voyage from New York having taken so much longer than anticipated, there was no hope at all.

Burgoyne was on his own. General Clinton might try to help him after reinforcements arrived from England, but Clinton wasn't likely to be strong enough to make a difference. As was the case the previous year, saving the colonies for the empire rested exclusively with the Howes. One thing was clear, General Howe had to defeat Washington and take Philadelphia. If Burgoyne was beaten in the north, and the main army defeated in Pennsylvania, the king's dominion in America was over. On the other hand, if Howe defeated Washington and forced him to surrender, the consequences for the patriots would be dire. The British would be holding Philadelphia and New York, while the rebels would be without their main army. The chances of the rebellion surviving would be dramatically lessened, even if General Gates and his army succeeded against Burgoyne. France would undoubtedly lose interest in an alliance, perhaps even in any further involvement.

Howe intended to proceed directly to the Schuylkill River, cross it, and march into Philadelphia, which he believed abounded with Tories waiting to give him a rousing welcome. All that stood in his way was the somewhat smaller rebel army. He planned to draw Washington into a major battle, confident that he'd win and the accursed war would be over. He had defeated Washington before; there was no reason to believe he couldn't do it again. The key was to force a surrender. If Washington escaped, as he had in the past, the result would be inconclusive, and the war would drag on. At the moment, except for the surprising lack of support from Tories outside Philadelphia, Howe's prospects looked good.

Washington, as it turned out, intended to confront Howe directly, risking his army, precipitating the battle that Howe always wanted. The British had about two thousand more men than Washington, roughly sixteen thousand to fourteen thousand. "The army that I have had under my immediate command," Washington wrote later, "has not, at any one time since General Howe's landing at the Head of Elk, been equal in point of numbers to his." It didn't matter; Washington was going to fight.

He made no attempt to attack Howe when he landed, or immediately after, which was a blessing for the British troops, who had just spent forty-seven interminable days cooped up in stifling transports during a steamy summer. Many died. So did their horses—perhaps one hundred fifty of them. The first thing Howe needed to do was resuscitate his men and scour the countryside for fresh meat and horses, conscious all the time that Washington was hovering close by with an army of unknown size. Washington left him alone. He planned to keep between Howe and the city and engage him at the most advantageous spot.

After resting, Howe began marching toward the Schuylkill River, expecting to skirmish with Washington and then fight a full-scale battle. On September 6 a brief, inconclusive skirmish developed between advance units at White Clay Creek. Afterward, Washington pulled back, positioning his army on the Philadelphia side of Chadd's Ford on Brandywine Creek, blocking Howe's path to the city. Both armies now prepared for a major confrontation.

On September 11 at around 10:30 in the morning, eighteen days after Howe had landed, the battle that he had to win began on Brandywine Creek. General Knyphausen conducted an impressive demonstration against the middle of Washington's line at Chadd's Ford to draw his attention. General Greene and Brigadier General Anthony Wayne were opposite Knyphausen with the main army. When Knyphausen did not follow his initial artillery barrage with an attack, Washington suspected that he might be holding his attention while the main action went quietly elsewhere, to one of the fords farther up the Brandywine. In fact, he had been receiving reports of the movement of a large column in that direction. If, as Washington suspected, Howe was at the head of that column, moving, once again, to envelop him, he was considering foiling him by attacking Knyphausen with Greene and Wayne. The German had less than seven thousand troops. After routing Knyphausen, Washington could then turn on an unsuspecting Howe, whose army would have been considerably weakened. Washington was about to give the order to attack when he received a report from Sullivan, who was in command of the American right, claiming that the intelligence was incorrect—that Howe was not moving in that direction. Believing that Sullivan's report was more credible, Washington held back.

Unfortunately, Sullivan's report was wrong. Washington's first impulse had been correct; Knyphausen was indeed only holding his attention, while the main thrust was on the far right. Howe and Cornwallis were engaged in another classic envelopment movement to outflank Sullivan and get in the rear of the American army with over eight thousand men. Washington was as completely fooled as he had been on Long Island. If he had acted on his first impulse and attacked Knyphausen, he would have upset all of Howe's plans.

While Knyphausen continued holding Washington's attention, Howe and Cornwallis crossed undefended Trimble's Ford on the west branch of the Brandywine and then unguarded Jeffries' Ford on the east branch, fourteen miles west of Chadd's Ford, with a little over half their army, enveloping Washington as they had on Long Island. The prominent Philadelphia Loyalist Joseph Galloway had alerted Howe to the fords and had sent men to guide him. Once across, Howe gathered his force on nearby Osborne Hill in the patriots' rear, gave his troops time to rest after a long march, and prepared a powerful strike.

Independently, Thomas Cheyney, a local farmer and strong patriot in what was Loyalist country, managed somehow to see Washington in the early afternoon and told him that the original story was accurate— that a large British column was moving to outflank the American right wing. Others reported the same thing. Washington sent word to Sullivan, who by then knew he had been wrong: He had a major fight on his hands. Washington left Sullivan to fight the battle until after 5:00, when he received hurried messages from him and heard so much of the battlefield noise that he became worried and went himself with Greene and his division, which hadn't been employed yet, to support Sullivan, who was being overwhelmed.

Howe's attack had commenced at close to 4:30 p.m. The outnumbered patriots fought back hard, with Generals Sullivan, Stirling, and

Stephen leading them. But the British were too strong and were over-powering them when around 5:30, Washington arrived on the scene and took command.

Greene was right behind him with his division. A wild melee developed as the commander in chief risked his life riding through the battlefield and organizing resistance. The badly outnumbered Americans had the worst of it and were forced back, as Knyphausen's force pushed ominously across Chadd's Ford to join Howe and Cornwallis. But General Wayne checked him, fighting valiantly against great odds, holding Knyphausen for a critical hour and preventing a total rout. Meanwhile, Greene's division pulled back as Cornwallis pressed his attack. Washington was retreating slowly toward Chester, fourteen miles away on the Delaware River. It was now 7:00, and with daylight diminishing, it looked as if he was going to be saved. By this time his army was disintegrating into a mob seeking refuge.

Howe might have won a complete victory and compelled Washington to surrender had night not fallen. It had taken so long for the battle to develop that darkness overtook the combatants before Howe could administer the coup de grâce.

Washington gathered his men at Chester for the night. Howe did not follow. He remained on the battlefield and rested his exhausted troops. They were still there on September 12, when Washington took his army along the northern bank of the Delaware until he reached the Schuylkill, which he crossed, and established a camp near Germantown, five miles northwest of Philadelphia. He had lost a tenth of his men—200 killed, 500 wounded, and 400 captured. The unfortunate prisoners would be turned over to Cunningham, who had accompanied Howe. On the British side, 90 had been killed, 448 were wounded, and 6 were missing.

Much of the Brandywine story was reminiscent of what had taken place on Long Island the year before. Howe won the battle, but Washington's army survived and could be strengthened, whereas Howe had no easy way to replace his fallen men. He had hoped that Pennsylvania Loyalists would come to his aid. He imagined they were far more numerous than in New York, which they were, but they were no more inclined to risk life and limb for the king than their New York brethren were.

Washington was as disappointed as Howe at not receiving more help from Pennsylvanians. It was their state he was defending, after all, and their capital. Maryland and Delaware did not give the support he thought they should, either. "How different the case in the Northern Department!" he wrote later. "There the state of New York and New England, resolved to crush Burgoyne, continued pouring in their troops, till the surrender of that army [at Bemis Heights, near Saratoga]; at which time not less than fourteen thousand militia, as I have been informed, were actually in Gates' camp, and those composed, for the most part, of the best yeomanry in the country, well armed, and in many instances supplied with provisions of their own carrying."

Despite what happened, Washington's men did not feel defeated. There was a big difference between the aftermath of the battle on Long Island in 1776 and the one at Brandywine in 1777. Nothing like the demoralization of the American army after the Battle of Brooklyn occurred after the drubbing on Brandywine Creek. The patriots were not disheartened.

They were angry but still tired when Washington roused them and crossed back over the Schuylkill on September 15 to have another go at Howe. Washington must have felt that he had let his troops down by not reconnoitering the Brandywine and its forks and fords more thoroughly—an amateurish, inexcusable oversight. Howe, in the meantime, had also recovered and was marching toward Philadelphia, anxious to finish off Washington. He wasn't aware that Washington was coming on fast to get at him. For a brief time, Washington had the initiative. But on September 16, near Warren Tavern, twenty miles from Philadelphia, just as the armies met for another full-scale battle, a massive cloudburst ruined Washington's chance, overwhelming both sides and making firing impossible. The ferocious gale continued for a day and a half.

After the deluge, Washington retreated to the big supply depot at Reading Furnace to rearm and then crossed to the north side of the

Schuylkill, moving, in the process, a total of thirty miles. He left General Wayne on the south side of the Schuylkill to hang on Howe's rear with 1,500 men, waiting for an opportunity to strike. It was an odd, ill-thought-out decision that would soon have disastrous results. Wayne's success depended on secrecy, but with the countryside honeycombed with Tories that was manifestly impossible.

Wayne's movements were reported to Howe, who sent General Charles Grey, one of the more accomplished officers in the British army, after Wayne with a force substantially larger than his. Grey waited for his opportunity and attacked Wayne in the dead of night at his camp in Paoli on September 20–21.

Grey's well-planned assault was a surprise, but Wayne reacted quickly. His guards opened fire, while Wayne, sensing that the British force was much larger than his, organized a retreat. The patriots closest to Grey's leading units engaged them, covering their retreating comrades and paying a dreadful price. Grey charged the defenders, using the bayonet only. Wayne's men bravely continued firing and falling as Grey's column came on. Wayne pulled back as fast as he could to a place of advantage with the bulk of his force, while the survivors near Grey's units never ceased fighting. Eventually Grey decided not to continue the attack, allowing Wayne to withdraw. In the end, although exact figures are not known, Grey killed over fifty and took eighty prisoners, some of whom were wounded. Wayne's swift retreat had saved most of his men.

It was a bloody night, but not as bad as patriot propaganda made it out to be, or as General Howe proudly proclaimed. Grey was accused by the Americans (with Howe in agreement) of wantonly stabbing to death four hundred, which was a gross exaggeration. Killing over fifty patriots who never should have been where they were in the first place was bad enough; the story did not need embellishment.

Foremost among the officers assisting Grey was his aide-de-camp, Major John André, as aggressive and bloodthirsty as anyone. "We ferreted out their Piquets and advanced guards," André gloated, "surprised and put them to death, and, coming in upon the camp, rushed on them as they were collecting together and pursued them with a prodigious slaughter." André gloried in the enterprise, noting that afterward they celebrated with some "good gin" they discovered in the camp.

Meanwhile, on September 18, Congress, not wanting to take any chances, adjourned to Lancaster, Pennsylvania, and from there to York, one hundred miles from Philadelphia. Washington urged them to go. He was determined to defend the city and did not want them in the way. He needed more men, however, and on September 23 he sent General Putnam an urgent message, ordering him to dispatch twenty-five hundred troops to Pennsylvania immediately.

Putnam wasn't happy with the order and took his time. Sending the troops would seriously weaken his defenses on the Hudson, especially in the Highlands. It would also put a crimp in some vague plans he had of mounting an attack on either Staten Island, Paulus Hook, Manhattan, or Long Island. Governor Trumbull encouraged him. Washington's order put an end to Putnam's dreams. Which was just as well: The possibility of Old Put's pulling off a successful raid of the kind he was talking about was nonexistent.

The following day Washington wrote to General Gates asking—not ordering—him to send Colonel Morgan and his corps back to Pennsylvania. Gates could not, at that moment, part with Morgan, however. Burgoyne was still very much in the field, preparing to attack again. Washington wasn't aware that a major (but inconclusive) battle had taken place at Freeman's Farm, near Bemis Heights, on September 17, and that Burgoyne was getting ready to have at it again. Gates sent his refusal on October 5.

On September 21, Howe began a feint north toward the Reading Furnace depot, causing Washington to hastily move north to protect it. Howe then suddenly whirled and turned south, crossing to the east side of the Schuylkill at Fatland and Gordon fords during the night of September 23. He sped toward Philadelphia, stopping at Norristown, seventeen miles from the city. Washington was over twenty miles away, totally outmaneuvered again.

On September 26 Cornwallis marched into Philadelphia unopposed with three thousand troops and ten field pieces. He immediately erected batteries on the waterfront to fend off an attack by the minuscule Pennsylvania navy, supported by the Continental frigate *Delaware*. When the attack came, it was disorganized, and Cornwallis easily defeated it. The *Delaware* ran aground and was captured, repaired, and made part of Lord Howe's fleet. All the while, General Howe kept his main army at Germantown.

Washington was watching him, waiting for an opportunity to spring a sudden counterattack—a repeat of Trenton. He wrote to Governor Trumbull of Connecticut, "Many unavoidable difficulties and unlucky accidents . . . helped to promote [Howe's] success. [It] will be attended with several ill consequences; but I hope it will not be so detrimental as so many apprehend, and that a little time and perseverance will give us some favorable opportunity of recovering our loss, and of putting our affairs in a more flourishing condition."

In fact, Washington was preparing a surprise attack on the British at Germantown. It began suddenly on October 4 in thick fog. His plan was so needlessly complicated that the bad weather caused enough confusion to ruin whatever chance he had of succeeding. Washington also committed a glaring tactical error that hurt his prospects: He wasted a full hour assaulting the Chew House, a heavily shuttered stone mansion of no particular importance. He used a brigade to kill four enemy soldiers. The fog, Washington's delay, and general confusion caused by inexperienced troops attempting to carry out the plan of attack allowed Howe to bring up reinforcements from the city just in time to avoid disaster. He was lucky. Washington came very close to inflicting a major setback. In the end he failed and had to withdraw.

The following morning he reported to the president of Congress, "The day was rather unfortunate than injurious. We sustained no material loss of men, and brought off all our artillery, except one piece which was dismounted. The enemy are nothing better by the event; and our troops, who are not in the least dispirited by it, have gained what all young troops gain by being in combat."

A short time later, Washington discovered that his losses were far greater than he had initially thought: one thousand killed, wounded, or missing—the last either captured or deserting. Howe's casualties totaled five hundred. Washington was not wrong in suggesting that his army had given a good account of itself. As General Howe knew only too well, if the rebels had had a better strategy and good weather, they probably would have won, since he was taken completely by surprise, as he had been at Trenton.

By taking Philadelphia and surviving Germantown, General Howe had at least avoided an immediate collapse of the king's cause in America. On the other hand, Admiral Howe's ability to open the Delaware River remained uncertain. Cornwallis had gained control of the Delaware around Philadelphia, but the rest of the river remained in patriot hands. Until the Delaware was secured, Philadelphia was in danger. Gaining possession of the river would not be easy. Its defenses were already formidable, and Washington intended to strengthen them.

Chapter 16

CLINTON AND BURGOYNE

While Howe was holding his own in Pennsylvania, Burgoyne's troubles mounted in New York. His army had shrunk from disease and desertion to less than seven thousand. On September 13–14 he crossed to the west side of the Hudson, moving to Saratoga, committing himself irrevocably to fighting all the way to Albany or giving up, something he had no intention of doing. His situation was becoming desperate, however. Only seven miles ahead, the American army waited in strongly fortified positions on Bemis Heights, its numbers much greater than his and increasing daily.

Five days later, on September 19, Burgoyne attacked Gates at Freeman's Farm. He did well, considering the handicaps he was operating under, and at the end of the day he remained on the battlefield while the Americans retired. He did not hesitate to claim victory, but it was a hollow one. There were 160 dead, 364 wounded, and 42 missing—undoubtedly deserters. Gates had lost 319, but they could be replaced; Burgoyne's men could not. Nonetheless, he prepared to fight on, even though he knew now that he faced terrible odds.

Two days later, he received a communication from General Clinton that made him think all was not lost yet. It was dated September 11. Clinton promised that in about ten days he would send two thousand men up the Hudson to create a diversion—just what Burgoyne wanted. He was hoping that Gates, who had limited battlefield experience, might be unnerved enough to dispatch a large part of his army to confront Clinton. Burgoyne decided to wait for Clinton to make his move before attacking Gates a second time. It was his only hope.

Time was critical. Burgoyne needed Clinton to surprise Gates right away and panic him. In fact, he had needed help from New York for a long time. And Clinton had been anxious to provide it, but until now, the army in New York had been too small to both safeguard the city and succor Burgoyne. Clinton had only four thousand regulars. Three thousand Loyalists supplemented them, but he had no faith in them. As far as he was concerned, they were untrained, unreliable provincials. He needed reinforcement from British regulars. He could not move until he received them. When they arrived, he planned to immediately attack the Highland forts, something he had always wanted to do. He told Burgoyne that if he did well, he would consider moving farther north along the river. The reinforcements had not yet arrived when Burgoyne received Clinton's letter.

For reasons that remain obscure, on September 12 Clinton led an army of two thousand into New Jersey and rounded up some cattle, returning to Manhattan on the sixteenth. His purpose may simply have been to give the troops some exercise. He did arouse the interest of General Putnam, who was headquartered on the east side of the Hudson. Putnam sent Lieutenant Colonel Aaron Burr across the river with a small party to observe and engage any stragglers. Burr encountered some, killed a few, and captured others. Like everyone else, Putnam was puzzled as to what Clinton was up to. The only effect Clinton's action had seemed to be on the New Jersey militia. Their superb leader, General Philemon Dickinson (John Dickinson's younger brother), became more alert to the possibility of a future raid.

———

Clinton's reinforcements finally arrived on September 24. At last, he was going to get his chance at the Highlands. He knew that they were weakly defended and that Putnam's reduced force would not be an obstacle. He did not waste any time. On October 3 he sailed up the Hudson with three thousand troops and a strong naval contingent. Two days later, he landed near Peekskill, forcing the shorthanded Putnam to retreat with his fifteen hundred men. Clinton then made a feint at Putnam before crossing to the west side of the river with two thousand troops. Fog concealed his movements. As soon as he landed, he attacked undermanned Forts Montgomery and Clinton. The defenders, led by Governor Clinton and his brother James, fought valiantly but were overwhelmed. "They gained possession of both posts [forts]," Governor Clinton reported to the New York Council of Safety. "I immediately posted my men in the most advantageous manner for the defense of the post (Fort Montgomery), and it was not many minutes before . . . our post . . . [and] Fort Clinton were invested on all sides, and a most incessant fire kept up till night; and soon after dusk, when the enemy forced our lines and redoubts at both posts, and the garrisons were obliged to fight their way out, as many as could, as we were determined not to surrender, and many have escaped. . . . [In the end] we were overpowered by numbers." By five o'clock on October 6 all firing ceased, with the British in complete control. Since General Clinton had no way to occupy the forts he destroyed them.

The naval contingent accompanying Clinton attacked as vigorously as he did. The 50-gun *Preston*, the frigates *Tartar* and *Mercury*, the brig *Diligent*, the sloop tender *Hotham*, and the row galleys *Crane*, *Dependence*, and *Spitfire* all participated. Commodore William Hotham and Captain James Wallace led the aggressive attack on the forts, as well as on a pitiable collection of Continental warships that Governor Clinton had put together.

Hotham and Wallace exchanged fire with the forts briefly, but most of the action centered around a chain stretched across the Hudson from

Fort Montgomery in the west to Anthony's Nose in the east. The chain was designed to prevent enemy ships from traveling upriver. Defending the north side of the chain were the two Continental frigates built at Peekskill, the 28-gun *Congress* and the 24-gun *Montgomery*, as well as the row galleys *Lady Washington* and *Shark*, and a privateer sloop, the 20-gun *Camden*. Governor Clinton placed Continental navy captain John Hodge of the *Montgomery* in charge of defending the chain against impossible odds.

The American frigates were still unfinished, even though they were started over a year and a half earlier. During the fighting, the *Montgomery*, with her inexperienced crew, drifted closer to the chains until she became entangled in them. To prevent her capture Hodge burned her while the crew escaped in the ship's boats. When flames reached the magazine, the doomed ship exploded, sending chilling echoes reverberating through the mountains.

Meanwhile, the *Congress* fled north, but the green crew accidentally ran her aground, and she had to be burned to keep her out of British hands. The two New York row galleys were set on fire and the *Camden* captured. Commodore Hotham easily cut through the chain, and the Hudson was now open.

The next big question was where Clinton was going from here. He knew the northern army desperately needed him. Burgoyne feared that the next encounter with Gates might be his last. And there was no ready avenue of retreat. He was trapped. If he went forward he had a growing American army itching for a fight, and if he retreated he had Generals Benjamin Lincoln and John Stark to contend with, along with Gates. Clinton was still his only hope. But communication between them was poor, and Burgoyne was running out of supplies and time. He'd be forced to make a move soon.

He did not realize, and neither did Clinton, how fast the American army was growing. During the seventeen days after the battle at Freeman's Farm, Gates's force had markedly increased. Militiamen by the hundreds were flooding into camp from New York, New Hampshire, Massachusetts, and Connecticut. Governor Clinton's efforts and the efforts of many others in New York's counties and in New England were producing a remarkable turnout.

Burgoyne had less than half their number, and many more of his men were deserting as supplies dwindled and food grew scarce. When he imposed strict rationing, it was obvious to the ranks that the army was in desperate trouble.

As the days passed and Clinton did not appear, Burgoyne felt compelled to attack Gates again without him. On October 7, with food running out, he desperately lunged at his nemesis. By this time his force had dwindled to less than sixty-five hundred, while Gates's had grown to over fifteen thousand. The numbers were increasing so fast that even Gates did not realize how large his force had become. The armies met at Bemis Heights, and this time there was no doubt about the outcome. The Americans, led by Benedict Arnold and Daniel Morgan, crushed Burgoyne, who lost six hundred more men.

One of the oddities of this great battle was that Gates and Arnold had been feuding before it, to the extent that Gates tried to keep Arnold from participating. Before the fighting started, Gates, in a fury, removed Arnold from command. But Arnold would not be denied and he rode out onto the battlefield without orders, threw himself into the fight, and made a major contribution to victory, getting badly wounded in the process.

General Gates directed from two miles behind the lines, never exhibiting any interest in getting near the actual fighting. Afterward, Burgoyne attempted a desperate retreat that failed, and in ten days formally surrendered his army and a substantial amount of small arms, artillery, ammunition, military stores, and equipment.

The terms of surrender were remarkable. Gripped by an inordinate fear of Clinton's approaching from the south, Gates was more than a little anxious to put a quick end to the fighting, granting Burgoyne terms that were embarrassingly lenient. The final document was not even called a surrender; it was softened down to "Articles of Convention between Lieutenant General Burgoyne and Major General Gates." Included in it was the striking provision that Burgoyne's army was to march to Boston and embark for England. The only stipulation was that they not serve against the United States during the present war, which meant that they could be assigned garrison duty anywhere in the empire, replacing regiments that could then be sent to America.

Gates needlessly gave way to such an extent that Burgoyne grew suspicious and actually delayed signing, hoping that Clinton would still come to the rescue. Finally, on October 17 he gave up. In spite of his delay, the generous terms remained. New Yorkers like Governor Clinton, John Jay, and Gouverneur Morris were not happy with the concessions. They worked hard to get Congress to change them, and they were successful. Burgoyne's army, instead of returning to England, was imprisoned in Virginia.

The fear growing in General Gates's mind of the column coming up from the south was entirely unwarranted. Instead of dreading Clinton's approach, he should have welcomed it. In fact, had Clinton pushed far enough north, he would have been in serious danger from the huge, and growing, American army. Clinton—without any idea of the disaster that awaited him—did resume his push north, with the intention of seeing how well he could do. The thought of reaching Burgoyne and gaining control of the Hudson must have dazzled him.

After securing the Highland forts, he dispatched General Vaughan on October 13 to penetrate north with two thousand men, supported by a naval squadron under Wallace. Two days later, Vaughan reached Kingston, the new capital of New York State, and destroyed it, in as vicious an undertaking as any of the war. Not a house or building was left standing. Vaughan meant to show the illegitimacy of rebel institutions. By destroying their capital he was symbolically destroying their movement. He had no appreciation of how his brutality was only adding to their strength.

Clinton supported General Vaughan's scorched-earth tactics. Politically tone-deaf, he apparently thought that the brutal destruction of Kingston would be an object lesson for the rebels. Instead it swelled their ranks throughout New York.

Vaughan continued north to Livingston Manor, forty-five miles south of Albany, planning to continue his mindless rampage, but when he observed large numbers of militiamen gathering on both sides of the Hudson and increasing as he went, his progress slowed. Fortunately for him, just at that moment, Clinton received orders from General Howe to send four thousand reinforcements to Philadelphia immediately and return to New York with all his troops. Howe was not thinking of Burgoyne's problems, or of Clinton's; he was reacting to the near calamity at Germantown, and the difficulties Lord Howe was experiencing opening the Delaware River.

Not having any idea of the disaster that lay ahead if he continued north, Clinton was furious with Howe for tying his hands at this critical moment. He wanted to press forward. Nonetheless, he quickly obeyed and ordered Vaughan back, which saved him, although Clinton never had any idea that it did. He returned to New York convinced that Howe was making a monumental mistake in pulling him back and giving up the Highlands.

Clinton's partial victory there became immense in his mind. He was certain that his capture of the two forts could have secured the Hudson and won the war, if only Howe had supported him. Clinton never understood—even years later—how potent the American army at Bemis Heights had become and what a threat it posed to him.

As far as Clinton was concerned, his was the only real achievement of British arms in 1777. He did not think Howe won anything by taking Philadelphia other than a big headache. He was convinced that if Howe saw the overriding importance of keeping the Highland forts, he would have reinforced him and secured them. In his memoirs, he wrote:

> I had . . . hope[d] that as soon as [Howe] found I had opened the important door of the Hudson, he would have strained every nerve to keep it so and prevent the rebels from ever shutting it again— even though he had been obliged to place the whole back of his army against it.

And I hope I shall be pardoned if I presume to suggest that, had this been done, it would have most probably finished the war. And Sir William's southern move [to Philadelphia], instead of being censured, would perhaps have been extolled as one of the operative parts of a judicious and well combined plan, and even the loss of General Burgoyne's army looked upon as a necessary sacrifice, as having both essentially contributed to draw off the two grand armies of the enemy to a distance from that very strong and important hold [the Hudson Highlands], which might possibly have been placed beyond our reach had either remained in its neighborhood.

While Clinton was brooding over his lost opportunity, London was becoming increasingly concerned about the course of events. Particularly worrisome were rumors of Burgoyne's troubles. Lord North was anxious enough to take the unusual step of writing to Lord Howe directly on October 26 and 28, reminding him of the urgent need to end the war. North had been receiving reports of the increasing movement of war matériel from France, Spain, and Holland to America. He reminded Howe of how important it was to crush the rebellion before France and perhaps the other two countries actually entered the war. He also warned him that the British people were in no mood to support another inconclusive campaign. North's missives had the king's full approval.

Britain's leaders would have been even more anxious had they known that Lord Howe was having great problems gaining control of the Delaware River. Its defenses were more formidable than they imagined, consisting of strategically placed forts; an array of river obstructions, including massive *chevaux-de-frise*; and a large assortment of row galleys, warships, floating batteries, and fireships. Not until November 23 did the first British transports sail unimpeded from the Delaware capes to Philadelphia's waterfront.

On the same day, Admiral Howe asked to be relieved of command. He knew that a month earlier, on October 22, General Howe had also asked to be relieved—even before the general had received the doleful news of Burgoyne's fate. The Howes had a high appreciation of the fact that in the eyes of their superiors they had failed to defeat the rebellion for two years running, and they were anxious to go home and defend their conduct. They believed that they had done an excellent job with an inadequate army and navy and were now being blamed for not subduing the colonies, when the responsibility rested with London for not providing them with sufficient resources.

Four days after General Howe's resignation, a disgruntled Henry Clinton requested leave from Howe to go home as well. Clinton had been unhappy serving under Howe for a long time. He was convinced that Howe's strategy and tactics were consistently wrongheaded. Thus, the year that had started with such promise for Britain ended with the high command in America frustrated, and their superiors in London waiting to excoriate the Howes for what had gone wrong.

Chapter 17

FRANCE DECLARES
WAR ON BRITAIN

When word of Burgoyne's disaster reached London the last week of November, it created an alarm, even panic, and a good deal of anger. Attacks on the ministry in Parliament, especially on Germain, were ferocious. Criticism from the politically weak opposition had always been loud—and compelling—but now more members were paying attention. North was afraid support for the war might collapse. If Germain were cashiered, the ministry might fall with him, something neither His Majesty nor the first minister wanted.

Even more troubling for North was the reaction in Paris. Spies were reporting that it looked as if France, in a matter of weeks, if not days, would sign a treaty of alliance with the Americans. North tried desperately to head it off. Racing against time, he offered—for the first time—real negotiations to the rebels. He began his effort even before he knew Philadelphia had been taken, and long before Admiral Howe opened the Delaware River. North was now willing to concede every point at issue except independence. He offered the Continental Congress, or the state legislatures acting separately, every power they sought, including over taxation, if they would remain in the empire under a common sovereign. His proposals were so generous the king's supporters naturally wondered what the fighting had been about. A disgusted Horace Walpole wrote in his journal, "Disappointed, defeated, disgraced, alarmed, but still depending on a majority in both houses, and on the blindness and indifference of the nation, the Administration ventured on taking the very opposite part to all they had been doing; and as if there was not shame but in losing their places, presumed to tell the three kingdoms that they must abandon all the high views with which they had been lulled, and must stoop to beg peace of America at any rate."

No matter what criticism came from friend or foe, North persisted. He was determined to make a maximum effort to keep the colonies. Had his offer come in 1774 or 1775, or even in the early months of 1776, it could have served as a basis for serious discussions, but in 1778 it was too late. Many Americans, like Washington, viewed North's proposals as aimed, "under offers of peace, to divide and disunite us." At this point, patriots were not going to listen to any proposal until Britain withdrew her troops and conceded independence, which the king was not prepared to do.

On February 6, 1778, the dreaded event occurred. France signed both a Treaty of Alliance and a Treaty of Amity and Commerce with the United States. On March 13 Paris made the treaty of commerce public, converting a colonial dispute into a world war. The Comte de Vergennes thought the moment well chosen. Britain was peculiarly vulnerable. The success of patriot arms at Saratoga and the near success at Germantown demonstrated that the Americans were resolved to continue fighting for their independence, and that they had enough strength, with French aid, to do it. If Britain foolishly continued the war, she would have to commit greater and greater resources, with no guarantee of success. If she chose instead to cut her losses, America would be free and beholden to France. That would be satisfaction enough for Vergennes. But he did not think London would make that choice. He thought it more likely that she would continue the war, regardless of the mounting costs. The hubris of England's rulers was too great for them to suffer a humiliation of this kind at the hands of American provincials. That the hated English had created a robust modern economy capable of withstanding the stress of war far better than France escaped Vergennes' notice.

Britain's diplomatic isolation further encouraged Vergennes. For the first time in the eighteenth century, London had no European allies to act as a check on France. Paris was free to concentrate on England alone, which meant that the home islands would be threatened, as well as Britain's overseas possessions. Vergennes was confident that America, supported by France—and quite likely Spain, would prevail. He was not interested in crushing Britain. The other European powers, no matter how much they might enjoy seeing the haughty British embarrassed, would not sit by and have France become too powerful.

Before signing the alliance, Vergennes worked hard to make Spain a partner. He needed her navy. Britain had fifty-two sail of the line in commission, an additional forty-four in ordinary (storage), and ten building, while France had forty-eight. A combined Franco-Spanish fleet, on the other hand, could potentially deploy ninety sail of the line.

The dons resisted, however. They were content to keep helping the Americans on a small scale, slowly bleeding the English. They had no interest in having America actually win. It would set a bad example for their own colonies, not to mention their fear that the United States might in the future actively aid other independence movements.

Vergennes thought that Spain's concerns were unwarranted. He saw no danger that America's republican ideals would spread. Thirteen squabbling states would emerge from the war, he believed, not a united colossus. The best example of how weak the Americans would be was their consistent refusal to tax themselves. They paid for the war by recklessly printing money that had no backing and begging loans from Paris and any other place they could find them. The Articles of Confederation, which Congress had been obliged to produce after declaring independence, was a notoriously weak document. It failed to establish a strong central government, leaving real power with the states. Even then, it had taken Congress until November 1777 to agree to it. What's more, approval of the final document by the individual states was still in doubt. Even if they eventually agreed to confederate, Vergennes was convinced they would go on bickering, perhaps even fighting.

Madrid's principal objective was retrieving Gibraltar and Minorca, possibly East and West Florida, and Jamaica, not in humbling the annoying English. The Spanish foreign minister, Conde de Floridablanca, was more bellicose than his monarch. He was willing to enter into an alliance against Britain, but Charles III wanted to explore the possibility of negotiations first. Only if the British refused would he consider declaring war. Floridablanca told London that if Gibraltar and Minorca were returned, Madrid would remain neutral.

No matter what the preference of Charles III, however, Vergennes remained confident that Spain would soon be an ally. The British were never going to give up Gibraltar or Minorca—or Jamaica, for that matter. And Madrid had a real interest in keeping America and Britain apart. Together they threatened Louisiana. Spain also had the prospect of regaining East and West Florida and Jamaica in a peace settlement.

★

THE DRAMATIC CHANGE IN THE CHARACTER OF THE WAR brought forth yet another grand strategy from the king to deal with the American rebellion—the third since the war began in 1774 with passage of the Coercive Acts. His Majesty now saw North America as a secondary theater. After protection of the home islands, his first priority became the West Indies. Britain's lucrative sugar islands were in danger. Jamaica (the most important), Antigua (which contained English Harbor, the main British naval base in the eastern Caribbean), Barbados, St. Vincent, Nevis, Montserrat, St. Kitts, Tobago, Grenada, and Dominica were all vulnerable. France had eight thousand troops in the Caribbean; Britain had only one thousand fit for duty. Unless something was done, all the British islands could fall.

During March 1778, Germain issued a series of new orders for General Clinton. To begin with, he was to evacuate Philadelphia and proceed by sea to New York. Once there, he was to await the results of the king's peace commission, which Lord North sent to America to advance his initiative. Known as the Carlisle Commission after its obscure, inept chairman, Lord Carlisle, it was taken seriously by no one except North and the commissioners. The members had not even been informed of the king's new military strategy, especially concerning Philadelphia. The order came as a complete surprise to Lord Carlisle. The weakness it demonstrated cut the ground out from under the commission and made its mission look even more ridiculous than it already was. The reason given for leaving Philadelphia's Loyalists in the lurch was the pressing need for troops. The king judged that he could not hold the rebel capital and at the same time provide enough soldiers to defend the sugar islands.

Abandoning Philadelphia was only a small part of Germain's extensive new instructions. Once Clinton returned to New York, he was to send five thousand men to St. Lucia. London intended to seize the island from the French and use it as Britain's major base in the Windward Islands. Not only was the harbor at Gros Islet Bay large and serviceable, but St. Lucia was the perfect place to maintain surveillance of the important French naval base at Fort Royal Bay in nearby Martinique.

Clinton was also instructed to send three thousand men to St. Augustine for duty in West Florida, and to return six hundred marines ashore in Halifax to their ships. He was then to bring Washington to a general action, which seemed absurd, since his army would be seriously depleted. As a result, he ignored this order for the time being and hung on to his troops.

If fighting Washington proved impossible, he was to cooperate with the navy and conduct raids along the New England coast, as well as help establish a tight naval blockade from Chesapeake Bay to Canada. After that, Clinton was to invade the South, beginning with Georgia and South Carolina. The king's intention, Germain explained, was to bring about the "entire reduction of all the colonies to the southward of [the] Susquehanna." The provinces to the north would be dealt with by the blockade and by savage raids on their ports. The focus, however, was to be on the South.

The new strategy puzzled General Clinton. He continued to believe that control of the Highlands and the Hudson River was the key to winning the war. Much of the criticism of the government's record in 1777 assumed that if only the Howes had pushed up the Hudson River instead of focusing on Philadelphia, they would have won the war. Debate over the debacle of 1777 reinforced the belief that the old strategy would have worked, if only it had been tried. The fact that it hadn't been added to its luster.

Although the king was changing failed policies, he was not replacing the men who had made them. Germain was left in place as if he had had no share in the mistakes of 1776 and 1777. Sandwich also survived, as did the North ministry, which, under the British system, was nominally responsible for all policy during those years.

The opposition in Parliament was calling for Germain's head, and Sandwich's as well. As early as November 18, 1777, when only rumors of Burgoyne's troubles were circulating in London, Charles James Fox, who, along with Edmund Burke, was the most persuasive of the government's critics, declared that Burgoyne's army "was not equal to the task." Fox ridiculed the notion that Howe could both take Philadelphia and help the northern army. "No man with common sense," he shouted at Germain on the floor of the House of Commons, "would have placed the two armies in such a position as from their distance made it . . . impossible that the one should receive any assistance from the other." Fox went on to ridicule, as he had many times before, the whole idea of conquering America. No matter who the generals were, he argued, they were bound to fail.

Unfortunately for Fox, and for the country, it didn't matter what he said. The king had no intention of replacing Germain. The inability of British arms to end the rebellion in either 1776 or 1777 was to be blamed on the field commanders, not on those who had directed them. Replacing the American secretary and the first lord of the Admiralty could precipitate the fall of the North ministry, and the king did not like what might replace it. There was a good deal of talk about aging Lord Chatham (William Pitt) leading a government of national unity, something the king found repellent. He was comfortable working with North. Bringing the Howes home was much easier than replacing the first minister. The men most responsible for the disasters of 1776 and 1777 remained in place, which clearly showed that Parliament was a glorified debating society. The king held sway. The deeply corrupted House of Commons did his bidding.

It was also the case that when England was fighting her traditional rival France, patriotic sentiment in the country rose and coalesced around the king. War against the French was far more popular than against the colonies, however misguided and infuriating they might be. With France's direct involvement, George III's war on America, which had been flagging in popularity, gained new life.

General Clinton knew that with France in the war, a new strategy was inevitable. When he saw what it actually was, however, he wasn't happy. He was being forced into the same trap that had ruined General Gage in 1775 and General Howe in 1776 and 1777—namely, grandiose objectives not matched by adequate resources. London was once again expecting the theater commander to reclaim the colonies without providing the necessary troops or naval support. The only difference between Clinton and his predecessors was that the gap between what was expected and what was provided had grown much larger. Clinton requested more support, as Gage and Howe had, and he received soothing replies from Germain, but the forces Clinton required were never forthcoming. And even more infuriating, Germain could not resist giving Clinton detailed tactical instructions, which got under Clinton's skin more than anything else.

★

WHILE LONDON WAS DEVELOPING A NEW STRATEGY, VER-gennes was planning to deliver a punishing blow in the opening weeks of the war, using the French navy. He did not want a prolonged war.

Forty-eight-year-old Vice Admiral Charles-Hector, Comte d'Estaing, was to take a fleet that was much stronger than Admiral Howe's and sail from Toulon directly to the American coast and conduct joint operations with Washington that Vergennes expected would end the war fast.

The fleet assembling at Toulon was indeed strong. It consisted of the 90-gun flagship, *Languedoc*; one ship of 80 guns; six 74s; three 64s; one of 50 guns; and six frigates. It also carried a complement of four thousand marines.

John Paul Jones happened to be in France at the time operational details were being worked out. He had a close, although at times uneasy, relationship with Franklin, who probably arranged for him to meet d'Estaing in Franklin's suite at the Hôtel de Valentinois. Franklin was the only American included when Vergennes' inner circle was devising strategy—a good indication of how much the French trusted him. "His conduct leaves nothing for Congress to desire," Vergennes said of Franklin. "It is as zealous and patriotic, as it is wise and circumspect."

The possibility of trapping Lord Howe's inferior squadron in the Delaware River drew their attention. Franklin had detailed knowledge of the river's defenses, having played a leading part in devising them. He and Jones suggested that d'Estaing's primary objective should be containing Howe in Delaware Bay. Without his protection, General Clinton would be caught between Washington's army and part of the French fleet. Vergennes found the plan irresistible.

To aid d'Estaing's entry into the Atlantic, the French planned to hold London's attention with a convincing threat to the home islands. They continued strengthening their main fleet at Brest and worked hard to make Spain a partner—activity that spies regularly reported to London. Lord Sandwich and Admiral Augustus Keppel, commander of the Channel Fleet, were attentive. The Admiralty had known about d'Estaing for weeks, indeed months. There had been plenty of time to prevent him from leaving the Mediterranean. Lord Germain had been a strong advocate of doing so, but Sandwich had demurred. He did not want to send a large fleet to the Gut of Gibraltar when it might be needed at home. At the moment, three sail of the line were in the

Mediterranean; Sandwich did not want to add to them. He also pointed out that London did not know d'Estaing's actual destination. He might be headed for Brest or for the Spanish base at Cádiz—or for America.

While the British were debating what to do, d'Estaing was delayed. Even though speed was essential, Vergennes wanted Britain to strike first. He postponed d'Estaing's departure from Toulon in hopes that the British would fire the opening shots of the war. The Dutch had a defensive pact with Britain that required them to join her if she was attacked anywhere. Vergennes wanted to avoid activating that alliance. As a result, even though he was ready much earlier, d'Estaing did not sail from Toulon, until April 13, 1778, over two months after the treaty of alliance was signed.

The delay would not be d'Estaing's last, either. He did not clear the Straits of Gibraltar until May 16. The trip from Toulon, which should have taken days, consumed over a month. He escaped into the Atlantic with no difficulty, charting a course for the American coast, where he planned to remain until hurricane season was over and then sail to the Caribbean for an expected British attack there.

London made no attempt to stop him. Instead, Sandwich stationed the frigate *Prosperine* (Captain Evelyn Sutton) at Gibraltar to shadow the Toulon fleet and report its likely destination. Sutton discreetly followed d'Estaing for two hundred miles into the Atlantic before returning to Falmouth on June 2. He reported that the fleet was making for either the West Indies or the American coast.

On June 9, when Sandwich was fairly certain that d'Estaing was indeed sailing for America—although he could not be absolutely certain, since the fleet could always turn back—the Admiralty dispatched thirteen sail of the line and one frigate under Vice Admiral John Byron to reinforce Lord Howe and to act in the West Indies if d'Estaing went there. If Byron was able to combine with Howe in a timely fashion, the British fleet would be superior. Paris was aware of the danger but chose not to send reinforcements. D'Estaing was on his own.

Sandwich and Admiral Keppel were still concerned about the main French fleet at Brest. They had been unhappy about dispatching Byron.

And, as things turned out, they had good reason to worry. In fact, one of the more important naval battles of the war occurred between the two main fleets off Ushant on July 27, 1778, not long after Byron departed. Admiral Keppel, fifty-three, and Admiral Louis Guillouet, Comte d'Orvilliers, seventy, led the two roughly equal squadrons into the critical fight. It ended in a draw, although both sides claimed victory. Had Keppel defeated d'Orvilliers, French naval power could not have been employed in America over an extended period. England would have kept French warships blockaded in Brest and Toulon. France would never have been able, even for a brief period, to achieve naval supremacy along the American coast, which Washington considered absolutely essential.

Chapter 18

ADMIRAL HOWE
SAVES NEW YORK

While the British were changing strategies and commanders, Washington, unaware of developments in either London or Paris, was at Valley Forge trying to hold his army together. He did not learn of the French alliance or of Lord North's peace commission until the end of April. During December and January, he was struggling just to keep his men from freezing or starving. The departments—if they could be called that—tasked with provisioning the army, already poor to begin with, had broken down. The clothier general, quartermaster general, and commissary general had practically ceased to function.

The suffering of ordinary soldiers was heartrending. Lack of food, inadequate clothing, a scarcity of blankets, and widespread illness plagued them as they shivered in thin tents while building log huts as fast as they could. Their hardships were made all the more terrible by the knowledge that they could have been prevented. Over twenty-five hundred young patriots were needlessly lost in a matter of a few weeks, either deserting or dying.

And yet the army held together. "No history . . . can furnish an instance of an army's suffering such uncommon hardships and bearing them with the same patience and fortitude," Washington wrote. Through it all, the commander in chief persevered, as he always did, and at length got the quartermaster, commissary, and clothier departments functioning again, albeit imperfectly. After February, the crisis eased, and Washington was able to turn to a project he had long planned, and desperately needed—making the Continental army into a more professional fighting force. Friedrich Wilhelm von Steuben, a minor Prussian aristocrat who had served in Frederick the Great's splendid army, provided critical help. He was one of a large number of European officers, mostly French, who landed on Washington's doorstep, seeking to make a name for themselves with the army. For the most part, they were incompetent, if not outright frauds.

Steuben was a welcome exception—a considerable asset for the beleaguered commander in chief. He instilled a higher degree of order and discipline in the troops; reorganized their camp, with particular attention to sanitation; and markedly improved their training, especially the handling and use of weapons in formation, including the bayonet. By May the Continental army was decidedly more proficient. Washington was so pleased with the results that he treated Steuben as the army's unofficial inspector general.

The quartermaster, commissary, and clothier departments, although not as bad as before, continued to be problems. "Such have been the derangement and disorders in them," Washington wrote on May 18 to Henry Laurens, Hancock's successor as the president of Congress, "that we must be greatly embarrassed for a considerable time yet. . . . Half the army are [still] without shirts."

With the appointment of Jeremiah Wadsworth of Connecticut as commissary general and Nathanael Greene as quartermaster general, both departments, which Congress placed directly under Washington, began to improve. Clothing continued to be scarce, except for brief periods, when supplies from France reached the troops.

As if he did not have enough to worry about, Washington was, at

the same time, fending off a political stealth attack designed to undermine his authority and replace him with General Gates. From the
moment Burgoyne surrendered, Gates was promoting his star, con-
trasting his great victory at Saratoga with Washington's defeats in
Pennsylvania. Gates began distancing himself from the commander in
chief, as he had the previous year in Trenton, acting independently to
the degree he could. He pointedly refused to officially apprise Washington of the victory at Saratoga, sending his announcement directly to
Henry Laurens rather than through the commander in chief. Laurens
took the slight to Washington for what it was, an attempt by a faction in
Congress to boost Gates as a general who could lead the army to victory.
Laurens was a strong supporter of Washington, but he sensed that
there would be a serious attempt to unseat him.

In spite of Washington's critics in and out of Congress, most of the
officers in the army had a high opinion of him. This included Lafayette,
whose attitude was critical because of his political strength at home.
Faced with Washington's strong support in the officer corps and from
Lafayette, the conspiracy failed. When it did, the plotters moved quickly
to cover their tracks, protesting their innocence, pretending that noth-

Washington fought back with consummate skill, developed over
many years in Virginia and national politics. And he succeeded. The
conspirators included Gates, General Mifflin, and General Thomas
Conway; Doctor Benjamin Rush; congressmen from Massachusetts,
led by Samuel Adams, and from Virginia, among them Richard Henry
Lee; and delegates from Pennsylvania and Maryland. Rush spoke for
them when he wrote to John Adams, who was not one of the conspirators but was unhappy with Washington's performance, asking him to
compare the records of Gates and Washington. Rush asserted that
Gates's army was "well-regulated," while Washington's was a "mob."
He thought Gates was on "the pinnacle of military glory," while Washington was "outgeneraled . . . and twice beaten . . . forced to give up a
city the capital of a state." If Congress did nothing about this intolerable
situation, Rush argued, "I shall think we have not shook off monarchi-
cal principles."

ing had happened. But Washington knew better. "That there was a scheme of this sort . . . admits of no doubt," he wrote later. ". . . [I]t originated . . . with three men [Gates, Conway, and Mifflin] who wanted to aggrandize themselves; but finding no support, on the contrary, that their conduct and views, when seen into, were likely to undergo severe reprehension, they shrunk back, disavowed the measure, and professed themselves my warmest admirers."

Fortunately for the patriots, General Howe, although well informed about the problems of the American army at Valley Forge, had no interest in attacking it. Again, he was passing up an excellent opportunity to defeat Washington and end the war. The rebels seemed to be the last thing on his mind. He had already submitted his resignation, and it was happily accepted, as he knew it would be. He simply wanted to remain in Philadelphia and enjoy a winter's respite with Mrs. Loring and his friends. "Indolence and luxury" were the hallmarks of his winter, according to Charles Stedman, an eyewitness.

Following General Howe's lead, the British high command in Philadelphia carried on as they had during the winter of 1776–77. General Clinton did the same in New York. He and Howe had sumptuous quarters; Clinton's were shared by Mary O'Callaghan Baddeley. The daughter of an Irish country gentleman and the wife of a soldier, she had started in 1775 as Clinton's housekeeper in Boston and soon became something more. Their relationship continued throughout the war and beyond.

Official holidays such as the king's or queen's birthdays were celebrated with fireworks and a grand ball. Receptions, dinners, and dances were held on a regular basis, as were plays, concerts, and horse races. Lord Howe, again, participated very little in the entertainment and general debauchery.

Cricket, cockfights, and eating clubs with names like the Yorkshire Club were established. Philadelphia's Tory belles attended weekly dances with young officers at places like Smith's Tavern. Supper parties in the city's finest homes contributed to the gaiety. Among those seen in the most fashionable circles was Margaret (Peggy) Shippen, often in the company of Major John André. André and a few friends revived the Southwark Theater, built in 1766. They became known as Howe's Thespians, putting on thirteen plays in five months—always before a packed house.

Gambling was the favorite entertainment. Nothing was more popular than the French card game faro. Large sums were bet every night at City Tavern on Walnut Street, the main gaming house. General Howe was a regular. His love of gambling was well known, and his officers, young and old, were anxious to oblige him. The amount of money won and lost in an evening was often measured in the thousands of pounds.

While the king's officers indulged themselves, their prisoners were being subjected to the same treatment that Loring and Cunningham had been inflicting on rebel captives since the Battle of Brooklyn. Eight unnecessary deaths a day was common. The five hundred men taken at Brandywine were incarcerated in gruesome jails. Thirty were at times crowded into a single cell, where they could not all lie down. Food and drink were awful and scarce, and the men had rags for clothes. Many were given the choice of either starving or deserting. Perhaps three hundred—not wanting to die of hunger—were forced into His Majesty's service. Provost Marshal Cunningham orchestrated the torture, with the full knowledge of General Howe and his brother. Cunningham was known to dump a bucket of soup just at the edge of a cell door and laugh while gaunt, hollow-eyed men tried to lick it off the floor. And while he wasn't indulging his twisted humor, he continued making money by selling the scarce provisions allotted for prisoners.

★

ON MAY 8, 1778, GENERAL CLINTON ARRIVED IN PHILADEL-phia from New York aboard HMS *Greyhound* to take command from General Howe. The following day the sloop of war *Porcupine* arrived at the waterfront with orders for Clinton that reflected the new overall strategy for the war developed by Germain and the king and approved by the cabinet on March 21. The order to immediately evacuate Philadelphia must have come as a complete surprise. Clinton now had to direct a massive withdrawal from the largest city in the colonies, a city he was convinced never should have been taken in the first place.

Ten days later, while Clinton was in the midst of this gigantic operation, John André and twenty-two officers threw a dazzling farewell party for departing General Howe. Even though he had failed in his mission, there was no doubt that Howe was a hero to his young officers. They described their extravaganza as a Meschianza, or medley. The entertainment was on such a grand scale that many people were offended. The festival went on for hours and hours, and when it was over, Ambrose Serle, reflecting the opinion of most people who saw it, called it shameful. "Our enemies will dwell upon the folly and extravagance of it with pleasure," he wrote. "Every man of sense among ourselves, tho' not unwilling to pay a due respect, was ashamed of this mode of doing it."

Before leaving for London on May 25, Howe attempted one last stab at Washington. Lafayette was his immediate target. Washington had, unaccountably, sent the young Frenchman with 2,200 men—a third of the American army—to Barren Hill, eleven miles from the city, to watch the enemy's movements. When Howe found out, he decided to attack, and came very close to trapping the young, inexperienced Frenchman. Fortunately, Lafayette was warned in time, and Howe's thrust was neatly parried, saving Washington from an egregious blunder.

Recognizing the futility, and indeed the danger, of going forward, Howe returned to the city. His time in America was now over, and he prepared to leave, knowing that the road ahead was not going to be easy. Waiting in London was a great political battle with Germain, as each would try to blame the other for the colossal failure of British arms in America.

By June 18 the evacuation of Philadelphia was complete. All of Clinton's troops, their animals, wagons, baggage, and equipment, were ready to cross the Delaware and begin the ninety-mile trek to New York. The heat was oppressive and the air unhealthy. The men were lucky to be escaping the city's summer.

Governor George Clinton of New York was watching events in Philadelphia closely and was as amazed as everyone else that the British were leaving. He knew where they were going, and he wasn't happy about it. He told the Senate and Assembly in a joint meeting, "The enemy by the evacuation of Philadelphia, and their removal to the city of New York have again made this state the principal seat of war."

General Clinton had decided to march to Manhattan instead of sailing. Lord Howe did not have enough transports to accommodate the army and the hundreds of overwrought Loyalists who were clamoring for passage out of Philadelphia to escape retribution from the patriots. Over three thousand forlorn souls, unable to obtain guarantees of safety from Congress, demanded help. Clinton could not turn them down. He wrote to Germain explaining that if he went by sea "a great part of our cavalry, all our provision train, and the persons whose attachment to the government has rendered them objects of vengeance to the enemy, must have been left behind." He was aware that Germain cared little about the Loyalists. As far as he was concerned, they were expendable. Clinton did not agree, and let them have the troop transports.

The arguments that Clinton had with General Howe and Germain the previous year about the folly of taking Philadelphia must have run through his mind often during these difficult days. He still had no idea that Howe had saved him when he ordered him back to New York. Clinton remained convinced that when he seized the Highlands he began a process that would have won the war if only Howe had supported him.

With Lord Howe's warships stationed nearby, Clinton on the eighteenth moved the bulk of his men across the Delaware River south of the city to Gloucester Point in New Jersey. Cornwallis was with him; he had returned with the peace commissioners to become Clinton's second, and perhaps his successor. The two were still like oil and water, finding it nearly impossible to work together.

The next day, Admiral Howe weighed anchor and steered downriver with his warships, accompanied by over two hundred transports containing the three thousand Loyalists and their baggage. The admiral had been forced to impress a large number of Philadelphia seamen in order to accomplish all the loading, which, of course, they bitterly resented. It then took Howe ten exasperating days to reach the Delaware capes. Adverse winds and perfect calm alternated to slow his progress. Once out into the Atlantic he shaped a course for New York, racing for Sandy Hook to move Clinton's army as quickly as possible to Manhattan.

It wasn't at all clear that Clinton would get there. Crossing New Jersey would not be easy. He was taking a big chance by marching. Washington was sure to attack him, and Clinton was uncertain of the enemy's strength. He believed he had no choice, however. Since he would be traveling with an immense supply train of hundreds of wagons, he needed his entire army to protect it. Using all the troops in this way was a violation of orders, which required him to send detachments to St. Lucia and to St. Augustine, but he simply could not spare them at the moment.

While Clinton was moving out of Philadelphia, Major General Benedict Arnold was moving in. The day after the British army left, Arnold, the new military governor, led a contingent of troops into the capital, riding in a handsome carriage, his leg wound from the great battle at Bemis Heights not yet healed. A throng of patriots cheered as he rode in grand style to the Richard Penn mansion at the corner of Sixth and Market streets, the same fine residence that General Howe had used as his headquarters. For some who were watching, Arnold's splendid entrance was a bit incongruous for a republican military governor.

Washington had known since April that Clinton was going to evacuate Philadelphia and travel to New York. The mountainous collection of baggage and military stores that Clinton was assembling in Philadelphia could not be missed, nor could the preparations for receiving the army in Manhattan and Staten Island. "The enemy are making every preparation, and seem on the point of leaving Philadelphia," he wrote to General Henry Lee. "In my own judgment, and from many corresponding circumstances, I am convinced they are bound to New York;

whether by land or water, whether as a place of rendezvous, or to operate on the North [Hudson] River, is not so clear."

Washington did not know until close to the date of departure how
Clinton planned to travel. When he discovered that Clinton was marching with a huge wagon train, he had a momentous decision to make.
Clinton was presenting him with a perfect opportunity to attack him
and perhaps end the war. But it would be risky. Clinton had advantages
that Washington did not—namely, a professional army, well equipped,
with an experienced cavalry. Washington had around ten thousand
effective fighters—roughly the same as Clinton. Whether they were
equal in quality after their training at Valley Forge remained to be seen.
Four thousand others were sick from smallpox and other disorders.

Washington had hoped to have a much larger force, and he was
angry that he didn't. The states had not provided nearly the number of
men they were supposed to. If they had, the Continental army would
have been at least twice the size it was, and he could have crushed Clinton. Adding to his frustration was the knowledge that the New Jersey
countryside would give him strong support. A clear victory over Clinton, coupled with the arrival of a large French fleet offshore, would
surely end the war.

On the other hand, a defeat could be disastrous. Washington hesitated, wondering if he should risk all in a final showdown in New Jersey
when the French fleet was approaching the coast. He could just as well
let Clinton reach Manhattan, and then engage in a joint attack with
d'Estaing. That was the safest plan, but Clinton's long column was very
inviting.

Washington held conferences with his senior officers to discuss the
problem. General Charles Lee, who had recently been exchanged, advocated doing nothing, allowing Clinton a clear path to New York, on the
grounds that it was safer to take him on after the French fleet arrived.
Others wanted limited action. Greene, Steuben, and Lafayette advocated striking Clinton's rear, or his baggage train, which stretched for
twelve miles. Washington's young aide Alexander Hamilton—who, of

course, kept quiet—could not believe how timid the senior officers were. He hoped Washington would launch a full-scale attack.

The reconstituted rebel army did not intimidate Clinton. He was confident in the superiority of his regulars. To be sure, he did not welcome a grand encounter of the kind that Germain envisioned. He was not going to initiate an action. He had only ten thousand men; Washington might have many more. Clinton knew that the patriots were watching his every move and would attack if the opportunity arose, but he was ready for them.

Still uncertain how to proceed, Washington sent New Jersey major general Philemon Dickinson and his one thousand militiamen to destroy bridges and causeways, foul wells, and create other obstacles along Clinton's likely route, which they did, measurably slowing him down. At the same time, General William Maxwell's brigade was sent to Hopewell, along Clinton's probable route, to observe.

Eventually, Washington made up his mind to attack Clinton's rear. The British force was divided into three divisions—a third in front, followed by the twelve-mile-long wagon train, and a third in the rear. Cornwallis was in charge of the rear guard. On June 21 Washington crossed the Delaware River at Coryell's Ferry, thirty-three miles above Philadelphia and forty miles from Valley Forge. From the ferry he moved down toward Clinton, and by the twenty-seventh he was within six miles of his column, near Monmouth Court House (now Freehold).

Washington did not waste any time. As soon as he was within striking distance, he went on the attack. On the morning of the twenty-eighth, he sent General Lee with the van of the army to attack the British rear as soon as Clinton resumed marching east. Washington felt obliged to place Lee, his second in command, in charge of the forward units, even though Lee had not changed his mind about the wisdom of attacking. Clinton's regulars were so superior to the Americans, in Lee's view, that he thought it would be disastrous to fight them without the French fleet. His opinion of the French appeared to be very high. He assumed that they would dominate Lord Howe, which was a very big assumption. Lee, as it turned out, was not the best strategist in the world.

Allowing a man to lead an attack when he was opposed to doing it was, to say the least, dangerous. Prior to his capture, Lee had given Washington nothing but trouble and was obviously angling to replace him. Why Washington gave him this appointment is puzzling. Evidently it was because Lee ranked second in the army and had asked for it.

Washington planned to follow Lee with the main army in support. It was an extremely hot day; temperatures were in the nineties—not a day to be fighting a major battle. Lee's instructions were to bring on an action against Clinton's rear, if that appeared feasible, with Washington to come up in support with the rest of the army and act according to circumstances. Early in the encounter, Washington, to his dismay, was informed that Lee's troops, instead of moving forward, were retreating in disarray. Lee had not bothered to inform the commander in chief what was happening, in good part because he didn't know himself. Confusion reigned.

Lee, who had never commanded a battle in the field, appeared befuddled. He seemed unable to grasp what was going on around him and issued no specific orders to subordinate commanders, such as Anthony Wayne. This resulted in the patriots' falling back in disorder rather than attacking.

On being informed that the forward units were pulling back for no discernible reason, Washington galloped ahead of the main army, which was coming on fast, found Lee, and demanded to know why he was retreating instead of attacking. The glib Lee was tongue-tied for once. Washington had some harsh words for him and took command, rallying the troops behind a nearby hedgerow on a hill that had protection on left and right.

Clinton, who by now realized he had a chance to win a significant victory, sent his wagon train ahead and counterattacked with the rest of his army. He quickly ran into Washington's now much stronger position behind the hedgerow, however, where a stand was made long enough to allow the main army, which was advancing fast, to form upon advantageous ground. "Here," Washington wrote, "our affairs took a favorable turn, and, from being pursued, we drove the enemy back over the ground they had followed, and recovered the field of battle."

Having checked Clinton and forced him to retreat, Washington understandably wanted to pursue, but by then it was almost 6:00 p.m., and all the troops on both sides were worn down from the heat. Men were dropping everywhere; they could not go on. The fighting ceased, and Clinton withdrew.

Both sides appeared to rest on their arms during the night. Washington's men certainly did. He was hoping to attack in the morning, but when the sun rose, Clinton was nowhere to be found. He had slipped away during the night, pushing on to Sandy Hook, where he prayed Lord Howe would be waiting to whisk him to New York. Clinton's hasty withdrawal was an indication of a new respect for the American army that was bound to affect his future behavior.

Although Washington missed an excellent opportunity to defeat Clinton at Monmouth, at least he had prevented Lee's fumbling from becoming a disaster. He was convinced that, had he not saved the day, Lee's disorderly retreat could well have proven fatal to the army.

Deeply angered both by his confrontation with Washington and for having been exposed as a grossly inadequate battlefield commander, Lee went on the offensive and managed to show enough public contempt for the commander in chief to get himself thrown out of the army. His all too public tirades demonstrated, finally, that he was contemptuous not only of Washington but of the Continental army and, most importantly, of Congress and the democratic process itself.

As Clinton raced to Sandy Hook, he worried that the American army might attack him again, but Washington wasn't interested in that right now. He wanted to rest his weary army (and himself) for the major confrontation that was ahead. He planned to get on to the Hudson River at a leisurely pace, secure the defenses there, and prepare to conduct joint operations against Manhattan with the approaching French fleet, if that proved practicable, or against Newport, Rhode Island, if it did not. The coming showdown, he believed, had the potential to end British rule in America.

To get the army into a position to respond to any eventuality, he moved across the Hudson at King's Ferry with no difficulty and settled in White Plains. From Westchester County he could protect against a British move up the Hudson and cooperate with the French. At the moment, moving up the Hudson was the last thing the British were considering; Clinton was entirely preoccupied with the defense of Manhattan.

★

WHILE WASHINGTON WAS TRAVELING TO WESTCHESTER, Lord Howe had been moving rapidly from the Delaware capes to Sandy Hook. On June 29 he met the frigate HMS *Grantham* off the New Jersey coast with dispatches from London, indicating that d'Estaing would be off the coast momentarily and that Byron's squadron had been dispatched to Halifax. Howe sent orders for Byron to join him in New York as soon as possible. If Byron's thirteen sail of the line combined with Howe's, they would be stronger than the French. In the crucial matter of leadership, however, Admiral Howe was far superior to d'Estaing.

After receiving this vital information, Howe hurried on to Sandy Hook with a fair wind and had his fleet safely within the bar by July 1. On the same day, he received a communication from Clinton reporting that he was at nearby Navesink, having arrived the day before. It was just chance that they met so conveniently. Any number of things could have prevented it. Acting with great speed because of d'Estaing's expected arrival, Howe had Clinton's entire force—wagon train and all—deposited on Staten Island, Manhattan, and Long Island by July 5.

Two days later, Howe received word that d'Estaing's fleet had been spotted off the Virginia coast on July 5 by one of the string of cruisers he had sent out to watch for the French. Howe now moved quickly to establish a defensive position just inside the entrance to the Lower Bay that would give his nominally inferior fleet a distinct advantage, such that he hoped the French admiral would attempt to cross the formidable bar at the Hook and run into New York Harbor.

Howe assumed that Washington and d'Estaing were planning a joint attack on Manhattan. It was up to him to disrupt it. His splendid fighting qualities came to the fore in this desperate crisis. He demonstrated his inestimable value, and why he should never have been permitted to return to London and hand over command. Admiral Horatio Nelson believed that in the management of a fleet, Howe had no peer.

Chapter 19

THE FRANCO-AMERICAN
ALLIANCE MISFIRES

While Lord Howe was inside Sandy Hook organizing the defense of the harbor, the long-awaited French fleet arrived off Chesapeake Bay after a grueling sixty-seven-day voyage. By July 8 d'Estaing was off the Delaware capes. He missed trapping Howe's warships and transports in Delaware Bay by only a few days, disappointing the hopes of Vergennes and Franklin.

After sending Silas Deane and the new French ambassador, Conrad Alexandre Gérard, to Philadelphia on the frigate *Chimère*, d'Estaing moved on to Manhattan for what he hoped would be a joint attack with Washington. He planned to burst into the harbor with his powerful fleet and smash Howe, after which he and Washington would force Clinton's surrender. Without command of the water, no army could survive in Manhattan.

On the afternoon of July 11 the French squadron was approaching Sandy Hook. Washington was moving from Monmouth Court House to White Plains; when he got news that the French fleet had finally arrived, he was in Paramus, New Jersey. He immediately dispatched

his aide Colonel John Laurens, who spoke excellent French, to coordinate with d'Estaing, while he hurried on to White Plains.

Before Washington got there, d'Estaing was off Sandy Hook, viewing the masts of Howe's fleet inside the bar. He was anxious to get at
him. He knew that Byron was coming from England, and he did not
want to face the combined fleets. Unfortunately, just getting across the
bar at the Hook proved an insurmountable problem. Every pilot, no
matter how much money he was offered, refused to guide d'Estaing
across—even at the height of the high spring tide. D'Estaing allowed
them to decide the matter for him.

Admiral Howe was watching carefully and concluded that there
were three days when tide and wind were good enough for d'Estaing to
make the attempt and when, had their positions been reversed, he
would have done it. Of course, he had plenty of experience moving over
the bar and d'Estaing had none, which made all the difference.

The bar was not the only problem for the French commander. The
way Howe had positioned his fleet inside the bar dramatically increased
the chances of d'Estaing's suffering extensive damage, if not an outright defeat, when he entered. Howe had organized his defense so that
the great French warships would be attacked as they tried to come over
the bar, not only by Howe but by an impressive array of artillery on
Sandy Hook, which Clinton had installed on July 19, along with eighteen hundred men.

If d'Estaing passed the bar, he would then face an even greater
obstacle as he made his way into the Lower Bay. He would be receiving
concentrated fire from seven of Howe's largest ships, without being able
to make an effective reply.

D'Estaing also had to consider that once inside the bar, he might
have to face Byron when attempting to exit. Getting out might be harder
than getting in. He even had to worry about Byron bursting into the
harbor and attacking his injured fleet there.

It was not surprising that, given all these obstacles, d'Estaing began
thinking that attacking Rhode Island was a much better idea. Newport
was a far more inviting target. The ease of entry into Narragansett Bay

made it much more attractive than New York's Lower Bay, and there was a sizable British army at Newport—in excess of six thousand, under General Sir Robert Pigot. A victory over such a large army would not only be relatively easy, given the fact that the allies could bring to bear more than twice the number of Pigot's troops, but would have a profound impact on London—perhaps enough to end the war.

On July 17 d'Estaing gave up on New York and prepared to attack Newport. He later explained to Congress that "the pilots procured by Colonels Laurens and Hamilton . . . unanimously declared that it was impossible to carry us in." Whether that was strictly true or not, having to confront Admiral Howe if d'Estaing was able to negotiate the bar, and perhaps Byron later, certainly made an entry foolhardy.

D'Estaing did not count his time off Sandy Hook a failure. While there, he captured twenty supply ships, which had an immediate impact in New York. It was a measure of how mismanaged the military occupation of the city was that just by seizing a relatively small number of vessels, d'Estaing could dramatically affect Manhattan's food supply. Even though the British occupied all of Long Island, which should have been able to supply all the food Manhattan needed, there was a continual shortage in the city, causing prices to escalate over three hundred percent. The problem arose because farmers were not growing food. The British were paying so little for it by artificially fixing prices, and at times simply taking crops, that farmers refused to plant. Large quantities of food thus had to be imported from England. D'Estaing's brief blockade almost caused a famine.

D'Estaing used the provisions he obtained for his own ships, and after July 17 he moved his squadron to nearby Monmouth on the New Jersey coast to continue resupplying and bringing fresh vegetables aboard for his scurvy-ridden crews. Five days later, he weighed anchor and, after pausing briefly at Sandy Hook, disappeared out to sea. Lord Howe had no specific intelligence about his destination, but he suspected it would be Newport. His suspicions were confirmed when the French fleet appeared off Narragansett Bay on July 29.

During this time, Washington had been preparing for an attack on

Maj.^r Genl Greene.

Major General Nathanael Greene

ENGRAVED BY WILL^M SKELTON.

HIS MOST EXCELLENT MAJESTY
GEORGE THE THIRD,
BY THE GRACE OF GOD, OF THE UNITED KINGDOM
OF GREAT BRITAIN & IRELAND, KING, DEFENDER OF THE FAITH &c. &c. &c.

George III

Burgoyne surrendering his sword to Horatio Gates at Saratoga

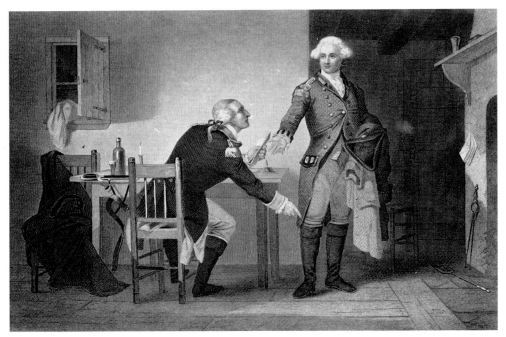

Arnold persuades André to conceal incriminating papers in his boot

Lieutenant General Sir Henry Clinton

George Washington

Admiral Lord Howe, commander in chief of the British fleet in North America

Marquis de Lafayette

Engraved for RAYMOND's History of England.

Metz delin.   Fregt sculp.

COUNT DE GRASSE, the French Admiral, resigning his Sword to ADMIRAL RODNEY, after being defeated by that gallant Commander in the West Indies, on April 12th. 1782.

Admiral de Grasse resigning his sword to Admiral George Rodney

Charles Gravier, Comte de Vergennes

General Washington and Governor Clinton leading the procession into liberated New York City

Newport. On July 17 he ordered General John Sullivan in Providence to organize an assault, authorizing him to immediately request help from the governors of Massachusetts, Rhode Island, and Connecticut, which he did, getting a tremendous response. His force of three thousand Continentals soon increased dramatically to over ten thousand, as New England militiamen came to help. John Hancock himself led the Massachusetts contingent. Colonel Paul Revere was with him, leading an artillery regiment. Washington also dispatched brigades under Generals Glover and James Varnum.

Having Sullivan in command of a major operation made Washington uneasy. The New Hampshire general had well-known weaknesses. Washington gave the matter a good deal of thought but in the end left Sullivan in charge, in part because General Gates wanted the job, and Washington was never going to let him gain the plaudits that would come from a victory of this magnitude.

It was also the case that Sullivan had been with Washington on that freezing Christmas night when they saved the revolution at Trenton. Sullivan's loyalty and bravery, when so many others—most notably Gates—had given up on him, meant a great deal to Washington.

By the same token, he had serious doubts about Sullivan, who had made costly mistakes in Canada, Long Island, and Brandywine. Washington did not want another one in Newport. In order to put a check on Sullivan's often impetuous behavior, he sent Greene and Lafayette to Rhode Island and ordered Sullivan to divide his force into two divisions, one under Greene and the other under Lafayette. Greene, who came from Rhode Island, was naturally delighted with the assignment, and of course Lafayette wanted to cooperate in every way he could with d'Estaing, his countryman. In addition to helping lead the attack on Newport, Lafayette would be invaluable as a liaison.

D'Estaing's sudden appearance off Point Judith at the entrance to Narragansett Bay on July 29 touched off a surge of enthusiasm in the American camp. He brought with him not only a fleet superior to Howe's but four thousand marines to swell Sullivan's now formidable army.

Adding to the growing confidence among the patriots, on the mere appearance of the French, General Pigot sank the four frigates anchored off Newport to prevent them from falling into d'Estaing's hands. Victory seemed assured. D'Estaing immediately concerted plans with Sullivan, Greene, and Lafayette, but it took several critical days for the troops Washington had sent, and especially the New England militiamen, to get integrated with Sullivan's. During that time, when Newport essentially lay at their feet, Admiral Howe was racing toward Narragansett Bay, which Sullivan and the others were unaware of.

On August 9, just as Sullivan and the French were about to commence their attack on Pigot, Admiral Howe suddenly appeared in the offing with a reinforced fleet, changing everything. The fifty-five-year-old d'Estaing, who was more of a soldier than a seaman, seemed to get rattled. For no discernible reason, he turned his attention entirely on Howe and ignored the plans for the attack he had already made with Sullivan. D'Estaing had his entire fleet in Narragansett Bay and would have immediately gone after Howe had it not been for the wind, which was blowing directly into the bay, making it impossible to sortie. He spent the day reembarking his four thousand marines while a horrified Sullivan looked on in disbelief.

Actually, there was no need for d'Estaing to do anything more than block the entrance to the bay so that the British fleet could not enter, which he easily could have done. He could then have carried out the plan he had worked out with Sullivan to force Pigot's surrender and dealt with Howe later when the wind permitted an easy exit from the bay.

It's true that on the day Howe first appeared, he might have taken the opportunity to make a run at the French in the bay with the wind at his back, but he chose not to. His squadron had been reinforced, but it was still not as strong as d'Estaing's, nor did fighting in the close confines of Narragansett Bay appeal to him. Howe's fleet had gained the 64-gun *Raisonable* and the 50-gun *Centurion*, both from Halifax; the 50-gun *Renown* from the Caribbean, and the 74-gun *Cornwall*, the first of Byron's storm-tossed squadron to arrive from Britain.

In their passage from England, Byron's ships met with brutal storms that scattered them. Only three days after "Foul-Weather Jack" left England, a gale struck and dispersed his squadron. Dreadful weather then plagued the individual warships all the way across the Atlantic. The first to arrive in New York did not get there until July 30. The next came fifteen days later. At the end of August only eight had reached New York. Byron himself did not arrive until the end of September.

On August 10, the morning after Lord Howe's fleet appeared off Narragansett Bay, the wind swung into the northeast and blew hard, allowing d'Estaing to run out of the harbor directly at Howe. Before departing, he left a message for Sullivan, promising that the attack on Newport would resume when he returned. Merely by appearing, Lord Howe had destroyed Sullivan's attack plans—at least for the moment.

When Howe saw the French getting under way, he pulled out to sea, away from the oncoming fleet, adopting a strategy of gradually maneuvering until he had the wind at his back (the weather gauge) before engaging. As d'Estaing exited the bay, he had the weather gauge, giving him a significant advantage. He could attack or not as he pleased.

Howe spent the next hours working his fleet to windward of the inept French commander. It was a masterful performance. During the next day and a half, Howe obtained his objective and was about to strike when, on August 12, a nor'easter of historic size blew with a vengeance, severely damaging and dispersing both fleets. They now had to fight for survival against the elements. Both squadrons were hit hard, but d'Estaing's received the most punishment.

Howe managed to get his fleet assembled back in New York faster than d'Estaing could gather his widely scattered ships. In the meantime, Sullivan, who was deeply annoyed at d'Estaing's sudden departure, decided to attack Pigot without him. The stupendous storm that struck on the twelfth brought all action to a halt, however. Sullivan was forced to wait for d'Estaing's return, expecting that once the storm abated, the siege of Newport would begin. D'Estaing's battered force reappeared off Narragansett Bay on the twentieth. Sullivan was shocked and angered when the count explained that he was abandoning the attack on Newport and sailing to Boston to repair his fleet. The American high command, except for Lafayette, remonstrated against his decision, but to no avail.

In the shape his fleet was in, d'Estaing could not risk an engagement with Byron. And there was still Admiral Howe to think about; d'Estaing did not know the condition of his fleet. He did not want to face both Howe and Byron with his ships needing extensive repairs. He had no choice but to retreat to Boston.

As it turned out, d'Estaing was in real danger from Howe. The British fleet had been quickly repaired in New York and was strengthened by the 64-gun *Monmouth*, the second of Byron's ships to arrive. Howe raced to Newport, hoping to catch d'Estaing, but when he got there he found that the French fleet had already gone to Boston.

Howe forgot about Newport, and about Clinton's three thousand reinforcements that were coming on fast to support Pigot, and raced to Boston to catch d'Estaing. But he arrived too late. D'Estaing was already safely within the confines of well-defended Boston Harbor.

In the meantime, the patriot force in Rhode Island had shrunk to less than five thousand, as hundreds, then thousands, of militiamen ran away from a losing cause, giving Pigot, who knew Clinton was coming, an opening. He attacked, forcing Sullivan to retreat, which he did with consummate skill, and escaped from Rhode Island just before Clinton arrived. Sullivan's prompt action saved hundreds of men from New York's jailers.

Washington was still unhappy with Sullivan for his all too typical lack of diplomacy in handling d'Estaing. His intemperate outbursts forced Washington, Lafayette, and others to smooth over the hurt feelings of the French—the patriots' great ally and only hope.

Although Washington hid it well, his anger at losing Newport was far greater than Sullivan's. It was the opportunity he had been praying for, and it was lost because of poor decisions and bad luck. "The whole may be summed up in a few words," he wrote later, "and amounts to this; that an unfortunate storm . . . and some measures taken in consequence of it by the French admiral, perhaps unavoidably, blasted in one moment the fairest hopes that ever were conceived; and, from a moral certainty of success, rendered it a matter of rejoicing to get our own troops safe off the island. If the garrison of that place, consisting of nearly six thousand men, had been captured, as there was, in appearance at least, a hundred to one in favor of it, it would have given the finishing blow to British pretensions of sovereignty over this country, and would, I am persuaded, have hastened the departure of the troops in New York, as fast as their canvas wings could carry them away."

★

AT THIS POINT, LORD HOWE HAD HAD ENOUGH. HE WAS determined to go home. General Clinton tried to keep him by suggesting they attack Boston, but Howe was not interested. Whether Clinton was actually serious is doubtful, although his biographer, William B. Willcox, thought he was.

It was impossible to tell when Clinton was committed to his frequent proposals for military action. A *coup de main* against Boston probably struck Howe as bizarre. He had heard similar proposals from Clinton ever since arriving in America, and he wasn't impressed by them. Even if they could mount a successful attack on Boston, what would it matter? It would be another dead end, as Philadelphia had been. The British had left Boston three years before; Howe could not see any good strategic reason to go back now.

He had sent in his resignation long before, and it had been swiftly accepted, which he expected. Neither Lord Sandwich nor any of Britain's leaders had any inkling that relieving Howe would be a critical turning point in the war. If there had been any hope of winning, when Howe left, that hope went with him. His importance remained unrecognized, and to a large extent still does. For Britain to bring her best naval commander home when, as Washington never tired of pointing out, supremacy on the water was crucial turned out to be a large gift to the Americans.

On September 24, Howe left New York for Newport to meet Byron at last and turn over command of the North American station. He then sailed home, understandably gloomy about Britain's prospects in America and bitter about the inept leadership in London, particularly that of Sandwich and Germain, and, of course, North. By this time, the politically adept North had turned against Howe. Instead of keeping him on the job or seeking his advice, the government acted meanly toward him. North refused to appoint him as the new treasurer of the navy and even postponed his promotion to vice admiral of the red, which would place him last in the class of flag officers promoted to that rank.

On November 1 Byron reached Boston, hoping to engage d'Estaing. The very next day, however, another nor'easter struck, scattering Byron's fleet again. Foul-Weather Jack just could not escape the dark cloud that seemed to hover over him. The ferocious storm blew for two days. When it subsided, d'Estaing took advantage of the opening and escaped from Boston before Byron could return, shaping a course for the West Indies. His battered fleet had been rapidly repaired. Since he was paying in hard money, work on his ships took priority—even over those of the Continental navy.

On November 3, the day before d'Estaing departed Boston, British major general James Grant left New York with five thousand troops. Commodore William Hotham escorted him with two 64-gun ships, three of 50 guns, and three smaller vessels. They were headed for Barbados to join Admiral Samuel Barrington's squadron for the long-delayed attack on St. Lucia.

Barrington, who was one of the more capable officers in the British service, had no trouble capturing the island on December 14, just before d'Estaing's fleet arrived from Boston and attacked Barrington's ships and troops. Barrington had much the better of the fight and forced d'Estaing's men back to their ships, securing St. Lucia and its important naval base.

Meanwhile, Byron, after the storm off Boston subsided, gathered his fleet in Newport for repairs. He then sailed for St. Lucia to strengthen

British forces and battle d'Estaing. He arrived on January 6 and for the next six months fought inconclusive duels with the French fleet.

The year ended with Washington feeling that the patriots had come close to winning the war three times during 1778, but they could never capitalize on their considerable advantages. He was, to say the least, frustrated. If the states had provided anywhere near the number of troops they should have, he could have destroyed Clinton's army on its march through New Jersey. And if the French fleet had not experienced one delay after another on its voyage to the Delaware capes, Admiral Howe could have been trapped in Delaware Bay, leaving Clinton's army exposed and vulnerable in New Jersey. Washington's third chance came at Newport, where a combination of factors, including poor decisions by the allied commanders, particularly d'Estaing, brought defeat instead of an easy victory. Thinking back, Washington could only count the year as one of missed opportunities, for which the patriots themselves and their French ally were largely to blame. How many more chances the allies would have he did not know, but, as always, he intended to fight on.

Chapter 20

WITHDRAWAL FROM
RHODE ISLAND

W hen General Clinton returned to New York from Rhode Island, he began implementing the king's plan for subduing the South, starting with Georgia. On November 27 Lieutenant Colonel Archibald Campbell stood out from New York with Commodore Hyde Parker Jr. and a fleet of twenty-seven warships and transports loaded with thirty-five hundred men to attack Savannah. The weather was benign, and on December 23 they stood off Tybee Island at the mouth of the muddy Savannah River. Six days later, Campbell, aided by slaves, marched into Savannah, after defeating a much smaller, ill-equipped patriot force under General Robert Howe, commander of the Southern Department.

At the same time, General Augustine Prevost, the British commander in East Florida, marched from St. Augustine the first week of January with two thousand men and joined Campbell. By the end of January all of Georgia was in British hands. Former royal governor James Wright returned from London in July, and Georgia was once again a British colony, albeit a thinly populated one.

Clinton's next objective was Charleston, the key to the king's southern strategy. Although Clinton was originally skeptical of concentrating on the South, after the quick victory in Georgia he began changing his mind. Once in possession of Charleston, the South's most important city, he assumed that the rest of South Carolina would soon submit. North Carolina would quickly follow, he supposed, and Virginia after that. His knowledge of any of these states was minimal and came solely from hardened Loyalists.

Clinton's orders specified that while conquering the South, he was also to hold all the territory currently in His Majesty's possession, which meant New York and Newport, Rhode Island. Despite the new emphasis on the South, Clinton still believed that the war could be won by seizing the Highlands. He began thinking, however, that the war should be pursued in both places—that his already small army would have to be divided between North and South. If that was the case, if he meant to operate substantial bases in Charleston and New York, reinforcements were essential, and so was maintaining continuous naval superiority. The departure of Lord Howe was inopportune, to say the least.

The decision on Admiral Howe's replacement became critically important, but every indication was that Lord Sandwich would not make it a priority. He had already sent the incompetent Rear Admiral James Gambier to replace Lord Howe in 1778. But Howe remained longer than intended, because of d'Estaing's arrival and Byron's being delayed by storms. Howe dealt with the Gambier problem by giving him the post of port admiral in New York, where he could do the least harm.

When Howe left America in September 1778 he turned over command to Byron, not to Gambier. But in November Byron had to chase d'Estaing to the West Indies, which meant leaving Gambier in command of the North American station, where he stayed until April 1779. Although the Admiralty recalled him in November of 1778, he did not actually leave for home until April 5. Clinton characterized him as "a horrid performer in every respect." Few disagreed with him.

London's new emphasis on the South did not surprise Washington. He had long been concerned about it. Congress, following his recommendation, had already appointed Major General Benjamin Lincoln to take command of the weak Southern Department on September 25, 1778. Lincoln, a hero of Saratoga, was delayed, however, and did not reach Charleston until December 7, narrowly missing a chance to save Savannah.

During the next weeks and months, Lincoln and Prevost fought for control of Georgia and Charleston. The British hung on to Georgia, while Lincoln kept control of Charleston. By July of 1779, with the onset of hot, humid, unhealthy summer weather, fighting was suspended.

Meanwhile, Clinton waited impatiently for reinforcements. He could not begin operations against Charleston until the proffered troops arrived. He complained to London that since he was forced to send five thousand men to the West Indies with Grant and two thousand more to Canada, he was left with only around fifteen thousand fit for duty. Germain promised that 6,600 would reach New York in the spring of 1779 and more in the summer. Carolina Loyalists were supposedly going to augment them. After Philadelphia Loyalists had been cruelly abandoned, however, southern Tories were bound to be more reluctant to take up arms.

When reinforcements failed to arrive in the spring, Clinton worried that few, if any, were coming, and he would be stuck with an inadequate army, as Howe had been, and General Gage before him. If that was going to be the case, he asked to be recalled. The king would not hear of it, however; Clinton just had to bide his time.

While waiting for more troops, the British high command enjoyed themselves in New York in the early months of 1779, as they had every winter. Indolence and self-indulgence was the order of the day. General Clinton, although a much different character than his predecessor, set the tone, just as General Howe had. Clinton had the same agreeable mistress, Mary O'Callaghan Baddeley, he had before.

His townhouse in Manhattan, the finest in the city, continued to be his official residence, although he also spent time with Mrs. Baddeley at his country estates in Manhattan, Queens County, Kings County, and on Staten Island. He was devoted to fox hunting, as much as General Howe was to faro, and he apparently thought that these various estates were essential for recreation.

Clinton shunned officers who had been personally close to Howe, with the notable exception of John André, who managed to ingratiate himself with Clinton, in part by the clever way he lampooned his former chief, and in part because he was a superb actor. Clinton was so taken with André that he made him acting adjutant general and chief of his secret service. They were so close that some of their enemies speculated that there was a sexual relationship, although this was undoubtedly idle gossip.

During the winter of 1778–79 Washington was marking time as well, waiting for another French fleet to appear, so that he could attack New York. He thought there was a good chance that d'Estaing would come north again during hurricane season in the Caribbean. He stationed his army in a semicircle around Manhattan at Middle Brook, Elizabeth, and Ramapo in New Jersey; West Point and Fishkill in New York, and at Danbury, Connecticut. Headquarters were at Middle Brook. The weather was comparatively mild—nothing at all like the previous winter at Valley Forge. Spreading the camps over a wide area increased the supply of food and other necessities. And French aid, which now came in larger quantities, contributed to the more benevolent atmosphere. The men even had warm uniforms, overcoats, and shoes for a change.

With nothing else to do, Washington spent six weeks in Philadelphia discussing policy with various congressional committees, arriving on December 21, 1778. He stayed with Henry Laurens, who was no longer president of Congress, John Jay having succeeded him. Martha was there to greet him when he arrived. She joined him every winter, even at Valley Forge.

Washington was concerned that excessive reliance on France might undermine the war effort, and that's exactly what was happening. Philadelphia turned out to be a huge disappointment. Washington was upset with the state of Congress, which had shrunk in both numbers and quality. The states were not sending their best people. An even greater shock was the extent of profiteering. While his army was being starved of money, even to pay its officers, speculators were buying goods meant for the army and making a profit reselling them to the government.

Benedict Arnold was the military governor of Philadelphia. Washington was an admirer, but there were questions and rumors about him. Joseph Reed, president of the Executive Council (governor) of Pennsylvania, was particularly upset with Arnold's lifestyle, his reckless pursuit of money, and his close relations with Loyalists. Reed was shocked by how Arnold managed his everyday business as if he were an imperial overlord rather than a subordinate officer. He consistently showed disrespect for local authorities, which outraged Reed. Arnold's aristocratic friends seemed of greater importance to him than patriot officials or the well-being of the great majority of Philadelphia's citizens.

Answers to two of Washington's more important questions were not available in Philadelphia. He wanted to know whether d'Estaing was coming north, and if Spain was likely to ally herself with France. Finally, in late April, Ambassador Gérard visited Middle Brook and told him there was a good possibility that d'Estaing would come north. Washington wanted to coordinate another attack on either New York or Newport, but only if d'Estaing came with overwhelming strength. If not, perhaps an alternative could be helping General Lincoln recover Savannah.

Don Juan de Miralles, the Spanish agent in Philadelphia, accompanied Gérard, but he could not confirm that Spain and France were allied, although he thought it likely. In fact, the secret alliance between the Bourbon powers had been signed on April 12, 1779, at Aranjuez, near Madrid. In reaching agreement with Paris, Madrid pointedly did not recognize American independence, although presumably the compact would benefit the patriots.

The new alliance meant that the energies of the three European powers, Britain, France, and Spain, would likely be absorbed battling each other during 1779. Charles III, the Spanish king, wanted to invade England in the summer. He hoped the war would be quick and that he would regain lost territory, while the French would have the satisfaction of seeing Britain humiliated. Vergennes did not want to invade England; he preferred concentrating on America and the West Indies, but, since Spain was so important to France, he was compelled to go along.

Charles III was so anxious to get after the British that planning for the invasion started before the treaty with Paris was signed. He knew that actually conquering Britain was impossible; what he was aiming for was seizing an important coastal city like Portsmouth, which might lead to a negotiation that would force London to give up at least Gibraltar, and perhaps Minorca.

The immediate impact of the Bourbon alliance on America was hard to judge. Spain would be cooperating with France in the Caribbean and the Floridas, which would be a help. And Britain would be forced to defend her homeland, as well as the West Indian islands, which meant less emphasis on America. What exactly that would mean, however, was unclear.

★

WHILE WASHINGTON WAS TRYING TO GET A MAJOR FRENCH fleet to return to the American coast, Clinton was receiving the first feelers from General Benedict Arnold about defecting. It was an intriguing development that immediately drew the British commander's attention. In early May 1779 Clinton's trusted aide John André reported having received an inquiry from General Arnold about changing sides. The message came through an intermediary whom André considered reliable.

Arnold had finally made the decision to betray his country for money. His motivation, apart from a voracious appetite for gold, appeared to be unhappiness at how Congress and Pennsylvania authorities were treating him. He had many complaints, some of them unquestionably valid, about the way Congress handled his promotions and finances. His lavish lifestyle added to the problem. The unnecessarily large household he maintained, the handsome carriage he went about town in, the fabulous parties he threw, the social milieu he liked to travel in, his stylish eighteen-year-old wife—all contributed to an endless need for more money. It left him deeply in debt and made him a number of powerful enemies, particularly Joseph Reed, who felt that Arnold's public persona and quest for profit were unseemly.

Watching Congress up close in Philadelphia could not help but contribute to Arnold's cynicism, as did, no doubt, all the war profiteering he saw going on. He may have simply concluded that the British were going to win the war, and he wanted to profit from it. Whatever his reasons, by the spring of 1779 he had decided to offer his services to the enemy for as large a sum as he could get.

Making the initial overture was a delicate and dangerous undertaking. Arnold was aided throughout by his talented, resourceful wife, Peggy Shippen Arnold. He chose as his initial contact Joseph Stansbury, an inconspicuous Philadelphia Loyalist who owned a china shop. After lengthy conversations with Arnold, Stansbury got in touch with the Rev. Jonathan Odell, a Loyalist clergyman and writer in New York who was a friend of André's. The patriots had roughly handled Odell, and he was ready to pay them back. After listening to Stansbury's story, Odell arranged a meeting with André.

André was interested enough in what Odell had to say to meet Stansbury in New York on May 10, 1779. Satisfied that Stansbury was who he claimed to be, André mentioned their conversation to Clinton, who indicated that he would like to explore the matter. When André met Stansbury again, the first thing he did was tell him to assure Arnold that the British would persevere until they won the war. Arnold was fearful that after he betrayed his country, there could be a reconciliation. André also assured Arnold that if he performed an important service, his compensation would be generous. If Arnold failed but made a good faith effort, he'd still be paid, although a smaller amount. An elaborate cipher was arranged so that they could communicate safely.

After the initial contact, relations proceeded slowly, primarily because Arnold did not have enough to trade in order to justify the amount of money he was asking. By July the negotiations were at an impasse over the same issue. Arnold simply did not have enough to offer. In a letter sent at the end of July, André suggested for the first time that if Arnold could be instrumental in securing West Point, with a garrison of over three thousand men, the sum he was after would be forthcoming.

What sum, specifically, wasn't mentioned, which did not please Arnold. André wrote, "I am sorry any hesitation should still remain as I think we have said all that prudence [will allow]. . . . I can only add that as such sums as are held forth must be in some degree accounted for, real advantage must appear to have arisen from the expenditure or a generous effort must have been made." André then thanked Arnold for the information he had already provided. Since it still wasn't nearly enough, he again suggested West Point as a prize that would elicit the gold Arnold was looking for.

André's letter angered Arnold. Such a vague response, particularly about his reward, was unsatisfactory. At this point, their tortuous dialogue ceased until the spring of 1780, when Arnold's need for money grew acute.

★

THE REINFORCEMENTS CLINTON WAS WAITING FOR FINALLY left England on June 4, 1779. Sixty-eight-year-old Vice Admiral Marriot Arbuthnot, Lord Howe's replacement, was bringing them. His appointment showed clearly, if there were not already an abundance of other evidence, that for Lord Sandwich America was indeed a secondary theater. Clinton had asked for Admirals Robert Roddam or Barrington, or Commodores John Elliot, Jervis, or Hotham, but his preference was ignored. Instead he got a physically impaired admiral who had been fifty-five years in the service and should have been retired, not handed one of the navy's toughest assignments.

During the spring and summer of 1779 the war in America had become much less important for the British. London was preoccupied with defending the country against the Bourbon powers. A sizable army was forming on the French coast and two large fleets combining to gain control of the English Channel. The capacity and determination of France and Spain were not to be taken lightly. The home island was under a real threat. Until the planned amphibious attack was thwarted, the war in America had to have a low priority. The fact that by the end of August the threat had dramatically lessened did not negate the concern felt in England during the spring and summer. In the end, the French and Spanish fleets could not work together, and even if they had, the British fleet with its copper-bottomed ships would have been hard to defeat.

Given all that was happening in Europe, delays in sending more troops to America were to be expected. Admiral Arbuthnot did not arrive in New York with reinforcements until August 25. In the interim, Sir George Collier was in command of the fleet in America, and Clinton got along well with him. Collier was a first-rate fighting sailor who knew how to work with the army. But unlike Lord Howe (and very much like Clinton), he had no understanding of the political dimensions of his job.

While waiting for Arbuthnot, Clinton followed Germain's orders and conducted a series of coastal raids. The first was against Portsmouth, Virginia. On May 5 Commodore Collier left New York with eighteen hundred troops under Major General Edward Matthews. They arrived in Chesapeake Bay five days later and easily took Portsmouth. Much to their surprise, the people appeared friendly, so much so that Collier thought Portsmouth would be an excellent outpost.

He and Matthews spent the next two weeks ravaging nearby Norfolk, Suffolk, Gosport, Kemp's Landing, and adjacent areas without opposition. Collier returned to New York on May 29. His success encouraged Clinton to think again about establishing a permanent post in Chesapeake Bay, one that could prevent Washington from sending troops and supplies south to aid General Lincoln when Charleston was attacked.

★

AS SOON AS COLLIER RETURNED, CLINTON MADE A PROBE UP the Hudson that he had been planning for some time. Leaving Manhattan on June 1, he drove forty-five miles upriver with six thousand men for an attack on the two forts guarding King's Ferry, the main crossing point south of Peekskill. Collier was in command of the one hundred fifty flatboats and seventy-odd transports and warships carrying the troops. The two fortified points on opposite sides of the river were considered the gateway to the Highlands. Washington likened them to the Pillars of Hercules.

Fort Lafayette guarded Verplanck's Point on the east bank, and Stony Point protected the west. They were lightly defended, and Clinton easily seized both. But that's as far as he went. The fortress that now stood at West Point was thirteen miles farther north on the west side of the Hudson. Heavily defended Constitution Island was on the east side opposite West Point. A thick iron chain with supporting river obstacles stretched across the water between them. Washington had been strengthening all the defenses in the Highlands ever since Clinton had so easily penetrated them in 1777.

Testing this stronghold would be a major undertaking, and Clinton was planning to do it at some point, believing it was a sure way to end the war, but now was not the time. His force was not large enough, and he withdrew. Before leaving, he strengthened both forts at King's Ferry in preparation for a possible strike on West Point later.

After returning to New York, Clinton, following Germain's instructions, began raids along the Connecticut coast at New Haven, Fairfield, and Norwalk led by General (former Governor) Tryon. They took place at the end of June and early July.

Washington unexpectedly countered on July 15–16 with a surprise night attack on Stony Point. Concerned that the army appeared too passive, he was looking for a spectacular enterprise to show the public, and Congress, that it wasn't. He reconnoitered the post himself and thought it would be difficult to take but, under the circumstances, necessary. Surprise was the key. He gave the difficult assignment to thirty-four-year-old Brigadier General Anthony Wayne and his corps of light infantry. On the fifteenth, in the dead of night, Wayne set out quietly from Fort Montgomery with fourteen hundred men—about twice the size of the British garrison.

After shooting the sentries, Wayne's men fixed bayonets and entered the fort a little after midnight, surprising the confused garrison and taking it easily without firing a single shot. Using bayonets only, his soldiers killed 63 redcoats, wounded 70 more, and took an amazing 543 captive. The patriots suffered 15 killed and 83 wounded. Many more redcoats could have been killed, but Wayne's fighters refused to slaughter the sleepy young men in front of them who were pleading for mercy. In his report to Washington, Wayne wrote, "The humanity of our brave soldiery, who scorned to take the lives of a vanquished foe calling for mercy, reflects the highest honor on them, and accounts for the few of the enemy killed on the occasion." Wayne meant to contrast his policy toward captives with what the British and Hessians practiced.

A simultaneous attack against the fort at Verplanck's Point on the opposite side of the river miscarried, but Washington was still pleased with the evening's results. He soon withdrew all his troops from both sides of the river back to the Highland forts. He knew that Clinton would counterattack, and he did not want a major engagement at Stony Point, where he'd be at a great disadvantage. He had already achieved his objective. Wayne's gambit had caught the public's imagination. Widespread approval was exactly what Washington was aiming for. It was good for the army's morale—and for the commander in chief's.

When Washington withdrew, Clinton, as expected, retook Stony Point and hurriedly strengthened the fort and the garrison. Despite heightened vigilance along the river, he was again taken by surprise when, on August 19, Major Henry "Light-Horse Harry" Lee attacked Paulus Hook, capturing one hundred fifty redcoats before retiring. An angry Clinton retook that as well, but it was another embarrassment.

At the same time that he was retaking Paulus Hook, Clinton brought Tryon and his raiders back to New York. He had never been enthusiastic about Tryon's work. He was only doing it to please London. He thought that the attacks were a waste of time and resources.

On July 21, 1779, Cornwallis arrived back in New York after the death of his wife. Clinton then attempted to resign, assuming Cornwallis would take his place, but the answer to his request did not arrive until seven months later, and it was turned down. Part of the delay stemmed from indecision over a successor. The king and cabinet had no intention of appointing Cornwallis; they favored Carleton. In the end they kept Clinton, even though his resignation showed his negative frame of mind and made the decision puzzling. Many far abler generals could have taken his place. Carleton and Charles Grey were good examples.

Three weeks later, on August 13, Commodore Collier appeared suddenly in Penobscot Bay off the coast of Maine with a strong squadron from New York and won a decisive victory over a large Massachusetts fleet led by the grossly incompetent Continental navy captain Dudley Saltonstall, who was afterward drummed out of the service for his bizarre, cowardly behavior. The British now had a critical base in Castine to use against privateers, and to protect Maine's all-important white-pine masts being shipped to the North American squadron at Halifax. The Royal Navy had been using Maine pine for its ships since the seventeenth century.

While Collier was away, New York Harbor was undefended, and d'Estaing was sailing from the Caribbean to the American coast with a massive fleet of thirty-three warships. Admiral Arbuthnot did not arrive in New York until the twenty-fifth of August, and even so, he could not have countered d'Estaing's powerful fleet had it appeared, which it might well have. The naval supremacy that Clinton required was compromised with surprisingly little thought given to it.

★

WHEN ADMIRAL ARBUTHNOT FINALLY ARRIVED, HE WAS A huge disappointment for Clinton. He was supposed to be bringing 6,600 troops, but he actually had only 3,800, and many were sick with a variety of maladies, which in turn infected the troops in New York, disabling the army through the rest of the summer and early fall. The *New York Journal* reported, "Arbuthnot's fleet with the reinforcements of British troops between three and four thousand men, are at last arrived at New York. The troops are . . . in a very feeble condition, being much emaciated by sickness and a long passage of thirteen weeks." Clinton had planned to attack Charleston as soon as Arbuthnot arrived, but with his troops riddled with sickness, a major operation of that kind had to be postponed. It was an inauspicious beginning.

Lesser action could not be avoided, however. As soon as Arbuthnot dropped his hook, Clinton received an urgent request from the governor of Jamaica for help to defend the island against a possible attack by d'Estaing's fleet. Clinton responded, sending Cornwallis with four thousand troops. Arbuthnot transported them. Three days after leaving New York, however, a chance meeting at sea with a friendly ship provided critical intelligence indicating that d'Estaing was actually off the coast of Georgia (not Jamaica) with a huge fleet, and that Arbuthnot was steering right for him.

In fact, d'Estaing had appeared off Tybee Island on September 1. His fleet was enormous—twenty sail of the line, two 50-gun ships, eleven frigates, and supporting transports carrying six thousand troops.

Cornwallis immediately returned to New York with the news, and Clinton reacted fast. There was a good possibility that d'Estaing was coming to New York, as he had the previous year. The report on d'Estaing provided the first opportunity for Arbuthnot and Clinton to work together. It did not go well. To Clinton's dismay, he found that the relationship he had with Lord Howe and George Collier was not going to continue.

Problems developed right away, when Clinton decided to abandon Rhode Island and bring the troops back to New York for its defense. It was a major decision that meant turning over the finest harbor on the Atlantic coast to the enemy. Arbuthnot was needed to transport the men, their animals, and equipment. Clinton was dismayed to find that Arbuthnot had no idea how to proceed and kept changing his mind. The admiral was obviously worried about his fleet should d'Estaing appear. He wanted to avoid any engagement at all costs. Finally, ninety vessels were assembled and the whole garrison brought off all at once. The lighthouse at the entrance to the harbor was burned as they left.

Clinton was concerned with d'Estaing as well, and he wanted the troops moved quickly. He felt the same about the men he had at Stony Point and Verplanck's Point: He wanted them withdrawn. In the end Arbuthnot accomplished the tasks, but friction with Clinton became intense, to the point where they found it difficult to communicate. Nonetheless, by the end of October, all the troops were assembled in New York, bringing the strength of the garrison to twenty-five thousand. The ill will generated between admiral and general during the exercise, however, did not bode well for the future.

Washington, meanwhile, hoped that d'Estaing would bring his entire fleet to New York or Rhode Island, but if not, he wanted the Frenchman to cooperate with Benjamin Lincoln and attack Savannah. D'Estaing had no intention of going to New York again, but when he received an appeal the first week in August from Lincoln to take Savannah, he responded, setting sail with his entire fleet on August 16, 1779, from Cap François, the large French naval base in Haiti, arriving off the Georgia coast sixteen days later. Unfortunately, his attempt on Savannah failed, but his appearance on the American coast had precipitated Clinton's withdrawal from Rhode Island, which would have great benefits the following year, and the year after that.

On October 19 d'Estaing left the American coast and went home, much to Washington's regret. On October 20, before he knew d'Estaing wasn't coming to New York, Washington wrote to Lafayette:

We have been hourly in expectation, for the last fifteen days, of seeing the Count d'Estaing off Sandy Hook. We have not heard a syllable from Charleston since the 8th of September. The accounts then mentioned that the Count intended to make his attack the next day. Under such circumstances, you may easily form an idea of our impatience and anxiety. We are making every preparation in our power for an extensive and perfect cooperation with the fleet, if it comes; while the enemy, whose expectation of it keeps pace with ours, are equally vigorous in preparing for defense. They are throwing up strong works at the Narrows, both on Long Island and Staten Island. They are fortifying the point at Sandy Hook, on which the lighthouse stands, and every other spot which can contribute to the defense of the harbor or city. Besides which, they have already sunk eight large ships and have twelve more to sink in the channel within the lighthouse. . . . In a word, if they are not horribly frightened, they certainly are in horrid confusion.

Under the circumstances, Clinton breathed an enormous sigh of relief when d'Estaing disappeared. Once it was clear that he was not coming north, Clinton could get on with planning the long-delayed attack on Charleston. He now believed that capturing the city would be the beginning of the end for the rebels.

Germain, Sandwich, and the king felt the same. They seemed to believe that the head of their naval force in America was a satisfactory substitute for Admiral Howe. They appeared confident that, even with the shockingly small squadron Arbuthnot had assigned to him, he could easily accomplish the immensely difficult task of dealing with the French West Indian fleet should it reappear.

★

ON DECEMBER 1, 1779, WASHINGTON SETTLED DOWN WITH his army at Morristown again for the winter. It was a depressing time for him and for the revolution. The conditions that his troops and officers had to cope with were gruesome. They had not been paid for months. Food was scarce. In a country swollen with produce, the army was starving. How the men tolerated their circumstances was a mystery, even to the commander in chief. Washington was preparing for outright mutiny. Even if the soldiers received their back pay, its worth would be questionable, as the value of the currency continued to plummet. The one hope Washington had was France. Would she come to the rescue? Another fleet was essential, and a large loan, but he had no idea if either would be forthcoming.

Of the few military successes Washington had had during this difficult year, there was one about which he had decidedly mixed feelings. From the end of July to the middle of September General Sullivan, General James Clinton, and Colonel Daniel Brodhead led a three-pronged expedition, retaliating against the Iroquois nations in Tryon County, New York, led by the gifted Mohawk chief Joseph Brant.

Fighting over territory had been endemic to Tryon County and nearby northern Pennsylvania for years, with blood being shed in large quantities by both sides. Washington's inclination was to stay out of it, but the alliance of Brant with the British in Canada added a dimension he could not ignore. Before Sullivan and the others began their march, Washington made a feint on Canada to keep General Frederick Haldimand from sending an army to help Brant. Washington's ploy worked. Haldimand stayed away, and Brant, who survived personally, was badly defeated.

After many years thinking about the immense problem of hostile tribes, Washington had come to the conclusion that when the situation warranted, a devastating blow should be aimed at the offending nations, and with the approval of Congress, that's what he did on this occasion. It was effective, in the sense that the tribes involved were crushed to a point where they were not going to be a problem for some time. Washington wished there was another way, for he knew that although Brant was defeated, he, or someone like him, would be back fighting for his nation's lands again. It was a conundrum Washington had no answer for. He had no Indian policy that had any possibility of achieving an amicable relationship with the tribes. He had been part of the relentless expansion of American speculators and settlers into Indian lands since before the French and Indian War.

Chapter 21

CHARLESTON

On December 26, 1779, while Washington was getting settled in Morristown for another difficult winter, General Clinton finally began his voyage to Charleston, leaving General Knyphausen in charge of New York. The weather could not have been worse. Bitter cold and ferocious storms plagued the task force as it struggled south with eighty-five hundred freezing soldiers, their horses, and equipage. Five thousand sailors manned the huge fleet of fourteen warships and ninety transports. Lord Cornwallis accompanied Clinton as second in command, while Admiral Arbuthnot directed the fleet. Relations between the three were still sour and continued to deteriorate.

While Clinton struggled south, Washington, as expected, was suffering from the most diabolical winter the army had ever experienced, including that of 1777–78 at Valley Forge. He was spending most of his time trying to feed demoralized troops and keep them warm. Ice on the Hudson was so thick that horses pulling heavily loaded wagons and artillery had no trouble crossing. Desertion was rampant. Desperate men were leaving camp and roaming the countryside looking for food.

At the same time that Washington was dealing with the cold, he was keeping a close eye on the South. He wanted to dispatch a body of troops to help General Lincoln, but he could not spare them without dangerously weakening his own force. He had only ten thousand, and he had to use them to protect the Hudson and threaten Manhattan. He judged that General Knyphausen had more than eleven thousand in New York. The actual number was closer to sixteen thousand.

Washington voiced his concerns to Philip Schuyler, then a member of Congress. "I feel many anxious moments on account of the Carolinas," he wrote, "which are increased by the daily diminution of our force in this quarter, the little prospect of getting it augmented in time to answer any valuable purpose, and other obvious embarrassments."

Washington planned to have Lord Stirling make an attack on Staten Island with twenty-five hundred men on January 15, 1780, to obtain food. If Lord Stirling (Washington always referred to him as "your lordship") succeeded, it would not only raise morale but also help stop the soldiers from going about the countryside in large numbers seeking sustenance. Things were so bad that Washington, who was embarrassed by what his men were doing, still refused to take any action against them. Although anxious for Stirling to succeed, he had to cancel the mission at the last minute, when he found that the British were aware of his plans.

Meanwhile, Clinton's voyage south became a nightmare, as terrible storms lashed his armada. The trip, which normally would have taken ten days, took nearly five weeks. A particularly vicious blizzard off Cape Hatteras almost destroyed the entire expedition. Ships were scattered. The first to regroup found Tybee Island on January 30. It was not until February 11 that Clinton was finally able to get established on John's Island, thirty miles south of Charleston.

Once the army was ashore, Arbuthnot began a blockade of Charleston Harbor. He was worried about a large French fleet appearing, even though it wasn't hurricane season in the Caribbean. He did not have nearly enough sail of the line to battle a fleet of the kind that d'Estaing had brought to the coast the last two years. The likelihood of the French West Indian fleet's appearing in February, however, was nonexistent. Nonetheless, Arbuthnot worried, which could not help but negatively influence the mission. His disinclination to take any risks was a serious handicap.

When he left New York, he had five sail of the line, but he lost the 64-gun *Defiance* to the weather, and now had only four—his flagship, the 64-gun *Europa*, along with the 74-gun *Robust*, the 74-gun *Russell*, and the 64-gun *Raisonable*. He had no intention of risking any of them attempting to cross Charleston's notoriously difficult bar, eight miles southeast of the city. He planned to use the seven smaller warships he had for the attack on Charleston. The largest were the 50-gun *Renown*, the 44-gun *Roebuck*, and the 44-gun *Romulus*. Two of the others were British frigates: the 32-gun *Richmond*, and the 32-gun *Blonde*. But the remaining two—the 32-gun *Raleigh* and the 32-gun *Virginia*—had been made in America for the Continental navy. The British had easily captured both of them and had taken them into the Royal Navy.

Arbuthnot transferred his flag to the *Roebuck*. He would direct the battle from her quarterdeck. He anticipated serious problems just getting the *Renown*, the *Roebuck*, and the *Romulus* into Charleston Harbor. He would first have to cross over the bar to the broad anchorage called Five Fathom Hole and then run north for a thousand yards, down the main ship's channel to the southern end of Sullivan's Island, at which point he would have to run by the island's guns on Fort Moultrie, which had devastated a large British squadron under Admiral Parker in 1776.

He would also have to contend with a sizable American fleet in Charleston, under the command of Continental navy captain Abraham Whipple of Rhode Island. Arbuthnot assumed that Whipple would challenge him from Five Fathom Hole as he was coming over the bar, and later when he attempted to run by the guns of Fort Moultrie.

Unfortunately, his concerns were unwarranted. Whipple turned out to be even less inclined to fight than Arbuthnot. Whipple had been in Charleston observing the situation for weeks, arriving on December 23. His fleet was impressive. He had three Continental frigates—the 24-gun *Boston*, the 28-gun *Providence*, and the 28-gun *Queen of France*—as well as John Paul Jones's famous 18-gun *Ranger*. And that was not all. When Whipple first sailed into Charleston Harbor he found two powerful French warships already there, the 44-gun *Bricole* and the 26-gun *Truite*, as well as ships of the South Carolina navy: the 20-gun *General Moultrie*, the 16-gun *Notre Dame*, the 26-gun *L'Aventure*, and the 18-gun polacre *Zephyr*.

The obvious strategy for Whipple was to contest Arbuthnot's entrance over the bar. Had he done so, he would have had a good chance of preventing any British ships from entering the harbor at all, which would have defeated Clinton's entire enterprise with profound repercussions in Britain, perhaps even ending the war. To float the *Renown*, the *Roebuck*, and the *Romulus* over the bar, guns, water, and stores had to be removed completely, making them defenseless against fully loaded American men-of-war waiting in Five Fathom Hole on the other side of the bar. Given Arbuthnot's jitters, when he saw a powerful array of Whipple's ships waiting on the other side of the bar he might not even have attempted a crossing. On the other hand, if he tried, the North American squadron might have ripped apart his stripped-down men-of-war.

Given Whipple's reluctance to fight, however, Arbuthnot did not have to worry about crossing the bar. The British fleet intimidated the American commodore. He was looking for any excuse to avoid engaging Arbuthnot. General Lincoln had urged Whipple to challenge the British when they attempted to cross the bar, but Whipple flatly refused. He claimed that he could not challenge Arbuthnot when he drove his ships over the bar because his own men-of-war could not find sufficient anchorage in Five Fathom Hole, which was nonsense. There was plenty of anchorage in Five Fathom Hole. It's hard to imagine John Paul Jones or John Barry, or any of the other great Continental navy captains, making a similar excuse.

Lieutenant Colonel John Laurens, a South Carolinian, was on the scene reporting to his chief in Morristown. He wrote, "The Commodore and all his officers renounce the idea of defending the passage over the bar; they declare it impracticable for the frigates to lie in a proper position for that purpose. The government has neglected to provide floating batteries, which might have been stationed there."

It's hard to understand how frigates were not floating batteries, but Whipple and his timid officers were not John Paul Jones, shouting, "I have not yet begun to fight." They were men looking for excuses not to go up against the vaunted Royal Navy. They could look out at Arbuthnot's warships and see that two of them were former American frigates now being used against them. They were not anxious to have their own warships suffer a similar fate.

In Washington's opinion, if Arbuthnot got over the bar the battle was lost, and Lincoln should evacuate Charleston to save his army. "I have the greatest confidence in General Lincoln's prudence," he wrote later, "but it really appears to me, that the propriety of attempting to defend the town, depended on the probability of defending the bar, and that, when this ceased, the attempt ought to have been relinquished."

As an alternative to disputing Arbuthnot's entrance over the bar, Whipple proposed fighting him when he attempted to run by the guns on Fort Moultrie at the tip of Sullivan's Island. But when the time came, Whipple invented more excuses, abandoned that idea, and retreated to the Cooper River. Once there, he helped build a log and chain defense. After completing that, he removed the cannon and men from all his ships, except for two, which he kept behind the obstructions. The men and guns that he removed were sent into the town to help defend it.

When the time came for Arbuthnot to cross the bar and fight his way into the harbor, he was surprised and gratified to find literally no opposition. He could hardly believe it. He reported to the Admiralty:

After seeing to the landing of the army, preparations were next made for passing the squadron over the Charleston bar, where at high water spring tides there is only 19 feet of water. The guns, provisions, and water were taken out of the *Renown*, *Roebuck*, and

Romulus to lighten them, and we lay in that situation on the open coast in the winter season of the year, exposed to the insults of the enemy for sixteen days, before an opportunity offered of going into the harbor, which was effected without any accident on the 20th of March, not withstanding the enemy's galleys continually attempted to prevent our boats from sounding the channel. . . . The enemy naval force . . . made an appearance of disputing the passage up the river at the narrow pass between Sullivan's Island and the Middle Ground, having moored their ships and galleys in a position to make a raking fire as we approached Fort Moultrie, but on the squadron arriving near the bar and anchoring on the inside, they abandoned that idea, retired to the town, and changed their plan of defense.

Whipple's plan of defense was to make no defense at all. The Continental navy had never participated in an important battle, where so much was at stake, and Whipple's highest priority seemed to be keeping out of harm's way. While he and his officers did their utmost to save themselves, they threw away an excellent chance to deliver a significant, if not fatal, blow to the enemy.

Once Arbuthnot's warships were in the harbor, he was of little help to Clinton; he merely observed. When he received a request from Clinton to attack Whipple's meager force on the Cooper River, remove the obstructions in the water, and close Lincoln's only escape route out of the city, he refused. He claimed that his ships were vulnerable to artillery fire from shore, another of his lame excuses. Naturally, Clinton was furious and the rift between them widened.

Other than problems with Arbuthnot, Clinton's attack progressed steadily with no opposition. As was his wont, he moved cautiously from John's Island, where he had originally landed, toward Charleston peninsula, intending to lay siege to the city. He expected that by the time he arrived, Arbuthnot's warships would be in the harbor and in control of both the Ashley and Cooper rivers. General Lincoln would then be trapped in the city. With Lincoln receiving fire from land and sea, Clinton anticipated a quick surrender.

His first move was to cross the Stono River. He seized the Stono Ferry, connecting John's Island with James Island, and sped across with no trouble. Needless to say, Whipple never thought of challenging Clinton as he negotiated the waterways leading to Charleston peninsula.

From the Stono River Clinton kept slowly making his way toward the city, ultimately crossing the Ashley River onto the Charleston peninsula on March 29—again, without opposition. He moved slowly because of his innate caution and because he set up posts as he went along to ensure a safe retreat to his ships, if necessary.

General Lincoln was in the city all the time, preparing to defend it with half the troops and far less artillery than Clinton had, and with the Royal Navy in complete control of the harbor. Lincoln had no way of knowing that the British fleet was of little use to Clinton, especially in sealing off the Cooper River. Clinton considered it an obvious escape route for Lincoln, but the American commander appeared to be committed to fighting it out. The situation being what it was, Lincoln should have retreated over the Cooper long before now.

To prevent Lincoln from retreating over the Cooper, Clinton on April 14 dispatched fifteen hundred men under Lieutenant Colonel Banastre Tarleton—the same spirited officer who had captured General Lee in New Jersey—and Major Patrick Ferguson to seize control of the far side of the river, which they did by defeating General Isaac Huger at Monck's Corner. This action, not Arbuthnot's warships, closed off any chance Lincoln had to escape. Clinton soon had over two thousand men on the Cooper blocking Lincoln.

Meeting no resistance on water or land, Clinton began his formal bombardment of the city on April 13. It was obvious that General Lincoln should have retreated. He had fifty-five hundred men, half of whom were Continentals, the rest militia, while Clinton, who had received reinforcements, now had ten thousand regulars. Charleston's leaders argued vociferously for Lincoln to stay, and he gave way to their entreaties. On May 12, bowing to the inevitable, Lincoln surrendered his entire army.

His soldiers paid a high price for his decisions throughout the ordeal. Afterward, they were thrown into four improvised, grossly over-crowded prison ships off Haddrell's Point on Mount Pleasant. Many defected to avoid dying. A high percentage of the others suffered excru-ciating deaths.

★

CLINTON MOVED QUICKLY TO FOLLOW UP HIS VICTORY AND establish royal authority in the rest of South Carolina. His time was limited: He had just received word that a sizable French force was steer-ing for the American coast. He had to get back to New York to counter a possible attack on Manhattan. He did not know exactly where the French would land or how large their task force was, or, indeed, what their immediate objective was, but he guessed it was either New York or Rhode Island. With his army now divided between Manhattan and Charleston, command of the sea was more important than ever. Hav-ing Arbuthnot directing the fleet was cause for great concern.

Before leaving South Carolina, Clinton tried to subdue as much of the countryside as possible. Cornwallis, who would be taking com-mand in the South, assisted. Unfortunately, neither of them had any political sense, and in the short time Clinton remained, he threw away his military victory by making political decisions that, instead of secur-ing the countryside, ignited a vicious civil war that Cornwallis inher-ited and could never stamp out.

There were probably sixty to seventy thousand people in South Carolina, and perhaps 20 percent were Tories. In order to regain control for the king, Clinton had to win over the uncommitted, which he had no idea how to do. Converting a military victory, even one as decisive as this one, into a lasting political transformation of the state was beyond him. His political missteps, instead of securing victory, only served to swell patriot ranks.

As a mark of Clinton's naiveté, he employed rabid Tories exclusively and let them settle scores. The estates of prominent landowners were confiscated, adding to the ranks of the guerrillas who would bedevil Cornwallis. The worst of Clinton's mistakes was allowing the wild romp of twenty-six-year-old Lieutenant Colonel Tarleton, who led a detachment of dragoons known as the British Legion into the Waxhaws, in the Piedmont region, and did more for the patriot cause in an afternoon than General Lincoln's entire army did in months.

On May 29 the aggressive, talented, utterly ruthless Tarleton caught up with a unit of retreating Virginia Continentals under the command of Colonel Abraham Buford. The patriots actually outnumbered the British dragoons, but in the course of the afternoon, Tarleton's cavalry slaughtered the patriots, slashing with sabers helpless men on the ground who were pleading for mercy. "Tarleton's Quarter" became a famous patriot rallying cry.

Another example of Clinton's more egregious political mistakes was in the beginning paroling all males in the colony, which was widely popular, and then immediately reversing himself. His initial announcement meant that men could go about their business and be left alone, which a great many did, but when he reversed himself he kicked over a political hornet's nest with no idea he had done so. His new proclamation made every male take an oath of allegiance to the king, requiring each to "be ready to maintain and defend the . . . [oath] against all persons whatsoever." This meant that every man might be required to fight against his countrymen, something most would never do. South Carolina's political divisions were polarized, and many young fighters were added to the patriots' ranks.

Before leaving, Clinton believed he had the political situation well in hand. He assumed that Cornwallis would have no trouble holding South Carolina and that he would use it as a base to conquer the rest of the South. But he was wrong. Cornwallis had no more idea of how to treat the country people than Clinton did. He needlessly stirred up a mountain of trouble when he ordered his men to go into the interior and "extinguish the rebellion." This they attempted, but the bitter partisan fighting that had already started grew far more intense, marked by wanton destruction and murder. Allowing Lieutenant Colonel Tarleton, Major Patrick Ferguson, Major James Wemyss, Captain Christian Huck, and their colleagues free rein had the effect of swelling rebel ranks. William Moultrie accused the British of exercising "the most savage cruelty."

Cornwallis, who should have known better, was demonstrating, not just to the South but to the entire country, what was in store if the British succeeded in putting down the rebellion. As an example of his ham-handed tactics, his rampaging men burned down the home of Brigadier General Thomas Sumter after he became head of the South Carolina militia. Sumter sought his revenge by becoming an important guerrilla leader, along with Francis Marion, Andrew Pickens, William Harden, Charles McDowell, Griffith Rutherford, Henry William Harrington, and several others. Some months later a bewildered Cornwallis would look back and declare that there were times when he felt that "there was scarce an inhabitant . . . that was not in arms against us." He had no idea why, or what to do about it, other than to impose more vicious repression.

★

WHEN CLINTON AND ARBUTHNOT DEPARTED CHARLESTON on June 8, they were being hailed in London and New York as heroes. In the eyes of George III and his New York Loyalists, the victory at Charleston was enormous. They expected the king's southern strategy to finally suppress the cursed rebellion. Clinton was the man of the hour, just as General Howe had been after the Battle of Brooklyn. Even though Arbuthnot had been of little help, Lord Sandwich and the ministry credited him with being an essential partner in the great victory. His reputation at the Admiralty soared.

Before leaving Charleston, Clinton made it clear to Cornwallis that securing the city and the rest of South Carolina must be his first priority. He was to move into North Carolina and Virginia only when South

Carolina was secure. In issuing these instructions Clinton was confident that keeping South Carolina would not present any great difficulties. He thought that he had already accomplished almost all that needed to be done.

Cornwallis, for his part, was delighted to see the back of both Clinton and Arbuthnot. He had become so unhappy with them that on May 13, long before Clinton left for New York, he requested that Lord Amherst recall him and send him to any other place in the world. Oddly, neither Amherst nor anyone else in authority in London took the request seriously.

In ten days Clinton was in New York, arriving on June 18 with four thousand men. His unhappiness with Arbuthnot had not abated; he was disgusted with him, feeling that he could never trust him. The man was a complete mystery to him. Arbuthnot felt the same about Clinton, whose icy treatment infuriated him. Their personal feud became more important than their mission and would have a profound effect on the war.

Chapter 22

BENEDICT ARNOLD'S
BETRAYAL

The Clinton-Arbuthnot feud did not cause any alarm in London. Although known, it was not considered a big enough problem to warrant recalling either of them. Success in Georgia and Charleston was proof that it did not interfere with the war effort. Of far greater importance was that at long last victory seemed within reach. Germain was particularly sanguine. He wrote to Clinton on May 3, 1780—even before receiving news of Charleston—informing him that all the private letters he was receiving from America announced great distress and a "universal wish for peace. The middle provinces are said to be so disinclined to support the Congress . . . no recruits are to be had, and the militia will not submit to be drafted. Their only resort for continuing the war seemed to be a foreign aid, which, however, has not been sent to them; and therefore I flatter myself that you will have met but little interruption in your progress northward after the reduction of Charleston, and that you will have sufficient time to execute your plan in the Chesapeake, or at least to establish yourself there beyond the power of any force, which can be brought to dislodge you."

At the time, there appeared little to stop Clinton's "progress northward." America's southern army was in shambles, and Washington's main army in New York, after a dreadful winter, was in no condition to be of service in the South. The feckless states (now twelve in number) refused to give Congress the powers necessary to carry on the war. They jealously withheld the indispensable ability to tax—even imports. Without the capacity to raise money, Congress could not support the currency. Reliance on the states was near total, and soldiers' wages were five months in arrears. They were not even certain where their next meal was coming from. The only thing that could save the rebellion was French aid, and that was uncertain.

After much debate, Congress responded to the Charleston disaster and the rampaging of Cornwallis's lieutenants by appointing General Horatio Gates to command the Southern Department. Washington was deliberately not consulted. He never would have recommended Gates, which was well known. Gates had eagerly sought the assignment, insisting, no doubt, that he would carry on an offensive campaign against the enemy, in contrast to Washington, who had been on the defensive for months.

Gates knew that he faced a daunting task rebuilding the southern army. His supporters in Congress were hoping that he'd work the magic he was supposed to have performed at Saratoga and draw a large militia army to his banner.

Washington would be of little help. He did not want to send troops south to fight under Gates. He thought that if he were forced to reduce his army, he could never take action in the North. As far as he was concerned, New York was still where the war would be won or lost.

At the moment, there was little hope for Washington to go on offense. He had all he could do to hold his shrinking army together. Even though Clinton and Arbuthnot had taken a huge chunk of the British army south, Washington still could not muster enough troops to threaten Manhattan. By April 1780 only seven thousand Continentals remained in the New Jersey camps, and thirteen hundred of them would terminate their service on May 1.

On May 28, Washington wrote to Joseph Reed, the president of Pennsylvania: "I assure you, every idea you can form of our distresses will fall short of the reality. There is such a combination of circumstances to exhaust the patience of the soldiery, that it begins at length to be worn out, and we see in every line of the army the most serious features of mutiny and sedition."

Deserters were going to New York in numbers that hadn't been seen before. William Smith, the Tory lawyer and Clinton confidant, interviewed many of them and became convinced that Washington was far weaker than Clinton imagined. Smith saw unmistakable signs that the patriot political base was shrinking dramatically. A vigorous attack on Washington, he thought, might end the war right then.

While Washington was lamenting his situation, help was on the way. Lafayette was returning from France, where he had been since the winter of 1779, and he was bringing very good news. On May 10 he arrived in Morristown and informed Washington that seven French sail of the line, under Charles-Henri-Louis d'Arsac, Chevalier de Ternay, and five thousand soldiers, under Jean-Baptiste Donatien de Vimeur, Comte de Rochambeau, were on the way to America. He also told Washington that a second, more potent, expeditionary force was being prepared as well, and it would sail from Brest soon. Of course, a British blockade offshore was always possible, but the ever-optimistic Lafayette thought that the second task force would get to sea as easily as the first. The Admiralty had been aware of preparations at Brest for Ternay and Rochambeau and had made no effort to stop them. Lafayette could not be certain that Sandwich would be indifferent a second time, but he thought it was likely.

Germain informed Clinton that the French were coming, and probably heading for Newfoundland, Halifax, or Quebec. He directed him to reinforce General Haldimand in Canada, which Clinton did.

The news was a great boost for Washington, who felt an overpowering need to take advantage of the French force and attack New York as soon as possible. He was growing increasingly worried about the prospect of a prolonged war. Neither the patriots nor the French could sustain one, he thought. In a long war, France—even combined with Spain—would falter. France's war effort rested on an archaic financial system. Britain, on the other hand, with her solid commercial base and modern economy, could survive a lengthy fight. "The maritime resources of Great Britain are more substantial and real than those of France and Spain united," Washington wrote to Joseph Reed. "Her commerce is more extensive, than that of both of her rivals; and it is an axiom, that the nation which has the most extensive commerce will always have the most powerful marine." He thought that it was imperative for the Franco-American alliance to strike a mortal blow soon. And, as it turned out, Paris, for different reasons, felt the same.

Washington hoped to coordinate a joint attack on New York while Clinton and Cornwallis were occupied in the South. During the first week in June, he used the authority Congress had given him to call up troops. On the second he sought a draft of militia from New England and the Mid-Atlantic states of seventeen thousand, which would have brought his army up to twenty-five thousand. What he actually received were six thousand raw recruits.

For an attack on New York, Washington needed not only a larger army but a much stronger navy. Command of the sea was essential. He asked Lafayette to communicate with Admiral Luc Urbain de Bouëxic, Comte de Guichen, France's most accomplished admiral, whose huge fleet was in the Caribbean, to come north and participate in an attack on Manhattan. If Ternay combined with de Guichen, the allies would dominate the water.

To allow him to make important decisions faster, Washington asked Congress to appoint a select committee to be at his side. His intention was that certain decisions that only Congress could make would be decided quickly and not hamper military operations. But Congress did not like the idea, and it was dropped.

Even though Washington failed to mount an attack on New York before Clinton and Arbuthnot returned from Charleston, he had high hopes of doing so when the French arrived. If nothing else, they would certainly boost the lagging spirits of the patriots, who seemed to be floundering.

The French had already succeeded in weakening the enemy. By sending a relatively small task force to the American coast, they forced Clinton to hurry back to Manhattan and divide his army.

★

WHEN CLINTON LEFT CHARLESTON, HE WAS UNCERTAIN where Rochambeau would land, but he soon received intelligence from Benedict Arnold confirming that it would be Rhode Island. Arnold was trying desperately to reestablish communications with the commander in chief, and he had succeeded. Clinton was now convinced that the traitor was for real. He was putting great stock in the information Arnold was feeding him.

Sometime during the winter of 1780 Arnold made the final decision to betray his country. Before doing so, he made one last attempt to solve his money problems by brazenly asking the new French minister in Philadelphia, the Chevalier de la Luzerne, for a large loan. Luzerne turned him down. After this humiliating episode, he approached his influential friend Congressman Philip Schuyler and inquired about appointment to command West Point. The position included not only the fortress itself on the west side of the Hudson but the forts at Stony Point and Verplanck's Point, the posts on the east side of the river from Fishkill to King's Ferry, and a corps of Continentals whose domain stretched down to North Castle.

Peggy Shippen Arnold used her friendship with Chancellor Robert R. Livingston, the powerful New York congressman, to convince him that Arnold should have command of the Hudson fortress. Livingston had no qualms about pressuring Washington. Livingston's family had always admired Arnold for his close association with their hero Major General Richard Montgomery (Livingston's brother-in-law) and for his gallantry at Lake Champlain in 1776 and at Saratoga in 1777.

Apart from monetary gain, Arnold's motivation for selling out his country remains a mystery. He may have thought that the American war effort had sunk so low it was beyond recall. The defeat at Charleston, the condition of the army at Morristown, and the state of the currency were signs that the revolt was on its last legs. Congress hadn't improved. And the profiteering going on in Philadelphia had only become more outlandish. He may have concluded that he had better act and exact a large price from the British before it was too late. Whatever his motivation, he did act, and he had a powerful impact on Clinton and the war.

Once Clinton knew where the French were going, he made plans to destroy their task force. Even though his army was divided, it was still powerful enough to keep Washington at bay while he attacked Newport. Clinton now had twenty thousand men, with close to fifteen thousand fit for duty in New York and Long Island. Cornwallis had almost seven thousand, with five thousand fit for duty, and an additional fifteen hundred in Georgia.

Overwhelming naval superiority made Clinton's task much easier. And the Admiralty was sending six sail of the line, under Rear Admiral Thomas Graves, to bolster Arbuthnot. If all went well, Graves, with copper-bottomed ships, would arrive in America at the same time the French did.

Unfortunately, Graves would be junior to Arbuthnot. Clinton would still be saddled with a colleague he wasn't even speaking to. When they left Charleston, they were communicating by letter and messenger only. Their relations had become actively hostile. Arbuthnot would have been difficult for anyone, but so, too, was Clinton. Throughout the war, he found it impossible to work with either superiors or equals. His biographer wrote, "As a colleague, he would have tried the patience of a saint."

The first order of business for Clinton after he got to New York was a strike on Washington in New Jersey. He hoped to hit him hard before the French arrived. If he could defeat Washington in New Jersey and the French in Newport, Paris might conclude, after the debacle at Charleston, that the rebel cause was never going to prosper, and that a settlement should be negotiated with London.

When Clinton reached Manhattan, however, he found that Knyphausen had already made a surprise attack in New Jersey on June 6 with five thousand men. To Knyphausen's great surprise, his troops met determined opposition not only from Washington and Greene but from New Jersey militiamen. Clinton took over command of the attack, but his intervention didn't work out as he had hoped, and he returned to New York to prepare for the strike on Newport, which was of far greater importance to him.

He had in mind an immediate attack to prevent the French from even landing. He thought that when they discovered that Newport was closed to them, they would find another place—Boston, the Delaware, or the Chesapeake. Whichever it was, it would be greatly inferior to Newport and would make any attempt on New York far more difficult, if not impossible.

By June 22 Clinton had 6,700 troops ready to attack, but Arbuthnot would not cooperate. He claimed that they needed more accurate intelligence on where the French actually were going before making a move. Clinton dismissed his excuse as nonsense and took it as a personal rebuke, which it certainly was.

The mission that Clinton felt held so much promise was suspended while Arbuthnot waited for intelligence he didn't need. He was not convinced that the French were going to Newport—or so he claimed. He thought the Delaware or the Chesapeake were more likely places. Clinton was livid, but there was nothing he could do about it. Finally, on July 5 Arbuthnot's frigates spotted Ternay off Virginia. Their reports reached him on July 7, but by then Ternay's squadron had vanished. Arbuthnot's frigates lost him, which gave the admiral another excuse to delay.

———

At the same time that Clinton was planning his campaign against the French, he received information from Mr. Moore (Benedict Arnold) that would color all his thinking. On June 12 Arnold, using the elaborate cipher he had worked out with André the year before, told Clinton that Washington had given him command of West Point. Although he did not actually have the appointment, he felt certain he would have it soon. Actually, he was given command on August 3. Clinton could not have been more pleased. Capturing West Point was what he wanted more than anything else. He still believed it was a quick and relatively easy way to win the war.

The knowledge that West Point was now within his grasp made attacking Newport less urgent. Of course he still wanted to. Defeating the French and seizing West Point would go a long way toward ending the war.

Clinton had a high appreciation of the chance he was taking. He could not be absolutely certain that communications from Arnold were not part of an elaborate plot concocted by Washington. Naturally cautious, Clinton proceeded with the intention of going along with Arnold, whom he was inclined to trust, but watching carefully for any sign of betrayal. It was, at best, a dicey business, but the rewards were potentially so enormous he could not pass up the opportunity.

On July 11, while Arbuthnot was still searching for the French, Rochambeau and Ternay, who had departed Brest on May 2, slipped into Narragansett Bay with troops and ships in desperate need of care after their long voyage. It took Arbuthnot and Clinton a full week to discover they were actually there. Apparently they had no lookouts on the ground or frigates offshore watching Narragansett Bay.

Clinton wanted to attack immediately, while the French were most vulnerable, but, again, Arbuthnot would not agree. He continued to delay, which allowed the French not only to recover but to organize a stout defense. Washington supported them in a number of ways, including sending New England militiamen to Newport and making a timely feint against New York.

All of this happened while the British were far superior to the French. Arbuthnot had one 90, four 74s, four 64s, two 50s, plus a heavy frigate; Ternay had one 80; five 64s, and five frigates. And Clinton's regulars were more than a match for French soldiers not yet recovered from their voyage.

On July 13, two days after the French arrived, Rear Admiral Thomas Graves landed in New York with six sail of the line—all of them faster, more maneuverable, and far more durable than the French ships, which didn't have copper bottoms. The British now had even greater superiority on the water. Seven hundred of Graves's men were sick, but they recovered quickly.

Despite missing the opportunity to strike the French when they were at their weakest, Clinton still planned to attack them. Six days later, on July 19, Arbuthnot was ready to put to sea with the combined squadrons. His refurbishing of Graves's ships was done so fast that it looked as if he were finally going to cooperate, but that was misleading. While Clinton was drawing up specific plans for the attack and submitting them to Arbuthnot, the admiral continued to dither.

It appeared that Arbuthnot, without saying so, was determined not to get involved in another joint operation with Clinton. He was not going to have a repeat of Charleston. It looked as if he would only fight if the French fleet in Newport came out to challenge him, which was highly unlikely. Thus on the nineteenth, instead of pressing the attack, he announced that he was sailing to Narragansett Bay to reconnoiter, which wasn't needed. In the meantime, he suggested that Clinton move his 6,700 troops to Huntington Bay on Long Island to be closer to the enemy. There was nothing Clinton could do but comply. He arrived in Huntington Bay with his men on July 28.

Two days later, he received word from Arbuthnot that an attack on Newport wasn't possible—the French were too well fortified, and the rebels had significantly reinforced them. Clinton knew this was more of Arbuthnot's foot-dragging, but since he could do nothing without him, he gave up and withdrew to New York, leaving the French to grow stronger by the day. Clinton's chance of winning a decisive victory and possibly ending the war was thus needlessly lost, while a major French base was established within striking distance of New York.

Later, in a letter to Lord Sandwich, Admiral Sir George Brydges Rodney explained why occupying Rhode Island was so important. In his opinion, Narragansett Bay contained

> the best and noblest harbor in America, capable of containing the whole navy of Britain, and whence they could in all seasons lay in perfect security; and from whence squadrons, in forty-eight hours could blockade the three capital cities of America, namely, Boston, New York, and Philadelphia. France wisely took advantage of our misconduct, and had used every endeavour to make it almost impregnable.
>
> Had not this place [Newport] been evacuated [in 1779], the French must have sheltered themselves in the Delaware or Chesapeake, where they could have been easily blockaded, which is not the case at Rhode Island, off which it is too dangerous for squadrons to cruise in the spring, autumn, or winter months, as your Lordships may perceive by Mr. Arbuthnot's laying with his squadron in Gardiner's Bay, which is eighteen leagues to leeward of Rhode Island, and where, if Monsieur Ternay's squadron sails with the wind, from N.W. to N.E., Mr. Arbuthnot cannot possibly move in time to intercept him.

Having stopped the momentum for a joint attack on Newport, Arbuthnot brought his entire fleet to Gardiner's Bay, at the eastern end of Long Island, seventy miles closer to Newport than Huntington Bay. He planned to keep watch on Ternay from there. He then issued a tantalizing invitation to meet Clinton face-to-face. It was immediately accepted, and after a difficult overland journey, Clinton arrived at Gardiner's Bay on August 18. To his amazement, Arbuthnot wasn't there. He had left with his fleet; they had gone to sea, ostensibly to counter Ternay, who had supposedly sortied from Narragansett Bay, which he hadn't. Clinton couldn't believe he was being stood up, and left in a rage. Any slim chance remaining for an attack on Newport went with him.

Although the French were now well established in Newport, their force wasn't nearly enough to do what Washington and Rochambeau wanted. They had to wait for the second French task force. Lafayette was anxious to fight right then, but Rochambeau, who was his senior and far more experienced, would not budge. Neither would Ternay, who demanded unquestioned naval superiority before attacking New York. Even with the expected second expeditionary force, the allies might not have enough. To defeat Clinton in New York Washington needed an additional French fleet similar to the one d'Estaing had brought to Savannah the previous year.

It was possible that one would be coming from the Caribbean after the start of hurricane season. In the meantime, Washington worked hard to bring his army up to twenty-five thousand or thirty thousand men. He solicited help from governors and ordered General Knox to gather all the cannon and stores in the patriots' possession for a siege and the service of a campaign. "Apply to the Board of War, to the Quartermaster General, and to the executives of those states where the cannon and stores now are, for the requisite assistance," he told Knox.

★

WHILE WASHINGTON WAS BUSY AND HOPEFUL IN THE NORTH, the Southern Department was going from bad to worse. On August 16 Lord Cornwallis defeated General Gates in an important battle five miles north of Camden, South Carolina. The news was a shock. Washington briefly considered rushing south with his army, and perhaps Rochambeau's, but then thought better of it. He needed to guard West Point, and Rochambeau was unlikely to agree to a southern campaign under existing conditions. Washington also thought that he could help the southern army more by threatening New York and preventing Clinton from sending reinforcements to Cornwallis.

When Congress appointed Gates on June 13, his supporters had high hopes for a repeat of Saratoga. But the Gates they imagined to have won in upstate New York was not the Gates Cornwallis beat decisively at Camden. On July 25 Gates had arrived full of energy and ambition at Deep River, a small branch of the Cape Fear River, to take command of what was left of the southern army. Major General Johann (Baron) de Kalb, a solid, experienced officer, was there to greet him. Washington had sent de Kalb south in April with fourteen hundred Continentals from Maryland and Delaware to reinforce General Lincoln at Charleston, but de Kalb arrived too late. His well-trained corps was now the heart of the southern army.

De Kalb was surprised to find that Gates was anxious to take the offensive—much too anxious, under the circumstances. Gates's personal strength was in organization and administration. He could have spent at least some time building the southern army before fighting experienced British regulars under Lord Cornwallis. Daniel Morgan, who liked Gates and had kept up with him after Saratoga—even visiting his plantation in Virginia—was coming on with men he was gathering to fight in the southern army. But Gates would not even wait for Morgan, the finest combat leader in the American army.

For some reason, Gates wanted immediate action. With little preparation, and troops that were in no condition for a long march, he set out two days later—against de Kalb's advice—to surprise Lieutenant Colonel Francis Rawdon, Cornwallis's second in command and an excellent fighter. Gates had around 3,050 men, two-thirds of whom were inexperienced militiamen; Rawdon had 2,000 regulars camped near Camden. Gates intended to pounce on Rawdon and win a quick victory that he hoped would give heart to the entire southern enterprise, as well as impress his political supporters in Philadelphia.

In order to get to Rawdon as quickly as possible, Gates took a direct route rather than the one recommended by officers who knew the ground. Instead of marching through Mecklenburg County, where he would have political and material assistance, he marched through barren Loyalist country ill-suited to the troops' needs. His movements were anything but secret. Cornwallis soon had wind of them and quietly moved reinforcements to the area, catching Gates by surprise.

On August 16 the battle was joined, and Cornwallis badly mauled Gates's militiamen, who were in full retreat almost from the start. And what was far worse, their general ran with them. Baron de Kalb stood with the experienced Continentals and fought well, but they were overwhelmed. Gates, who seemed to have somehow gotten caught up in the hysterical retreat, abandoned de Kalb while he was still fighting and fled to Charlotte, a distance of sixty miles, and then quickly moved on to Hillsborough, one hundred and eighty miles from Camden. While he did, 1,050 patriots remained on the battlefield, either dead or wounded—the worst casualty totals for the Americans of any battle during the war.

On August 25, only nine days after Gates had been defeated, Washington received even more bad news. The second French expeditionary force wasn't coming after all. He wasn't sure why.

Chapter 23

RODNEY

As if Washington did not have enough problems, on September 14 an even bigger one suddenly arrived off Sandy Hook—Admiral Sir George Brydges Rodney with ten sail of the line. No one was expecting him. All of a sudden, it looked as if Clinton had an opportunity to end the war by acquiring Newport and West Point, as well as opening a second southern front on Chesapeake Bay to aid Cornwallis.

After Lord Howe, sixty-two-year-old George Rodney was Britain's premier fighting admiral. Unlike Howe, he was someone Sandwich got along with, although not all the time. Over the years, he and Sandwich had had serious disagreements—usually about money. Fortunately for both of them, Rodney's politics were the same as the first lord's and the king's. He had no desire to negotiate a settlement with the rebels; he simply wanted to crush them.

Rodney came from an old family that traced its ancestry back to Tudor times in the sixteenth century. He had had a life of privilege, with all the benefits that wealth and family connections brought to a young man in eighteenth-century England. After education in the rough-and-tumble of Harrow he joined the navy at the age of fourteen and was a midshipman the following year. He was promoted to lieutenant in 1749, and to captain three years later. Appointment to post captain came five years after that. Advancement to admiral was a matter of seniority. Rodney was finally promoted to rear admiral of the blue in May 1759. His naval career was extensive. He had served with distinction in the War of the Austrian Succession during the forties and the Seven Years' War the following decade.

He would have been employed early in the American war, and certainly against France when she entered, had it not been for his personal life, which was in complete disarray from his having run up huge gambling debts he could not pay. Even though he had been needed long before, he did not get involved in the fighting until September 16, 1779, when, relieved of his crushing burden of debt by, of all people, a French aristocrat, the duc de Biron, he was appointed commander in chief of the Leeward Islands station.

Rodney's reputation as a talented, aggressive sea warrior was well known. In fact, at the moment, he was a great hero in England, having saved Gibraltar in spectacular fashion from a long Spanish siege. His celebrated mission began on December 23, 1779, shortly after his appointment to command the Leeward Islands station. He was on his way there via Gibraltar when he departed Spithead with twenty-two sail of the line and eight frigates. Persistent gout was bothering him, but he carried on. His squadron was guarding three hundred fully stocked transports on their way to relieve Gibraltar.

Throughout his career, Rodney had had remarkably good luck, and it was no different during this voyage. On January 9 he happened on a luckless Spanish fleet off Cape Finisterre. Fifteen transports, loaded with supplies, and seven warships were suddenly there for the taking. In a few hours he captured every one of them, before moving on, integrating the Spanish supply vessels with his own as he went.

When he sailed down the Iberian coast toward Gibraltar, his good fortune continued. On January 16 lookouts spotted fourteen Spanish sail of the line off Cape St. Vincent. Their admiral, Don Juan de Langara, aghast at seeing the immense British fleet, naturally tried to run, but Rodney's copper-bottomed ships caught him as night approached. The weather was tempestuous, and Rodney's gout was enough to send him to bed, but he wasn't going to let this opportunity pass. He pressed a night attack, directing the fight from his bed, and either captured or destroyed every one of Langara's ships.

When the one-sided battle was over, Rodney moved on to break the siege of Gibraltar and become the toast of London. After this immense achievement, he sailed for the West Indies to take up his command and battle the French West Indian fleet.

When Rodney arrived in New York in September of 1780 (with his gout still acting up), he was in pursuit of the very same French fleet he had been battling in the Caribbean under the Comte de Guichen. They had dueled during April and May without result. Their first encounter was off Martinique on April 7, the second on May 15, and the last on May 19. Although not decisive, Rodney had the better of it, which he wasn't fully aware of. De Guichen was too banged up to come north, and in any event he had no orders to do so. While Rodney rushed to New York, de Guichen limped back to Europe licking his wounds. Making his return even more painful, his son, whom he doted on, wasn't with him. He had been killed in the April battle. Rodney's son also fought with him, but he survived unharmed.

Rodney had no idea de Guichen was returning to France; he naturally assumed he would come north to the American coast during hurricane season, just as d'Estaing had done the previous two years. Rodney felt he had to counter him, especially since a friendly vessel in the Caribbean warned him that a French squadron of seven sail of the line had anchored in Narragansett Bay. Rodney feared that de Guichen might be headed for New York to combine with Ternay and give the French and Americans an overwhelming advantage at sea.

As Rodney made his way up the American coast, he planned to combine forces with Arbuthnot and Clinton to fight both de Guichen and the French in Newport. Since de Guichen wasn't there, Rodney assumed that taking Newport would be comparatively easy. He expected to be welcomed with open arms in New York by Clinton, but not by Arbuthnot. He was bringing enough firepower to accomplish whatever Clinton had in mind, but he would be taking over command from Arbuthnot, who would not be pleased.

Actually, he was in for a bit of a surprise. Arbuthnot's negative reaction was beyond anything Rodney had anticipated. Arbuthnot threw a tantrum, behaving as if he had been handed a poisonous snake. No sooner had Rodney dropped anchor off New York than he unceremoniously informed Arbuthnot that he was taking over command. It was something Arbuthnot feared the moment he heard that Rodney was at Sandy Hook. Rodney might have been more gentle in giving the news to Arbuthnot, but it would not have made any difference. Arbuthnot was about to lose a lot of money. Rodney would now control all patronage and prize money on the North American station, which Arbuthnot felt were his, and which he was counting on for his retirement. None of this mattered to Rodney; he was going to take whatever he wanted, and he did. Clinton could not have been more pleased to see Arbuthnot's discomfort.

Long before Rodney got to New York, he had formed a low opinion of Arbuthnot. On his way up the American coast from the Caribbean he had seen none of His Majesty's warships—not a single one—but he had seen plenty of what he assumed were enemy privateers, as well as merchant vessels. He wondered why the admiral at New York couldn't spare even a single frigate to patrol those waters.

Needless to say, Henry Clinton was overjoyed to see Rodney. He could scarcely believe his good luck. Since Rodney was now the senior naval officer on the North American station, he solved the Arbuthnot problem for Clinton. At this particular moment, Arbuthnot had become an even bigger headache than he had been before. His refusal to work with Clinton was about to become a major obstacle to the cherished goal of obtaining West Point. Clinton and André were making final arrangements with General Arnold for turning over the fortress. In a matter of days, as soon as André and Arnold worked out the details, Clinton would need a potent amphibious force to race up the Hudson and seize the fort, whose garrison now had 3,086 men. If Arbuthnot continued to evade any joint action, he could destroy all of Clinton's plans. With Rodney on the scene there was nothing to worry about.

Rodney was captivated when he heard the details about West Point. The story of how Arnold was about to hand it over delighted him. For Rodney, capturing West Point meant gaining control of the Hudson and the entire corridor to Canada, which, in his mind, meant winning the war. As he explained to Sandwich, "The rebels look upon it [West Point] as their *dernier resort,* and would have been undone had the scheme with Arnold succeeded."

Since Arnold was going to give them West Point, Rodney expected to take Newport as well. He also wanted to establish a secure base at the mouth of Chesapeake Bay. He thought that they could do all three in a relatively short time and win the war. The prospect of being the hero who solved the American conundrum excited him like nothing else had.

It soon became apparent, however, that Clinton did not want to embark on a joint operation against Newport or the Chesapeake right away. Even with Arnold's indispensable help, he did not think that West Point was going to fall easily. He wanted to be prepared for whatever happened, and that meant concentrating exclusively on capturing the fortress. Matters were swiftly coming to a head; Clinton did not want to be distracted by anything else.

Rodney's sudden appearance forced Washington and Rochambeau to rethink their plans. Rodney's fleet foreclosed any possibility of an attack on New York, unless de Guichen also appeared. They had urged him to come north and still hoped that he might. Lafayette and Luzerne sent him letters pointing out how important he would be to the allied cause. Unfortunately, on August 16 de Guichen had already sailed from Cap François to Europe with a fleet in need of extensive repairs.

Clinton, meanwhile, continued gathering the troops and ships for the strike on West Point and making final arrangements with Arnold.

André and Loyalist Beverley Robinson had arranged to meet face-to-face with Arnold on September 11, but the meeting was aborted when Arnold's barge was fired on by a patrol boat. Six days later, while André was in the middle of making other arrangements, he was presented with another incredible opportunity—capturing Washington. On September 15 Arnold sent a hurried message to André: "General Washington will be at King's Ferry Sunday evening [September 17] next on his way to Hartford, where he is to meet the French admiral and General. And will lodge at Peekskill."

Washington had informed Arnold that he would cross the Hudson at King's Ferry and stay in Peekskill at the home of Joshua Hett Smith, William Smith's brother. A more inappropriate place for the American commander in chief was hard to imagine, which Washington would soon find out. But for now, he had no inkling of what was afoot. He intended to have dinner there and invited Arnold so that he could speak with him about strengthening West Point against a possible attack now that Rodney was on the scene.

Fortunately, Arnold's message did not reach André in time. Clinton was left to ponder what would have happened had he been able to capture both West Point and Washington at the same time.

Not only was Arnold trying to hand over Washington, he was attempting to give Clinton the identities of as many patriot spies in New York as possible. He approached Lafayette for the names of the spies working for him, but Lafayette refused to give him any. He did not think that the request was unusual, since it was coming from the commandant of West Point.

Arnold tried to pry the same information out of General Robert Howe, his predecessor at West Point, but Howe also refused. Unlike Lafayette, he thought the request, and the way it was made, more than a little odd, but he never dreamed it was part of Arnold's attempt to get the maximum amount of money from Clinton.

Meanwhile, plans to capture West Point moved forward. On September 15 Arnold sent another message to André, proposing that they meet on September 20 between 11:00 and midnight. It was the same day that Arnold received the message from Washington indicating he would be at Peekskill.

By September 19, the day before André and Arnold were to meet, everything was proceeding as planned. Clinton and Rodney were readying troops and ships, and André was preparing for his face-to-face encounter with Arnold. Clinton still did not know for sure that Arnold wasn't playing a part in an elaborate deception. André had to decide if Arnold was legitimate when he met him, but he had no doubts. He trusted Arnold and eagerly looked forward to seeing him in the flesh.

Clinton gave André specific orders to protect him if things went awry and he was taken prisoner. When he met Arnold, he was to be in uniform, refuse any incriminating papers, and never cross enemy lines. If he followed these simple instructions and got caught, he would be a prisoner of war, not a spy subject to hanging.

After missing each other again the night of September 20, André and Arnold finally met on the twenty-first, at Joshua Hett Smith's House, the same place Washington had stayed four days earlier. André came up the Hudson in the 14-gun sloop of war *Vulture*, dressed in his uniform, expecting to go back the same way.

The most important question for him was whether Arnold was for real. Arranging their meeting had become so difficult—their plan having misfired again only the day before—that Clinton had to think that maybe the whole business was a trap. Arnold had no trouble convincing André that it wasn't, however. André, for his part, told Arnold what he most wanted to hear—namely, that he would receive £20,000 if the plot against West Point and its garrison came off and £6,000 if it did not. While going over detailed plans, Arnold gave André a written statement on the overall condition of Washington's army, the garrison at West Point, the number of men considered necessary for the defense of it, a return of the ordnance, and the disposition of the artillery corps in case of alarm. André, demonstrating what a novice he was, accepted the papers he was offered, even though none of them were actually needed to take the fortress.

When André was finished with Arnold, he assumed that Smith

would be taking him back to the *Vulture*, but the sloop had come under fire earlier and had been forced to sail downstream. Instead of waiting for the *Vulture* to return, André took off his uniform and put on a civilian disguise, placing Arnold's papers inside his boot. He and Smith then crossed from the west side of the Hudson to the east side and rode through patriot-held territory toward British lines near White Plains. André, posing as Mr. John Anderson, was nervous about doing everything Clinton had ordered him not to do—taking off his uniform, going into enemy territory, and carrying incriminating documents, but, conscious of the need to act fast, he decided that he could get away with it.

Before long they reached sentries guarding American lines, and after a perfunctory check, they were permitted to rest for the night. In the morning André continued on alone into Westchester County's neutral ground, the no-man's-land between the American and British lines. It wasn't long before he was stopped suddenly by three patriot militiamen, John Paulding, Isaac Van Wart, and David Williams. Paulding had on a Hessian overcoat, which led André to think he had run into friendly troops. He let down his guard and revealed who he was, sealing his fate. Andre's own account of the incident was that he simply was taken "by three volunteers who, not satisfied with my pass [given by Arnold], rifled me and, finding papers, made me a prisoner."

Washington's meeting in Hartford with the French leaders on September 20 went well. With Lafayette acting as interpreter, he spent a full day closeted with Rochambeau and Ternay, going over plans for defending Newport, which was now at great risk with Rodney in the picture. They discussed the general outlines of a strategy to attack New York City and Brooklyn Heights, if the opportunity presented itself.

Washington explained their thinking to Brigadier General Knox: "In the conference between Count Rochambeau and myself it was agreed, if by the aid of our allies we can have a naval superiority through the next campaign, and an army of thirty thousand men, or double the force of the enemy at New York and its dependencies, early enough in the season to operate in that quarter, we ought to prefer it to every other object, as the most important and decisive. And applications have been made to the court of France in this spirit, which it is to be hoped will produce the desired effect."

Rochambeau and Washington were going for the jugular, but they obviously could not make specific plans about New York until they knew if de Guichen was coming north. Nonetheless, they both thought that the conference had been a success. Perhaps as important as anything else, at the end of an exhausting day, they felt confident that they could work together harmoniously—a significant achievement in itself.

All during the conference, West Point was on Washington's mind. Given the new strength and vitality Rodney brought to British operations, the fortress would be a natural target. Washington needed to make certain it was ready for an assault. He had confidence in Arnold, but he wanted to view the defenses for himself.

After leaving Hartford, he rode with Lafayette, Knox, Hamilton, and other aides toward the fort. On the way, he met Luzerne, the French minister, by chance, and spent a day with him in Peekskill before resuming his trip. Their meeting, although not planned, turned out to be important. Washington went over what had been discussed at Hartford, and then impressed on Luzerne how important it was for the commander of the West Indian fleet to have specific orders to come to the American coast with his entire squadron during hurricane season and cooperate in a joint attack on New York. Luzerne needed no convincing. He had long held the view that a huge French fleet was crucial.

Washington left the French envoy on September 25 and proceeded directly to West Point. When he was approaching Arnold's headquarters (the former home of Beverley Robinson), he sent two aides ahead to prepare the household for his arrival. Everything appeared in order when the aides reached the mansion. Arnold greeted them cordially and appeared ready to receive the commander in chief, until a mysterious letter was delivered to him. He opened it, read it without changing expression, and went upstairs to talk with his wife. Returning shortly, he called for his horse and left abruptly.

When Washington arrived later, Arnold wasn't there. His aide, Major David Franks, informed Washington that an emergency at the fort had required Arnold's personal attention. Washington couldn't imagine what it might be, but he graciously told Franks to prepare breakfast, and said that he would see Arnold at the fort when he inspected it. Peggy Shippen Arnold, who remained upstairs, was said to be unwell.

Actually, Arnold was racing to get away. He had been found out. The letter he had received was from American lieutenant colonel John Jameson, in command at North Castle, revealing André's capture and the incriminating documents found on him. The three patriots who had originally captured André had brought him to Jameson.

Arnold had to move fast or he was done for. When he reached his barge—actually, a bateaux—he ordered his men to row downstream to the *Vulture*, which had returned to Haverstraw Bay. When they got there, Arnold told the rowers that they could join him and receive promotions as British soldiers or return. Two joined him; three others returned.

Meanwhile, Washington, unaware of Arnold's treason, had breakfast and went across the river to have a look at West Point. The inspection was disconcerting, not only because of the fort's dreadful condition but because Arnold failed to appear, and Washington was informed that he had never come to the fort that morning at all. Washington did not find out the real reason for Arnold's sudden departure until Alexander Hamilton handed him a packet at 4:00 p.m. containing the papers in Arnold's handwriting that were found on André, revealing Arnold's intention to hand over West Point. Washington was thunderstruck.

He immediately made an attempt to catch Arnold before he reached the *Vulture*, but it was too late. Poor André, on the other hand, was a captive, a spy caught out of uniform within American lines, carrying incriminating papers—a capital offense. Clinton worked hard to get him back, but Washington insisted that the only way Clinton could save André was to hand over Arnold. Clinton could not agree to an exchange, however. As much as he loved André, he could not give up Arnold. British policy had been to entice rebel officers to desert, and now that a famous one had, Clinton could not very well send him back to a certain death, even to save André's life. In a few days, André, the great actor, managed to work up unexpected sympathy and respect for himself among the Americans, including Washington, who, nonetheless, had him tried and hanged on October 2.

Washington moved swiftly but with great difficulty to strengthen West Point, expecting an attack momentarily from Clinton and Rodney, assisted by Arnold. Fortunately, it did not come. Instead, Clinton welcomed Arnold to the fold and left West Point alone, which made no sense to either Rodney or Arnold. As far as they were concerned, the attack was all prepared, so why not go ahead with it? Arnold predicted that the fort would be theirs in ten days. But Clinton, who had had his heart set on capturing West Point for a long time, suddenly decided not to unleash the planned assault. No one could explain why. Rodney was bewildered. "To my infinite surprise," he wrote to Sandwich, "cold water was immediately thrown on [the idea] not withstanding it had but a few days before the arrival of Arnold been told me that it was of infinite consequence, and if taken would ruin the rebels."

Washington, in the meantime, was doing everything he could to get Arnold back and make an example of him. He ruled out assassination, which would have been easy to arrange. Plenty of patriot agents in Manhattan would have done the job, but Washington wanted Arnold alive. A scheme to capture him was developed, using a civilian named Baldwin and an army sergeant major of cavalry, John Champe, who was serving under Henry "Light-Horse Harry" Lee of Virginia. Pretending to be a deserter, Champe made his way to New York and joined a body of Loyalist troops that Arnold was raising for service in the South. Champe and Baldwin planned to kidnap Arnold and, with the help of a third associate, row him across the Hudson to New Jersey. On October 20, the day Arnold was supposed to be taken, Light-Horse Harry Lee was waiting in Hoboken with some men ready to receive Champe, Baldwin, and Arnold, but they never appeared.

The day before Arnold was to be captured, he moved his quarters to a better location for supervising the loading of troops for an invasion of Virginia. When men were moved from their barracks to troop transports, John Champe was among them. He was trapped on a ship and went with Arnold to Chesapeake Bay. It was a long time before he could extricate himself from the British army and regain his real identity.

Instead of attacking West Point or Newport, Clinton was now concentrating on establishing a base in Chesapeake Bay at the mouth of the James River. He wanted to open a second front to aid Cornwallis, who was having problems that neither of them had anticipated when Clinton left Charleston in June. South Carolina was not as easily pacified as they had expected.

A particularly vicious partisan war was raging, and Cornwallis needed help. The rebels were far more numerous and angry than anticipated, and they had competent, aggressive leaders like Thomas Sumter, Francis Marion, John Thomas Jr., and James Wilson, who were drawing hundreds to their ranks. To cope with the problem, Cornwallis decided to move into North Carolina, even though South Carolina was not yet secure. He now insisted that to subdue South Carolina it was necessary to invade North Carolina, and he wanted a second front established in Virginia to help him.

Clinton thus turned away from the Hudson and focused on the South, even though, as far as Rodney was concerned, he could perfectly well have done both. Rodney was certain that they could still take West Point and Newport and create a solid post in Virginia with no difficulty.

Three years earlier, Clinton had been incensed with General Howe for giving up the Highlands after he had taken them. He believed then, and continued to believe, it seemed, that control of the Hudson River was essential to reestablishing British rule in America. He was convinced that if he had succeeded with Arnold in taking West Point, they would have won the war. Every other objective paled in comparison. Why, then, was he forgoing a perfect opportunity to do it now?

Rodney had no idea. He was perplexed and angry. Clinton was being presented with the opportunity to crush Rochambeau, sink Washington's hopes, and end the war, yet he was refusing to grasp it. Rodney became convinced that the American theater needed a new commander. "I must freely confess," he wrote to Sandwich,

> that there appears to me a slackness inconceivable in every branch of [the operation in New York], and that briskness and activity which are so necessary, and ought to animate the whole, to bring it to a speedy conclusion, have [been] entirely forsaken.
>
> Believe me, my dear Lord, you must not expect an end of the American war till you can find a general of active spirit.

Rodney had become just as fixated on the Hudson as Clinton had been. He believed that West Point was of supreme importance. He told Sandwich, "This was the post that Arnold was to have betrayed to us. The rebels . . . would have been undone had the scheme with Arnold succeeded. At all events it must be recovered in the ensuing summer." He was certain that once the British controlled the Highlands they could "cut off all communication with the northern and southern provinces" and gain control of the entire river, and that "with little difficulty" they "might have opened a passage to Canada." For Clinton to ignore this was, for Rodney, inexplicable and intolerable.

If Clinton was now looking exclusively to the South as the most fertile ground for accomplishing the king's objectives, an event soon occurred that should have made him think again. Scottish Major Patrick Ferguson, one of Cornwallis's chief lieutenants, a man with extensive combat experience who was bringing the fight to the rebels with a vengeance, was defeated and killed on October 7, 1780, at King's Mountain, twenty miles from Charlotte. Four hundred of Ferguson's 1,100-man detachment were killed—including the wounded who were murdered in retaliation for British crimes—and nearly 700 captured. The totally unexpected event blunted Cornwallis's northward thrust, forcing him to pull back to Winnsboro, South Carolina, sixty-six miles south of Charlotte.

In spite of the obvious need to rethink the southern strategy, Clinton went ahead as if nothing untoward had happened. He organized an expeditionary force of twenty-five hundred for Virginia, under Major General Alexander Leslie. Leslie had orders to create a secure base at the mouth of the James River and to place himself under Cornwallis's command. This was to be the beginning of the second front that both Clinton and Cornwallis thought would be of great service. Leslie arrived in the Chesapeake on October 20 and easily established himself at Portsmouth, Virginia, where he ingratiated himself with the people by allowing his men to run riot.

A week earlier, on October 14, Congress responded to the unexpected victory at King's Mountain by appointing General Greene to replace Gates as head of the Southern Department.

Greene arrived at Hillsborough to pick up the reins at the end of November. With him were two of the army's finest units, under superb leaders: cavalry commander Colonel Henry "Light-Horse Harry" Lee and General Daniel Morgan. Morgan finally arrived with the troops he had promised Gates. Colonel William Washington (a second cousin of the commander in chief) was already in Hillsborough with his light dragoons. He would be important to Greene, as would the veteran Maryland colonel Otho Williams.

Washington and Greene behaved toward the deflated Gates much differently than Gates had anticipated. Washington did not gloat or retaliate. Instead, he treated Gates, who during this time lost his only son, with the utmost kindness, offering him the command of the left wing of the main army. Gates was touched, but he did not accept Washington's offer. It's hard to believe that Gates would have treated Washington and Greene in the same way had the situations been reversed.

———

General Leslie remained in Portsmouth for a month, before Cornwallis unexpectedly moved his entire corps to the Cape Fear River and then to Charleston. From there Cornwallis ordered Leslie to join him in North Carolina. With Leslie's detachment absorbed by the main army, Clinton sent Arnold with seventeen hundred men to establish a post similar to Leslie's. Arnold reached the mouth of the James River on December 30.

While Clinton and Cornwallis were busy with the South, a puzzled, irate Rodney departed for the West Indies on November 16, taking nine sail of the line with him. He had accomplished little, which he blamed entirely on the dysfunctional pair in command in New York. He left feeling that, but for Arbuthnot and Clinton, Britain would have won the war in the fall of 1780. He was furious with them for depriving him of a great victory and the laurels he sought.

Unlike Lord Howe, Rodney had implicit faith in the sword. That the colonies could be forced to submit by military means alone seemed to him self-evident. The idea that there was a political dimension to the conflict never entered his mind. What did impress Rodney was the need to replace Arbuthnot and Clinton. From the moment he had arrived in New York back in September, he had concluded that Arbuthnot was a hopeless incompetent, but he had expected more from Clinton. When Clinton failed as well, Rodney could not see how the war could ever be won with these two in charge.

London ignored Rodney's warning about the dire consequences of leaving Arbuthnot and Clinton in place. They were both still there the following year when he was again in the Caribbean, and it was time for him to decide if he would come north during hurricane season to counter another French fleet. Did he really want to be involved with this bewildering duo again and risk his reputation, or should he leave the job to a competent subordinate and hope for the best? His decision would go a long way toward determining the outcome of the war.

Chapter 24

FACING SOUTH

During the first week of December 1780, Washington established his main winter camp at West Point and a satellite at Morristown. His headquarters were at New Windsor, in the vicinity of West Point. As always, Washington was on the alert to capture General Knyphausen at his headquarters in Morris House or Sir Henry Clinton at his headquarters at the Kennedy house in the city. On December 23 he ordered Lieutenant Colonel David Humphreys, one of his trusted aides, to take two officers and twenty-eight men and kidnap either general. He left the selection and the plan to Humphreys.

Two days later, Humphreys and his party pushed off from Dobbs Ferry at night in two whaleboats and a barge. Using the password "Success," they set out to capture Clinton at the Kennedy house, which stood on the lower tip of Manhattan Island. The wind was high and carried them down smartly to the end of the island, but the breeze became so strong they could not land and were driven out into the Upper Bay. One of the whaleboats sped past Staten Island, through the Narrows, and almost went aground on Sandy Hook. The other careened onto the beach at Staten Island with the barge. Their bad luck did not remain with them the entire night; they all managed to rendezvous at Brunswick on the Raritan River, the designated point, and made their way back to camp, more than a little embarrassed. Their failure might not have been unfortunate—often Clinton had more than twenty-eight troops guarding his headquarters, sometimes twice that many. Humphreys's detail might have run into more than they could have handled and been captured themselves.

Washington hoped that seizing General Clinton would cause a sensation and improve the dreadful state of the army's morale. The winter of 1780–81 was threatening to be the worst yet for the commander in chief, his officers, and his men. A crisis was brewing. Pay was a year in arrears. Food and clothing were even more difficult to come by than in previous winters. Mutiny was in the air. Washington continued to plead with Congress and the states for sustenance.

He sympathized with the plight of the discontented soldiers, but he could not countenance mutiny and still have an army. If widespread defiance occurred, his first instinct was to deal with it harshly, particularly with the leaders. Given the extremity to which dissatisfaction in the ranks had progressed, he wasn't surprise when, on January 1, 1781, perhaps as many as thirteen hundred men of the Pennsylvania Line, which consisted of six regiments under Brigadier General Anthony Wayne, mutinied at Morristown and killed several officers.

Washington did not blame the officers. He said that they "have given convincing proofs, that everything possible was done by them to check the mutiny upon its first appearance, and it is to be regretted, that some of them have fallen sacrifices to their zeal." He might have added that they died from the neglect of a feeble Congress and selfish, shortsighted state governments. But since he believed so strongly in civilian control of the military, he would never say openly what must surely have been on his mind.

The Pennsylvania mutineers began marching to Philadelphia intending to pressure Congress into paying more than lip service to their complaints. But they never made it—never even crossed the Delaware River. General Wayne was on the scene, and he took charge of confronting them. Negotiating with mutineers went against the grain as much for Wayne as it did for Washington; it inevitably undermined discipline. Washington was ready to employ loyal troops against the mutineers, but that proved unnecessary. Wayne wanted to avoid more bloodshed by conducting tough negotiations, which he did. In the end he agreed to give six hundred men discharges and seven hundred furloughs until April—all of them with back pay. He then executed a dozen of the ringleaders in front of the troops. The sight of these young men with legitimate grievances being shot down in the name of army discipline, although deemed necessary, was deeply disturbing. Of course, they were the same men who had led the way in killing innocent officers, who were in no way to blame for their plight.

Washington was apprehensive about what might come next and did not have to wait long. On January 21 the New Jersey Line in Pompton also mutinied. Two hundred angry men marched toward Trenton. This time Washington came down hard on them. By January 27 the ugly business was over. He had to execute only two sergeants, but he knew that if conditions did not improve, more might follow. He warned Congress and the governors of all the states that the "aggravated calamities and distresses that have resulted from the total want of pay for nearly twelve months, the want of clothing at a severe season, and not infrequently the want of provisions, are beyond description, and would inevitably produce worse disruptions if not remedied."

General Clinton was keeping a close eye on the disturbances. His agents were out encouraging desertion, which was increasing. But he wasn't contemplating taking advantage of the situation by an attack on West Point or Newport, as he might have been. The hostility between the British chiefs foreclosed any joint action. Clinton was not looking to do anything in the North during the winter. His eyes were on the South, where Germain and the king wanted them to be. They still thought the war would be won there. Germain wrote to Clinton, reminding him again of London's overall strategy, which had not changed since the French entered the war in 1778. "I am commanded by His Majesty," he told him, "to acquaint you that the recovery of the Southern Provinces and the prosecution of the war, by pushing our conquests from south to north, is to be considered as the chief and principal object for the employment of all the forces under your command, which can be spared from the defense of the places in His Majesty's possession."

London's assumptions (and Clinton's) about the South continued to be based on wishful thinking. Their view of the South was as much of a fantasy as their notion of the Hudson–Champlain corridor. British tactics in South Carolina were not leading to the submission of what was deemed a basically loyal population but to a guerrilla war in which the rebels showed surprising strength, as demonstrated at King's Mountain and other places.

Lord Rawdon explained their basic dilemma in October. He wrote to General Leslie:

> No force has presented itself to us, whose opposition could be thought serious to this army, but then we have little hope of ever bringing the affair to an action. The enemy are mostly mounted militia, not to be overtaken by our infantry, nor to be safely pursued in this strong country by our cavalry. Our fear is that, instead of meeting us, they would slip by us into this province were we to proceed far from it, and might again stimulate the disaffected to serious insurrection. This apprehension must greatly circumscribe our efforts.

The British were in the middle of a guerrilla war they had started with no idea how to end. Going about terrorizing the population certainly wasn't the answer, but they had nothing else to offer.

Ferocious and widespread fighting in the South left Clinton with the dilemma of where to commit his limited number of troops. The threat from Washington and Rochambeau, and the ever-present danger of a French fleet appearing off Sandy Hook, meant that he had to keep substantial forces around New York. At the same time, Cornwallis needed more troops to counter both the guerrillas and the American southern command, which was being reconstituted under the formidable General Greene and a remarkable set of lieutenants.

Once again, uninformed superiors in London were insisting that the commander in America accomplish unrealistic goals with insufficient resources. To make Clinton's problem tougher, he did not have a naval commander he could work with, and, what was worse, the first lord of the Admiralty insisted that it didn't matter. Sandwich was adamantly opposed to replacing Arbuthnot just because Clinton could not get along with him. As far as Sandwich was concerned, Arbuthnot was perfectly fine, other than the fact that his health was poor.

Meanwhile, much to Washington's chagrin, Arnold was having great success in Virginia. In spite of Leslie's having landed twenty-five hundred men unopposed at Portsmouth in October and ravaged the countryside, the state remained unprepared for Arnold. He had only half as many men as Leslie, but he did far more damage. Only twelve hundred redcoats (including John Champe) landed with him at the end of December. They came ashore near Portsmouth, on the Elizabeth River, a tidal estuary that, along with the Nansemond and James rivers, formed Hampton Roads. Since Arnold was still an unknown quantity, Clinton assigned two of his best fighting units to accompany him—Colonel John Simcoe's Queen's Rangers and Hessian Captain Johann Ewald's light infantry.

Although raging storms had buffeted Arnold's winter voyage south from New York and a quarter of his force was lost, as soon as he landed he was off and running, despoiling both sides of the James River, working his way toward the new capital at Richmond, ninety-five miles away. By January 5 he strode into the city, having encountered almost no opposition. He was so contemptuous of Virginians that he had the effrontery to demand from Governor Thomas Jefferson a large ransom to prevent the despoliation of Richmond. Jefferson of course refused. Arnold then quickly burned and pillaged before pulling back downriver and setting up a base at Portsmouth, his original objective.

Perhaps Governor Jefferson and the Virginia militia would have acted with more energy had they been faced with a slave uprising instead of a foreign invasion. Virginia was comparatively untouched by the war swirling around it, yet the state wasn't ready to repel even an assault on its capital by twelve hundred men, the majority of whom were American deserters. The state's militia was more organized to repress a slave revolt than they were a tiny British attack.

Baron von Steuben was in command of Virginia's practically non-existent defense force. When Congress appointed General Greene to command the southern army, Washington assigned Steuben as his second. Steuben and Greene rode south together in November, but when Greene saw the sad state of Virginia's defenses, he left Steuben to breathe new life into them. Steuben was doing so, albeit with great difficulty, when Arnold arrived.

Virginia's nonresponse to Arnold bothered Washington, who was deeply concerned about the South. He needed far more troops to send there than he had. "The situation of the southern states is alarming," he wrote to the president of Congress, "as the measure of providing a regular and permanent force was by my last advices still unattested. If the states don't act together, we have little to expect but their successive subjugation."

Washington dearly wanted to get his hands on Arnold. He was particularly anxious to stop him from coordinating with Cornwallis and destroying Greene's tiny army in North Carolina. In what would turn out to be a dress rehearsal for the fatal entrapment of Cornwallis at Yorktown a few months later, Washington orchestrated a land and sea attack on Arnold's base in Portsmouth. To begin with, he sent Lafayette with a corps of Continentals to Virginia to work with Steuben. He would have sent more, but he feared that Clinton might storm up the Hudson and attack West Point if he did.

Lafayette's troops crossed the Hudson at Peekskill on February 20 and marched south with strict orders not to treat Arnold as a prisoner of war but to summarily execute him. Capturing him alive would not be easy. If anyone got near him, he'd probably fight it out with the brace of pistols he always carried.

On the same day that Lafayette's men began their long journey, Washington wrote to Steuben, "Convinced that naval operations alone will probably be ineffectual, and that militia would be unequal to the reduction of Arnold in his works, I have detached a corps of twelve hundred men from this army . . . commanded by the Marquis de Lafayette." Needless to say, Steuben was very happy to be getting reinforcements.

To trap Arnold, Washington also needed the French warships at Newport. The fleet commander was now senior captain Commodore Charles-René-Dominique Sochet, Chevalier Destouches. He was replacing Admiral de Ternay, who died on December 15. Destouches was younger than Ternay and more willing to take risks.

Destouches' squadron had not been as strong as Arbuthnot's, but when a ferocious gale devastated the British fleet on January 22, the two squadrons suddenly became more evenly matched. Arbuthnot, who was ailing, and spending most of his time in Manhattan, had three sail of the line badly damaged in the storm.

Since Destouches' warships could come and go as they pleased from Narragansett Bay, he seized the opportunity, and on February 9 sent a sail of the line and two frigates, under Captain Armand Le Gardeur de Tilly, racing to Lynnhaven Bay, inside the Chesapeake capes, a short distance from Arnold at Portsmouth. Steuben tried to work with de Tilly, but when the French captain discovered that Arnold's small force was situated too far up the Elizabeth River to get at it, he returned to Lynnhaven Bay, captured some unsuspecting privateers and the 44-gun *Romulus*, and took them to Newport. He could not remain in the Chesapeake long for fear Arbuthnot might trap him.

The unwelcome news from Virginia was more than offset by a surprising patriot victory on January 17, 1781, at Cowpens, South Carolina, twenty-five miles west of King's Mountain. The southern army that had worried Washington so much performed what looked from New York like a miracle. Brigadier General Daniel Morgan, ably supported by Lieutenant Colonel William Washington's cavalry, administered a stunning defeat, and effectively wiped out murderous Lieutenant

Colonel Banastre Tarleton's famous Legion, a blend of well-trained cavalry and infantry composed largely of Loyalist Americans and British officers that Cornwallis relied on.

Cowpens was a severe, unexpected setback for Cornwallis, who had confidently dispatched Tarleton to get Morgan when he saw that Greene had divided his army and sent Morgan southwest to work with the partisans in the backcountry who were giving the British so much trouble. With no regard for his opponent and blood in his eyes, Tarleton had swooped down on Morgan with eleven hundred men, expecting to make quick work of his backwoods rebels. When Tarleton was five miles from the American camp, Morgan was alerted and quickly got ready. So did Lieutenant Colonel Washington's cavalry. Exact numbers aren't known, but Morgan probably had around nineteen hundred men.

"Boys, get up, Benny's coming," he shouted, referring to Banastre Tarleton. And they did, assembling in prearranged places in front of the Broad River. Soon Tarleton appeared with his infantry and green-jacketed cavalry, rushing toward Morgan in complete ignorance of what awaited him. A well-prepared and brilliantly executed defense stopped him in his tracks. Tarleton was lucky to escape with his life. Morgan killed 110, wounded 200, and took 500 prisoners—nearly all of Tarleton's force and a quarter of Cornwallis's army, while suffering 148 casualties.

Clinton, whose relations with Cornwallis had not improved by their separating, was quick to note that making detachments of this sort was a mistake he would never have made.

Cornwallis did not respond to Cowpens in the way he did to King's Mountain. Instead of pulling back, he dispensed with as much baggage as he dared and charged after the rebels, hoping to get back the prisoners Morgan had taken and prevent him from reuniting with Greene. If Morgan reached Greene, their army would be almost equal to Cornwallis's, even with Leslie's reinforcements. But Morgan wasn't easy to catch. After sending away his prisoners for safekeeping, he continued slogging doggedly over muddy spring roads and crossing dangerously swollen rivers and streams toward Salisbury, staying just ahead of

Cornwallis. Some of Morgan's militiamen left him along the way, while others joined him.

In the midst of Morgan's extremely difficult retreat, General Greene, with only a few men, appeared suddenly at his camp on the Catawba River. Greene had ridden 125 miles over difficult terrain from the Pee Dee River to coordinate with Morgan. He was a welcome sight. Morgan's health was deteriorating badly.

Before leaving the Pee Dee, Greene had ordered Brigadier General Isaac Huger to bring the main army toward Salisbury to combine with Morgan. Racing to keep ahead of Cornwallis, Greene organized a rendezvous of the two parts of his army at the tiny hamlet of Guilford Courthouse, north of Greensboro. As they moved on, they managed to stay ahead of Cornwallis and reach the courthouse, where they reunited with Huger.

Greene now had two thousand men. He quickly retreated fifty miles to the Dan River, on the border of Virginia and North Carolina, hoping to cross it and be reinforced. Before he reached it, Morgan, overtaken by severe sciatica, had to leave and go to his home in Virginia. With Cornwallis not far behind, Greene crossed the Dan, taking all the available boats with him to the Virginia side.

When Cornwallis arrived at the banks of the river a short time later, he could not cross easily. Since he needed to regroup anyway, he fell back, giving the patriots a much-needed breather. Greene immediately sought help from Governor Jefferson, who responded with more energy than expected. The tiny southern army (around fourteen hundred now) began to grow. As it did, Greene sent men back across the Dan to harass Cornwallis.

Soon Greene's army approached four thousand, and he was anxious to get after the British. Cornwallis was looking to fight now as well, even though he had only half as many men as Greene had. Of course they were regulars—tired, perhaps, but regulars nonetheless—while so many of Greene's were inexperienced militiamen. They met at Guilford Courthouse on March 17, 1781. It was a critical encounter. If Greene lost, Cornwallis would then have only the partisans in the Carolinas to deal with, and they would be demoralized. If Greene won, the Loyalist partisans would be even more disheartened, and any hope of Cornwallis's holding on to the Carolinas would be in doubt.

Greene organized his men in roughly the same way Morgan had at Cowpens, and the plan worked well, except that at the end of the day, Cornwallis was on the field and Greene was in retreat. But it was a Pyrrhic victory, and Cornwallis knew it. He lost a quarter of his army, including a large number of his best officers, who could never be replaced.

He sorely missed Tarleton's Legion, which might have made the difference. He did what he could to disguise his failure, particularly from his superiors, but he could not hide it from himself and his officers. They knew that another victory like it and they were done for. Immediately afterward, Cornwallis began a retreat all the way to Wilmington on the Cape Fear River to recuperate. Greene, for his part, pursued him for a short distance before moving south toward Charleston to take advantage of Cornwallis's absence.

While Greene was reversing patriot fortunes in the South, Washington continued with his plan to trap Arnold. On March 6 he rode to Newport to convince Destouches and Rochambeau to send their whole fleet after the traitor and prevent him from combining with Cornwallis. Rochambeau received the American commander with great ceremony and told him that they had already made the decision to send their entire squadron, and, what's more, Destouches was ready to depart right away, with a fine complement of 1,100 French regulars, under General the Baron de Viomenil. Washington could not have asked for more.

At the same time that the allies were preparing their attack, Clinton was hoping that Arbuthnot would grasp the need to counter Destouches. Convinced that Arbuthnot would—since this would not be a joint undertaking—Clinton prepared reinforcements for Arnold that he planned to send to Portsmouth as soon as Arbuthnot cleared the way by defeating the French fleet. Major General William Phillips, who was personally close to both Cornwallis and Clinton, was to lead the expedition.

At the moment, Arbuthnot was in such poor health that he asked Sandwich to relieve him. He did not know, nor did Clinton, that the ministry, against the advice of Sandwich, had already decided in December 1780 to recall Arbuthnot. He hadn't been informed yet, and his successor had not been picked. He was in charge and, for once, eager to take on the French fleet.

On March 8 Destouches sortied from Narragansett Bay and shaped a course for the Chesapeake. His destination was no secret, and Arbuthnot was ready to go after him. His fleet had partially recovered from the January storm. Two of his damaged sail of the line had been repaired, and he was now superior in numbers and firepower to Destouches. He was also stronger in another area that was not so readily seen. All of his ships had copper bottoms, and only three of Destouches' eight had them. It made a big difference.

When Arbuthnot determined for sure that Destouches had sailed on March 9, he got under way the following day, confident that he'd catch the slower French squadron. This was a different man than the one Clinton had been struggling with for months.

Washington wrote to Lafayette on March 11, reporting that the British had left Gardiner's Bay on March 10 with their whole fleet. He thought that whichever squadron got to Chesapeake Bay first would have the advantage.

Arbuthnot had no trouble finding his prey. He spoke a ship on the thirteenth, confirming that a French squadron was sailing south. On the sixteenth, during the early morning, Arbuthnot's lookouts spotted Destouches off the Virginia coast, and their duel began. After maneuvering for a time, the two fleets came together in a light fog off Cape Henry.

With an inferior squadron but an extraordinary degree of skill and bravery, Destouches had the better of the engagement, which lasted for an hour. He badly damaged four British ships while suffering injury to only one of his. Clearly he was the victor, even though he did not immediately follow up by driving into Chesapeake Bay and landing Viomenil's troops for a combined attack on Arnold.

Instead, he sailed back to Newport, allowing Arbuthnot to hobble into Chesapeake Bay and pretend he was the victor, although when the Admiralty received his report it was obvious how badly he had bungled things. He did succeed in one respect, however; his presence in Lynnhaven Bay saved Arnold from the combined attack that Washington had orchestrated. It was, to say the least, a frustrating moment for the commander in chief, one he could not talk about for fear of alienating his French allies, on whom everything depended. On March 23 Destouches arrived back in Newport a victor. He had shown that the Royal Navy was not invincible, but his primary objective, which apparently he misunderstood, was lost.

With Destouches out of the way, and Arbuthnot in Lynnhaven Bay for protection, Major General Phillips brought the two thousand troops he had assembled in New York into Portsmouth to reinforce Arnold, arriving on March 26. Steuben and Lafayette were forced to withdraw. Phillips was senior to Arnold and would now be in charge, which is what Clinton wanted. Like the rest of the British army, particularly the younger officers, he was uneasy about Arnold, still not convinced he could be trusted.

Clinton's orders for Phillips reflected how out of touch he was with realities on the ground in the Carolinas. He told him that if Cornwallis was successful, he was to move up to Baltimore and take a post near the Susquehanna. Clinton imagined that there were numerous Loyalists on Delaware Neck waiting to show themselves and help with an amphibious drive in that area. Clinton emphasized the great importance of supporting "on both sides of the Susquehanna, and between the Chesapeake and the Delaware the friends of the king's interests."

Clinton supposed, from the meager reports he was getting from Cornwallis, that things were proceeding as expected in the Carolinas, and would in Virginia as well. The king's grand southern strategy appeared to be moving along nicely. The reality was just the opposite, of course. Things were going very badly for Cornwallis. He had actually been defeated at Guilford Courthouse and in desperation sought refuge in Wilmington, his army continuously reduced by sickness and desertion to perhaps fourteen hundred worn-out men.

Clinton's lack of understanding was in part due to the sparse, misleading information Cornwallis was feeding him. To protect himself and keep his options open, Cornwallis was disguising the true state of affairs—to the extent he even knew them. The truth was that he had little appreciation of the kind of war he was in. Greene and the guerrillas were, in fact, very close to defeating him and forcing him back to Charleston.

At this point, Cornwallis might have retreated from Wilmington to Charleston and regrouped. Obviously, his strategy wasn't working, but he could no more accept the onus for what inevitably would be seen as a backward movement than Burgoyne could in 1777. Instead, on April 10 he wrote to his dear friend Phillips that he was coming to join him in Virginia and hoping to make it the center of the war. "If we mean an offensive war in America," he wrote, "we must abandon New York, and bring our whole force to Virginia."

Cornwallis also wrote to Clinton on April 10, advocating the same thing. "I cannot help expressing my wishes that the Chesapeake may become the seat of the war," he told him, "even, if necessary, at the expense of abandoning New York. Until Virginia is in a manner subdued, our hold upon the Carolinas must be difficult if not precarious." The unhealthy climate in Virginia during the hot months of the year was of little concern—although Cornwallis was certainly aware of it—to a general who was desperate to find a way out of the mess he was in.

On the same day, he wrote a longer, equally deceptive letter to Germain, explaining why he had to move to Virginia in order to win the South. His original orders were to move from south to north, from the Carolinas to Virginia, not the other way around. Now, he needed to move to Virginia to disguise his failure in the Carolinas. He had no place to go from Wilmington, other than back to Charleston and admit failure, or pretend that all was well and move to Virginia.

Without waiting for an order from Clinton, the nominal commander in chief, Cornwallis left Wilmington on April 25 and marched his dwindling army slowly to Virginia to meet Phillips and Arnold.

————

A frigate, the *Amphitrite*, arrived in New York on April 20 with Cornwallis's letter of April 10, and Clinton was understandably startled by its contents—then irate. Here was clear evidence, finally, that things in the Carolinas were not as he had been led to believe. They were, in fact, far worse than he might have imagined. The large detachments he was sending south were not having the desired effect. Why else would Cornwallis want to move to Virginia and change the whole focus of the war?

Clinton did not blame failure on the southern strategy, he blamed Cornwallis's poor execution, and thereby drew all the wrong conclusions. He continued to believe there was an abundance of Loyalists in the Carolinas whom Cornwallis was failing to connect with simply because he was moving around too much, chasing Morgan and Greene. Even though Clinton had found Loyalists to be universally unreliable, he still clung to the idea that they were out there in large numbers.

In any event, Clinton had no intention of leaving New York and handing it over to Washington, which, he was convinced, would end the war. Besides, it was the king's policy to hold New York, and sending more troops south was impossible until he was reinforced.

Instead of moving "the seat of the war" to Virginia in the manner Cornwallis was suggesting, Clinton accepted Cornwallis's surprising move and proposed that he establish a deepwater post on the Chesapeake and send three thousand reinforcements to New York.

Thus, even though Cornwallis was marching to Virginia without orders, he succeeded in getting Clinton to approve the move. Beyond that, however, neither man had a clear idea of where to go from there. And neither was willing to face the fact that their southern strategy had failed, not only through military ineptness but because they had no political plan that might bring the great majority of southerners to their side. They did not even think one was necessary.

Washington was unaware of the confusion that Greene was causing in the British high command. He was watching developments closely, however, trying to judge where he should place his troops, particularly

Lafayette's detachment, which was still in Virginia. With all the activity in the South, Washington did not have to worry about a sudden British push up the Hudson. Nonetheless, he had to be prepared. If Clinton all of a sudden became active, Washington planned to call up the state militias in New Jersey, and also in the New York counties of Orange, Ulster, and Dutchess, to defend the several works in the vicinity of West Point. He felt that he could count on these militias to be ready to repair to the aid of the fortress at the first alarm and the firing of the beacons.

He also needed to protect King's Ferry and wrote to Major General Heath to have his Westchester County militia ready at a moment's notice. Washington ordered Heath to defend Stony Point and Verplanck's Point "to the last extremity." The beacons on Butter Hill and the mountain opposite Fishkill were to be kept in condition to "fire at a moment's warning."

The likelihood of Clinton's making a move on West Point, however, was nil. Adding to his natural caution was a much reduced force in Manhattan, continuing problems with Arbuthnot, and now things going badly in the South. Clinton reported to Germain on April 5, describing the state of his army. "I am preparing for every exertion within the compass of my very reduced force," he wrote, "which, after the several large detachments sent to the southward, amounts to no more than 6275 auxiliary troops, 4527 regular British, and 900 provincials, ready for the field." Obviously, he needed help; he was in no position to think about an offensive.

Chapter 25

PRELUDE TO VICTORY

By April 6, 1781, Washington had decided where to station Lafayette's detachment. Still worried that Arnold and Phillips might link up with Cornwallis and turn on Greene, he ordered him to join the southern army. Lafayette followed orders, of course, but he much preferred being with the commander in chief on the Hudson, where he assumed the war would be decided. Washington knew his young protégé wanted to be where the action was, and he assured him that it would not be in the North. "We [in the north] shall from all appearances remain inactive," he told him

How wrong he was. In a month he would be informed that Louis XVI had ordered a large fleet to be off the American coast during hurricane season with specific instructions to cooperate with Washington and Rochambeau. The minister of marine, Charles Eugène Gabriel de la Croix, Marquis de Castries, issued the orders. The news arrived in Boston on May 6 aboard the frigate *Concorde*. In addition to a considerable sum of gold for Rochambeau, the French warship carried vital dispatches and letters promising that Rear Admiral Joseph François

Joseph Paul de Grasse would be on the American coast with a substantial fleet sometime after July 15. The king's purpose, and of course Vergennes', was to end the war this campaign season. France had been supporting the American cause for a long time now; if victory was not achieved this year, a negotiated peace with London was likely. The ugly compromise that would undoubtedly result wasn't anything the Americans or the French wanted.

Sixty-year-old veteran Admiral Jacques-Melchior Saint-Laurent, Comte de Barras, commander of d'Estaing's van (the front third of his fleet) at Newport in 1778, brought the news. Barras would now take over the squadron in Narragansett Bay from Destouches, who had been a temporary replacement.

Donatien-Marie-Joseph de Vimeur, Vicomte de Rochambeau, the general's son, was also a passenger aboard the *Concorde*. He carried a letter for his father from de Grasse, written on March 29, only a week after the admiral had left Brest for the West Indies, where he had gone to fight the Royal Navy before coming to America. De Grasse informed Rochambeau that he would not arrive on the American coast until July 15, at the earliest, and he cautioned that he would be able to stay only a relatively short time, which meant that everything had to be in readiness when he got there. He speculated that if all went well, he would have twenty-two sail of the line with him, and perhaps more.

Rochambeau père understood and immediately dispatched a vessel to Cap François with plans that he and Washington had worked out for attacking New York. Rochambeau recommended that de Grasse bring five to six thousand troops and stop in at Chesapeake Bay, where he could strike a blow before proceeding to New York. He also sent pilots who knew Chesapeake Bay as well as New York; de Grasse had especially requested them.

By the time the *Concorde* reached Boston with its letters and dispatches, Admiral de Grasse had long since left France and reached the West Indies. He had departed Brest on March 22 with twenty ships of the line, including the three-deck *Ville de Paris*, his 110-gun flagship, and, in convoy, one hundred fifty transports with provisions for the islands. His orders required him to be in the West Indies until the middle of the summer battling the British West Indian fleet before coming to America. All the hopeful plans that Washington and Rochambeau had worked out could be for naught if de Grasse suffered serious reverses in the Caribbean at the hands of George Rodney.

Although Admiralty spies had been observing and reporting for weeks on preparations for de Grasse's massive fleet, no attempt had been made to stop him from leaving Brest. He was being left entirely to Rodney, who was already in the Caribbean, with Rear Admiral Samuel Hood as his second. Giving Rodney sole responsibility for de Grasse meant that Rodney would have another chance to decisively influence the American war. He had the resources to counter the French fleet, and he was, after Admiral Howe, England's finest fleet commander. His Majesty's interests appeared to be in good hands.

After leaving New York in November 1780, Rodney had returned to the Caribbean, happy to be in a warm climate and away from Clinton and Arbuthnot. When he arrived in Barbados on December 6 he had another mess waiting for him. A mammoth October hurricane had destroyed or damaged much of the British fleet, and he had to repair it. He also needed replacements for the ships that were lost. On December 10 he moved to St. Lucia, which the hurricane had hit hard. He brought nine sail of the line with him and got right to work restoring them. On January 7, Hood arrived with 8 more battleships and a huge convoy of 118 merchantmen loaded with supplies.

During January, Rodney resuscitated four more ships of the line, expanding his fleet to twenty-one battleships. Within days he put them to work on an enterprise dear to his heart—seizing the Dutch island of St. Eustatius. On January 27, he received orders to seize all the Dutch islands in the West Indies, especially St. Eustatius, which the Dutch had set up as a free port, open to traders from all countries. In December 1780, Britain had finally declared war on neutral Holland. London was fed up with the Dutch for openly supporting the Americans, particularly for allowing huge quantities of munitions, especially gunpow-der, to be funneled to them through St. Eustatius.

One of the smaller of the Leeward Islands, St. Eustatius was only five miles long and two and a half wide, but her port, Oranjestad, had a mile and a half of warehouses—six hundred of them—filled with goods of all kinds, especially war matériel, from a number of nations, including Britain herself. A continuous flow of munitions from Oran-jestad went to Washington's army in the North and to rebels in the South. Of course, many other islands traded war matériel with Amer-ica, particularly French islands like Martinique, but St. Eustatius stood out from the rest.

Rodney had had his eye on the notorious traffic for some time, and on February 3 he attacked the island with army commander Major Gen-eral Sir John Vaughan—the same General Vaughan who in 1777 had mercilessly ravaged Kingston, the capital of the new State of New York. Hood was with Rodney as they swooped down on Oranjestad with fif-teen warships and three thousand men, easily capturing the island, along with one hundred fifty traders and six warships in the harbor. And that was not all. Rodney raced after and caught a Dutch convoy of thirty merchantmen that had just left port accompanied by two warships.

For the next three months, through the end of April, Rodney remained on the tiny island, inflicting untold suffering on its people, lining his pockets, seemingly unconcerned with the likelihood that the French West Indian fleet might appear at any time off Martinique. His conduct toward the inhabitants of St. Eustatius was unrestrained—a "nest of vipers," he called them. As far as he was concerned, they were all engaged in pernicious arms trafficking with America, except per-haps for a few sugar planters, whom he favored.

Rodney brushed aside mounting criticism of his methods and greed, claiming that by destroying the island as a base of supply, he was making a major contribution to the war effort in America—even if he was making a huge personal profit while doing it. This was the golden age of peculation; he was only doing what others of his social class did routinely at home and abroad.

While Rodney was preoccupied with milking St. Eustatius, he dispatched Hood with twelve battleships on February 12 to watch the French at Martinique. Rodney had heard from a merchant—not London—that a French fleet had departed Brest, bound for the Caribbean. The Admiralty had sent a sloop of war to warn Rodney, but the ship did not reach the Caribbean until May 17, long after the information would have been of use.

Rodney ordered Hood to search for the French fleet off Martinique, which he did, but, finding that the report was inaccurate, he continued to patrol off Fort Royal Bay for weeks, grumbling all the time about the difficulties a blockade carried with it and blaming Rodney for his discomfort. A squadron of six British sail of the line, under Admiral Francis Drake, was already off Fort Royal Bay, bringing the total of British warships in the area to eighteen. Both Hood and Drake, and, indeed, Rodney, expected a French fleet to appear soon.

Their long wait was over on April 28 when Admiral de Grasse arrived off Martinique with his warships and one hundred fifty transports only thirty-six days after leaving France. Rodney had no official warning that he was coming, and neither did Hood, but an enemy fleet was certainly expected. Rodney should have been at St. Lucia to welcome it. He was leaving Hood with an inferior squadron to engage the enemy for no other reason than personal greed.

De Grasse had no trouble slipping his transports past Hood into Fort Royal Bay during the evening of the twenty-eighth and the morning of the twenty-ninth, much to Hood's embarrassment. His squadron was out of position, a fact he tried, not very successfully, to blame on Rodney's orders. Hood's criticism was no doubt sharpened by the fact that he failed to stop even a single one of de Grasse's transports. He could not possibly put all the blame for that on Rodney, much as he would have liked to. There was nothing wrong with Rodney's orders. He had far more experience in the Caribbean than Hood, and even more in the neighborhood of Martinique and St. Lucia. The real problem was Hood's lack of local knowledge, although after spending weeks in the area, he should have done much better than he did.

On the morning of the twenty-ninth, de Grasse, who had kept his warships outside Fort Royal Bay during the night, went after the British fleet with twenty-four sail of the line. Four French battleships that were stationed in Fort Royal Bay were added to his fleet. Hood had eighteen copper-bottomed ships of the line. Less than half of de Grasse's fleet was copper-bottomed. Hood was understandably angry that Rodney had not returned to St. Lucia to prepare for what would certainly be the decisive naval battles of the season.

The duel between Hood and de Grasse went on inconclusively for three days. Hood, with his faster, more maneuverable ships, managed only to survive, and immediately afterward sailed to rejoin Rodney. De Grasse was forced to return to Fort Royal Bay empty-handed. He was frustrated and furious with his captains, but his convoy was safe, and he could repair his ships in safety. On May 8, he attacked St. Lucia with twelve hundred troops. Hood wasn't there, of course—he was with Rodney—but shore batteries drove off the French.

When Hood met up with Rodney and informed him of de Grasse's arrival, they set out on May 5, not for St. Lucia but for Barbados, arriving to resupply on the eighteenth. Rodney feared that, after de Grasse attacked St. Lucia, he might go after Barbados. But that's not what he did. While Rodney and Hood were at Bridgetown, on Barbados, de Grasse attacked the British island of Tobago, two hundred miles to the south, which surrendered on June 2.

When Rodney found out, he went after de Grasse and caught up with him on June 6, but he did not engage. Rodney had twenty sail of the line, while de Grasse had twenty-three. A major battle might have developed, but Rodney judged that conditions were not right; he did not want to find himself at a disadvantage to leeward, while de Grasse descended on Barbados, which Rodney thought could happen. Instead of fighting the French fleet, he retired with his much faster ships to Barbados to protect it, while de Grasse took his fleet back to Fort Royal Bay. From Martinique, he sailed with his fleet and a large merchant convoy for Cap François on July 5, arriving on the sixteenth to prepare for his fateful involvement in the American war. Time was rushing by. He had promised to be off the American coast after July 15, and here it was already the sixteenth. He needed to hurry.

★

WASHINGTON AND ROCHAMBEAU HAD BEEN PLANNING (AND praying) for de Grasse's arrival ever since the *Concorde* had sailed into Boston on May 6. Immediately after the frigate arrived, Rochambeau arranged a meeting with Washington on May 22 at the Joseph Webb House, on Main Street in Wethersfield, Connecticut, to go over strategy. Barras, at the last minute, could not attend because of movements in the British fleet. Arbuthnot, for some unknown reason, had taken a large portion of his squadron to Block Island. Nothing came of it, but it prevented Barras from being at the conference.

No one knew if de Grasse would survive Rodney and Hood in the Caribbean, but both Washington and Rochambeau wanted to discuss strategy on the assumption that he would. Washington obviously wanted to attack New York, believing, as he had for a long time, that a victory there would end the war. He thought that all the detachments Clinton was sending south made Manhattan vulnerable.

Following the conference, he wrote to Luzerne, explaining the general plan he and Rochambeau had worked out and emphasizing how essential de Grasse was to its success. He told him that Rochambeau intended to march his army to the North (Hudson) River, and that the French fleet at Newport, if circumstances permitted, would move in the same direction for an attack on New York and Brooklyn, depending, of course, on the timely arrival of de Grasse.

When Rochambeau was away from Newport with his army, the only force protecting Narragansett Bay would be Rhode Island militiamen, which made Barras a tempting target. Whether the state could protect him against a determined British effort was doubtful. In view of this, Washington and Rochambeau agreed that Barras should move his ships to Boston when Rochambeau departed Newport.

With Washington and Rochambeau threatening New York, there was probably nothing for Barras to worry about. The British fleet would have to stay close to Manhattan. On the other hand, if Rochambeau was away from Newport for any length of time before de Grasse appeared, then Barras might be in trouble. Neither Rochambeau nor Washington was aware that relations between Arbuthnot and Clinton had reached a state where a joint attack on Newport was inconceivable.

In any event, the French West Indian fleet was the key to success in New York. Washington concluded his letter to Luzerne by telling him:

> It is not for me to know in what manner the fleet of His Most Christian Majesty is to be employed in the West Indies this summer, or to inquire at what epoch it may be expected on this coast; but the appearance and aid of it in this quarter are of such essential importance in any offensive operation, and so necessary to stop the progress of the enemy's arms at the southward, that I shall be excused, I am persuaded, for endeavoring to engage your good offices in facilitating an event on which so much depends. For this I have a stronger plea, which I assure you, that General Rochambeau's opinion and wishes concur with mine, and that it is at his instance principally I make to you this address. . . . An early and frequent communication from the Count de Grasse would lead to preparatory measures on our part, and be a means of facilitating the operation in hand, or any other, which may be thought more advisable.

Washington's preference for attacking New York was clear to everyone. As he explained to the president of Congress, Samuel Huntington, "in every point of view, an operation against New York has been deemed preferable to making further detachments to the southward, while they can only be sent by land."

Two days later, he wrote to former general John Sullivan, now in Congress, explaining the reasons for selecting New York. "The weakness of the garrison, the central position for drawing together men and supplies, and the spur, which an attempt against that place would give to every exertion," were among the reasons. Washington also pointed out that if Clinton were forced to draw troops from the South to defend New York, it would be a big help to Greene.

Two days later, Washington wrote in confidence to Lafayette explaining that New York would be the main target of the allies. The letter never reached him. An enterprising spy intercepted it and brought it to General Clinton. He was so delighted that he gave the man two hundred guineas. Clinton was convinced that the letter was not a plant. How long he held that view is impossible to tell, but later, when Washington wanted Clinton to believe that New York was the target when it really wasn't, the wayward letter probably helped.

Luzerne, like Rochambeau, was willing to do whatever was necessary to win a decisive victory. After all, that was the king's objective. But it would become increasingly clear to the ever-sensitive and perceptive Washington that the French had their doubts about making Manhattan the primary target, mainly because they knew that, after d'Estaing's experience, their naval officers did not want to deal with the problem of taking their large warships, which drew more water than their British counterparts, over the bar at Sandy Hook. They did not want to thread that needle and expose their fleet.

Rochambeau, who was as skilled a diplomat as Washington, did not immediately inform him of his qualms but moved slowly and gently to suggest a more attractive alternative. When it became known that Cornwallis had unexpectedly moved his entire army to Virginia, Rochambeau was handed a perfect argument for making Chesapeake Bay the target rather than New York. When Cornwallis combined his troops with Phillips's and Arnold's, he created an army of more than seven thousand—large enough for a defeat to precipitate negotiations that would end the war favorably.

Whether New York or Chesapeake Bay was the target, Washington needed a much larger army. On May 24 he sent letters to the governors of the New England states, urging them to fill their quota in the Continental army, hold their militias ready to march at a week's notice, and arrange for certain supply and transportation. He also asked the governors of Massachusetts (Hancock) and Connecticut (Trumbull) for a loan of gunpowder. Rhode Island was exempted from this request; the state might need it to protect Newport.

Two days later, on May 26, Washington received a report from John Laurens that Louis XVI had once again opened the French treasury and agreed to supply the Americans with an additional six million livres. It was glorious news at this particular moment, but at the same time, it was indicative of France's drive to settle the American war in the next few months. The decisive moment for the patriots had clearly arrived.

They almost ruined their chances of getting more French money by sending Laurens to Paris instead of relying on Franklin. Laurens's appointment was an unsubtle and unnecessary slap at Franklin by a Congress under the influence of members like Arthur Lee, Richard Henry Lee, and Samuel Adams, who had no appreciation of the magnificent job Franklin was doing or how absurd they looked in the eyes of Vergennes and the king, not to mention how angry they were making them.

It was Franklin who had actually obtained the money. Laurens had no idea how to do it. He had no diplomatic experience and was entirely out of his element. The congressional faction who sent him almost destroyed any chance of getting the loan. Vergennes was annoyed with Laurens and with the congressmen who were using him; above all, he detested their idiotic animus toward Franklin. In the end Vergennes sent the money, which he knew was vital, and Franklin remained in Paris, although he was understandably offended, and nearly came home, which would have been a great tragedy for the United States and would have cost the country dearly.

By early June, Washington was more aware of how powerful French misgivings about New York were, and he began adjusting his thinking. He did not make a firm decision about where the attack should be, because a "decisive plan," as he called it, was not needed yet. That would come later, if and when he had more particulars from de Grasse. Knowing that Cornwallis was now in Virginia with a large army helped Washington immeasurably to look more favorably on Chesapeake Bay. He later wrote in his diary that the "disinclination of their naval officers to force the harbor of New York, the feeble response of the states to his requisitions for men hitherto, and the little prospect of great exertion in the future," led him to be ready to give up all ideas of attacking New York.

On June 13 Washington suggested to Rochambeau that perhaps the Chesapeake might be better than New York, and that it would be best to let de Grasse choose between them. If he came to Sandy Hook, Washington felt that he could "block up" any fleet there and "have a very good chance of forcing the entrance." On the other hand, if the enemy was in Chesapeake Bay, de Grasse could follow them there. The Chesapeake "is always accessible to a superior force," he wrote.

Much would depend on what Cornwallis and Clinton were going to do, now that Cornwallis was in Virginia. It would have surprised Washington to know that Cornwallis had come to Petersburg without orders, and that there was no concerted British plan about where to go from there. Cornwallis's move to Virginia was as much of a surprise to Clinton as it was to Washington.

Cornwallis arrived in Petersburg on May 20, deeply saddened to find confirmation of news he had heard en route: His close friend General Phillips had succumbed, on May 13, to a sudden illness. Cornwallis had been looking forward to being with someone he could talk with openly. Now he was forced to work with the renegade Arnold, whom he detested. Together, they had an army of 7,200.

Once Clinton found out about Cornwallis's new location, he recalled Arnold to New York. For once, Cornwallis must have been happy with his boss. Clinton was upset that Arnold was communicating with Germain behind his back, making proposals that Clinton knew nothing about and that might be in conflict with his own. Clinton suspected that Arnold was telling Germain that he wasn't aggressive enough, which Clinton knew Germain would agree with. By this time Clinton hated Germain. He called him "the falsest man alive," adding, "he was not to be trusted and meant to ruin" him.

Arnold's uninhibited pursuit of prize money also angered and embarrassed Clinton. The traitor's outsized greed was impossible to overlook. Clinton planned to let him cool his heels in Manhattan for a while and then send him to attack New London, Connecticut—putting him far away from the main theater of action, where Clinton knew Arnold dearly wanted to be.

Now that Cornwallis was in Virginia, he had to decide what to do. In a general sense, he needed to defeat the army arrayed against him and win over the people—the same objectives as in the Carolinas. The problem was, he had no realistic strategy that would accomplish either. Although he really did not know quite what to do, he thought that action of some kind was called for, and decided that the first order of business was to deal with Lafayette, who was twenty-three miles away, across the James River at Richmond, with a force less than half the size of his. Once that was accomplished, he was going to base himself at Williamsburg, which he had heard was comparatively healthy during the summer months. He also planned to establish a deepwater base on Chesapeake Bay and attack Steuben's militia, as well as the Virginia government at Charlottesville, hoping again to embolden Loyalists, as well as slaves, to join him. Although Loyalists in the Carolinas did not support him in the numbers he had anticipated, he hoped to do better in Virginia.

Cornwallis assumed that he would make quick work of "the boy," as he liked to call Lafayette. But he found that the boy was not easily caught. Thus began a cat-and-mouse game that went on for nearly a month, with Lafayette remaining tantalizingly close, and skirmishing, but never fully engaging. At the same time, Cornwallis sent Simcoe's Rangers after Steuben's militia, and Tarleton's cavalry to Charlottesville to shut down the state government. None of this worked out, and Cornwallis pulled back to Williamsburg, reaching it on June 25. In the meantime, General Anthony Wayne and what was left of the Pennsylvania Line had joined Lafayette.

Cornwallis was finding that fewer Loyalists were coming out to support him than had in the Carolinas, and he was sorely disappointed. Many slaves did, however, just as they had joined Arnold and Phillips—much to the embarrassment of owners like Thomas Jefferson and Patrick Henry and, indeed, George Washington, James Madison, and James Monroe. Over two dozen fled Mount Vernon.

Virginians who were sympathetic with the patriot cause were not rushing to join Steuben, either. Their reluctance to turn out was notable, as was the extensive profiteering going on in the state. Enthusiasm for the war seemed most pronounced in an embarrassingly large class of entrepreneurs. They were more interested in making money than fighting.

On June 26 Cornwallis was in Williamsburg when he received a dispatch from Clinton urging, but not ordering, him to speedily establish a naval base and send three thousand troops back to New York to help with its defense—if he could spare them. Clinton was increasingly feeling that New York was going to be attacked soon.

Cornwallis was upset. Clinton's letter meant that Cornwallis's strategy of emphasizing Virginia was being rejected. He began to think that he'd be better off simply sending the troops Clinton wanted, and maybe more, and retreating to Charleston, leaving Virginia completely. With his anger mounting, he marched down to Portsmouth and threatened to send all his troops to New York while he personally returned to Charleston. Actually, under the circumstances, that would not have been a bad plan.

But Clinton did not interpret it that way. He was aghast at Cornwallis's gross misinterpretation of his message and backed off, allowing Cornwallis to keep all his troops in Virginia and settle on a suitable base. Cornwallis had his way, although having a third of Clinton's army in Virginia during the hot summer establishing a small port on Chesapeake Bay seemed absurd. If there was any point at which Clinton should have asserted his authority over a recalcitrant subordinate it was here. But he failed to do so, primarily because he had no clear overall strategy.

Cornwallis consumed another month marching back and forth from Williamsburg to Portsmouth, jousting with Lafayette, and then to Gloucester and Yorktown, although he hadn't yet chosen Yorktown as his base. He was flailing about as he had in the Carolinas. In fact, the whole southern strategy appeared to make less and less sense, except to London. On June 27 Clinton received yet another letter from Germain insisting that he pay more attention to the Chesapeake.

Clinton, meanwhile, continuing to observe all the threatening preparations being made in Westchester County, was bolstering New York's defenses as much as he could. He was confident that Rodney, whom he still regarded as a friend, would return from the Caribbean and counter any French fleet that showed up at Sandy Hook. Clinton had no idea what Rodney really thought of him, which wasn't surprising. Any ability to understand, sympathize, and get along with colleagues was beyond him. He had famously described himself as a "shy bitch," whatever that meant. No one knew, but it certainly did not mean that he was a figure beloved by colleagues, his men, or the officer corps, as William Howe had been.

Chapter 26

RODNEY'S DILEMMA

The all-important decision on whether the allied attack would be in the Chesapeake or at New York ultimately rested with Admiral de Grasse. The well-known difficulty of getting his giant warships over the shifting sandbar at Sandy Hook made him prefer the Chesapeake, but New York had not been entirely ruled out. Washington and Rochambeau could gather their forces in Westchester County and plausibly make it appear that Manhattan was their target, because it was one. At the same time, they could be preparing for a quick march to Virginia.

During the first week of July, Rochambeau's splendidly equipped army joined Washington's ill-clad Continentals at Dobbs Ferry on the Hudson, thirteen miles above Kings Bridge. The stark contrast between the two armies startled the French and embarrassed the patriots. America's dependence on France had never been more obvious. What wasn't so obvious was that French help was coming to an end. Something decisive had to come from this campaign. The patriots were at the end of their tether, or so it appeared, and the French were as well. The splendid uniforms and weaponry of Rochambeau's soldiers masked the fact that the French treasury was being exhausted.

Washington thought that by being active around Manhattan he was keeping Clinton from helping Cornwallis, and taking the pressure off Greene. He was fortunate to have Clinton as his adversary. Even though the British army was superior to Washington and Rochambeau combined, Clinton never entertained the idea of attacking them in Westchester County. He expected them to come to him. His mind was fixed on defending Manhattan against an attack he was sure would come from adversaries who could not help but know that they were much weaker than he was. The man who had been full of daring strategic advice for his superiors, Howe and Gage, was now lacking initiative, quiescent when he should have been aggressive.

The fact that Barras' squadron at Newport was vulnerable when Rochambeau left to join Washington did not escape Clinton's notice. A successful surprise attack on the French fleet could have a major impact on the war. The British squadron in New York was far superior. Admiral Graves was all for using it. But Clinton demurred. His excuse was that Cornwallis had not sent the three thousand troops to New York that he had requested. Since he had plenty of troops even without reinforcements from Cornwallis to both defend New York and attack Rhode Island, Clinton's reasoning was hard to fathom.

Rochambeau and Washington had urged Barras to take his fleet to the protection of Boston Harbor, but he refused, preferring Narragansett Bay. Although Boston was unquestionably safer, it was also much farther away from the potential scene of action in either New York or Chesapeake Bay, and Newport was much easier to get in and out of.

Clinton's unwillingness to go after Barras was another major mistake that contributed a good deal to Britain's ultimate defeat. As commander in chief, Clinton always wanted overwhelming superiority before undertaking any action. His basic approach seemed to be to never take chances. He told William Smith that the reason he never attacked West Point, even when he had Rodney and Arnold to help, was that he needed a twelve-to-two margin of superiority, which, of course, ruled it out. A two-to-one margin was usually considered adequate. Despite all of Clinton's strategic proposals over the years, it's doubtful that he would have acted on any of the major ones. He made many plans, and even preparations, that never materialized.

Clinton's lack of spirit and enterprise mystified and angered Loyalists in Manhattan. They did not understand why he was not attacking Washington's obviously inferior force in Westchester County. In spite of Washington's unceasing efforts to strengthen the army, he had fewer than six thousand men. Even after Rochambeau arrived, they had less than eleven thousand troops between them. Benedict Arnold, who had been recalled to New York, was relentless in stirring up the Tories, bemoaning Clinton's inexplicable unwillingness to take advantage of rebel weakness in a number of places, including Rhode Island, Westchester, and Philadelphia.

Washington kept the pressure on the indecisive British commander by making a surprise raid on the north end of Manhattan Island on July 3. Before his troops moved, he warned Governor Clinton, "I intend to make an attempt by surprise upon the enemy's position on the north end of York [Manhattan] Island on Monday night." The surprise did not succeed, but the incessant activity near Kings Bridge held General Clinton's attention and contributed to his unease.

After Rochambeau arrived in Westchester, he and Washington explored in greater detail the feasibility of an attack on New York. Washington was to concentrate on Manhattan, while Rochambeau focused on Brooklyn and Long Island. As their thinking sharpened, Rochambeau became less concerned about failing in New York. His preference was still the Chesapeake, but when he gave de Grasse details of a possible attack on New York, they appeared more plausible than they had in the past.

It was still almost certain that de Grasse would make for the Chesapeake, however. When the time came, Washington and Rochambeau had to keep Clinton's focus on Manhattan while they moved most of their troops to Virginia. So much intelligence was coming in to Clinton confirming New York as the target that he must have wondered if it was all an elaborate deception, but watching the activity in Westchester County and in New Jersey made him think it probably wasn't.

Washington, meanwhile, kept in close touch with Lafayette. He had to know right away when Cornwallis made a move. He did not know if Cornwallis would continue dueling with Lafayette and Steuben in Virginia, or carry the war back to the Carolinas, or even come to New York with some or all of his army. His seven thousand troops could make a big difference wherever they went. To ensure rapid communication, Washington had Lafayette set up a chain of express riders. He particularly wanted to know if Cornwallis was creating a deepwater base on the Chesapeake and sending a detachment to bolster Clinton in New York. He did not know, of course, that Germain, reflecting the king's view, was urging Clinton to do exactly what the allies wanted—namely, while holding New York, emphasize the South, especially Virginia.

While Washington was preoccupied with the South and Manhattan, he did not forget the North. A quick British advance down from Canada—perhaps aided by Vermont separatists—was a possibility. On June 21 he wrote to Governor Clinton to make sure he was prepared for a raid from Canada. At the moment, the British were quiet, their activity low; they had "not made any movement in force," but that could change.

A few days later Washington appointed Major General John Stark to be commander of the northern front, telling him to make Saratoga his headquarters. Stark was in New Hampshire when he got the message, and was on the move quickly, picking up strong support from Green Mountain Boys as he went.

★

SINCE BOTH SIDES KNEW THAT THE NAVIES WOULD DECIDE who won the impending showdown, there was every reason for Rodney to be in command of the West Indian squadron when it came to the American coast. Rodney was aware of his responsibility, but at the same time, he had no desire to go near the American war. In fact, he had already taken steps to avoid getting trapped in it again.

After being occupied for a month with the messy but immensely profitable business of St. Eustatius, he wrote to the Earl of Sandwich on March 7, 1781, requesting leave to come home and get away from "this climate during the rainy season." He needed to restore his health, he told the first lord.

Given the circumstances, it's hard to imagine that health was his only reason, or even the primary one. He did not expect to receive Sandwich's reply until June, or even July. By that time, if he had not gotten permission to go home, he would likely be sailing for America to counter a French fleet. Normally, Rodney would have been anxious to have the opportunity to defeat the French in a dramatic showdown that had the potential to win the American war. He was a gifted fighter, with no hesitation about taking risks. But on this occasion, racing for the American coast, as he had the year before, was the last thing he wanted to do. As far as he was concerned, with the leadership the British government had in place in New York, the war could well be lost, and he did not want to be the scapegoat. He had no desire to risk his reputation battling alongside Arbuthnot and Clinton, the same dysfunctional pair who, he was convinced, had cost His Majesty an easy victory in 1780. Rodney had urged London to replace them, but as far as he knew, they were still directing the war. He did not want to share the blame for another missed opportunity or, worse, an outright defeat.

Having permission from Sandwich to return to England for health reasons was a perfect way out. Even though Rodney's ailments had not handicapped him when he was plundering St. Eustatius or fighting the Spanish and French, they were a good excuse for returning home.

Then there was the money. He had amassed a fortune looting St. Eustatius, and it was being sent to England, where he could use it to get rid of all the money problems that had plagued him for years. Ironically, he kept very little of the money he took from the island. He sent much of it home in a convoy that Admiral Toussaint-Guillaume de la Motte-Picquet captured as it approached the English coast and took to France.

The rest was lost in successful lawsuits brought against him by English merchants whose goods and money he had stolen.

Making Rodney's decision easier was the arrival of Admiral Hood, who would be sent to America in his stead. Rodney had confidence in Hood. The only problem was that Hood would not have seniority. Arbuthnot would be his superior, which meant that Hood, regardless of his ability, would be no replacement at all for Rodney.

As hurricane season approached in the summer of 1781, Rodney had to decide what he was going to do. He still had not made up his mind. He knew that his decision would have far-reaching consequences, and his conscience was bothering him.

Lord Sandwich appeared indifferent. With apparently little thought, he had already granted permission for Rodney to return to England and tend to his health. On the sidelines was an admiral even better than Rodney, Lord Howe, but Sandwich had never wanted to send him to America; he certainly was not going to send him now. Nor would Howe have gone, unless the king himself asked personally, which His Majesty was not inclined to do.

Even though Rodney was preparing to evade his responsibility and return to England, he continued to worry about what would happen without him. He wrote to his wife explaining what was at stake. "In all probability, the enemy, when they leave these seas, will go to America," he told her, "wherever they go I will watch their motions, and certainly attack them if they give me a proper opportunity. The fate of England may depend upon the event."

★

WHEN DE GRASSE, HAVING LEFT OFF DUELING WITH RODNEY, arrived at Cap François on July 16 from Fort Royal Bay in Martinique with the large merchant convoy, he found four sail of the line waiting for him, along with the frigate *Concorde*, fresh from Boston with messages from Rochambeau and Washington.

After reading their letters, de Grasse decided to take the unusual step of leaving the merchant convoy at Cap François while he brought his whole task force to Virginia. Normally, he would have split his fleet, assigning half to guard the convoy on its way to France and taking the other half to America. The merchantmen would now remain where they were until he returned. It was a bold move with momentous consequences. De Grasse was gambling that by hitting the British with all he had, he could accomplish what Vergennes and the king really wanted—a quick end to the war.

At the same time, de Grasse chose Chesapeake Bay over New York. The showdown with Britain, if there was to be one, would be there. It was hoped that Cornwallis would cooperate and remain with his full army at a post where the allies could trap him. The latest intelligence suggested that he would, but would he?

De Grasse could make all these plans because Rodney had failed to engage him in a general battle in the Caribbean during the campaign season of 1781. Rodney's best opportunity had been on April 28, when de Grasse first arrived off Martinique, but Rodney was nowhere to be found. He was at St. Eustatius. He had left Hood, who had no experience in those waters, with an inferior fleet to deal with de Grasse. The result was predictable.

De Grasse could now bring a huge fleet north to decisively affect the outcome of the American war and still plan to be back in the Caribbean to combine with the dons in attacking the British islands. If de Grasse succeeded, Rodney would have much to answer for.

Washington wrote in his diary that he and Rochambeau had received dispatches from de Grasse on July 14, announcing that he would depart Cap François with twenty-five to twenty-nine sail of the line and thirty-two hundred French troops. De Grasse emphasized that he had to be back in the West Indies by the middle of October for joint operations with the Spanish. Having to coordinate with the dons made his task far more complicated. The able Spanish governor of Louisiana, thirty-six-year-old Bernardo de Galvez (Galveston is named after him), who was working closely with de Grasse, agreed to cooperate and allow him to take the French troops that had been slated for an invasion of West

Florida in November, to the Chesapeake, provided de Grasse returned by the end of October.

On July 21 Washington wrote to de Grasse in Rochambeau's cipher, describing the situation of the joint armies just above Manhattan and the enemy's strength. He also suggested possible plans for future operations. Washington entrusted the letter to General David Forman at Monmouth, New Jersey, with instructions to deliver it personally to de Grasse the moment his fleet was sighted.

As if to cooperate with French and American plans, Clinton stuck to the idea of keeping Cornwallis's entire seven-thousand-man army in Virginia and establishing a deepwater base. On August 2, Cornwallis began debarking troops at Yorktown and at Gloucester, directly across the York River. Establishing a base there at this particular moment served no immediate purpose. It would not impact Greene and the southern guerrillas or the war in general. Cornwallis, with Clinton's connivance, appeared to be doing it simply to give his army something to do.

While Cornwallis had been running around Virginia with no results, General Greene had been taking advantage of his absence and systematically pushing the British back to Charleston. Working with guerrilla leaders Francis Marion, Thomas Sumter, Andrew Pickens, Elijah Clarke, William R. Davie, and others, Greene was seeing the Union Jack hauled down everywhere in the South. Soon, the only places flying it would be Savannah and Charleston. And their collapse would be only a matter of time.

The loss of Lord Rawdon, Cornwallis's chief lieutenant in the Carolinas, contributed to Greene's success. Rawdon had become seriously ill, and was returning home to recover when de Grasse captured him while Rawdon was sailing north from Charleston to Chesapeake Bay. General Leslie took his place in Charleston.

While Rochambeau and Washington were absorbed with preparations for the coming showdown in the Chesapeake, on August 14 Admiral de Barras suddenly announced that he was going to attack Newfoundland with his fleet and some of the five hundred French troops remaining in Newport. Amazed and horrified when they heard the news, Washington and Rochambeau protested so vehemently that he backed off. Washington pointed out how dangerous a move it would be "under the probability of Rodney coming up this coast." The problem, Washington discovered later, was that Barras was senior to de Grasse and was uncomfortable, indeed annoyed, at having to serve under him—thus the bizarre Newfoundland proposal. Fortunately, Barras changed his mind before any damage was done.

On July 28 de Grasse sent the *Concorde* north with dispatches for Rochambeau, Barras, and Luzerne indicating that he would begin his journey north the first week of August. On the fifth he sailed from Cap François, and on the thirtieth he reached Chesapeake Bay. The following morning a dumbfounded Cornwallis awoke to find a gargantuan French fleet parked at his back door.

Chapter 27

NEW YORK AND
YORKTOWN

Success or failure for de Grasse and the allies now depended on Rodney's decisions. He had already failed to prevent the French fleet from sailing to Chesapeake Bay, and he had no idea how many battleships were in it. He assumed that de Grasse would bring only half his fleet and send the other half to escort the huge merchant convoy that regularly traveled from Cap François to France. But he could not be sure. D'Estaing had twice brought the entire West Indian squadron to America; de Grasse could do the same.

It was to Rodney's advantage not to learn the true size of de Grasse's fleet: If he knew for certain that de Grasse was bringing his entire squadron north, he would have felt compelled to come himself. Otherwise, he could, in good conscience, avoid coming to America. If he assumed that de Grasse would not do what d'Estaing had done, there would be enough copper-bottomed British battleships to counter him. Graves's fleet in New York, combined with Hood's fourteen and perhaps the two Rodney had ordered Admiral Parker to send from Jamaica, would be sufficient.

Rodney remained uncharacteristically ambivalent about what to do for a long time. He knew that he should lead the squadron going north, but his distaste for Arbuthnot and Clinton was simply overpowering. Finally, on July 25, when he could wait no longer, he wrote to Hood from St. Eustatius, ordering him to "secure the outward bound convoy for Jamaica" and then take fourteen sail of the line and four frigates to North America immediately.

It was late in the day to be sending these critical orders. At the time, Rodney was unaware that on July 4, Rear Admiral Thomas Graves, a fifty-five-year-old veteran, had replaced Arbuthnot. When Rodney found out, he was somewhat relieved. It's true that he would not be leading the North American squadron, and neither would Hood, since Hood would still be junior, but Graves was perfectly capable, in Rodney's eyes, and de Grasse was not the most formidable fighter in the French navy.

Admiral Graves was actually an interim appointment. He was not Arbuthnot's successor; forty-nine-year-old Rear Admiral Robert Digby was. Appointing him at this particular moment was awkward, if not bizarre. Digby was junior to Graves, who was bound to feel humiliated. Sandwich obviously didn't care what effect that would have on Graves or the war.

In early July Digby was still in England, however, and Graves was still unaware of Digby's appointment; he continued to labor under the impression that he was Arbuthnot's permanent replacement. Digby did not sail for America until July 19 and would not reach New York until September or even October. Sandwich felt no sense of urgency. He only allowed three sail of the line to accompany Digby—a shockingly small number. The first lord continued to be out of touch with realities in the American theater, where far more battleships were needed.

In his July 25 letter to Hood, Rodney prescribed the route Hood was to take to New York, directing him "first to make the capes of the Chesapeake, then those of the Delaware, and so on to Sandy Hook." In this letter Rodney seemed unsure if Hood would be the senior commander on the American station, but it's safe to say that since either Arbuthnot or Graves would still be there, Hood would not be the senior officer.

On August 1 Rodney left the roadstead at St. Eustatius and sailed for England with the huge homeward-bound convoy. Two old sail of the line accompanied the one hundred fifty merchant vessels, along with Rodney's 80-gun *Gibraltar* and the fast frigate *Pegasus*. Aboard the *Gibraltar* with Rodney were three of Benedict Arnold's children, Benedict, Richard, and Henry. They were going to England to be with their father, when and if he got there. In the brief time Rodney had gotten to know Arnold in the fall of 1780, he had become a great admirer, believing that if the savvy, dynamic Arnold had been in command of His Majesty's forces instead of the inscrutable, inactive Clinton, the British would have already won the war.

Even at this late date, Rodney still had not totally made up his mind to turn away from the American maelstrom. He fancied that at the last moment he could transfer to the *Pegasus*, race for New York, and assume command. When he judged that the moment had finally come to make a choice, however, he sent the *Pegasus* off to New York with word of Hood's imminent arrival, while he went on to England and a holiday. He arrived at Plymouth on September 19.

As it turned out, he waited too long. *Pegasus* did not reach New York until September 2, four days after Hood arrived at Sandy Hook and one day after Admiral Graves left New York with the combined fleets to battle de Grasse in Virginia. Rodney later insisted that he had done everything possible to prevent the disaster that followed. In addition to sending Hood with fourteen sail of the line, he ordered the commander in chief in Jamaica, Peter Parker, to send the 90-gun *Torbay* and the 64-gun *Prince William* to America with the "greatest dispatch." He further protested:

> I had sent also to the commander in chief in America, desiring he would collect his whole force and meet me with it off the Capes of Virginia, and in case he could not meet me, that he would acquaint me with it by one of his frigates, but no answer was sent either to Sir Samuel Hood or myself, for I was then so ill, that I was coming home. I had sent twice to the admiral in Jamaica, and three times to the

admiral at New York. . . . If the admiral in America had met Sir Samuel
Hood near the Chesapeake, the probability was that de Grasse would
have been defeated, and the surrender of Cornwallis prevented.

Rodney's explanation was an embarrassing blend of gross exaggeration, fabrication, and wishful thinking. He never exhibited a com-
pulsion to race to the American coast. In fact, he did everything he
could to avoid it. Illness was his excuse. The notion that Graves with
nineteen sail of the line would have beaten de Grasse with twenty-eight
if they had met near the Chesapeake was, to say the least, doubtful,
particularly in view of what happened later, when the odds were not as
heavily in de Grasse's favor. The truth was that having General Clinton
and Admiral Arbuthnot managing the war was anathema to Rodney, a
sure recipe for a disaster he did not want to be associated with. Even
though he learned at the last minute about Admiral Graves taking over
command, there was still Clinton.

At this critical juncture, the Admiralty, seemingly oblivious of the
momentous events taking shape in the Caribbean and the need for
the British fleet to be in New York, sent the sloop of war *Hornet* to
warn Graves that a large French convoy was heading for Boston with
essential supplies for the rebel army. Stopping it would, in their lordships' view, have a serious impact on the war. The order for Graves
was written as if there were no impending crisis, that Graves's fleet
wasn't needed to stave off the deadly blow being aimed by the Franco-
American allies. Nothing could have better illustrated how out of
touch the Admiralty was.

Graves might have ignored the communication. Instead, on July 21,
not taking the movements of the allies and the probability of a French
fleet's coming to New York or to Chesapeake Bay too seriously, he went
in search of the enemy convoy, leaving New York undefended. He never
found a convoy, but he did get stuck in thick fog near Boston and had
two of his large warships seriously damaged. He did not get back to New
York until August 16. De Grasse was already racing for Chesapeake Bay.

Clinton was understandably shocked when Graves left. Washington and Rochambeau were threatening Manhattan, and a potentially huge French fleet was coming, which Clinton had been apprised of. A more inopportune time to withdraw the fleet from New York would be hard to imagine. It was as if Paris were sending Graves his orders rather than London.

Clinton was still counting on Rodney to save him. He had written to him as if they were the closest of friends, pleading with him to come to New York as he had the previous year, and expecting that he would. It was more than a little ironic that Clinton was the principal reason Rodney wasn't coming.

On August 10 Hood left Antigua with fourteen sail of the line, shaping a course directly for Chesapeake Bay. He had already received a letter from Admiral Graves, warning about a French fleet, but not its size. Hood sent word that he was coming to the rescue, but his letter never reached Graves. By August 25 Hood was at Chesapeake Bay, and, finding no French fleet there, he sailed on to New York, arriving on August 28.

When Hood reached Sandy Hook, he was amazed to find no sense of urgency in Manhattan. No one had any idea that the expected French fleet, which they all knew about, was so large. Graves had just returned from his fruitless search for the French convoy off Boston, and he was refurbishing his ships. Two of them, *Robust* and *Prudent*, needed major repairs and could not sail. His fleet was reduced to five sail of the line. But he wasn't overly concerned. He suggested that Hood move his squadron into the harbor while he prepared. Hood was dumbfounded. Time was of the essence, and he tried to impress that on Graves by remaining outside the Hook. Taking fourteen battleships into and out of the Lower Bay could have consumed days.

By the time Graves was ready and his ships were out in the Atlantic it was August 31. He now had nineteen copper-bottomed sail of the line, a 50-gun ship, a fireship, and seven frigates, including the *Iris*, which was the former Continental frigate *Hancock*. Graves was confident that he could handle the French. He knew that Barras had already left Newport with his eight battleships, but he still did not know how many sail of the line de Grasse had. Even so, Graves could not imagine that de Grasse was bringing his whole West Indian fleet to the Chesapeake, and so he wasn't overly concerned. No ship had appeared to tell him how large the French squadron really was. De Grasse had managed to scoop up every vessel he found on his way north, so that his numbers would remain a secret.

★

THE FRANCO-AMERICAN ARMY, IN THE MEANTIME, WAS PRE-paring to march from the Hudson to Yorktown. On August 15, Washington wrote to Lafayette, telling him that de Grasse had planned to depart Cap François for Chesapeake Bay the first week of August with twenty-five to twenty-nine sail of the line and a large detachment of soldiers. Washington ordered Lafayette to "take such a position as will best enable you to prevent . . . [Cornwallis's] sudden retreat through North Carolina, which I presume . . . [he] will attempt the instant . . . [he] perceive[s] so formidable an armament."

Two days later, Washington wrote to de Grasse from Dobbs Ferry:

> In consequence of the dispatches received from your Excellency by the frigate *Concorde*, it has been judged expedient to give up for the present the enterprise against New York, and turn over our attention to the South, with a view, if we should not be able to attempt Charleston itself, to recover and secure the states of Virginia, North Carolina, and the country of South Carolina and Georgia.
>
> For this purpose we have determined to remove the whole of the French army, and as large a detachment of the American as can be spared, to the Chesapeake, to meet your Excellency there.

Washington asked de Grasse "[t]o send up the Elk River, at the head of the Chesapeake Bay, all your frigates, transports, and vessels proper for the conveyance of the French and American troops down the bay."

On the same day, Washington wrote to his old friend Robert Morris, the superintendent of finance, requesting food and other supplies, which Morris was doing his utmost to provide, "I shall also stand in need of a sum of specie for secret services, I suppose about 500 guineas." Morris wrote back immediately, explaining that he didn't have the money but would do his best to get it.

At the same time, Washington was providing for the safety of the Hudson and particularly West Point. Clinton had a sizable army of at least sixteen thousand in Manhattan capable of driving up the Hudson when the allied armies moved south. Making matters more uncertain, on August 11 three thousand German troops arrived to reinforce Clinton. Washington told General Heath, "The security of West Point and the posts in the Highlands is to be considered the first object of your attention."

The following day, Washington's army crossed King's Ferry to Stony Point, beginning the movement of the allied armies to Virginia. Washington was understandably worried that Cornwallis might suddenly burst out of Yorktown before he got there. On August 21, he wrote to Lafayette, emphasizing again that "my most earnest wish, that the land and naval forces, which you will have with you, may so combine their operations, that the British army may not be able to escape."

British agents flooded Clinton with reports that the allied army was on the move. Even at this late date, Clinton thought that they were going to attack Manhattan, Brooklyn, or Staten Island. Washington encouraged the illusion by marching the American and French armies by different routes south to Trenton. The French moved through Springfield and Brunswick, making it appear that they were positioning themselves to cooperate with the French fleet that Clinton had been warned was coming and attack Staten Island and Sandy Hook,

Rochambeau set up a French bakery at Chatham, New Jersey, making it look as if he was there to stay. Clinton was taken in. He believed until September 1 that the attack was going to be on New York. He apparently gave no thought to attacking the allied armies in New Jersey. With the British fleet at sea going to Chesapeake Bay, he felt confined to Manhattan. The defenses on the island were strong; moving beyond them at the moment was unthinkable, even though he had probably seven to eight thousand more men than the combined allied armies— nineteen thousand to their eleven thousand. Even that ratio wasn't nearly enough to tempt him out of the city.

Lack of money continued to bedevil Washington. The country was bankrupt; Congress had no hard money. On August 27 he wrote again to Robert Morris, telling him of the urgent need for transports to get the troops to the battle zone, for flour and salt provisions, and especially for one month's pay in specie for the detachment "which I have under my command. . . . Part of those troops have not been paid anything for a long time past, and have upon several occasions shown marks of great discontent." Morris responded by securing a loan of 20,000 in hard currency from Rochambeau.

Washington was also wondering where Admiral de Grasse was. He hadn't heard as yet. He knew that a British fleet was racing to get to the Chesapeake ahead of de Grasse and worried that it would get there first, defeating all his plans for trapping Cornwallis.

★

EARLY ON THE MORNING OF SEPTEMBER 5, AS ADMIRAL Graves and the British fleet approached Cape Charles at the northern edge of Chesapeake Bay, Graves dispatched the frigates *Richmond* and *Solebay* to search for the enemy. When they returned, their report indicated a French fleet of at least twenty-four battleships and perhaps more. All of a sudden, Graves was confronting a much different reality than the one he, and everyone else in the British high command, including Hood and Rodney, had long expected. Instead of having a superior fleet, his squadron was significantly smaller than the enemy's. He had to quickly adjust his thinking. For the first time, he had to consider the consequences of a defeat and what it would mean, not just for North America, but for the West Indies.

What to do? Graves could not return to New York and wait for reinforcements; he had a responsibility to Cornwallis. But he was understandably reluctant to enter the bay and challenge de Grasse's larger fleet, particularly with Barras about to arrive with reinforcements. Given the new situation, Graves decided to remain offshore. If he did, de Grasse would be forced to sortie and challenge him in order to protect Barras. It was unlikely that Barras had already arrived in Chesapeake Bay. With the entire British squadron having copper bottoms, Graves stood a good chance of beating the larger French fleet, and he began preparing to fight.

Fortunately for Graves, when he arrived, de Grasse was in the middle of debarking the thirty-five hundred soldiers he had brought with him. Over twelve hundred seamen and their officers were engaged in the unloading. He wasn't ready for an enemy fleet to appear just at that moment, even though he knew one was coming.

Nonetheless, despite being surprised, de Grasse did not hesitate. The moment his ships signaled the approach of a British fleet, he began preparing to exit the bay for a major battle. He could not let Barras run into Graves unexpectedly. Barras was still on his way from Newport, having left on August 25 with eight sail of the line, four frigates, and eighteen transports carrying the indispensable French siege guns for Washington and Rochambeau. De Grasse had to defeat the British fleet or, at a minimum, draw it away from the mouth of the bay so that Barras could enter safely.

De Grasse hurried to get officers and men back to their ships. Many would not make it. He ordered four big warships to remain in the bay and twenty-four others to get under way. Unfortunately, wind and tide were against him. He was forced to wait until noon for the tide to turn before beginning to beat out of the Chesapeake against the wind.

When the French ships crawled out piecemeal, Graves, with his fast, maneuverable sail of the line and a fair wind at his back, had an excellent opportunity to attack the stragglers a few at a time and even the odds. As the slow French battleships moved gradually beyond Cape Henry into the Atlantic, separated from the main fleet, it seemed obvious that Graves should have exploited this perfect opening and attacked them. But he chose not to. Instead, he formed a conventional line of battle with his entire fleet outside the bay and, inexplicably, waited for de Grasse to sortie and form his line of battle. Graves's officers, particularly Hood, were baffled by his tactics.

When Rodney later studied reports of the encounter, he was furious at Graves for throwing away the clear opportunities he had to win. There's no doubt that Rodney would have acted differently. He certainly would have attacked the French battleships as they struggled singly into the Atlantic or later, when de Grasse's van got separated from the main fleet. Caution appeared to mark Graves's every move, and caution rarely won a battle where the opponent had a significant advantage, although, since only half of de Grasse's ships had copper bottoms, how much of an edge the latter really had was questionable.

While waiting for de Grasse to bring his ships out of the bay, Graves had his sail of the line moving slowly away from the Chesapeake's entrance in a traditional line of battle formation, with a third in the van, a third in the middle, and a third in the rear. Graves directed the fight from his flagship, the 98-gun *London*, situated in the middle of the battle line, as was customary.

By four o'clock the British van and middle, which were positioned at an angle to de Grasse, got close enough to fire with effect, and Graves gave the order to engage. The fight that would determine the outcome of the American war was on. It lasted two and a half hours and was inconclusive. Naturally, much debate over tactics followed. Hood, who never had a good word for any superior, was unrestrained in his criticism of Graves's entire strategy. His complaints were colored by the fact that he had command of the seven ships in Graves's rear division and hardly became engaged in the battle at all, blaming his actions on Graves's confused signaling, which was unfair. Hood's tirade was reminiscent of the one he threw when he failed to stop any of de Grasse's one hundred fifty transports from reaching Fort Royal Bay in Martinique earlier in the year. He blamed the entire business on Rodney's orders, when the fault was his own. Rather than admit a mistake, he found it easier to point a finger at his superior.

After the initial encounter, the fleets remained close—within sight of each other most of the time—for three long, frustrating days, fixing their ships but not engaging again, although on the seventh de Grasse made an effort to do so, but failed. The following day, September 8, he made another attempt that failed, but found himself closer to the bay than the British, which was where he wanted to be. He was increasingly concerned about Barras. He did not want him to get cut off by Graves, and on the morning of the ninth, de Grasse raced back to the Chesapeake, hoping to get there before the British, and he succeeded. When he arrived, he found Barras already there.

Before de Grasse rushed back to the Chesapeake, Hood had been urging Graves to get into the bay ahead of the French, but Graves refused. He did not want to get trapped in the Chesapeake by a much larger French fleet. He remained where he was, while de Grasse entered and united with Barras.

With half his fleet needing repairs, Graves sent the frigate *Medea* to look into the bay and report back. What the *Medea* saw was thirty-six sail of the line—de Grasse's twenty-eight, plus Barras' eight. On the thirteenth she reported the baleful news to Graves, who was forced to admit defeat. His only alternative was to return to New York, where he arrived on September 20. He may have lost the battle, but he saved his fleet, except for the battleship *Terrible*, which was so badly damaged she had to be burned.

★

ON SEPTEMBER 5, AN EXPRESS RIDER CAUGHT UP WITH WASH-ington while he was on the road riding from Philadelphia to Yorktown and told him that de Grasse had arrived first in Chesapeake Bay, foreclosing any aid for Cornwallis by sea. The messenger added that de Grasse brought with him an eye-popping twenty-eight sail of the line and over three thousand troops. Needless to say, the commander in chief was ecstatic. This was wonderful news, of the kind he had been dreaming about for a long time. But what about Rodney and the British fleet? Where were they?

A short time later, Washington learned of the battle off Cape Henry, but not its outcome. He was obviously worried. He did not get the glorious news of de Grasse's victory until September 14. At the same time, he learned, again to his enormous relief, that the British fleet had suffered significant damage and had been forced back to New York.

The next day, Washington wrote to the president of Congress informing him of the magnificent victory and of the safe arrival of Barras in the Chesapeake. "I have the honor to inform Congress," he wrote, "that I have arrived at this place [Williamsburg] last evening; that soon after my arrival, I received the pleasing intelligence, that the Count de Grasse, who had put to sea on the 5th in pursuit of the British fleet, had returned to his former station at Cape Henry, having driven the British from the coast, taken two of their frigates, and effected a junction with the squadron of the Count de Barras." The news was almost too good to be true.

Washington also had the satisfaction of hearing soon after, in a meeting aboard the *Ville de Paris* with de Grasse, Rochambeau, and their staffs, that de Grasse had agreed to stay with his fleet until the end of October, which would give the allies enough time to force the surrender of Cornwallis, who was now securely trapped.

Clinton, in the meantime, had to decide how to help Cornwallis. He had plenty of options. After all, he still had the most powerful land force on the continent. His first instinct was to reinforce Cornwallis by sea. He wrote to him on September 6—before he knew the outcome of the great naval battle off Cape Henry—that he would come with support, which, of course, he could not until Admiral Graves established naval supremacy. At the time, Clinton assumed that Graves would. He never dreamed that de Grasse would bring twenty-eight battleships to the American coast.

Cornwallis, in order to deflect blame from himself, later insisted that Clinton had promised help, and that he, therefore, looked exclusively to New York for relief. Yet it was obvious that after de Grasse and Barras united in the Chesapeake, no aid could possibly come from Clinton. When Clinton promised relief in his letter of September 6, he was assuming that the British would continue to have naval supremacy. His letter did not reach Cornwallis until the middle of September, however, when it was obvious that Graves had lost control of the sea.

Cornwallis had only himself to blame for the predicament he now found himself in. He might have fought his way out of Yorktown earlier. He did not have to wait for Clinton to save him. When de Grasse unexpectedly appeared at the end of August, Cornwallis was much stronger than Lafayette and could have marched out of Yorktown and gone to a number of different places. Lafayette's force was too small to stop him and would have been forced to move out of the way.

Some of Cornwallis's officers, like Tarleton, urged him to fight his way out to the Carolinas. But a long march to the Carolinas in the heat of early September had no appeal for him. He had come to Virginia because he could not survive farther south. If he didn't go south, he could have marched north with his big army, even to New York. His force when combined with Clinton's would be formidable—more than twice the size of Washington and Rochambeau's combined. He chose instead to hope that the navy and Rodney would eventually get the better of the French, and that Clinton could supply enough force to deal with the Franco-American army.

Creating an even greater sense of urgency for Cornwallis's young officers was the sight of the handsomely clad French troops being unloaded from de Grasse's fleet beginning the first week of September. Tarleton and his colleagues had no idea how many there were, but they were obviously formidable French regulars who would have experienced leaders. In fact, the able Marquis de Saint-Simon was in command. Tarleton had hoped that Cornwallis would fight his way out of Yorktown before Saint-Simon had a chance to unite his troops with Lafayette's. Sitting in Yorktown and waiting for Clinton to save them did not appear to be a viable strategy.

While Cornwallis dithered, Lafayette and Saint-Simon joined forces and closed off Cornwallis's chance to march out of Yorktown, while de Grasse closed off Clinton's chance to send reinforcements by sea.

In spite of everything that had happened, Clinton still looked to the navy for help. Admiral Digby was coming to assume command of the

North American squadron. He could be bringing a large reinforcement; Clinton did not know how many battleships he would have with him, but he assumed the fleet would be substantial. When, on September 24, Digby finally arrived, Clinton could scarcely believe that he brought a stunning three sail of the line. It was as if the first lord of the Admiralty did not know a war was going on.

All was not lost, however. Even with the resources he had, Clinton could have done a number of things to help Cornwallis, other than sending him direct aid by sea. He could have attacked West Point and the Highlands with his still considerable army in New York, something Washington feared he might do. Clinton could also have attacked Philadelphia, which was largely defenseless. Arnold and others urged him to. Capturing the rebel capital might offset the advantage the allies were gaining in the Chesapeake. Clinton might even have taken Rhode Island as well as Philadelphia. Instead, after Graves's defeat, he did nothing but prepare with Graves an amphibious task force to rescue Cornwallis, even though it was doubtful it would be big enough or would get there in time. The task force itself might be vulnerable, which both Graves and Clinton worried about. Going by sea with the inferior fleet they had was, to say the least, tempting fate. A more unimaginative strategy would be hard to conceive.

Digby, after viewing the hopeless situation he was being placed in, refused to assume command from Graves until the present crisis had been resolved. He wanted no responsibility for the impending catastrophe that Rodney had predicted if Clinton were left in place. The same timid Clinton, the man who was cautious when he should have been bold, the leader whom Rodney was furious with the previous year because he wouldn't lead, was the same Clinton managing things now, mindlessly paddling toward the rapids.

The allies began the investment of Yorktown on September 28 with 16, 600 troops (7,800 French and 8,800 American), more than twice what Cornwallis had. It was eight days after Admiral Graves reached New York and began repairing his fleet—the ships that were supposed to rescue Cornwallis. The work dragged on and on. Graves's heart wasn't in it. In the end, he and Clinton did not leave Sandy Hook until October 19, the same day Cornwallis surrendered.

Cornwallis had put up a desperate fight against impossible odds, holding out against an incessant bombardment by the big French siege guns. On the sixteenth of October he finally attempted to break out over the York River to Gloucester at night; from there he intended to make an overland march to New York. Tarleton, who was at Gloucester, was ordered to organize wagons and animals. As if to underscore how absurd this attempt was, during the night a fierce gale struck in the middle of the operation, hitting the York River hard and putting an end to Cornwallis's scheme.

The next morning Washington's big guns resumed their bombardment; they had been crushing the British since the ninth. That was enough for Cornwallis; he asked for a parley to negotiate the terms of surrender. Two days later a final agreement was signed and the battle was over.

On October 23, Clinton and his task force finally arrived at the mouth of Chesapeake Bay to rescue Cornwallis. Even if he had gotten there sooner, he could hardly have been of any use, which had been perfectly clear long before he left New York. There were other, more promising schemes he might have tried. Why he chose this dead end is hard to understand. Had he attempted to run into Chesapeake Bay and attack de Grasse in spite of the odds, it surely would have been disastrous.

Instead of returning to New York, he hung around for six days, until October 29. Finally, he decided that, under the circumstances, as hard as it was, he would admit defeat. He knew the consequences would be devastating. Yet, as bad as Cornwallis's surrender was, the additional loss of Clinton's task force would have made things infinitely worse. He sailed back to Sandy Hook, not only humiliated, but knowing a major battle with Cornwallis lay ahead over who was responsible for the humiliation at Yorktown.

Chapter 28

BRITAIN STUNNED

On November 25, 1781, news of the Yorktown debacle reached London, and it was a shock. Support for continuing the war, which had been plummeting, fell further. Diehards like Germain, Sandwich, and the king were unmoved. They were determined to carry on. Even though almost a third of the British army in America had surrendered, they intended to pass off the defeat as only a single battle. His Majesty remained adamantly opposed to American independence.

There was a realization on the king's part, however, that although he was determined not to give in to the American radicals, another turning point had been reached that called for a new strategy. He now eschewed another great offensive in favor of a scaled-down effort designed to wait for the rebellion to collapse of its own weight. It would not take much longer. The rebel Congress was suffering grievously; its currency was worthless. Recruits for Washington's army were hard to come by, even with larger and larger bonuses being offered. The French would soon be ridding themselves of a losing enterprise. All Britain had to do was continue with the naval blockade and hold New York,

Charleston, and Savannah while the Royal Navy conducted punishing raids along the coast. Seeing Britain's continued commitment would encourage Loyalists and add to their ranks until the exhausted rebels were forced to submit.

A growing number of parliamentarians were not accepting these tired old arguments any longer. The usual critics condemned Germain and Sandwich in the House of Commons, but others now joined them. Opposition was growing. When Parliament returned from its Christmas recess the third week of January 1782, it was clear that Germain's days were numbered. The king decided that a peerage would ease his exit, and Germain did not resist, even though the House of Lords as a body made it clear it did not want him. By the end of February he was mercifully gone, and so, too, was his aggressive war in America. The House of Commons voted the very same week to halt offensive operations against the thirteen colonies. The king's new strategy was set aside.

Lord Sandwich hung on for another three weeks. Unlike Germain, who was wealthy, the first lord had only a small purse to fall back on. He did have considerable parliamentary influence, which Germain did not, and he fought to keep his position, but to no avail. He fell with the rest of the North ministry on March 20, 1782. Lord North resigned rather than suffer the indignity of being voted out of office.

Although still not reconciled to American independence, the king was forced to appoint Lord Rockingham (Charles Watson-Wentworth, 2nd Marquess of Rockingham), the leading advocate of independence, to form a new government. Rockingham's principle advisor was Edmund Burke, who for years had opposed the government's approach to America, believing it wrongheaded and bound to fail. Rockingham's foreign secretary was Charles James Fox, another longtime parliamentary critic of the king's American policies. When talk of peace being separated from independence was being bandied about by some of the king's supporters, Burke and Fox took strong exception. They found the idea unrealistic, as so much else about the American crisis had been.

Regrettably, Rockingham died on July 1, only three months after taking office. Lord Shelburne (William Petty, 2nd Earl of Shelburne), who had been a member of Rockingham's ministry, succeeded him. Shelburne was wealthy and devious, his views on America opaque. It was impossible to know just where he stood. Yet the king found him more congenial than Rockingham. As far as anyone could tell, Shelburne wanted to somehow obtain peace without recognizing American independence.

In this uncertain atmosphere, the king appointed General Guy Carleton to succeed Henry Clinton as commander in New York. Carleton was chosen even before the North ministry fell. He reached Manhattan on May 5, anxious to initiate a new approach to the colonies. He was not coming to America to fight; he was coming to work the political magic he had in Canada and keep the colonies, despite all that had happened, in the empire under a single monarch. It was what the king wanted, and certainly what the tens of thousands of American Loyalists wanted. But at this late date, it was hopelessly naïve.

Eight days after Carleton's arrival, a tired, sour, angry Henry Clinton, who had been marking time in New York, nursing his grievances since Yorktown, sailed home to do battle for his reputation, as Sir William Howe and Lord Richard Howe had done before him. The near-unanimous feeling of New Yorkers was good riddance.

However unrealistic Carleton's views were, he was a welcome relief from Clinton, who had become an odious figure. Not only had he mismanaged the war; he had mismanaged the city and every other occupied area. His lack of enterprise in conducting the war since returning from Charleston in June of 1780 was notorious. He seemed to have lost his nerve. His indecision and inertia were infuriating.

Just as maddening was his unwillingness to curb the gross corruption going on seemingly everywhere in Manhattan and its environs. He refused to see the need for civil government. He allowed his officers and other officials to make fortunes illegally while he led a life of luxury in a rarefied world of his own, unaware of and unconcerned with what was going on. Even George Rodney—no slouch at bending the rules to enrich himself—found Clinton's tolerance of corruption so egregious that he considered it one of the main reasons Britain was in danger of losing the war. He found "slackness in every branch of [the army]. . . . Quartermasters and their deputies *ad infnitum*; Commisaries and their deputies *ad infinitum*; all of which make princely fortunes and laugh in their sleeves at the general who permits it."

Loyalists in New York were even angrier with Clinton than they had been with General Howe. They thought that he could have done far more to save Cornwallis. Why, for instance, hadn't he attacked the allied armies in New Jersey when they were marching from the Hudson to Virginia? Why hadn't he taken Philadelphia as a diversion, or sent a task force up the Hudson against West Point while Washington and Rochambeau were away? In fact, Loyalists did not understand why the British had not won the war long before now.

Carleton's plans for peace without independence fit perfectly with the hopes of the thousands of Loyalists from nearby areas who were flocking to Manhattan. Many of them were not rich; they were middle class, some even poor, or "the lower sort," as they were called. They were, for the most part, people of British origin whose loyalty was to the crown. They had no comprehension of or sympathy with self-rule.

Their hope for peace without independence, however, was a forlorn one. Patriots were not going to make any peace agreement that did not recognize independence and require the complete withdrawal of British troops. Franklin and Vergennes liked to point out that America already was independent.

★

DURING THE UNCERTAIN PERIOD IMMEDIATELY AFTER YORKtown, Washington was doing his best to keep up America's guard. He did not have the luxury of assuming that Britain had had enough of the war. He had to prepare for the worst. He worried that the euphoria generated everywhere by the Yorktown victory would cause patriots to forget a war was still on. As far as he was concerned, Yorktown was only one battle. King George had not given up. The British army and navy were still on American soil.

He told Governor Trumbull that thinking the victory ended the war was "a delusive hope." To General Greene he confided, "I am apprehensive that the states, elated by the late success, and taking it for granted that Great Britain will no longer support so losing a contest, will relax in their preparations for the next campaign."

Washington was taking nothing for granted. Before leaving camp at Williamsburg, he divided his army, sending part of it south, under Major General St. Clair, to reinforce Greene, and the remainder north. New Jersey men went to Morristown, while two regiments from New York, under General James Clinton, went to Pompton, and the rest marched back to the Hudson and settled at New Windsor, close to Newburgh.

On November 5 Washington finally left Williamsburg. He planned to remain for a time in Virginia, tending to personal business—consoling Martha for the loss of her son Jacky Custis; dealing with his difficult mother, Mary; and getting brought up to date on affairs at Mount Vernon, where he arrived on November 13 for a few days' rest.

Of course, official business was always on his mind. He was very unhappy—even though he knew it was coming—when de Grasse stood out from Chesapeake Bay on November 4 and sailed for the Caribbean. Washington tried his best to get him to stay a little longer and attack Charleston or Wilmington, but de Grasse had commitments to the Spanish he could not put aside. At least Washington had the satisfaction of knowing that a little over a week after de Grasse left, Hood sailed back to the Caribbean with eighteen sail of the line, dramatically lessening the probability of any major British move in North America before spring. Washington asked de Grasse if he would return in 1782 for a possible attack on New York or Charleston, and de Grasse promised that he would ask his government.

On November 15 Washington wrote to Lafayette about the absolute necessity of naval superiority for the spring campaign. He lamented the inability of the allies to make a joint attack on Charleston after

Yorktown, which he was convinced would have ended the war. He hoped Lafayette's growing influence in Paris would result in orders to de Grasse to bring a huge fleet to America the following year.

After a few days at home, Washington left Mount Vernon with Martha on November 20 and traveled to Philadelphia, arriving six days later. He spent the next four months in the capital, trying to harden the country for the tough road ahead. It wasn't easy, nor did he expect it would be. Probably the most difficult problem he faced was finding money. He worked closely with finance superintendent Robert Morris to find a revenue stream. While searching, they needed to create the appearance of solvency so that they could carry on the war.

The basic problem they faced was whether the states were going to support a central government with the power to tax—in other words, whether or not there was going to be a United States of America. The states had not yet decided. At the moment, they were jealously guarding their right to raise money and refusing Congress any power to do so, while at the same time failing to send badly needed funds to Philadelphia. Governor Clinton, in particular, acted at times as if New York were an independent country.

If the states refused to grant Congress the power to raise any revenue, even on imports, the central government could not function. Rhode Island vetoed an impost duty that was proposed and put to a vote. The state assembly in Providence, led by John Brown, a prominent trader who made a fortune during the war, voted unanimously to reject a duty on imports. Virginia later did the same for ideological reasons, under the influence of Arthur Lee and Richard Henry Lee, who did not want a strong central government.

Neither Washington nor Morris let the matter rest. As Washington always had in the past, he carried on and tried, now with Morris's indispensable help, to find a way to keep the army together. If Congress had no way to raise money, it would have to be borrowed from France or Holland. Both countries ultimately came through, although obviously this method of funding—with the Americans refusing to tax themselves—was not going to continue. Morris employed a number of other expedients, but without the ability to tax they were bound to be short-lived.

★

DURING HIS TIME IN PHILADELPHIA, WASHINGTON APPROVED a plan to capture Prince William Henry, George III's son and third in line to the British throne. The seventeen-year-old was serving in New York as a midshipman aboard Admiral Digby's flagship, *Prince George*, and staying in the city with Digby. Washington planned to take them both.

The arrival of the prince on September 24 had been a complete surprise to everyone. Loyalists were quick to believe that his presence meant the British intended to stay, no matter what happened at York-town. A feeling of euphoria spread among them, something they hadn't felt for some time. They had been afraid of what was happening to Cornwallis, afraid that Britain might desert them if things went badly. De Grasse had already beaten Graves, and Cornwallis was in grave danger. Clinton, Graves, Digby, and Hood were frantically trying to cobble together a task force to rescue him.

In spite of the tense atmosphere, Loyalists celebrated the only royal to ever have visited New York or, indeed, America. Many felt that had the king himself come much earlier—even before the Tea Party—his presence would have made a significant difference in people's attitudes, and perhaps his own. The young prince's visit became more important to Loyalists than anything else.

Colonel Matthias Ogden of New Jersey proposed the plan to capture His Royal Highness, and Washington approved it on March 28, 1782. Attempting to capture high-ranking people was a common practice, which is why Generals Washington and Clinton always had a substantial guard around them. Seizing the king's son, however, was very different. It had the potential to create an enormous backlash in London and throughout England. Whether Washington realized the complications that might develop if he were successful isn't known. He was enthusiastic about the enterprise. He told Ogden, "In case of success, you will, as soon as you get . . . [the prisoners] to a place of safety [in New Jersey], treat them with all possible respect; but you are to delay no time in conveying them to Congress, and reporting your proceedings with a copy of these orders."

As things turned out, Ogden was forced to cancel the plot. General Clinton had gotten wind that something was up, although he did not know quite what. He probably thought that an attempt was going to be made on him. Guards were dramatically increased around him, Digby, and the prince. What would have happened had the mission succeeded can only be guessed at, but certainly it would have caused an uproar in England that might have given the king enough renewed political support to prolong the war, bringing about a result just the opposite of what Washington intended. Approving Colonel Ogden's daring proposal was not one of the commander in chief's better decisions.

Washington left Philadelphia on March 23 with Martha and arrived seven days later at Newburgh, New York, the army's winter quarters on the Hudson, fourteen miles above West Point. After dealing with politicians in Philadelphia, they must have felt some relief to be rejoining the army for the spring campaign. To be sure, the problems Washington faced in Newburgh were great, but not as infuriating and frustrating as those in the capital. Yet the state of the army was certainly troubling. The long winter was almost over; the men had suffered through cold, deprivation, and lack of pay once more. Last winter their legitimate grievances had produced heartrending mutinies. Washington was apprehensive about the mood of the troops now, knowing that he did not even have back pay to offer them.

He did have hope, however. By now it was clear—even to Washington—that Yorktown had had a much bigger impact on the British than he had originally thought. The king had been unable to brush off the defeat as a temporary setback. Fundamental changes were taking place in London. Washington wrote to General Greene on March 18 about the encouraging signs. "By late advices from Europe, and from the declaration of the British ministers themselves," he told him, "it appears that they have done with all thoughts of an excursive war, and that they mean to send but small, if any further reinforcements to America." Washington began thinking that the British would relinquish all their posts except New York and concentrate their forces there. To what end was unclear.

His optimism soon faded, however, when he heard of Admiral Rodney's stunning victory over de Grasse on April 12 at the Battle of the Saintes. Britain was now celebrating another classic victory by a great naval hero. Rodney was the man of the hour again. He had never been blamed for what had happened in America. People generally accepted poor health as a perfectly good excuse for his not having been at Chesapeake Bay. His failure to stop de Grasse in the Caribbean before the French fleet ever got to America was never mentioned.

Lord Sandwich was receiving plaudits for his appointment of Rodney. In the late fall of 1781, when Sandwich realized that the French were planning a major campaign in the Caribbean after hurricane season, he had plucked Rodney from retirement and sent him into action once more.

Jamaica was obviously a target of the French, and the other sugar islands were as well. Losing both America and Jamaica would be intolerable. Another major defeat would have certainly cost Sandwich his job as first lord of the Admiralty, which, at the time, he had been trying hard to keep. It was in desperation that he had sent for Rodney—who was at Bath tending to his gout and a stone, the same ailments that had plagued him for years, and that plagued most old sailors. The first lord had urged—begged would be a better word—him to take command of the Leeward Islands station once more and counter de Grasse. The king helped by having a personal interview with Rodney.

Sandwich had been indifferent the previous year when Rodney had made his request to come home for health reasons, even if it meant he would not be going to America. It did not seem to matter to Sandwich in 1781 which admiral led the fleet in America. Now, regardless of Rodney's health concerns, Sandwich pressured him to undertake an assignment that would have taxed any admiral at any age.

Rodney responded immediately, his ailments seeming to be of no concern, and on January 8, 1782, he stood out from Plymouth with a powerful squadron, reaching St. Lucia in the middle of February. He quickly discovered that the enterprising de Grasse had already taken St. Eustatius, St. Kitts, Nevis, Montserrat, and Demerara. Rodney had arrived just in time.

Hood was already at St. Lucia, and his fleet, combined with Rodney's, gave them thirty-six sail of the line. De Grasse had thirty-five. After refurbishing his ships, Rodney was ready, and when de Grasse departed Fort Royal Bay on April 8 Rodney was right after him, standing out from St. Lucia, thirty miles away. De Grasse, who had a large convoy to look after, would have preferred avoiding combat at the moment, but Rodney was determined to fight.

He did not get the full-scale battle he wanted until the twelfth, off Les Saintes, a tiny group of islands between the southern end of Guadeloupe and the northern end of Dominica. At the end of that unforgettable day, Rodney had defeated the French decisively. De Grasse and his *Ville de Paris* surrendered, along with four other sail of the line. The rest of the French fleet, some twenty-five battleships, got away. Hood, who was Rodney's second throughout, wanted to chase them, but Rodney, who had been maneuvering and fighting for four days, had had enough. Hood, not unexpectedly, was highly critical of standing down at this point. He insisted that twenty more enemy battleships could have been captured. "I am very confident," he wrote later, "we should have had twenty sail of the enemy's ships before dark. . . . Why he [Rodney] should bring the fleet to because the *Ville de Paris* was taken, I cannot reconcile."

In spite of Hood's criticism, Rodney's victory was a great triumph that had far-reaching effects, one of them being the end of any French naval support for Washington in 1782. To what degree the victory would change Britain's approach to the American war and peace negotiations remained to be seen. At a minimum, it would stiffen London's attitude and soften Vergennes'.

Rodney's stunning success inevitably led to conjecture about what would have happened had he been in command of the British fleet at the decisive battle off Cape Henry, Virginia, on September 5, 1781. It was widely believed that even with a numerically smaller fleet, Rodney would have won, and that that would have changed everything. Even Hood believed that Rodney would have been victorious. Of course, at the Saintes, Rodney had a numerical advantage, which he would not have had at the Chesapeake, although he would have had at least one more ship than Graves did.

Actually, during the decisive part of the battle off the Saintes—between noon and seven o'clock on the evening of the twelfth—Rodney had a six-ship advantage, thirty-six to thirty. It was not his six-ship advantage that brought victory, however, but rather a fortunate shift in wind direction and Rodney's using it to break the French line, which was moving in the opposite direction from his, into three disorganized groupings that made the French center especially vulnerable. A numerical advantage, a fortunate shift of wind, and unorthodox tactics won the day.

Rodney would certainly have had to improvise in order to beat de Grasse off Virginia, and there's no doubt that he would have done so. He probably would have begun with Barras, dealing with him before tackling de Grasse. It's hard to imagine Rodney not doing whatever he had to, regardless of tradition or outmoded rules of engagement, to win.

Rodney's behavior before, during, and after the Battle of the Saintes was more evidence that his anger at Clinton's inexplicable conduct in New York during September of 1780 was actually what made him decide to go home the following year and let Admirals Graves and Hood handle de Grasse and the French fleet. It's hard not to conclude that when Sandwich called him to go back to the Caribbean to deal with de Grasse in the late fall of 1781, he jumped at the chance, regardless of his ailments, because he had a guilty conscience about having avoided de Grasse and the Chesapeake earlier in the year.

Before Washington received news of the Saintes, he was aware of Parliament's momentous decision not to pursue offensive war in America, but he did not know if he could trust the hopeful trend after Rodney's victory. The British could change their minds. He was receiving newspapers from London and had an idea of parliamentary sentiment; still, he could not be sure. On June 24, 1782, he wrote to Rochambeau, who had kept his army in Virginia after Yorktown, proposing a meeting to discuss the implications of de Grasse's defeat. Obviously there would be no joint campaign in 1782. Both sides were in a defensive mode, waiting on events, especially the results of impending peace negotiations in Paris.

Chapter 29

PEACE

The diplomats were gathering in Paris during the summer of 1782 for peace talks. Benjamin Franklin was already there. John Jay joined him the first week of July, very happy to be away from Madrid, where the dons had treated him with contempt. John Adams was still in The Hague completing negotiations for an important loan. Henry Laurens, the final member of the negotiating team, was in Paris, but in such poor health that he would play no role in the talks until the very end. When he got word that his beloved son John had been killed in action in South Carolina, he withdrew even further.

As America's diplomatic team gathered, Lord Shelburne was still searching for a way to achieve peace without independence. He had support in Parliament and the country for his attempt, and, of course, from the king. Rodney's victory encouraged him. But the American delegation in Paris would never for a moment consider remaining in the empire under any circumstances, and neither would Congress. Franklin made it clear to Shelburne's negotiator, Richard Oswald, that a guarantee of American independence was a non-negotiable item in any peace agreement. The Americans' uncompromising stance forced the British to finally make a decision, and in the end they reluctantly accepted independence rather than continue the war, which Shelburne knew had almost no support in Parliament. If peace without independence could be achieved, Shelburne could get support for that, but continuing the war in America under any pretext was out of the question.

Shelburne was so slippery and unpredictable, however, that there continued to be considerable doubt as to whether he would in the end actually agree to independence. Benjamin Franklin and John Jay assumed he would and went ahead with serious talks in September. They were joined by John Adams on October 26, after he finally obtained the critical loan from the Dutch he had been working on for so long—five million guilders, an enormous sum, desperately needed by Robert Morris and Washington to keep the government and the army afloat.

The American diplomats were the finest team ever to represent the United States, and their final agreement was proof of it. Franklin, Jay, and Adams were the principal negotiators. Henry Laurens, although too ill to participate, was important as a representative of the South, which had to approve the treaty. In a little over a month, on November 30 both sides were ready to sign a preliminary peace agreement. It was a remarkable achievement. The United States secured recognition of her independence and settled on boundaries with the major powers that held the promise of a bright future. The borders agreed to were breathtaking. They reached from the Atlantic all the way to the Mississippi, rather than to the Appalachian Mountains; and from a generous northern border close to what now exists, to the 31st parallel along the northern border of the Floridas. Fishing rights off the Canadian coast and "free and open navigation" of the Mississippi River were also included.

At the end of the negotiations, Henry Laurens managed to insert into the final document an item regarding slaves. It forbid the British, when they evacuated New York, from taking "any negroes, or other property of the American inhabitants," with them. Laurens had been the leading slave trader in America when the Revolutionary War began, and he judged this item to be necessary to guarantee the South's approval of the final treaty. His son John, who had been ashamed of slavery and had hoped to eradicate it, would have been appalled. His father knew of John's attitudes very well and had some sympathy with them. He was responding to what he felt were political realities, as were the other American negotiators, none of whom were happy about having to include this noxious item in their otherwise marvelous peace treaty. It made them all look like hypocrites.

★

WITH PEACE CAME PROBLEMS WITH THE ARMY IN NEWBURGH. The troops, who were owed a great deal of money, were on the verge of being disbanded without a financial settlement. The enlisted men were, for the most part, happy to be going home to resume a normal life. There were, of course, many soldiers who liked life in the military for one reason or another and would miss the special relationships one forms when serving in the armed forces. For most, though, returning to a life that allowed them the freedom to do what they wanted had greater attractions. In any event, they were not in a mood to make a major protest about the fact that they had not been paid for a very long time, and that there was not even severance money to get them home. Most of them would have to work along the way, sometimes for weeks, to get enough cash just to get back to their loved ones.

Even more egregious was the fact that Congress ignored the land that had been guaranteed to the soldiers. Every man who had signed on for the entire war had been promised one hundred acres, but, as one of them explained, "when the country had drained the last bit of service it could screw out of the poor soldiers, they were turned adrift like old worn-out horses, and nothing said about land to pasture them upon."

Their officers, on the other hand, were not about to let Congress off the hook so easily. They refused to be dismissed without being paid the pension they had been promised—half pay for life. The record of Congress and the states gave them ample cause for concern. Their grumbling reached high intensity as time passed with no indication that the states were going to allow Congress to impose even a tax on imports to fund the government and allow it to pay the officers what they were due.

There was serious talk about marching on Philadelphia. A showdown occurred on March 15, 1783, when a large meeting of officers was organized at Newburgh and Washington unexpectedly appeared, turning their anger into tears as he pleaded with them to reject civil discord and accept the good intentions of Congress. Many officers broke down as he slowly took out his glasses to read what he had written. It was a virtuoso performance. The threat from the officers was deflected. The march on Congress, with all it implied, was averted.

Congress then responded to the urging of Washington and a group of nationalists, including Robert Morris, Alexander Hamilton, and James Madison, and passed a financial package for the army that was a national embarrassment. Members voted to give ordinary soldiers, who were asking nothing more than to go home, three months of back pay, even though they were owed far more. The officers, instead of half pay for life, received full pay for five years, and they were very happy to have that from a Congress whose treatment of its army can only be described as contemptible.

Compensation for ordinary soldiers was given in the form of certificates that were then sold by most of the men to speculators for very little. The need for ready cash was so great that the soldiers had little choice.

★

THE WEEKS AND MONTHS AFTER YORKTOWN WERE AGONY for Loyalists in New York. Their ranks kept growing in a never-ending stream, as people crowded into a city already bursting with refugees, perhaps as many as thirty thousand. They came mostly from nearby states to take advantage of London's offer of free transportation out of New York. They feared being abandoned, as Philadelphia's Tories had been in 1778, and Virginia's at Yorktown in the articles of surrender. Hundreds had already left New York after witnessing General Clinton's remarkable inactivity when Cornwallis needed help. They saw the handwriting on the wall. But most stuck it out, hoping for the best.

They had been shocked when, at the end of February 1782, Parliament had brought a halt to offensive operations in America. A few weeks later, they were buoyed by Rodney's victory at the Saintes. Nothing changed, however, and more time passed, as they waited to hear what the Paris peace negotiations would bring.

Finally, on February 14, 1783, as the Loyalists waited and prayed for good news, the king formally proclaimed an end to hostilities, and on April 6 the *Prince William Henry*, a packet from England, arrived with a copy of the document. Three days later, the proclamation was read from the steps of city hall. The war was over. The Loyalists were now in no doubt about their fate; they were going to lose everything.

Governor Clinton and the New York State legislature were making it plain, and had been for some time, that Tories should leave. There was no forgiveness in their hearts. The Loyalists had bet on the wrong horse and would suffer the consequences. If the situation had been reversed, would they have been easy on the rebels? It is hard to believe that they and their British masters would have been. In fact, they had given ample evidence throughout the war of how brutal they would be. The patriots had long memories. They recalled vividly the deep anger of former royal governor William Franklin and the merciless refugees he had organized into the Board of Associated Loyalists, as well as other smaller groups performing the same sort of bloody, clandestine raids against patriots.

A series of acts passed by the New York legislature made it clear that the state was going to be tough. A permanent commission was established "For Detecting and Defeating Conspiracies," and laws were enacted giving lawmakers extraordinary power to deal with suspected Tories. As early as 1777, when the new state government had just come into being, laws were written to harass Loyalists, depriving them of the right to vote, taking their property, and banishing them. On October 22, 1779, the Act of Attainder passed. It stipulated that the estates of

"Persons who have adhered to the enemies of the state" were subject to forfeiture. Fifty-nine individuals were specifically named in the legislation. In the end, probably fifteen hundred Tories had their property taken and hundreds more were identified as Loyalists, convicted, and banished—more than in any other state.

★

THE JOB OF BRINGING THE WAR TO A FINAL CONCLUSION IN New York fell to General Carleton. Evacuating the city in as peaceful a manner as possible was an enormous and delicate undertaking, requiring all his considerable political skill. He tried to work as much as possible with General Washington. On September 2, 1783, Carleton and his staff journeyed to Dobbs Ferry to meet with Washington, Governor Clinton, and their staffs to discuss how to make the coming evacuation and takeover of New York City as smooth and as free of bloodshed as possible. They met at the DeWint House in Tappan, which had been Washington's temporary headquarters on four separate occasions during the war. He had stayed there during the trial and subsequent hanging of Major John André. Samuel Fraunces, owner of Fraunces Tavern, came up from the city with his crew to prepare a special dinner for Washington and his guests.

Carleton brought along William Smith as an advisor. Governor Clinton and Smith knew each other well. As a young man, Clinton had read law in Smith's offices. Smith had a high regard for the ambitious young man, and it was reciprocated. Unfortunately, Smith, after much soul-searching and agonizing, had chosen to remain in the empire. It was a poor choice, one he must have regretted to some degree at this moment, when he was about to lose everything.

As the meetings progressed, there was general agreement between the two sides, except on the issue of slaves. Washington wanted all slaves in New York returned to their masters, and Carleton refused to return any. As far as he was concerned, any slaves within his jurisdiction were now free, and he would treat them as such. He and Washington did not allow this question to stymie them, however, and they proceeded with their plans to make the withdrawal as safe and seamless as possible.

New York Harbor was as busy as it had ever been, with huge numbers of transports moving Loyalists out of the country and troops going home or to other assignments in India or the Caribbean. The thousands of Tories who were leaving went in stages. Giant convoys moved them, five and seven thousand at a time. Perhaps as many as forty thousand or more embarked. Almost all went to Canada, but some traveled to the West Indies, and a few of the wealthy to England. The waterfront was always crowded with their pathetic belongings, remnants of a previous life now gone forever.

Also on the waterfront were prizes taken by Admiral Digby's warships. Digby was still pretending that there was a blockade on, capturing unlucky American vessels, bringing them into New York, and selling the contents and the ships. This was nothing but piracy, pure and simple. Admiral Digby obviously was not a great supporter of peace, although when Carleton finally departed the piracy stopped.

While Loyalists were leaving, over three thousand patriots who had fled when the British occupied Manhattan and Long Island came flooding back to reclaim their property. Slave owners arrived, looking to capture free people, claim they were their property, and cart them away. The American authorities, Washington included, encouraged them. But Carleton and Digby did not. Thousands of African Americans, enticed by British offers of freedom, had escaped from their masters at great personal risk during the war and wound up in New York. Their presence in such large numbers was a monumental embarrassment to patriots, who were preaching liberty while doing their utmost to deny it to former slaves. When the time came for the final evacuation, Carleton and Digby ignored the Laurens provision in the peace treaty and evacuated as many former slaves as they could, most of them going to a tough but free life in Nova Scotia.

Washington kept trying to stop them. He wrote to Carleton protesting that he and Digby were ignoring Article Seven of the peace treaty by carrying away hundreds of African Americans who were the property of slave owners like himself. Carleton responded by telling him that these men, women, and children were free human beings, not property. On May 12 he wrote to Washington, explaining that the "Negroes" who sailed away were persons who had been liberated when they came over to the British side. "I have no right to deprive them of that liberty they are possessed of," he insisted. Washington had heard this argument before, but he was not mollified. There was nothing he could do about it, however.

Patriot prisoners were also roaming the streets, happy to be alive. Carleton released them wholesale from places like the Jersey prison ship, where they had witnessed so many of their comrades being murdered. Gaunt, looking like beggars dressed in rags, they breathed the fresh air, waiting for the American army to appear. There was great disorder in the streets, where lawlessness continued. Policing was still at a minimum, crime rampant. Carleton, like his predecessors, Clinton and Howe, refused to return either New York or the surrounding counties to civil government.

He did attempt—not very successfully—to put an end to the rampant corruption that British officials had practiced since the Howes took over in 1776. In general, however, the military's gross mismanagement of the city continued to the end.

On November 21, General Carleton brought the long, complicated business of evacuating to a conclusion by loading the remainder of his troops on transports. Four days later, as the last of his men were being rowed to their ships, General Washington and Governor Clinton led a huge throng of cheering patriots into the city to formally reclaim it. Their unforgettable parade inspired a young female resident to write:

> We have been accustomed for a long time . . . to military display in all the finish and finery of garrison life; the troops just leaving

us were as if equipped for show, and with their scarlet uniforms and burnished arms made a brilliant display; the troops that marched in, on the contrary, were ill-clad and weather-beaten, and made a forlorn appearance; but then they were *our* troops, and as I looked at them, and thought upon all they had done and suffered for us, my heart and eyes were full, and I admired and gloried in them the more, because they were weather-beaten and forlorn.

The now-famous celebrations that followed went on day and night. Probably the most famous occurred on December 4, when Washington bid farewell to his officers at Fraunces Tavern, solemnly embracing each one in turn. There wasn't a dry eye in the place.

Chapter 30

CONCLUSION

After the passions of the moment have subsided, most wars appear to have been unnecessary, and none more so than this one. The king could have easily kept the thirteen colonies in the British Empire under a single monarch without bloodshed and without the expense of a long war, had he used peaceful means to settle their quarrels instead of rejecting negotiations out of hand and resorting to force. The differences between America and Britain were not irreconcilable; they were not even difficult to resolve. George III was not compelled to declare war in order to fashion an agreement on how the colonies could contribute their fair share of taxes to finance the growing budget of the kingdom after its enormous expansion following the great victories of the Seven Years' War.

Americans were proud of those victories. They were not refusing to pay taxes; they only wanted to be represented in the body that levied them. They believed it was their right as freeborn Englishmen to participate in governance. They were not seeking to change the government. The great majority of them were content to live under Britain's constitutional monarchy. In spite of its well-known defects, it was the freest, most liberal in the world. The standard of living of ordinary white Americans was higher than in any other country, including England, Scotland, Wales, and Ireland. The payment of reasonable taxes would not have constituted an undue burden. The questions of how colonial approval of taxes could be obtained, what taxes were to be imposed and how collected, could have been worked out over a conference table. Colonists did not have to declare independence and fight a six-and-a-half-year war to be free and prosperous.

The king and the small coterie of aristocrats who supported him needlessly condemned tens of thousands of young men to die before their time, or be maimed, their families and friends forced to suffer indescribable pain over a controversy that talks could have settled. At one time or another, both sides, realizing how small their differences really were, offered to negotiate—the patriots on many occasions, including in 1775 with the Olive Branch Petition, and Lord North in 1778. Unfortunately, their timing was off. The patriots were too early, Lord North too late.

If the king had only reached out, if he had even come to America himself with Lord North to preside over negotiations, it's hard to imagine that he would not have succeeded. At any time before the summer of 1776, his appearance in New York bearing an olive branch instead of a sword undoubtedly would have won over his subjects, dazzled them, and led to serious negotiations that might have kept America happily British for a very long time.

Instead of talking, he chose fighting. Pride got in His Majesty's way. He could not imagine lowering himself to negotiate with subjects who would have loved him for doing it. He would have abdicated first. His supporters in Britain, who spoke and acted as if they owned the colonies, would have been outraged. Their unquestioned belief in the power of the Royal Navy and of Britain's army would have made such a gesture seem unnecessary, indeed foolish, when a show of force would cow the American radicals quickly and avoid both great expense and having to share power. The king and his allies even seemed anxious to fight, anxious to knock heads. Their apparent need to show "their" colonies who was boss brought the exact opposite of what they wanted—rivers of blood, humiliation, and the loss of America. John Holt, the publisher of the influential *New York Journal and General Advertiser*, wrote, "They have acted inconsistent with their true interest from the beginning of the war." Indeed they had.

The king and his supporters never imagined that they could be defeated. And with the resources at their disposal, they never should have been. Their defeat was as unnecessary as their war. That they could have won with a different strategy, better leadership in London, and better commanders in the field seems incontestable. Even with poor leaders and bad strategy, they came close to winning a number of times. In the end, however, they failed, and nothing contributed more to their failure than their fixation with the watery highway connecting the Hudson River Valley with Canada. The fantasy that control of this great natural sea-land corridor was possible, and that it would inevitably lead to victory, played a decisive role in bringing about their two major defeats, the ones that cost them the war—Saratoga and Yorktown.

Saratoga brought France into the war, which made a patriot victory possible, although by no means inevitable. Saratoga also demonstrated how wrongheaded British strategy was. Burgoyne's defeat showed conclusively that Britain could never control, without the support of the inhabitants, even that portion of the corridor between Albany and Montreal. Reliance on military force alone, which the king insisted on, was a recipe for defeat.

At the decisive showdown on Bemis Heights, the patriot army, which was growing, numbered almost three times Burgoyne's, which was shrinking. He had no support from the countryside, while thousands of militiamen were continuously flocking into the patriot camp. Had the king thought it necessary to offer colonists something other than abject submission, Burgoyne might have found the going much easier.

Burgoyne was surprised when he found that he had practically no Loyalists fighting with him. He had assumed that the British had many supporters in that part of the world. When it turned out that there were essentially none helping him, the strategy he was pursuing looked more and more like a fantasy. The military resources he had, which before had seemed adequate, suddenly appeared ridiculously small. Instead of the corridor to Canada looking as if it were the perfect route to victory, it seemed more like the road to defeat.

There was no Loyalist help to speak of at Yorktown, either, even though London had long predicted strong support for the king throughout the South. But Cornwallis was not looking for Tories to save him; he was looking to the Royal Navy. In doing so, he had a much better chance of surviving than Burgoyne did. In spite of his many errors, Cornwallis might still have been saved if Admiral George Rodney had come to his rescue. But Rodney was purposefully staying far away.

Ironically, it was Rodney's almost religious belief in the viability of the king's old strategy of seizing the Hudson River Valley that led him to find an excuse to avoid his responsibility to Cornwallis. Rodney felt that, but for the inscrutable General Sir Henry Clinton, he could have seized West Point in September of 1780 with the help of Benedict Arnold, gained control of the corridor to Canada, and won the war. Misled by the enterprising traitor Arnold, Rodney had no idea how naïve his view was, no idea why Burgoyne lost.

Rodney feared that if he came to America in 1781 and got mixed up with Henry Clinton again, disaster would follow. He was simply not going to do it. Cornwallis, like Burgoyne, was left to suffer the consequences of his own folly. Rodney was not going to save him. The fantasy of the Hudson River Valley, which King George believed was the key to victory, thus became, instead, his undoing. Since there was no political dimension to his strategy, the burden on military leaders increased dramatically until it crushed them.

In the end, there were grave doubts about whether the king, even if he had won the war with a better strategy and better subordinates, could have won the peace. Would the man who found it impossible to negotiate with his subjects have been wise enough to handle them in a way that won their allegiance? John Holt wrote, "[T]he question remained, as it had from the beginning, could America be conquered, and if it could, could it be held for any length of time under the same British regime that initiated the war?"

Given all that had happened, it's impossible to imagine that it could have been. The imposition of a draconian regime designed to prevent another uprising was far more likely. And this, in turn, would have guaranteed permanent unrest, the need to keep a large military presence in the colonies, and another rebellion, aided by foreign powers. Thus, as Franklin maintained right along, independence was inevitable. The king's attitude made keeping America in the empire impossible. Even if he had won the war in the 1770s, he would not have gained a permanent victory.

Acknowledgments

oremost among those I would like to thank for their help is my agent, Rob McQuilkin, of Lippincott, Massie, McQuilkin. Knowing how many years I had spent studying the War of Independence, Rob suggested that I write a book entitled *Revolution on the Hudson*. He then helped craft the proposal, managed the contract negotiations, and provided critical advice throughout the long months it took to finish.

W. W. Norton's legendary editor Starling Lawrence lived up to his reputation, and then some, providing sage advice and amazingly detailed criticism. He is indeed a master of his craft. Janet Byrne, a brilliant editor in her own right, assisted him, examining every detail of the manuscript and saving me from a number of errors. All of us were fortunate to have Ryan Harrington, Star Lawrence's gifted assistant, attending to essential details, moving the publication process along, always with good humor.

Retired Vice Admiral George Emery provided invaluable assistance. No one knows more about the early American navy and life at sea during that era than Admiral Emery. He also happens to be an excellent writer and perceptive critic. I owe him an enormous debt of gratitude for going over the manuscript in detail and giving me his always sound advice.

Whenever I write a book I am reminded again of the influence my great teachers have had on me, including John Holden at the University of New Hampshire and Stanley Hoffmann, Samuel P. Huntington, and Henry Kissinger at Harvard. Samuel Eliot Morison was probably the greatest influence. His belief in the importance of the sea in America's history has been a constant source of inspiration.

I have also been fortunate in having had outstanding colleagues to work with at the various institutions where I have taught—Regis College in Weston, Massachusetts; the Air Force Academy; the University of Colorado; the University of New Hampshire; Connecticut College; Wesleyan University; and Harvard. I am indebted to Leo Chang, William P. Dickey, Ralph Hoffmann, Jon Parssinen, Harper Keeler, John Butterfield, Ted Finnegan, Wesley Posvar, Richard Rosser, Robley J. Evans, William Meredith, Charles Shain, Ivan Strenski, Philip Jordan, J. Barry Shepherd, Wayne Swanson, Lawrence Korb, William Cibes, Minor Myers, Ambassador Edward M. Korry, Louis Balthazar, and Frances McLaughlin. Four former students who have been significant in my intellectual life should also be mentioned: Susan Gorvine, Ruth Pulda, Peggy Brill, and Meg Gifford.

I have benefited over the years from collections in many outstanding institutions. First among them are Harvard's Widener and Houghton Libraries, followed by the American Antiquarian Society, the Massachusetts Historical Society, the New York Historical Society, the Pennsylvania Historical Society, the Maryland Historical Society, Britain's National Archives at Kew, the Maine Historical Society, the Boston Athenaeum, the Boston Public Library, the Bowdoin College Library, the Mystic Seaport Museum, the John Hay Library on the campus of Brown University, the Connecticut State Library, and the Franklin D. Roosevelt Presidential Library at Hyde Park.

I would especially like to thank Kia Campbell for her indispensable help in mining the seemingly inexhaustible resources of the Library of Congress, one of the nation's great treasures.

My wife, Kathleen (Kay), has been of great importance as well. She majored in history at the University of New Hampshire, where we were both undergraduates, and never lost her interest in early America. Her wise counsel shaped every part of the book.

I am also indebted to my family for their support. An author's life is at times a lonely one, and having encouragement from my daughter, Mary Sheft; her sons, Alex and Tyler; as well as her husband, Mark, has been invaluable. My brother, William (Jerry) Daughan, who knows the sea as well as anyone, having worked on developing America's nuclear fleet for many years, was a great help, as was his son, Michael Daughan, who has worked on the navy's ships all his life and has a deep knowledge of their early history.

Notes

Introduction

4 **"The difficulties in the way"**: Alfred Thayer Mahan, *The Influence of Sea Power upon History, 1660–1783* (New York: Dover Publications, 1987; Boston: Little, Brown, 1890), 342. The citation is to the Dover edition.

4 **"The importance of the North [Hudson] River"**: Washington to General Putnam, December 2, 1777, in *The Papers of George Washington: Revolutionary War Series* (hereinafter *Washington Papers*), ed. W. W. Abbot, Edward G. Lengel, et al., 24 vols. to date (Charlottesville: University of Virginia Press, 1988–), vol. 12, 498–99.

5 **"cut off all communication"**: Jefferson to Thomas Nelson Jr., February 4, 1776, in *Naval Documents of the American Revolution* (hereinafter *NDAR*), ed. William Bell Clarke et al., 11 vols. (Washington, DC: U.S. Government Printing Office, 1964–), vol. 3, 1127.

5 **"the North [Hudson] River is the nexus"**: John Adams to Washington, January 26, 1776, in *Washington Papers*, vol. 3, 37.

5 **"the jugular of America"**: Douglas Southall Freeman, *George Washington: A Biography*, 7 vols. (New York: Scribners, 1948–57), vol. 4, 500.

1. George III Declares War on America

7 **One hundred ten enemy vessels had arrived by June 30**: Washington to Hancock, June 30, 1776; General Howe to Lord George Germain, July 7, 1776, in *NDAR*, vol. 5, 962.

8 **"it must be treated as a foreign war"**: John Fortescue, ed., *The Correspondence of King George the Third from 1760 to December 1783*, 6 vols. (London: Macmillan, 1927–28), vol. 3, 234; Peter D. G. Thomas, *Lord North* (London: Allen Lane, 1976), 87–88.

9 **Lord North . . . found it impossible**: Dora Mae Clark, *British Opinion and the American Revolution* (Brasted, Kent, UK: Russell Publishing, 1966; New Haven, CT: Yale University Press, 1930), 1–16. The citation is to the Russell edition.

9 **"His Majesty's person, family, and government"**: Worthington C. Ford, ed., *Journals of the Continental Congress* (hereinafter *Journals of Congress*), 34 vols. (Washington, DC, 1904–37), vol. 2, 158–61.

10 **"It is folly to supplicate a tyrant"**: Quoted in George C. Daughan, *If By Sea: The Forging of the American Navy—From the Revolution to the War of 1812* (New York: Basic Books, 2011), 37.

10 **they signed the petition in the interest of solidarity**: John C. Miller, *Sam Adams: Pioneer in Propaganda* (Palo Alto: Stanford University Press, 1936), 339–41.

10 **There was no need to treat with them**: John Brooke, *King George III* (New York: McGraw-Hill, 1972), 175.

10 **royal proclamation**: Peter Force, ed., *American Archives*, 4th Series, 6 vols. (Washington, DC: M. St. Claire Clarke and Peter Force, 1837–46), vol. 3, 240–41.

10 **"The rebellious war now levied is become more general"**: Ibid.

10 **Terrified townspeople**: Letter of Jacob Bailey, Falmouth Collections; Narrative of Daniel Tucker, Tucker Manuscripts, Maine Historical Society, Portland, Maine.

11 **"as if the same were the ships and effects of open enemies"**: Force, *American Archives*, 4th Series, vol. 2, 211.

11 **Benjamin Franklin considered the noxious law**: Carl Van Doren, *Benjamin Franklin* (New York: Penguin, 1991; New York: Viking, 1938), 561. Citations are to the Penguin edition.

11 **"a complete dismemberment of the British Empire"**: Charles Francis Adams, *The Works of John Adams* (Boston: Little, Brown, 1850), vol. 2, 485–87; John Ferling, *John Adams, A Life* (New York: Henry Holt, 1996; Knoxville: University of Tennessee Press, 1992), 144 (citations are to the Holt edition); Merrill

Jensen, *The Founding of the Nation: A History of the American Revolution, 1763–1776* (New York: Oxford University Press, 1968), 650.

11 he would "effectuate [the subordination of his subjects]": William Cobbett, ed., *The Parliamentary History of England from the Earliest Period to the Year 1803* (hereinafter Hansard's Debates), 36 vols. (London: T. C. Hansard, 1814), vol. 18, 1365–66.

12 "the greatest sea officer the world has ever produced": Rodger Knight, "Richard Earl Howe, 1726–1799," in *Precursors of Nelson: British Admirals of the Eighteenth Century*, ed. Peter Le Fevre and Richard Harding (Mechanicsburg, PA: Stackpole Books, 2000), 279.

13 "Suppose the colonies do abound in men": N. A. M. Rodger, *The Insatiable Earl: A Life of John Montague, 4th Earl of Sandwich* (New York: W. W. Norton, 1993), 127.

14 Reconciliation was not in their vocabulary: Ira D. Gruber, *The Howe Brothers and the American Revolution* (New York: Atheneum, 1972), 82–83.

14 Once joined: Ibid.

15 The condescending attitude he had arrived with soon disappeared: Ibid., 25–26.

16 "The importance of preserving this force": Howe to Dartmouth, March 21, 1776, in Troyer Steele Anderson, *The Command of the Howe Brothers During the American Revolution* (New York: Oxford University Press, 1936), 100.

17 "there is no doubt": *New York Journal and General Advertiser*, March 21, 1776.

17 Washington certainly wanted to: Washington to Hancock, June 28, 1776, in *Washington Papers*, vol. 5, 132–35.

17 whoever controlled Manhattan and the Hudson River Valley would dominate the North American continent: *The Writings of George Washington from the Original Manuscript Sources*, ed. John C. Fitzpatrick, 39 vols. (Washington, DC: U.S. Government Printing Office, 1931–34), vol. 4, 399.

18 "As it is of the utmost importance": Washington to Governor Trumbull, January 7, 1776, in *Washington Papers*, vol. 3, 51–52.

18 Lee assumed: Phillip Papas, *Renegade Revolutionary: The Life of General Charles Lee* (New York: New York University Press, 2014), 36–37; Dominick Mazzagetti, *Charles Lee: Self Before Country* (New Brunswick, NJ: Rutgers University Press, 2013), 34–35; John Richard Alden, *General Charles Lee* (Baton Rouge: Louisiana State University Press, 1951), 67–69.

19 Old Put led a thousand men and occupied Governors Island: *New York Journal and General Advertiser*, April 11, 1776.

20 all they could do was fire a few shots and run: Daughan, *If By Sea*, 91.

20 "Our situation at present": George Washington to John Augustine Washington, July 22, 1776, in *Washington Papers*, vol. 5, 428–30.

21 Every warship thundered a salute: Ambrose Serle, *The American Journal of*

Ambrose Serle, Secretary to Lord Howe, 1776–1778, ed. Edward H. Tatum Jr. (San Marino, CA: The Huntington Library, 1940), 28.

2. The Importance of New York

23 **Clinton knew the ground well**: Sir Henry Clinton, *The American Rebellion: Sir Henry Clinton's Narrative of His Campaigns, 1775–1782, with an Appendix of Original Documents*, ed. William B. Willcox (New Haven, CT: Yale University Press, 1954), xiv–xvi.

23 **"an honorable and respected officer of the German school"**: Piers Mackesy, *The War for America, 1775–1783* (Lincoln: University of Nebraska Press, 1964), 213.

23 **a classic neurotic with an inability to handle authority**: William B. Willcox, *Portrait of a General: Sir Henry Clinton in the War for Independence* (New York: Alfred A. Knopf, 1964), 44.

24 **Richmond County**: Philip Papas, "Richmond County, Staten Island," in *The Other New York: The American Revolution Beyond New York City, 1763–1787*, ed. Joseph S. Tiedemann and Eugene R. Fingerhut (Albany: State University of New York Press, 2005), 84.

24 **the island's loyalty**: Howe to Germain, July 7, 1776, in *NDAR*, vol. 5, 962.

24 **"I have the satisfaction to inform your Lordship"**: Howe to Germain, July 7, 1776, in *The Writings of George Washington*, ed. Jared Sparks (hereinafter Sparks), 12 vols. (Boston: Russell & Co., 1834–37), vol. 5, 452–53.

25 **Oliver De Lancey narrowly escaped capture**: Carl Van Doren, *Secret History of the American Revolution* (New York: Viking, 1941), 14–15; Barnet Schecter, *The Battle for New York: The City at the Heart of the American Revolution* (New York: Penguin, 2002), 995–97.

25 **the patriots were in effective control of the city**: Schecter, *The Battle for New York*, 51.

26 **Vandeput had no trouble obtaining supplies**: "Journal of HMS *Asia*, Captain George Vandeput," in *NDAR*, vol. 1, 541; Cadwallader Colden to Lord Dartmouth, June 7, 1775, in *Documents Relative to the Colonial History of the State of New-York*, ed. Edmund B. O'Callaghan and B. Fernow, 15 vols. (1853–87; New York: AMS Press, 1969), vol. 7, 581–82. The citation is to the AMS Press edition.

26 **The landing**: Washington to Schuyler, July 11, 1776, in *Washington Papers*, vol. 5, 273–75.

26 **Kings County**: Edwin G. Burrows, "King's County," in Tiedemann and Fingerhut, *The Other New York*, 21–42.

27 **Queens County**: Joseph S. Tiedemann, "Queens County," in Tiedemann and Fingerhut, *The Other New York*, 43–61.

27 **New Jersey**: David J. Fowler, "Loyalty Is Now Bleeding in New Jersey," in *The Other Loyalists: Ordinary People, Royalism, and the Revolution in the Middle Colonies, 1763–1787*, ed. Joseph S. Tiedemann, Eugene R. Fingerhut, and Robert W. Venables (Albany: State University of New York Press, 2009), 45–77.

29 **Bonvouloir was to make contact**: Vergennes to Guines, August 7, 1775, in Henri Doniol, *Histoire de la participation de la France à l'établissement des États-Unis d'Amérique: Correspondance diplomatique et documents*, 5 vols. (Paris: Imprimerie Nationale 1886–92), vol. 1, 155–56; *NDAR*, vol. 1, 1357–58.

29 **British spies were working in the French embassy in London**: Louis de Loménie, *Beaumarchais and His Times*, trans. Henry S. Edwards (New York: Harper, 1857), 255–60.

29 **sided with Vergennes**: "Considerations on the Affairs of the English Colonies in America," in Doniol, *Histoire de la participation de la France à l'établissement des États-Unis d'Amérique*, vol. 1, 273–78; Benjamin Franklin Stevens, comp., *Facsimiles of Manuscripts in European Archives Relating to America, 1773–1783*, 24 vols. (London: C. Whittingham and Co., 1889–98), vol. 13, no. 1316.

31 **"upon assurances given by yourself"**: Lord Dartmouth to Governor Josiah Martin, November 7, 1775, in *NDAR*, vol. 3, 346–47.

3. The Great Hudson River Illusion

35 **"the leaders of the rebellion . . . manifestly aim at a total independence"**: Thomas, *Lord North*, 87.

36 **"was prompted and impelled to independence by necessity"**: Edwin G. Burrows and Mike Wallace, *Gotham: A History of New York to 1808* (New York: Oxford University Press, 1999), 222; Walter Stahr, *John Jay* (New York: Hambledon and London, 2005), 61; Jack Rakove, *Revolutionaries: A New History of the Invention of America* (New York: Houghton Mifflin Harcourt, 2010), 100–101.

37 **"Yesterday the greatest question was decided"**: John Adams to Abigail Adams, July 3, 1776, in *The Adams Family Correspondence*, ed. L. H. Butterfield et al., 12 vols. (Cambridge, MA: Harvard University Press, 1963–2015), vol. 2, 27–28.

37 **"to supply you with necessaries of every sort"**: Beaumarchais to the Committee of Secret Correspondence of the Continental Congress, August 18, 1776, in *The Revolutionary Diplomatic Correspondence of the United States*, ed. Francis Wharton, 6 vols. (Washington, DC, 1889), vol. 2, 129–31.

37 **"We will never submit to be hewers of wood"**: Stahr, *John Jay*, 62.

38 **Barrington, the secretary at war, wanted to rely on sea power alone**: Barrington to Dartmouth, November 12, 1774, December 24, 1774; Barrington to Lord

North, August 8, 1775, in Shute Wildman, *Political Life of William Wildman, Viscount Barrington* (London: Printed for Payne and Foss, 1815), 140–52.

38 **Admiral Howe was given nearly half of the king's sea force**: G. H. Barnes and J. H. Owens, eds., *The Private Papers of John, Earl of Sandwich First Lord of the Admiralty, 1771–1782* (London: Navy Records Society, 1932), vol. 1, August 1770–March 1778, 42; *NDAR*, vol. 6, 167–69.

39 **fleet was distributed over a wide area**: Admiral Howe to Philip Stephens, September 18, 1776, in *NDAR*, vol. 6, 891–94.

39 **over 90 percent of their gunpowder was imported**: O. W. Stephenson, "The Supply of Gunpowder in 1776," *American Historical Review* 30 (January 1925): 277–81.

41 **American privateers took 733 British merchantmen**: Samuel Flagg Bemis, "British Intelligence, 1777: Two Documents," *Huntington Library Quarterly* 24 (1960–61): 234–49; Gruber, *The Howe Brothers and the American Revolution*, 271.

41 **"The dread the people of New England etc. have of a war with the savages"**: Germain to Burgoyne, August 23, 1776, Historical Manuscripts Commission, *Report on the Manuscripts of Mrs. Stopford-Sackville, of Drayton House, Northamptonshire*, 2 vols. (London: 1904–10; hereinafter Historical Manuscripts Commission, Stopford-Sackville MSS), vol. 2, 40.

42 **If Manley led a squadron**: Daughan, *If By Sea*, 130.

4. HMS *Phoenix* and HMS *Rose* Provide a Lesson

44 **he wanted some idea of how strong the defenses were**: Shuldham to Philip Stephens, July 8, 1776, in *NDAR*, vol. 5, 975.

46 **Total casualties aboard from all the cannonading were three men wounded**: "Journal of Captain Hyde Parker Jr.," July 12, 1776, in *NDAR*, vol. 5, 1037; "Journal of Captain James Wallace," July 12, 1776, in *NDAR*, vol. 5, 1037–38.

46 **Several inexperienced artillerists were killed or wounded**: William Heath, *Memoirs of Major General William Heath*, ed. William Abbatt (New York: William Abbatt, 1901), 41–42.

46 **"proof of what I had long religiously believed"**: George Washington to John Augustine Washington, July 22, 1776, in *Washington Papers*, vol. 5, 428–30.

46 **"of infinite importance"**: *The Writings of George Washington from the Original Manuscript Sources*, ed. Fitzpatrick, vol. 4, 399.

46 **"Almost all our surplus of flour and no inconsiderable part of our meat"**: Washington to d'Estaing, September 11, 1778, in *Washington Papers*, vol. 16, 570–74.

48 **"insurrection of your own Tories"**: Washington to George Clinton, July 13, 1776, in *Washington Papers*, vol. 5, 291–92.

49 **Clinton gave orders**: Richard Carey Jr. to Colonel James Clinton, Schuyler Papers, vol. 15, New York Public Library; *NDAR*, vol. 5, 1040–41.

49 **William Smith, the prominent Tory lawyer, could not understand**: William Smith, *Historical Memoirs of William Smith from 16 March 1763 to 12 November 1783*, ed. William H. W. Sabine, 2 vols. (New York: New York Times/Arno Press, 1969 and 1971), vol. 2, 3; *NDAR*, vol. 6, 224–25.

49 **One of the first things Captain Hyde Parker Jr. did**: "Journals of Henry Duncan," *Publications of the Navy Records Society*, ed. John Knox Laughton (London: The Navy Records Society, 1902), vol. 20, 122.

50 **behavior was applauded in London**: Richard J. Koke, "The Struggle for the Hudson: The British Naval Expedition Under Captain Hyde Parker and Captain James Wallace, July 12–August 18, 1776," in *Narratives of the Revolution in New York: A Collection of Articles from The New-York Historical Society Quarterly* (New York: New-York Historical Society, 1975), 36–79.

51 **Tupper's aggressive small boat tactics**: Daughan, *If By Sea*, 92–93.

52 **made a second attempt on a frigate**: Ibid., 102–3.

53 **a complete defeat for Washington's river defense**: "Journal of Captain Henry Duncan of HMS *Eagle*"; "Journal of Captain James Wallace," August 18, 1776; "Journal of Captain Hyde Parker Jr.," August 1, 1776, in *NDAR*, vol. 6, 225–29.

53 **"On the night of the 16th"**: Washington to Governor Jonathan Trumbull, August 18, 1776, in *Washington Papers*, vol. 6, 70–71.

53 **the expedition had actually been "fruitless"**: Koke, "The Struggle for the Hudson," 79.

5. Attack Delayed

55 **lukewarm about attempting talks**: Gruber, *The Howe Brothers and the American Revolution*, 86–87.

56 **secret discussions with Benjamin Franklin**: Ibid., 74, 89–90.

56 **To make colonists aware that there was an alternative to fighting**: Declaration of Lord Howe, June 7, 1776, in Anderson, *The Command of the Howe Brothers During the American Revolution*, 152–54.

56 **the Continental Congress publicized his proclamation**: Anderson, *The Command of the Howe Brothers During the American Revolution*, 155–56.

57 **"This will be handed to you by Mr. Griffin"**: Washington to the president of Congress, July 15, 1776, in *Washington Papers*, vol. 5, 325.

58 **"The inhuman treatment"**: Ibid.

58 **Washington again refused**: Douglas Southall Freeman, *Washington*, an abridgement, by Richard Harwell, of Freeman's seven-volume biography, originally published by Scribners (New York: Simon & Schuster, 1995), 280–81.

59 **"Were it possible for *us* to forgive and forget"**: Franklin to Howe, July 30, 1776, in *The Papers of Benjamin Franklin*, ed. Leonard W. Labaree et al. (hereinafter *Papers of Benjamin Franklin*), 37 vols. (New Haven, CT: Yale University Press, 1959), vol. 22, 519–26.

60 **Clinton kept his troops sweltering**: William Moultrie, *Memoirs of the American Revolution*, 2 vols. (New York: Printed by David Longworth for the author, 1802), vol. 1, 180–85.

61 **The patriots still had the armed schooner *Liberty***: James L. Nelson, *Benedict Arnold's Navy* (New York: McGraw-Hill, 2007), 175–210.

61 **Arnold had been in Canada since December 1775 and knew the situation**: Arnold to Washington, August 25, 1776, in *NDAR*, vol. 5, 730–31.

61 **The three generals were anxious for Arnold to build a fleet to stop him**: William M. Wallace, *Traitorous Hero: The Life and Fortunes of Benedict Arnold* (New York: Harper, 1954), 97–98; Nelson, *Benedict Arnold's Navy*, 210–27. Of the many books and articles written about Arnold, Wallace's remains the best.

61 **"a matter of infinite importance"**: Washington to Hancock, June 28, 1776, in *Washington Papers*, vol. 5, 132–35.

62 **"The command of the water is of the last importance"**: Gates to Washington, July 29, 1776, ibid., 498–500.

62 **Most of the deaths were from disease**: Ibid.

6. The Battle of Brooklyn

63 **"All our hopes are now fixed on General Howe"**: William Knox to Lord Dartmouth, August 22, 1776, in *NDAR*, vol. 6, 565–66.

63 **he had had every intention of following the king's plan**: Howe to Germain, June 8, 1776, in Gruber, *The Howe Brothers and the American Revolution*, 84–85. For a different view, see Anderson, *The Command of the Howe Brothers During the American* Revolution, 125–30.

64 **Germain's requirement inevitably produced a long delay**: Anderson, *The Command of the Howe Brothers During the American Revolution*, 125–27.

64 **ten days later**: Vice Admiral Richard Lord Howe to Philip Stephens, August 1, 1776, in *NDAR*, vol. 6, 183; Anderson, *The Command of the Howe Brothers During the American Revolution*, 127; for a contrary view, see Gruber, *The Howe Brothers and the American Revolution*, 101.

65 **He estimated that perhaps eight or nine thousand troops landed**: Washington to John Hancock, August 23, 1776, in *Washington Papers*, vol. 6, 111–12.

65 **he had trouble deciding**: Colonel Joseph Reed to Governor Jonathan Trumbull, August 24, 1776, Trumbull Papers, 29, Letter Book 4, 334, Connecticut State Library, Hartford.

67 **"had committed already several depredations"**: Serle, *The American Journal of Ambrose Serle*, August 25, 1776, 77.

68 **At the same time, diversionary attacks could be made**: Clinton, *The American Rebellion*, 41–42.

69 **A few stray reports**: Schecter, *The Battle for New York*, 135–38.

69 **Their guns were run out**: Lord Howe to Commodore William Hotham, August 26, 1776, in *NDAR*, vol. 6, 309, 324–25.

69 **The warships also made a show of attacking Fort Defiance on Red Hook**: "Journal of Captain Andrew 'Snape' Hamond, HMS *Roebuck*, 14–29 August 1776," in *NDAR*, vol. 6, 351–54.

71 **"I well knew"**: Anderson, *The Command of the Howe Brothers During the American Revolution*, 136–37; Gruber, *The Howe Brothers and the American Revolution*, 115–16.

72 **they got no medical care**: Thomas Jefferson Wertenbaker, *Father Knickerbocker Rebels: How People Lived in New York City During the Revolution* (New York: Scribners, 1948), 162–71.

73 **What happened to the prisoners was so horrendous**: Edwin G. Burrows, *Forgotten Patriots: The Untold Story of American Prisoners During the Revolutionary War* (New York: Basic Books, 2008), 8–9.

7. A Masterful Retreat

74 **"I have the satisfaction to hear from General Howe"**: Lord Howe to Commodore Hotham, August 28, 1776, in *NDAR*, vol. 6, 337.

77 **heavy rain pelting down**: George Washington to John Augustine Washington, September 22, 1776, in *Washington Papers*, vol. 6, 371–74.

78 **The king made General Howe a Knight of the Bath**: Thomas Hutchinson, *The Diary and Letters of His Excellency Thomas Hutchinson . . .* , ed. Peter Orlando Hutchinson, 2 vols. (Boston: Houghton, Mifflin, & Co., 1884–86), vol. 2, 109–10; Alan Valentine, *Lord North*, 2 vols. (Norman: University of Oklahoma Press, 1967), vol. 2, 423–24; George H. Guttridge, *The Correspondence of Edmund Burke, July 1774–June 1778*, 10 vols. (Chicago: University of Chicago Press, 1958–70), vol. 3, 286.

79 **waiting to take them to Captain Christopher Billopp's landing**: Gruber, *The Howe Brothers and the American Revolution*, 116–18.

79 **Howe insisted that acceptable terms could be worked out after surrender**: Van Doren, *Benjamin Franklin*, 561–62.

79 **"Forces have been sent out"**: Ibid.

80 **British troops would become a permanent fixture**: *Papers of Benjamin Franklin*, vol. 22, 519–26.

80 **"[t]he three gentlemen were very explicit in their opinions"**: Lord Howe to Germain, September 20, 1776, in David Syrett, *Admiral Lord Howe: A Biography* (Annapolis: Naval Institute Press, 2006), 58; Sparks, vol. 4, 88.

81 **"Yesterday morning I returned with Dr. Franklin"**: John Adams to Abigail

Adams, September 14, 1776, *The Letters of John and Abigail Adams*, ed. Frank
Shuffelton (New York: Penguin Books, 2004), 228–29.

82 **"The ministry had become [unnerved by]"**: Silas Deane to Committee of
Secret Correspondence, October 1, 1776, in *The Revolutionary Diplomatic Correspondence of the United States*, ed. Wharton, vol. 2, 153.

8. The Howes Take New York City

83 **"Our situation is truly distressing"**: Washington to Hancock, September 2,
1776, in *Washington Papers*, vol. 6, 199–226.

84 **"No dependence could be put in a militia"**: Ibid.

84 **"If we should be obliged to abandon the town"**: Ibid.

84 **special care should be taken that no damage be done to the city**: Resolve of
Congress, September 3, 1776, *Journals of Congress*, vol. 4, 733.

85 **"Judging it expedient to guard against every contingency"**: Washington to
Hancock, September 2, 1776, in *Washington Papers*, vol. 6, 199–226

85 **"A general and speedy retreat is absolutely necessary"**: Greene to Washington,
September 5, 1776, ibid., 222–24.

85 **"Their designs we cannot learn"**: Washington to Hancock, September 6,
1776, ibid., 231–33.

86 **"On our side the war should be defensive"**: Washington to Hancock, September 8, 1776, ibid., 248–52.

86 **Washington ordered General Mercer in Perth Amboy**: Washington to Mercer,
September 3, 1776, ibid., 209.

87 **the city had to be abandoned as soon as possible**: Sparks, vol. 4, 87.

87 **"to get in our rear"**: Washington to Hancock, September 14, 1776, in *Washington Papers*, vol. 6, 308–9.

88 **"so terrible and so incessant a roar"**: Serle, *The American Journal of Ambrose
Serle*, September 15, 1776, 104.

89 **He was not anticipating that the landing place would be a mystery to the patriots**: Gruber, *The Howe Brothers and the American Revolution*, 122–24.

90 **Only one fireship got close**: Captain Francis Banks, "Journal of HMS *Renown*,"
in *NDAR*, vol. 6, 861.

90 **Hundreds would later sign a "Declaration of Dependence"**: Serle, *The American Journal of Ambrose Serle*, 107–8.

90 **"Sad complaints are made of the Hessians"**: Ibid.

90 **"The fortifications of the rebels particularly excited my astonishment"**:
Ibid., 109.

92 **"Fearing the enemy"**: Washington to Hancock, September 18, 1776, in *Washington Papers*, vol. 6, 331–33.

92 **"This affair"**: Ibid.

93 **General Howe believed that the entire city would have been in ashes**: Howe

to Germain, September 23, 1776, in Force, *American Archives*, 5th Series, vol. 2, 462.

94 **"The dependence which the Congress have placed upon the militia"**: George Washington to John Augustine Washington, September 22, 1776, in *Washington Papers*, vol. 6, 371–74.

94 **"The jealousy of a standing army"**: Washington to Hancock, September 24, 1776, ibid., 387.

94 **"to be enlisted as soon as possible"**: *Journals of Congress*, September 16 and 20, 1776, vol. 5, 760–64, 788–808.

9. Washington Evacuates Manhattan

95 **Hyde Parker Jr. had once again demonstrated the inadequacy of the river defenses**: "Narrative of Captain Andrew 'Snape' Hamond," October 9, 1776, in *NDAR*, vol. 6, 1182–83.

96 **"I have not the slightest prospect of finishing"**: Howe to Germain, September 25, 1776, Historical Manuscripts Commission, Stopford-Sackville MSS, vol. 2, 41.

97 **"The very strong positions the enemy had taken"**: Howe to Germain, November 30, 1776, in Anderson, *The Command of the Howe Brothers During the American Revolution*, 185.

98 **achieved his primary objective of getting Washington out of Manhattan**: Ibid., 184–90.

99 **remained on Pell's Point for another three days**: William Abbatt, *The Battle of Pell's Point, Pelham* (New York: W. Abbatt, 1901), 21.

100 **"At White Plains, the enemy advanced a second time"**: George Washington to John Augustine Washington, November 19, 1776, in *Washington Papers*, vol. 7, 102–5.

102 **"not only unworthy [of] the character of an officer"**: Catherine S. Crary, ed., *The Price of Loyalty: Tory Writings From the Revolutionary Era* (New York: McGraw Hill, 1973), 171.

102 **"I am . . . inclined to think"**: Washington to Greene, November 8, 1776, in *Washington Papers*, vol. 7, 115–16.

105 **"As soon as the enemy took possession of the fort the abuse and plunder commenced"**: "Isaac Van Horne Memoirs," excerpt printed in *A Salute to Courage*, ed. Dennis P. Ryan (New York: Columbia University Press, 1979), 52.

105 **one more indication of what awaited them if they submitted to His Majesty**: Burrows, *Forgotten Patriots*, 64.

10. Race for the Delaware

107 **"If the commanders of the galleys had acted with as much judgment as they did courage"**: *NDAR*, vol. 5, 13–19.

108 attacking Ticonderoga and having to garrison it for the winter was a bad idea:
Nelson, *Benedict Arnold's Navy*, 323–26.

110 "the public interest requires you coming over": Washington to Lee, November
21, 1776, in *Washington Papers*, vol. 7, 193–95.

112 He headed for Trenton: Freeman, *Washington*, abridged edition, 310–11.

113 Howe's vanguard was approaching the riverbank: Gruber, *The Howe Brothers
and the American Revolution*, 147–48.

114 Three thousand men accepted the terms immediately: William S. Stryker,
The Battles of Trenton and Princeton (Boston: Houghton, Mifflin, 1898), 206;
Howe to Germain, November 30, 1776, in Gruber, *The Howe Brothers and the
American Revolution*, 172.

115 Howe thought that Cornwallis had enough men to do the job: Willcox, *Portrait
of a General*, 115–20.

116 The unwillingness of the Howes to curb the miscreants: Charles Stedman,
The History of the Origin, Progress, and Termination of the American War, 2
vols. (London: J. Murray 1794), vol. 1, 24–26.

11. Redemption at Trenton

117 "Our affairs have taken an adverse turn": George Washington to John Augustine Washington, December 18, 1776, in *Washington Papers*, vol. 7, 369–70.

119 "Congress never thought of making him a dictator": Freeman, *Washington*,
abridged edition, 325.

124 "move down towards New York": Washington to Heath, January 5, 1777, in
Washington Papers, vol. 7, 531.

124 "if there is a fair opening": Washington to Heath, January 7, 1777, in *Washington Papers*, vol. 8, 10–11.

124 "as many valuable purposes": Washington to Heath, January 9, 1777, ibid.,
26.

125 "the sooner a panic-struck enemy is followed": Washington to Major General
Benjamin Lincoln, January 7, 1777, ibid., 11–12.

125 "Although the original design": Washington to Heath, January 27, 1777, ibid.,
164–65.

126 "The army is much reduced since we left Trenton": Washington to the Council
of Safety of Pennsylvania, January 19, 1777, ibid., 107–8.

127 "feasting, gunning, banqueting": Judge Thomas Jones, *History of New York
During the Revolutionary War, and of the Leading Events in the Other Colonies
at That Period*, ed. Edward Floyd De Lancey, 2 vols. (New York: New-York
Historical Society, 1879), vol. 1, 170–71.

127 "Not a stick of wood": Ibid., 171.

127 Loyalists were forced out of their homes: David Hackett Fischer, *Washington's
Crossing* (New York: Oxford University Press, 204), 349–50.

127 **with Howe anticipating a great victory in the coming summer**: Gruber, *The Howe Brothers and the American Revolution*, 189–95.

128 **"a strange mode of reasoning"**: Washington to Arnold, April 3, 1777, in *Washington Papers*, vol. 9, 45–46.

129 **"The hearts of the French people are universally for us"**: Jonathan Dull, *A Diplomatic History of the American Revolution* (New Haven, CT: Yale University Press, 1985), 82–83.

129 **Louis XVI presented the patriots with a loan of two million livres**: *The Revolutionary Diplomatic Correspondence of the United States*, ed. Wharton, vol. 2, 248–51.

12. Depraved Indifference

131 **"[N]othing can be more injurious"**: Smith, *Historical Memoirs*, vol. 2, 326.

131 **"If the military are to govern us"**: Ibid., 470–72.

132 **"Unwholesome smells"**: Nicholas Cresswell, *The Journal of Nicholas Cresswell, 1774–1777* (New York: L. MacVeagh, The Dial Press, 1924), 147–48.

132 **So did the other generals**: Thomas Jefferson Wertenbaker, *Father Knickerbocker Rebels: How People Lived in New York City During the Revolution* (New York: Scribners, 1948), 152.

132 **"Those who formerly wished our approach"**: Burrows and Wallace, *Gotham*, 255.

133 **tried and convicted of murder before a military court**: Jones, *History of New York During the Revolutionary War*, vol. 2, 92–93.

134 **Fewer than seven thousand patriots died in combat**: Burrows, *Forgotten Patriots*, x–xi.

134 **To avoid perishing from thirst**: Elias Boudinot, *Journal; or Historical Recollections of American Events During the Revolutionary War, from His Own Original Manuscript* (Philadelphia: Bourquin, 1894), 13–17.

134 **"If Mr. Howe's heart is not callous"**: John Adams to Abigail Adams, April 13, 1777, in *The Letters of John and Abigail Adams*, ed. Shuffelton, 26.

134 **One of them went back to England £150,000 richer**: Jones, *History of New York During the Revolutionary War*, vol. 1, 330–32.

135 **Lord Howe participated very little in the amusements and general debauchery**: Burrows and Wallace, *Gotham*, 247.

135 **Mrs. Loring**: Philip Young, *Revolutionary Ladies* (New York: Alfred A. Knopf, 1977), 76–80.

135 **His ability to forget that there was a war on**: Stedman, *The History of the Origin, Progress, and Termination of the American War*, vol. 1, 384–86.

136 **"The fair nymphs of this isle"**: Lord Rawdon to Lord Huntington, September 23, 1776, in Historical Manuscripts Commission, *Report on the Manuscripts of the Late Reginald Rawdon Hastings, Esq., of the Manor House, Ashby-de-la-Zouch [Leicestershire, UK]*, ed. Francis Bickley, 4 vols. (London, 1934), vol. 3, 179–80.

13. New War Plans

140 **"[If] the force I have mentioned [were] sent out"**: Anderson, *The Command of the Howe Brothers During the American Revolution*, 216.

142 **"to act defensively upon the lower part of Hudson's River"**: Howe to Germain, December 20, 1776, in Force, *American Archives*, 5th series, vol. 3, 1318.

142 **He replied on March 3, approving the whole strategy**: Germain to Howe, March 3, 1777, Historical Manuscripts Commission, Stopford-Sackville MSS, vol. 2, 58.

142 **"I pressed for more troops"**: Alan Valentine, *Lord George Germain* (New York: Oxford University Press, 1962), 173; Hansard's Debates, vol. 20, 684.

143 **Germain's reply**: Germain to Howe, May 18, 1777, in Anderson, *The Command of the Howe Brothers During the American Revolution*, 227, 256.

144 **"pass Lake Champlain"**: Germain to Carleton, March 26, 1777, Historical Manuscripts Commission, Stopford-Sackville MSS, vol. 2, 60.

145 **Once conquered, it would have to be held**: Willcox, *Portrait of a General*, 140–41.

146 **He assumed that General Howe's first priority would be the Hudson**: Lieutenant General John Burgoyne, *A State of the Expedition from Canada, as Laid Before the House of Commons* . . . (New York: New York Times/Arno Press; London: J. Almon, 1780), 189. Citations are to the Arno edition.

146 **"I shall endeavour to have a corps"**: Howe to Carleton, April 2, 1777, Historical Manuscripts Commission, Stopford-Sackville MSS, vol. 2, 64–65.

147 **he could do it just as well by moving up the Hudson**: Sir William Howe to General Henry Clinton, July 7, 1777, in Anderson, *The Command of the Howe Brothers During the American Revolution*, 264–66.

14. Duel for a Continent

150 **Washington was happy to find**: Washington to Major General Arnold, June 17, 1777, in *Washington Papers*, vol. 10, 58–60.

151 **positioned his army near the dramatic bend in the river known as West Point**: Freeman, *Washington*, abridged edition, 342–44.

152 **Burgoyne**: Richard M. Ketchum, *Saratoga: Turning Point of America's Revolutionary War* (New York: Henry Holt, 1997), 274.

155 **He expected his army to grow**: Burgoyne to Germain, July 12, 1777, in Mackesy, *The War for America*, 132.

156 **he was convinced that the heavy guns would be effective against inexperienced troops**: Burgoyne, *A State of the Expedition from Canada*, 88–94.

156 **expected to be in Albany by the twenty-third**: Burgoyne to Clinton, August 6, 1777, in Clinton, *The American Rebellion*, 70.

158 the great fleet had disappeared out to sea again: Daughan, *If By Sea*, 142.

158 he made a firm decision to march his army to the North (Hudson) River: Washington to the President of Congress, August 21, 1777, in *Washington Papers*, vol. 11, 21–27.

159 needlessly lost much of his rear guard: Washington Irving, *Life of George Washington*, in *The Works of Washington Irving*, 17 vols. (New York: P. F. Collier & Son, 1840), vol. 13, 526.

159 He immediately dropped plans for traveling to New York: Washington to Major General Sullivan, August 22, 1777, in *Washington Papers*, vol. 11, 48–49.

160 Tying the hands of local commanders: Valentine, *Germain*, 170, 285.

160 Lincoln was eventually able to close off any hope that Burgoyne had of retreating: David B. Mattern, *Benjamin Lincoln and the American Revolution* (Columbia: University of South Carolina Press, 1995), 41–51.

161 Washington urged Governor Clinton to do everything possible: Washington to Governor Clinton, August 13 and 16, 1777, in Sparks, vol. 5, 28–32.

161 "The prospect of the campaign . . . is far less prosperous": Burgoyne to Germain, August 20, 1777, in Burgoyne, *A State of the Expedition from Canada*, xxxix–xliv.

161 "I yet do not despond": Ibid.

15. New York and Philadelphia

163 "Our friend Phil has good qualities": Quoted in Max M. Mintz, The *Generals of Saratoga: John Burgoyne and Horatio Gates* (New Haven, CT: Yale University Press, 1990), 180.

163 In addition, Gates had a gifted group of militia officers: John F. Luzader, *Saratoga: A Military History of the Decisive Campaign of the American Revolution*, 185–88.

164 "The army that I have had under my immediate command": Washington to Patrick Henry, governor of Virginia, November 13, 1777, in *Washington Papers*, vol. 12, 240–43.

167 On the British side: Freeman, *George Washington*, vol. 4, 490.

168 "How different the case in the Northern Department!": Washington to Patrick Henry, governor of Virginia, November 13, 1777, in *Washington Papers*, vol. 12, 240–43.

169 the story did not need embellishment: Wayne to Washington, September 21, 1777, in Charles Janeway Stille, *Major General Anthony Wayne and the Pennsylvania Line in the Continental Army* (Gansevoort, NY: Corner House Historical Publications, 2000; Philadelphia: J. B. Lippincott, 1893), 82–88. For a different account of the battle see Stephen R. Taffe, *The Philadelphia Campaign, 1777–1778* (Lawrence: University of Kansas Press, 2003), 84–87.

170 **"good gin"**: Robert McConnell Hatch, *Major John André: A Gallant in Spy's Clothing* (Boston: Houghton Mifflin, 1986), 77.

170 **The possibility of Old Put's pulling off a successful raid**: Sparks, vol. 5, 73n.

170 **Gates sent his refusal**: Washington to Gates, September 24, 1777, in *Washington Papers*, vol. 11, 155.

170 **totally outmaneuvered again**: Christopher Ward, *The War of the Revolution*, 2 vols. (New York: Macmillan, 1952), vol. 1, 355–61.

171 **"Many unavoidable difficulties and unlucky accidents"**: Washington to Governor Trumbull of Connecticut, October 1, 1777, in *Washington Papers*, vol. 11, 364–65.

171 **"The day was rather unfortunate"**: Washington to the president of Congress, September 5, 1777, ibid., vol. 11, 150.

16. Clinton and Burgoyne

174 **more alert to the possibility of a future raid**: Clinton, *The American Rebellion*, 71; Willcox, *Portrait of a General*, 176.

175 **"They gained possession of both posts"**: *Journals of the Provincial Congress, Provincial Convention, Committee of Safety, and Council of Safety of the State of New-York, 1775–1776–1777* (Albany, 1842), vol. 1, 1063–64.

176 **the doomed ship exploded**: Hotham to Admiral Howe, October 9, 1777, in *NDAR*, vol. 10, 96–97.

177 **Arnold would not be denied**: Wallace, *Traitorous Hero*, 154–57.

178 **imprisoned in Virginia**: Star, *John Jay*, 84.

179 **"I had . . . hope[d] that as soon as"**: Clinton, *The American Rebellion*, 81–82.

180 **North's missives had the king's full approval**: North to Lord Howe, October 26 and 28, 1777, in Bemis, "British Intelligence, 1777: Two Documents," *Huntington Library Quarterly* 24 (1960–61): 234–49.

180 **Not until November 23 did the first British transports sail unimpeded**: For a detailed account of the battle for the river see Daughan, *If By Sea*, 155–59.

17. France Declares War on Britain

183 **His proposals were so generous**: *Annual Register; or A View of the History, Politics, and Literature for the Years 1777, 1778, 1781* (London: J. Dodsley, 1778, 1779, 1782), 1778 vol., 327–29.

183 **"Disappointed, defeated, disgraced"**: *The Letters of Horace Walpole*, ed. Paget Toynbee, 16 vols. (Oxford: Clarendon Press, 1904), vol. 10, February 18, 1778, 190.

183 **"under offers of peace, to divide"**: Washington to Governor Livingston, April 22, 1778, in *Washington Papers*, vol. 20, 166–67.

184 **A combined Franco-Spanish fleet**: Charles Lee Lewis, *Admiral de Grasse and American Independence* (Annapolis: Naval Institute Press, 1945), 60.

185 **Spain also had the prospect of regaining East and West Florida**: Vergennes to Comte Armand de Montmorin, the French ambassador in Madrid, December 13, 1777, in Stevens, *Facsimiles of Manuscripts in European Archives Relating to America*, vol. 17, no. 1775.

186 **Clinton was also instructed to send three thousand men to St. Augustine**: Clinton's orders were dated March 8, 12, and 21: Willcox, *Portrait of a General*, 220–25.

186 **the "entire reduction of all the colonies to the southward of [the] Susquehanna"**: Germain to Clinton, March 21, 1778, in Clinton, *American Rebellion*, 87.

187 **Burgoyne's army "was not equal to the task"**: John W. Derry, *Charles James Fox* (New York: St. Martin's, 1972), 71–72.

189 **"His conduct leaves nothing for Congress to desire"**: Vergennes to Luzerne, December 4, 1780, in Sparks, vol. 7, 379.

189 **The possibility of trapping Lord Howe's inferior squadron**: Van Doren, *Benjamin Franklin*, 602; Joseph Callo, *John Paul Jones: America's First Sea Officer* (Annapolis: Naval Institute Press, 2006), 41–43.

190 **April 13, 1778, over two months after the treaty of alliance was signed**: Jonathan Dull, *Diplomatic History of the American Revolution* (New Haven, CT: Yale University Press, 1987), 97–98.

18. Admiral Howe Saves New York

193 **"No history . . . can furnish an instance of an army's suffering"**: *The Writings of George Washington*, ed. Fitzpatrick, vol. 11, 191–92; James Thomas Flexner, *George Washington in the American Revolution, 1775–1783* (Boston: Little, Brown, 1968), 261–62.

193 **he treated Steuben as the army's unofficial inspector general**: Paul Lockhart, *The Drillmaster at Valley Forge* (New York: HarperCollins, 2010), 198–207.

193 **"Such have been the derangement and disorders in them"**: Washington to Henry Laurens, May 5, 1778, in *Washington Papers*, vol. 15, 154–56.

194 **"well-regulated"**: Benjamin Rush, *Letters of Benjamin Rush*, ed. L. H. Butterfield, 2 vols. (Princeton, NJ: Princeton University Press, 1951), vol. 1, 159–60.

195 **"That there was a scheme of this sort"**: Washington to Langdon Carter, May 30, 1778, in *Washington Papers*, vol. 15, 267–70.

195 **"Indolence and luxury"**: Stedman, *The History of the Origin, Progress, and Termination of the American War*, vol. 1, 309.

196 **subjected to the same treatment**: Burrows, *Forgotten Patriots*, 118–20.

197 **"Our enemies will dwell upon the folly and extravagance of it"**: Serle, *The American Journal of Ambrose Serle*, 294.

198 **"The enemy by the evacuation of Philadelphia"**: *New York Journal and General Advertiser*, November 2, 1778.

198 "a great part of our cavalry": Clinton to Germain, June 5, 1778, in Sparks, vol. 5, 396.

199 Using all the troops in this way was a violation of orders: Clinton to Germain, June 5–13, 1778, in Stevens, *Facsimiles of Manuscripts in European Archives Relating to America*, vol. 11, nos. 1084, 1093.

199 "The enemy are making every preparation": Washington to General Henry Lee, May 25, 1778, in *Washington Papers*, vol. 15, 216–17.

200 Four thousand others were sick from smallpox and other disorders: Washington to Gates, May 29, 1778, ibid., 254.

203 "Here," Washington wrote, "our affairs took": George Washington to John Augustine Washington, July 4, 1778, in *Washington Papers*, vol. 16, 25.

203 Clinton's hasty withdrawal: For a somewhat different view of the battle, see Willcox, *Portrait of a General*, 233–36.

205 Howe had no peer: Rodger Knight, "Richard, Earl Howe, 1726–1799," in *Precursors of Nelson: British Admirals of the Eighteenth Century*, ed. Le Fevre and Harding, 279–301.

19. The Franco-American Alliance Misfires

207 there were three days when tide and wind were good enough: Alfred Thayer Mahan, *The Major Operations of the Navies in the War of American Independence* (Gloucestershire, UK: Nonsuch Publishing, 1913), 50–51.

207 He would be receiving concentrated fire from seven of Howe's largest ships: Ibid.

208 "the pilots procured by Colonels Laurens and Hamilton": D'Estaing's letter to Congress, August 26, 1778, in Sparks, vol. 6, 12.

209 Lafayette would be invaluable as a liaison: Washington to the Marquis de Lafayette, July 22, 1778, and Washington to the president of Congress, July 22, 1778, in *Washington Papers*, vol. 16, 127–28.

210 when the wind permitted an easy exit from the bay: Syrett, *Admiral Lord Howe*, 83.

211 Byron himself did not arrive until the end of September: Mackesy, *The War for America*, 212.

212 Sullivan's prompt action saved hundreds of men: John Sullivan to Washington, August 13, 1778, in *Washington Papers*, vol. 16, 307.

212 "The whole may be summed up in a few words": George Washington to John Augustine Washington, September 23, 1778, in *Washington Papers*, vol. 17, 110–11.

213 General Clinton tried to keep him by suggesting they attack Boston: Willcox, *Portrait of a General*, 251–53.

214 **North refused to appoint him as the new treasurer of the navy**: Syrett, *Admiral Lord Howe*, 87.

20. Withdrawal from Rhode Island

218 **Clinton just had to bide his time**: Willcox, *Portrait of a General*, 268–70.

219 **he apparently thought that these various estates were essential for recreation**: Jones, *History of New York During the Revolutionary War*, vol. 2, 66–67.

220 **Arnold's aristocratic friends seemed of greater importance to him**: William B. Reed, *Life and Correspondence of Joseph Reed . . .* , 2 vols. (Philadelphia: Lindsay and Blakiston, 1847), vol. 2, 48.

223 **"I am sorry any hesitation should still remain"**: Van Doren, *Secret History of the American Revolution*, 453.

223 **Arnold's need for money grew acute**: Wallace, *Traitorous Hero*, 212–14.

224 **the British fleet with its copper-bottomed ships would have been hard to defeat**: Mackesy, *The War for America*, 278–97.

224 **unlike Lord Howe (and very much like Clinton)**: Clinton, *The American Rebellion*, 53.

226 **"The humanity of our brave soldiery"**: Wayne to Washington, July 17, 1779, in *Washington Papers*, vol. 21, 522–24; Stille, *Major General Anthony Wayne*, 182–98.

227 **The king and cabinet had no intention of appointing Cornwallis**: Herbert Butterfield, *George III, Lord North and the People, 1779–1780* (London: G. Bell and Sons, 1949), 176.

227 **The naval supremacy that Clinton required was compromised**: Daughan, *If By Sea*, 192–94.

228 **"Arbuthnot's fleet"**: *New York Journal and General Advertiser*, September 6, 1779.

229 **by the end of October, all the troops were assembled in New York**: *New York Journal and General Advertiser*, November 8, 1779.

229 **"We have been hourly in expectation"**: Washington to Lafayette, October 20, 1779, in *Washington Papers*, vol. 22, 557–62.

21. Charleston

232 **Relations between the three were still sour**: Clinton, *The American Rebellion*, 53.

233 **"I feel many anxious moments"**: Washington to Schuyler, March 31, 1780, in *The Writings of George Washington*, ed. Fitzpatrick, vol. 18, 185–87.

233 **Washington planned to have Lord Stirling**: Washington to Major General Lord Stirling, January 14, 1780, in *The Writings of George Washington*, ed. Fitzpatrick, vol. 18, 87–88.

234 **When he left New York, he had five sail of the line**: Daughan, *If By Sea*, 182–84.

236 **"The Commodore and all his officers renounce"**: Laurens to Washington, March 14, 1780, in *The Correspondence of the American Revolution: Being Letters of Eminent Men to George Washington*, ed. Jared Sparks, 4 vols. (Boston: Little, Brown, 1953), vol. 2, 413–15.

236 **"I have the greatest confidence in General Lincoln's prudence"**: Washington to Laurens, April 26, 1780, ibid., 298–300.

236 **"After seeing to the landing of the army"**: Arbuthnot's report to the Admiralty, May 14, 1780, in Gardner Allen, *A Naval History of the American Revolution* (Cranbury, NJ: The Scholar's Bookshelf, 2005; first published in 1913), 494–96. The citation is to the Scholar's Bookshelf edition.

239 **a high price**: Burrows, *Forgotten Patriots*, 201.

239 **political missteps**: Walter Edgar, *South Carolina: A History* (Columbia: University of South Carolina Press, 1998), 233–39.

240 **"Tarleton's Quarter"**: George F. Scheer and Hugh F. Rankin, *Rebels and Redcoats: The American Revolution Through the Eyes of Those Who Fought and Lived It* (New York: Da Capo Press, 1957), 401–2.

240 **"be ready to maintain and defend"**: Ibid., 403.

241 **"extinguish the rebellion"**: Russell F. Weigley, *The Partisan War: The South Carolina Campaign of 1780–1782* (Columbia: University of South Carolina Press, 1970), 10.

241 **"the most savage cruelty"**: Moultrie, *Memoirs of the American Revolution*, vol. 2, 219.

241 **"there was scarce an inhabitant"**: Edgar, *South Carolina: A History*, 235.

241 **reputation at the Admiralty soared**: Rodger, *The Insatiable Earl*, 284–87.

22. Benedict Arnold's Betrayal

243 **"universal wish for peace"**: Germain to Clinton, May 3, 1780, in Sparks, vol. 7, 30.

245 **"I assure you, every idea you can form of our distresses will fall short"**: Washington to Joseph Reed, May 28, 1780, in *The Writings of George Washington*, ed. Fitzpatrick, vol. 18, 434–40.

245 **A vigorous attack on Washington**: Smith, *Historical Memoirs*, vol. 2, 215–20.

245 **Lafayette could not be certain that Sandwich would be indifferent a second time**: Lafayette to Vergennes, May 1, 1780; Vergennes to Lafayette, August 17, 1780, in *American Historical Review* 8 (1903); Lafayette to Vergennes, May 20, 1780, in Stevens, *Facsimiles of Manuscripts in European Archives Relating to America*, vol. 17, no. 1625; Washington to Luzerne, May 11, 1780, in Sparks, vol. 7, 30–31; *The Writings of George Washington*, ed. Fitzpatrick, vol. 18, 347–48.

245 **reinforce General Haldimand in Canada**: Germain to Clinton, March 15, 1780, in Sparks, vol. 7, 53.

246 **"The maritime resources of Great Britain"**: Washington to Joseph Reed, May 28, 1780, in *The Writings of George Washington*, ed. Fitzpatrick, vol. 18, 434–40.

248 **Livingston's family had always admired Arnold**: George Dangerfield, *Chancellor Robert R. Livingston of New York, 1746–1813* (New York: Harcourt, Brace, 1960), 128–29.

248 **he had a powerful impact on Clinton and the war**: Wallace, *Traitorous Hero*, 212–14.

248 **Clinton now had twenty thousand men. . . . Cornwallis had almost seven thousand**: Mackesy, *The War for America*, 346.

248 **"As a colleague"**: Willcox, *Portrait of a General*, 93.

249 **Clinton dismissed his excuse as nonsense**: Ibid., 324.

251 **the British were far superior to the French**: Archibald Robertson, *Lieutenant General Royal Engineers: His Diaries and Sketches in America, 1762–1780*, ed. Harry M. Lydenberg (New York: New York Public Library, 1930), 237–38.

252 **"the best and noblest harbor in America"**: Rodney to the Earl of Sandwich, November 13, 1780, in Major General Godfrey Basil Mundy, *The Life and Correspondence of the Late Admiral Lord Rodney*, 2 vols. (London: John Murray, 1830), vol. 1, 428–33.

253 **"Apply to the Board of War"**: Washington to Knox, July 15, 1780, in *The Writings of George Washington*, ed. Fitzpatrick, vol. 19, 178–79.

254 **Gates would not even wait for Morgan**: Don Higginbotham, *Daniel Morgan: Revolutionary Rifleman* (Chapel Hill: University of North Carolina Press, 1961), 102–12.

255 **1,050 patriots remained on the battlefield**: Charles Royster, *A Revolutionary People at War: The Continental Army and American Character, 1775–1783* (New York: W. W. Norton, paperback, 1981; Chapel Hill: University of North Carolina Press, 1979), 282. The citation is to the Norton edition.

23. Rodney

258 **he sailed for the West Indies**: Rodney to Philip Stevens, January 27, 1780, in Mundy, *The Life and Correspondence of the Late Admiral Lord Rodney*, vol. 1, 220–25.

259 **Clinton could not have been more pleased to see Arbuthnot's discomfort**: Rodger, *The Insatiable Earl*, 286–70.

260 **"The rebels look upon it:"** Rodney to Sandwich, November 11, 1780, in Mundy, *The Life and Correspondence of the Late Admiral Lord Rodney*, vol. 1, 429.

261 **"General Washington will be at King's Ferry Sunday evening"**: Arnold to André, September 15, 1780, in Van Doren, *Secret History of the American Revolution*, 473.

262 **While going over detailed plans, Arnold gave André a written statement**: Washington to Major General Heath, September 26, 1780, in *The Writings of George Washington*, ed. Fitzpatrick, vol. 20, 88–89.

263 **"by three volunteers"**: Winthrop Sargent, *The Life and Career of Major John André* (1861), 350.

263 **"In the conference between Count Rochambeau and myself"**: Washington to Brigadier General Knox, February 10, 1781, in *The Writings of George Washington*, ed. Fitzpatrick, vol. 21, 208–12.

265 **he ordered his men to row downstream to the *Vulture***: Willard Sterne Randall, *Benedict Arnold* (New York: William Morrow, 1990), 565.

266 **"To my infinite surprise"**: Rodney to Sandwich, November 11, 1780, in Mundy, *The Life and Correspondence of the Late Admiral Lord Rodney*, vol. 1, 429.

267 **It was a long time before he could extricate himself**: "Light-Horse Harry" Lee, *Memoirs of the War in the Southern Department of the United States*, 2 vols. (Philadelphia: Bradford and Inskeep, 1812; New York: University Publishing Co., 1869, the latter edited by Robert E. Lee), vol. 2, 159–87 (the citation is to the Bradford and Inskeep edition); Wallace, *Traitorous Hero*, 272–73.

268 **"I must freely confess"**: Rodney to the Earl of Sandwich, November 13, 1780, in Mundy, *The Life and Correspondence of the Late Admiral Lord Rodney*, vol. 1, 428–33.

24. Facing South

272 **Humphreys's detail**: Washington to Lieutenant Colonel David Humphreys, December 23, 1780, in *The Writings of George Washington*, ed. Fitzpatrick, vol. 21, 6–7.

272 **"have given convincing proofs"**: Washington to General Anthony Wayne, January 3, 1781, ibid., 55–56.

273 **"aggravated calamities and distresses"**: Washington to Meshech Weare, president of New Hampshire, January 5, 1781; Washington to Brigadier General Knox, January 7, 1781, ibid., 61–65.

273 **"I am commanded by His Majesty"**: Clinton, *The American Rebellion*, 301–5.

274 **"No force has presented itself to us"**: Lord Rawdon to General Leslie, October 24, 1780, in Sparks, vol. 7, 347.

275 **As far as Sandwich was concerned, Arbuthnot was perfectly fine**: Rodger, *The Insatiable Earl*, 284–90.

275 **Arnold then quickly burned and pillaged**: Merrill D. Peterson, *Thomas Jefferson and the New Nation* (New York: Oxford University Press, 1970), 207–8.

276 **Steuben was doing so, albeit with great difficulty**: Washington to Steuben, February 20, 1781, in *The Writings of George Washington*, ed. Fitzpatrick, vol. 21, 256–58.

276 **"The situation of the southern states is alarming"**: Washington to the president of Congress, February 26, 1781, ibid., 300–302.

276 **he'd probably fight it out with the brace of pistols he always carried**: Washington to Lafayette, February 19, 1781, ibid., 253–56.

277 **"Convinced that naval operations alone will probably be ineffectual"**: Washington to Steuben, February 20, 1781, ibid., 256–58.

277 **Destouches**: Washington to Destouches, February 22, 1781; Washington to Rochambeau, February 24, 1781, ibid., 278–79, 285–86.

278 **making detachments of this sort was a mistake he would never have made**: Willcox, *Portrait of a General*, 370–71.

279 **Guilford Courthouse**: Higginbotham, *Daniel Morgan*, 135–54.

281 **catch the slower French squadron**: Arbuthnot to Clinton, March 11, 1781, in Sparks, vol. 7, 457.

281 **whichever squadron got to Chesapeake Bay first would have the advantage**: Washington to Lafayette, March 11, 1781; Washington to Destouches, March 31, 1781, in *The Writings of George Washington*, ed. Fitzpatrick, vol. 21, 333, 398–99.

282 **Destouches arrived back in Newport a victor**: The best account of this little-understood battle is in James L. Nelson, *George Washington's Great Gamble: And the Sea Battle That Won the American Revolution* (New York: McGraw-Hill, 2010), 58–71.

282 **"on both sides of the Susquehanna"**: Clinton to Phillips, April 11, 1781, in Sparks, vol. 7, 458.

283 **"If we mean an offensive war in America"**: Cornwallis to Major General William Phillips, April 10, 1781, in *Correspondence of Charles, First Marquis Cornwallis*, ed. Charles Ross, 3 vols. (London: John Murray, 1859), vol. 1, 87–88.

283 **"I cannot help expressing my wishes"**: April 10, 1781, Cornwallis to Clinton, in Sparks, vol. 7, 458.

285 **"to the last extremity"**: Washington to Major General Heath, February 23, 1781, in *The Writings of George Washington*, ed. Fitzpatrick, vol. 21, 280–82.

285 **"I am preparing for every exertion"**: Clinton to Germain, April 5, 1781, in Sparks, vol. 7, 458.

25. Prelude to Victory

286 **"We [in the north] shall from all appearances remain inactive"**: Washington to Lafayette, April 6, 1781, in *The Writings of George Washington*, ed. Fitzpatrick, vol. 21, 421–23.

287 **if all went well, he would have twenty-two sail of the line with him**: De Grasse to Rochambeau, March 29, 1781, in Sparks, vol. 7, 76.

287 **knew Chesapeake Bay as well as New York**: Lewis, *Admiral de Grasse and American Independence*, 99.

289 **"nest of vipers"**: Rodney to Lord Hillsborough, February 7, 1781, in David Spinney, *Rodney* (London: Allen & Unwin, 1969), 361.

290 **golden age of peculation**: Rodney to Philip Stephens, March 6, 1781, in Mundy, *The Life and Correspondence of the Late Admiral Lord Rodney*, vol. 2, 41–46.

292 **prevented Barras from being at the conference**: June 21, 1781, *The Diaries of George Washington*, ed. Donald Jackson, 6 vols. (Charlottesville: University of Virginia Press, 1978), vol. 3, *1771–1775, 1780–1781*, 217.

293 **a joint attack on Newport was inconceivable**: Ibid.; Sparks, vol. 8, 53–54n.

293 **"It is not for me to know"**: Washington to Luzerne, May 23, 1781, in *The Writings of George Washington*, ed. Fitzpatrick, vol. 22, 103–4.

293 **"in every point of view, an operation against New York has been deemed preferable"**: Washington to the president of Congress, May 27, 1781, ibid., 119–22.

293 **"The weakness of the garrison"**: Washington to John Sullivan, May 29, 1781, ibid., 131–32.

295 **Laurens's appointment was an unsubtle and unnecessary slap at Franklin**: Gregory D. Massey, *John Laurens and the American Revolution* (Columbia: University of South Carolina Press, 2000), 188–90.

295 **In the end Vergennes sent the money**: Ibid.

296 **"disinclination of their naval officers"**: *Diaries of George Washington*, ed. Jackson, vol. 3, 254.

296 **"block up" any fleet there**: Washington to Rochambeau, June 13, 1781, in *The Writings of George Washington*, ed. Fitzpatrick, vol. 22, 207–9.

297 **"the falsest man alive"**: Clinton's conversation with William Smith, October 2, 1781, Smith, *Historical Memoirs*, vol. 2, 450–51.

297 **he was going to base himself at Williamsburg**: Cornwallis to Clinton, May 26, 1781, in B. F. Stevens, ed., *The Campaigns in Virginia, 1781: An Exact Reprint of Six Rare Pamphlets on the Clinton-Cornwallis Controversy*, 2 vols. (London: Malby, 1888), vol. 1, 488.

298 **Enthusiasm for the war seemed most pronounced in an embarrassingly large class of entrepreneurs**: Rhys Isaac, *The Transformation of Virginia, 1740–1790* (Chapel Hill: University of North Carolina Press, 1982), 176–77.

299 **Clinton received yet another letter from Germain insisting that he pay more attention to the Chesapeake**: Willcox, *Portrait of a General*, 406.

26. Rodney's Dilemma

301 **His excuse was**: Mackesy, *The War for America*, 421.

301 **the reason he never attacked West Point**: Smith, *Historical Memoirs*, conversation with Clinton, October 2, 1781, vol. 2, 453.

302 **relentless in stirring up the Tories**: Ibid., 429.

302 **"I intend to make an attempt by surprise"**: A full account of this action may be found in *Diaries of George Washington*, ed. Jackson, July 2–6, 1781, vol. 3, 385–86; see also Sparks, vol. 8, 97ff.

303 **He particularly wanted to know if Cornwallis was creating a deepwater base on the Chesapeake**: Washington to Lafayette, July 13, 1781, in *The Writings of George Washington*, ed. Fitzpatrick, vol. 22, 367–69.

303 **"not made any movement in force"**: Washington to Governor Clinton, June 21, 1781, in *The Writings of George Washington*, ed. Fitzpatrick, vol. 22, 243–44.

303 **Washington appointed Major General John Stark to be commander of the northern front**: Washington to Brigadier General Stark, June 25, 1781, in *The Writings of George Washington*, ed. Fitzpatrick, vol. 22, 263–64.

304 **"this climate during the rainy season"**: Rodney to the Earl of Sandwich, March 7, 1781, in Mundy, *The Life and Correspondence of the Late Admiral Lord Rodney*, vol. 2, 47.

305 **"In all probability"**: Rodney to Lady Rodney, June 30, 1781, ibid., 139.

307 **Washington wrote to de Grasse in Rochambeau's cipher**: *Diaries of George Washington*, ed. Jackson, vol. 3, 409–10.

308 **"under the probability of Rodney coming up this coast"**: Ibid., vol. 2, 253–54.

27. New York and Yorktown

310 **"first to make the capes of the Chesapeake"**: Rodney to Hood, July 25, 1781, in Mundy, *The Life and Correspondence of the Late Admiral Lord Rodney*, vol. 2, 145–46.

311 **going to England to be with their father**: Spinney, *Rodney*, 378.

311 *Pegasus* **did not reach New York until September 2**: Mundy, *The Life and Correspondence of the Late Admiral Lord Rodney*, vol. 2, 145.

311 **"greatest dispatch"**: Debate in the House of Commons, December 4, 1781, ibid., 159–66.

314 **"take such a position"**: Washington to Lafayette, August 15, 1781, in *The Writings of George Washington*, ed. Fitzpatrick, vol. 22, 501–2.

314 **"[t]o send up the Elk River"**: Washington to de Grasse, August 17, 1781, in *The Writings of George Washington*, ed. Fitzpatrick, vol. 23, 7–11.

315 **"I shall also stand in need of a sum of specie for secret services"**: Washington to Morris, August 17, 1781, ibid., 11–12; Charles Rappleye, *Robert Morris: Financier of the American Revolution* (New York: Simon & Schuster, 2010), 268.

315 **"The security of West Point and the posts in the Highlands"**: Washington to

Major General Heath, August 19, 1781, in *The Writings of George Washington*, ed. Fitzpatrick, vol. 23, 20–23; Smith, *Historical Memoirs*, 429.

315 **"my most earnest wish"**: Washington to Lafayette, August 21, 1781, in *The Writings of George Washington*, ed. Fitzpatrick, vol. 23, 33–34.

316 **Even that ratio wasn't nearly enough to tempt him out of the city**: Willcox, *Portrait of a General*, 418.

316 **"which I have under my command"**: Washington to Morris, August 27, 1781, in *The Writings of George Washington*, ed. Fitzpatrick, vol. 23, 50–52.

316 **Washington was also wondering where Admiral de Grasse was**: Washington to Lafayette, September 2, 1781, ibid., 75–78.

316 **morning of September 5**: A detailed account of this critical battle is in James L. Nelson, *George Washington's Great Gamble: And the Sea Battle That Won the American Revolution* (New York: McGraw-Hill, 2010), 270–304.

319 **the commander in chief was ecstatic**: Washington to the president of Congress, September 5, 1781, in *The Writings of George Washington*, ed. Fitzpatrick, vol. 23, 87–88.

320 **"I have the honor to inform Congress"**: Washington to the president of Congress, September 15, 1781, ibid., 117–18.

323 **fierce gale**: Banastre Tarleton, *A History of the Campaigns of 1780 and 1781 in the Southern Provinces of North America* (London: T. Cadell in the Strand, 1787), 379–90.

28. Britain Stunned

324 **His Majesty remained adamantly opposed to American independence**: Valentine, *Germain*, 439–45.

327 **"slackness in every branch"**: Rodney to Sandwich, November 11, 1780, in Mundy, *The Life and Correspondence of the Late Admiral Lord Rodney*, vol. 1, 428–33.

328 **"a delusive hope"**: Washington to Governor Trumbull, November 28, 1781, in *The Writings of George Washington*, ed. Fitzpatrick, vol. 23, 359–60.

328 **"I am apprehensive"**: Washington to Greene, December 15, 1781, ibid., 389–92.

328 **he divided his army**: Washington to Governor Rutledge of South Carolina, October 31, 1781, ibid., 306–7.

328 **Washington asked de Grasse if he would return in 1782**: Washington to de Grasse, October 21, 1781, ibid., 248–50.

329 **they needed to create the appearance of solvency**: Rappleye, *Robert Morris*, 288–93.

329 **as if New York were an independent country**: John P. Kaminski, *George Clinton: Yeoman Politician of the New Republic* (Madison, WI: Madison House, 1993), 60–63.

329 **Virginia later did the same for ideological reasons**: Rappleye, *Robert Morris*, 326–29.

329 **Morris employed a number of other expedients**: Ibid., 325–30.

330 **"In case of success"**: Washington to Colonel Matthias Ogden, March 28, 1782, in *The Writings of George Washington*, ed. Fitzpatrick, vol. 24, 91.

331 **"By late advices from Europe"**: Washington to Greene, March 18, 1782, ibid., 72–74.

333 **"I am very confident"**: Mundy, *The Life and Correspondence of the Late Admiral Lord Rodney*, vol. 2, 234.

334 **A numerical advantage, a fortunate shift of wind, and unorthodox tactics**: Mahan, *The Major Operations of the Navies in the War of American Independence*, 143–58.

334 **Before Washington received news of the Saintes**: Washington to Greene, July 9, 1782, in *The Writings of George Washington*, ed. Fitzpatrick, vol. 24, 408–12.

29. Peace

337 **five million guilders, an enormous sum, desperately needed by Robert Morris and Washington**: Rappleye, *Robert Morris*, 313.

337 **"free and open navigation"**: Samuel Flagg Bemis, *The Diplomacy of the American Revolution* (Bloomington: Indiana University Press, 1957; New York: D. Appleton-Century, 1935), 259–64. The citation is to the Indiana University Press edition.

337 **"any negroes, or other property of the American inhabitants"**: Ibid., 262.

338 **"when the country had drained"**: Joseph Plumb Martin, *Private Yankee Doodle* (Boston: Little, Brown, 1962), 283.

339 **a Congress whose treatment of its army can only be described as contemptible**: Richard R. Kohn, *Eagle and Sword: The Beginnings of the Military Establishment in America* (New York: Macmillan, 1975), 17–39; John Ferling, *Almost a Miracle* (New York: Oxford University Press, 2007), 555–56.

340 **They recalled vividly the deep anger**: Sheila L. Skemp, *William Franklin: Son of a Patriot, Servant of a King* (New York: Oxford University Press, 1990), 239–50.

341 **"Persons who have adhered to the enemies of the state"**: Burrows and Wallace, *Gotham*, 257–58.

342 **Digby was still pretending that there was a blockade on**: Thomas Fleming, *The Perils of Peace: America's Struggle for Survival After Yorktown* (New York: HarperCollins, 2007), 277–78.

343 **"I have no right to deprive them of that liberty they are possessed of"**: Washington to Carleton, May 6, 1783; Carlton to Washington, May 12, 1783, in *The Writings of George Washington*, ed. Fitzpatrick, vol. 26, 408–9, 427–28.

343 "We have been accustomed for a long time": Washington Irving, *Life of George Washington*, in *The Works of Washington Irving*, vol. 15, chapter 33, 49.

30. Conclusion

347 "They have acted inconsistent with their true interest from the beginning of the war": *New York Journal and General Advertiser*, November 30, 1778.

348 "[T]he question remained, as it had from the beginning, could America be conquered": Ibid., September 13, 1779.

Select Bibliography

Primary Sources

Abbot, W. W., Edward G. Lengel, et al., eds. *The Papers of George Washington, Revolutionary War Series*, 24 vols. to date. Charlottesville: University of Virginia Press, 1985–.

Adams, John, and Abigail Adams. *The Letters of John and Abigail Adams*. Edited by Frank Shuffelton. New York: Penguin Books, 2004.

Annual Register; or A View of the History, Politics, and Literature for the Years 1777, 1778, 1781. London: J. Dodsley, 1778, 1779, 1782.

Barnes, G. R., and J. H. Owens, eds. *The Private Papers of John, Earl of Sandwich, First Lord of the Admiralty, 1771–1782*. London: Navy Records Society, 1936.

Beatson, Robert. *Naval and Military Memoirs of Great Britain, from 1727 to 1783*. 2nd ed. 6 vols. London, 1804.

Bielinski, Stefan, ed. *A Guide to the Revolutionary War Manuscripts in the New York State Library*. Albany: New York State American Revolution Bicentennial Commission, 1976.

Black, Jeannette D., and William G. Roelker, eds. *A Rhode Island Chaplain in the Revolution: Letters of Ebenezer David to Nicholas Brown*. Providence: Rhode Island Society of the Cincinnati, 1949.

Bolton, Charles Knowles, ed. *Letters of Hugh Earl Percy from Boston and New York, 1774–1776*. Boston, 1902.

Boudinot, Elias. *Journal; or Historical Recollections of American Events During the Revolutionary War, from His Own Original Manuscript*. Philadelphia: Bourquin, 1894.

Brigham, Clarence S., ed. *British Royal Proclamations Relating to America, 1603–1783*. Worcester, MA: American Antiquarian Society, 1911.

Burgoyne, Lieutenant General John. *A State of the Expedition from Canada, as Laid Before the House of Commons . . .* London: J. Almon, 1780.

Chadwick, French E., ed. *The Graves Papers and Other Documents Relating to the Naval Operations of the Yorktown Campaign, July to October, 1781*. New York: Naval History Society Publications 7, 1916.

Clarke, William Bell, et al. *Naval Documents of the American Revolution*. 11 vols. Washington, DC: U.S. Government Printing Office, 1964–.

Clinton, George. *George Clinton Papers, Public and Private, 1777–1795*. 47 vols. Edited by Hugh Hastings. Albany: Oliver A. Quayle, State Legislative Printer, 1904; State University of New York Library.

Clinton, Sir Henry, *The American Rebellion: Sir Henry Clinton's Narrative of His Campaigns, 1775–1782, with an Appendix of Original Documents*. Edited by William B. Willcox. New Haven, CT: Yale University Press, 1954.

Collier, Admiral Sir George, RN. "To My Inexpressible Astonishment: Admiral Sir George Collier's Observations on the Battle of Long Island." *New-York Historical Society Quarterly* 48 (October 1964).

Commager, Henry Steele, and Richard B. Morris, eds. *The Spirit of Seventy-Six: The Story of the American Revolution as Told by Participants*. New York: Da Capo Press, 1995.

Crary, Catherine S., ed. *The Price of Loyalty: Tory Writings from the Revolutionary Era*. New York: McGraw-Hill, 1973.

Cresswell, Nicholas. *The Journal of Nicholas Cresswell, 1774–1777*. New York: L. MacVeagh/ Dial Press, 1924.

Davies, K. G., ed. *Documents of the American Revolution, 1779–1783*. 21 vols. Dublin, Ireland: Irish University Press, 1972–1981.

Drinker, Mrs. Henry. "Journal." *Pennsylvania Magazine of History and Biography* 13 (1889).

Duncan, Henry. *The Journals of Captain Henry Duncan*. Edited by John Knox Laughton. London: Navy Records Society, 1902.

Ewald, Captain Johann. *Diary of the American War: A Hessian Journal*. New Haven, CT: Yale University Press, 1979.

Fitzpatrick, John C., ed. *The Writings of George Washington from the Original Manuscript Sources, 1745–1799*. 39 vols. Washington, DC: Government Printing Office, 1931–44.

Force, Peter, ed. *American Archives.* 4th Series, 6 vols. 5th Series, 3 vols. Washington, DC: M. St. Clair Clarke and Peter Force, 1837–53.

Ford, Worthington, ed. *Journals of the Continental Congress, 1774–1789.* 34 vols. Washington, DC: Government Printing Office, 1905.

Fortescue, Sir John, ed. *The Correspondence of King George the Third from 1760 to December 1783.* 6 vols. London: Macmillan, 1927–28.

Fraser, Henry S., ed. *The Memoranda of William Green, Secretary to Vice-Admiral Marriot Arbuthnot in the American Revolution.* Providence: Rhode Island Historical Society, 1924.

Gibbes, R. W., ed. *Documentary History of the American Revolution.* Columbia, SC: Banner-Steam-Power Press, 1853.

Gruber, Ira. *John Peebles' American War: The Diary of a Scottish Grenadier, 1776–1782.* Stroud, Gloucestershire, UK: Sutton, for the Army Records Society, 1997.

Gerlach, Larry R., ed. *New Jersey in the American Revolution, 1763–1783: A Documentary History.* Trenton: New Jersey Bicentennial Commission, 1775.

Guttridge, George H. *The Correspondence of Edmund Burke, July 1774–June 1778.* Vol. 3. Chicago: University of Chicago Press, 1961.

Heath, William. *Memoirs of Major General William Heath.* Edited by William Abbatt. New York: William Abbatt, 1901.

Historical Manuscripts Commission. *Report on the Manuscripts of Mrs. Stopford-Sackville, of Drayton House, Northamptonshire.* 2 vols. London: 1904–10.

Hutchinson, Thomas A. *The Diary and Letters of His Excellency Thomas Hutchinson . . .* Edited by Peter Orlando Hutchinson. 2 vols. Boston: Houghton Mifflin, & Co., 1884–86.

Jay, William. *The Life of John Jay: With Selections from the Correspondence and Miscellaneous Papers.* 2 vols. New York, 1833.

Jones, Judge Thomas. *History of New York During the Revolutionary War, and of the Leading Events in the Other Colonies at That Period.* Edited by Edward Floyd De Lancey. 2 vols. New York: New-York Historical Society, 1879.

Johnson, William. *Sketches of the Life and Correspondence of Nathanael Greene.* Charleston, SC, 1822.

Journals of the Provincial Congress, Provincial Convention, Committee of Safety and Council of Safety of the State of New-York, 1775–1776–1777. Albany, 1842.

Kemble, Stephen. *The Kemble Papers.* 2 vols. New York: Collections of the New-York Historical Society, 1884–85.

Laprade, William T., ed. *Parliamentary Papers of John Robinson, 1774–1784.* London, 1922.

Lee, "Light-Horse Harry." *Memoirs of the War in the Southern Department of the United States.* Washington, DC: F. Knight, 1844.

Mackenzie, Captain Frederick, *Diary of Frederick Mackenzie, Giving a Daily Narra-*

tive of His Military Service . . . 2 vols. Cambridge, MA: Harvard University Press, 1930.

Moultrie, William. *Memoirs of the American Revolution.* 2 vols. New York: Printed by David Longworth for the author, 1802.

Mundy, Major General Godfrey Basil. *Life and Correspondence of the Late Admiral Lord Rodney.* 2 vols. London: John Murray, 1830.

Neeser, Robert Wilden. *The Despatches of Molyneux Shuldham . . . January–July, 1776.* New York: DeVinne Press for the Royal Navy History Society, 1953.

O'Callaghan, E. B., and B. Fernow, eds. *Documents Relative to the Colonial History of the State of New York.* 15 vols. Albany, 1856–87.

The Parliamentary History of England from the Earliest Period to the Year 1803 (Hansard's Debates). Edited by William Cobbett. 36 vols. London: T. C. Hansard, 1814.

Peckman, Howard H., ed. *Sources of American Independence: Selected Manuscripts from the Collections of the William L. Clements Library.* Chicago: University of Chicago Press, 1978.

Reed, Wiliam B. *Life and Correspondence of Joseph Reed . . .* 2 vols. Philadelphia: Lindsay and Blakiston, 1847.

Robertson, Archibald. *Archibald Robertson, Lieutenant General Royal Engineers: His Diaries and Sketches in America, 1762–1780.* Edited by Harry M. Lydenberg. New York: New York Public Library, 1930.

Rochambeau, Count de. *Memoirs of the Marshal Count de Rochambeau, Relative to the War of Independence of the United States.* Translated by M. W. E. Wright. 1838. New York: New York Times/Arno Press, 1971.

Rodney, George. *Letter-Books and Order-Book of George, Lord Rodney, Admiral of the White Squadron, 1780–1782.* New York: Naval History Society, 1932.

Ross, Charles, ed. *Correspondence of Charles, First Marquis Cornwallis.* 3 vols. London: John Murray, 1859.

Rush, Benjamin. *Letters.* Edited by L. H. Butterfield. 2 vols. Princeton, NJ: Princeton University Press, 1951.

Russell, Peter. "The Siege of Charleston: Journal of Captain Peter Russell, December 25, 1779, to May 2, 1780." *American Historical Review* 4 (April 1899).

Scull, G. D., ed. *Memoir and Letters of Captain W. Glanville Evelyn of the Fourth Regiment (King's Own) from North America, 1774–1776.* Oxford, 1879.

Scheer, George F., and Hugh F. Rankin, *Rebels and Redcoats: The American Revolution Through the Eyes of Those Who Fought and Lived It.* New York: Da Capo Press, 1987.

Smith, William. *Historical Memoirs of William Smith from 16 March 1763 to 12 November 1783.* Edited by William H. W. Sabine. 2 vols. New York: New York Times/Arno Press, 1969 and 1971.

Sparks, Jared, ed. *The Correspondence of the American Revolution: Being Letters of Eminent Men to George Washington.* 4 vols. Boston: Little, Brown, 1853.

———. *The Writings of George Washington*. 12 vols. Boston: Russell, Odiorne, and Metcalf, 1834.

Stedman, Charles C. *The History of the Origin, Progress, and Termination of the American War*. 2 vols. London: J. Murray, 1794.

Stevens, Benjamin Franklin, comp. *Facsimiles of Manuscripts in European Archives Relating to America, 1773–1783*. 25 vols. London: C. Whittington and Co., 1889–98.

Stevens, Benjamin Franklin, ed. *The Campaigns in Virginia, 1781: An Exact Reprint of Six Rare Pamphlets on the Clinton-Cornwallis Controversy*. 2 vols. London: Malby and Sons, 1888.

Stokes, I. N. Phelps. *The Iconography of Manhattan Island, 1498–1909: Compiled from Original Sources and Illustrated*. 6 vols. Union, NJ: Lawbook Exchange, 1998.

Stone, W. L., ed. *Letters of Brunswick and Hessian Officers During the American Revolution*. New York: Da Capo Press, 1970.

Tarleton, Banastre. *A History of the Campaigns of 1780 and 1781 in the Southern Provinces of North America*. London: T. Cadell, in the Strand, 1787.

Uhlendorf, Bernard A., trans. and ed. *Revolution in America: Confidential Letters and Journals, 1776–1784, of Adjutant General Major Baumeister of the Hessian Forces*. New Brunswick, NJ: Rutgers University Press, 1957.

———. *The Siege of Charleston with an Account of the Province of South Carolina: Diaries and Letters of Hessian Officers from the von Jungkenn Papers in the William L. Clements Library*. Ann Arbor: University of Michigan Publications, History and Political Science, 12, 1938.

Walpole, Horace. *Journal of the Reign of George III from 1771 to 1783*. Edited by John Doran. 2 vols. London: Bentley, 1859.

Wharton, Francis, ed. *The Revolutionary Diplomatic Correspondence of the United States*. 6 vols. Washington, DC: Government Printing Office, 1889.

Webb, Samuel Blachley. *Correspondence and Journal of Samuel Blachley Webb*. Edited by Worthington C. Ford. 3 vols. New York: Burnet, 1894.

Willard, Margaret Wheeler, ed. *Letters on the American Revolution, 1774–1776*. Boston: Houghton Mifflin, 1925.

Secondary Sources

Abbott, Wilbur C. *New York in the American Revolution*. New York: Scribners, 1929.

Adelberg, Michael S. *The American Revolution in Monmouth County*. Charleston, SC: The History Press, 2010.

Allen, Gardner. *A Naval History of the American Revolution*. Cranbury, NJ: The Scholar's Bookshelf, 2005; Boston and New York: Houghton Mifflin, 1913.

Anderson, Troyer Steele. *The Command of the Howe Brothers During the American Revolution*. New York: Oxford University Press, 1936.

Alden, *General Charles Lee: Traitor or Patriot?* Baton Rouge: Louisiana State University Press, 1951.

Arnold, Isaac N. *The Life of Benedict Arnold.* Chicago: Jansen, McClurg, 1880.

Aston, Nigel, and Clarissa Campbell Orr, eds. *An Enlightenment Statesman in Whig England: Lord Shelburne in Context, 1737–1805.* Woodbridge, Suffolk, UK: Boydell and Brewer Press, 2011.

Atwood, Rodney, *The Hessians.* Cambridge: Cambridge University Press, 1980.

Bakeless, John. *Turncoats, Traitors, and Heroes: Espionage in the American Revolution.* New York: Da Capo Press, 1938.

Barck, Oscar T. *New York City During the War of Independence.* New York: Columbia University Press, 1931.

Baugh, Daniel A. "The Politics of British Naval Failure, 1775–1777." *American Neptune* 52 (1992).

Becker, Carl. *The History of Political Parties in the Province of New York, 1760–1776.* Madison: University of Wisconsin Press, 1909.

Bemis, Samuel Flagg. *The Diplomacy of the American Revolution.* Bloomington: Indiana University Press, 1957.

Berlin, Ira, and Leslie M. Harris. *Slavery in New York.* New York: New Press, 2005.

Billias, George Athan, ed. *George Washington's Opponents.* New York: William Morrow, 1969.

Bowman, Larry G. *Captive Americans: Prisoners During the American Revolution.* Athens: Ohio University Press, 1976.

Brookhiser, Richard. *Gentleman Revolutionary: Gouverneur Morris, The Rake Who Wrote the Constitution.* New York: Free Press, 2003.

Brown, Gerald S. *The American Secretary: The Colonial Policy of Lord Germain, 1775–1778.* Ann Arbor: University of Michigan Press, 1963.

———. "The Anglo-French Naval Crisis, 1778: A Study of Conflict in the North Cabinet." *William and Mary Quarterly,* 3rd ser., 13, no. 1 (January 1956).

Burrows, Edwin G., and Mike Wallace. *Gotham: A History of New York to 1808.* New York: Oxford University Press, 1999.

Butterfield, Herbert. *George III, Lord North and the People, 1779–1780.* London: G. Bell & Sons, 1949.

Callo, Joseph. *John Paul Jones: America's First Sea Officer.* Annapolis: Naval Institute Press, 2006.

Chernow, Ron. *Washington: A Life.* New York: Penguin, 2010.

Chidsey, D. B. *The Tide Turns: An Informal History of the Campaign of 1776.* New York: Crown, 1966.

Clark, Dora Mae. *British Opinion and the American Revolution.* Brasted, Kent, UK: Russell & Russell, 1966; New Haven, CT: Yale University Press, 1930.

Clearwater, Alphonse, ed. *The History of Ulster County, New York*. Kingston, NY: W. J. Van Deusen, 1907.

Clowes, William L., ed. *The Royal Navy: A History from the Earliest Times to the Present*. 7 vols. Boston: Little, Brown; London: S. Low, Marston, 1897–1903.

Curtis, Edward E. *The Organization of the British Army in the American Revolution*. New Haven, CT: Yale University Press, 1926.

Dakin, Douglas. *Turgot and the Ancien Régime in France*. London: Methuen, 1939.

Dangerfield, George. *Chancellor Robert R. Livingston of New York, 1746–1813*. New York: Harcourt, Brace, 1960.

Daughan, George C. *If By Sea: The Forging of the American Navy—From the Revolution to the War of 1812*. New York: Basic Books, 2008.

Decker, Malcolm. *Brink of Revolution: New York in Crisis, 1765–1776*. New York: Argosy Antiquarian Ltd., 1964.

Derry, John W. *Charles James Fox*. New York: St. Martin's, 1972.

Dull, Jonathan. *Diplomatic History of the American Revolution*. New Haven, CT: Yale University Press, 1987.

Edgar, Walter. *South Carolina: A History*. Columbia: University of South Carolina Press, 1998.

Ferling John. *Almost a Miracle*. New York: Oxford University Press, 2007.

———. *John Adams: A Life*. New York: Henry Holt, 1996. Originally published by the University of Tennessee Press, 1992.

Field, Thomas W. *The Battle of Long Island*. Brooklyn: Long Island Historical Society, 1869.

Fischer, David Hackett. *Washington's Crossing*. New York: Oxford University Press, 2004.

Flemington, Thomas. *New Jersey: A History*. New York: W. W. Norton, 1984.

———. *The Perils of Peace: America's Struggle for Survival after Yorktown*. New York: HarperCollins, 2007.

———. *1776: Year of Illusions*. Edison, NJ: Castle Books, 1975.

———. *Washington's Secret War: The Hidden History of Valley* Forge. New York: Smithsonian Books/HarperCollins, 2005.

Flexner, James Thomas. *George Washington in the American Revolution, 1775–1783*. Boston: Little, Brown, 1968.

Flick, Alexander, ed. *The American Revolution in New York*. Albany: State University of New York Press, 1926.

Fowler, David J. "Loyalty Is Now Bleeding in New Jersey." In *The Other Loyalists: Ordinary People, Royalism, and the Revolution in the Middle Colonies, 1763–1787*. Edited by Joseph S. Tiedemann, Eugene R. Fingerhut, and Robert W. Venables. Albany: State University of New York Press, 2009.

Freeman, Douglas Southall. *George Washington: A Biography*. 7 vols. New York: Scribners, 1948–57.

French, Allen. *First Year of the Revolution*. Boston: Houghton Mifflin, 1934.

Gee, Olive. "The British War Office in the Later Years of the American War of Independence." *Journal of Modern History* 26 (June 1954).

Gellman, David N. *Emancipating New York: The Politics of Slavery and Freedom, 1777–1827*. Baton Rouge: Louisiana State University Press, 2006.

Greene, Nelson, ed. *History of the Valley of the Hudson*. 2 vols. Chicago: S. J. Clarke Publishing Co., 1931.

Greene, George W. *The Life of Nathanael Greene, Major General in the Army of the Revolution*. 3 vols. New York, 1871.

Gruber, Ira D. *The Howe Brothers and the American Revolution*. New York: Atheneum, 1972.

———. "Lord Howe and Lord Germain: British Politics and the Winning of American Independence." *William and Mary Quarterly* 22 (1965).

Hannay, David. *Rodney*. London: Macmillan & Co., 1891.

Harris, Leslie M. *In the Shadow of Slavery: African Americans in New York City, 1626–1863*. Chicago: University of Chicago Press, 2003.

Hatch, Robert McConnell. *Major John André: A Gallant in Spy's Clothing*. Boston: Houghton Mifflin, 1986.

Higginbotham, Don. *Daniel Morgan: Revolutionary Rifleman*. Chapel Hill: University of North Carolina Press, 1961.

———. *The War of American Independence: Military Attitudes, Policies, and Practice, 1763–1789*. Boston: Northeastern University Press, 1971.

Higgins, W. Robert, ed. *The Revolutionary War in the South: Power, Conflict and Leadership*. Durham, NC: Duke University Press, 1979.

Hodges, Graham Russell. *Root and Branch: African Americans in New York and New Jersey, 1613–1863*. Chapel Hill: University of North Carolina Press, 1999.

Hoffman, Ross J. S. *The Marquis: A Study of Lord Rockingham, 1730–1782*. New York: Fordham University Press, 1972.

Irving, Washington. *Life of George Washington*. In *The Works of Washington Irving*. 17 vols. New York: P. F. Collier & Son, 1840.

Isaac, Rhys. *The Transformation of Virginia, 1740–1790*. Chapel Hill: University of North Carolina Press, 1982.

James, Bartholomew. *Journal of Rear Admiral Bartholomew James*. London: Navy Records Society, 1896.

Jensen, Merrill. *The Founding of the Nation: A History of the American Revolution, 1763–1776*. New York: Oxford University Press, 1968.

Johnson, Henry Phelps. *The Battle of Harlem Heights*. New York: AMS Press, 1897.

———. *The Campaign of 1776 Around New York and Brooklyn*. 2 vols. Brooklyn: Brooklyn Historical Society, 1878 and 1891.

Jones, Thomas. *History of New York During the Revolutionary War*. 2 vols. New York: New-York Historical Society, 1879.

Kaminski, John P. *George Clinton: Yeoman Politician of the New Republic*. Madison, WI: Madison House, 1993.

Kaplan, Roger. "The Hidden War: British Intelligence Operations During the American Revolution." *William and Mary Quarterly* 47 (1990).

Ketchum, Richard M. *Saratoga*. New York: Henry Holt, 1997.

———. *The Winter Soldiers: The Battles for Trenton and Princeton*. New York: Henry Holt, 1973.

Kirkland, Frederick R., ed. "Journal of a Physician on the Expedition Against Canada, 1776." *Pennsylvania Magazine of History and Biography* 59 (October 1935).

Koke, Richard J. "The Struggle for the Hudson: The British Naval Expedition Under Captain Hyde Parker and Captain James Wallace, July 12–August 18, 1776." In *Narratives of the Revolution in New York: A Collection of Articles from The New-York Historical Society Quarterly*. New York: New-York Historical Society, 1975.

Lacour-Gayet, Georges. *La marine militaire de la France sous le règne de Louis XVI*. Paris: H. Champion, 1905.

Lafayette to Luzerne, August 11, 1780. *American Historical Review* 20 (1915).

Larrabee, Harold A. *Decision at the Chesapeake*. New York: Doubleday, 1964.

Le Fevre, Peter, and Richard Harding, eds. *Precursors of Nelson: British Admirals of the Eighteenth Century*. Mechanicsburg, PA: Stackpole Books, 2000.

Leiby, Adrian. *The Revolutionary War in the Hackensack Valley: The Jersey Dutch and the Neutral Ground, 1775–1783*. New Brunswick, NJ: Rutgers University Press, 1991.

Lewis, Charles L. *Admiral de Grasse and American Independence*. Annapolis: Naval Institute Press, 1945.

Lockhart Paul. *The Drillmaster at Valley Forge: The Baron de Steuben and the Making of the American Army*. New York: Harper Perennial, 2010.

Lowell, Edward J. *The Hessians and the Other German Auxiliaries of Great Britain in the Revolutionary War*. New York: 1884.

Lucas, Reginald. *Lord North, Second Earl of Guilford, K.G., 1732–1792*. 2 vols. London: Arthur L. Humphreys, 1913.

Lundin, Leonard. *Cockpit of the Revolution: The War for Independence in New Jersey*. Princeton, NJ: Princeton University Press, 1940.

Mackesy, Piers. *The War for America, 1775–1783*. Cambridge, MA: Harvard University Press, 1964.

Mahan, Admiral Alfred Thayer. *The Major Operations of the Navies in the War of American Independence.* Gloucestershire, UK: Nonsuch Publishing, 1913.

Manders, Eric. *The Battle of Long Island.* Monmouth, NJ: Philip Freneau Press, 1978.

Mark, Irving. *Agrarian Conflicts in Colonial New York, 1711–1775.* New York: Ira J. Friedman, 1940.

Mazzagetti, Dominick. *Charles Lee: Self Before Country.* New Brunswick, NJ: Rutgers University Press, 2013.

Mercantile Library Association of New York City. *New York City During the Revolution.* 1861.

Middlekauff, Robert. *Franklin's Enemies.* Berkeley: University of California Press, 1996.

Mills, Louis V. "Attack in the Highlands, the Battle of Fort Montgomery." *Hudson Valley Regional Review* 17, no. 2 (September 2000).

Mitnick, Barbara J., ed. *New Jersey in the American Revolution.* New Brunswick, NJ: Rutgers University Press, 2005.

Murphy, Orville T. *Charles Gravier, Comte de Vergennes: French Diplomacy in the Age of Revolution, 1719–1787.* Albany: State University of New York Press, 1982.

Namier, Lewis, and John Brooke. *The History of Parliament.* 3 vols. London: Her Majesty's Stationery Office, 1964.

Narratives of the Revolution in New York: A Collection of Articles from the New-York Historical Society Quarterly. New York: New-York Historical Society, 1975.

Nelson, James L. *Benedict Arnold's Navy.* New York: McGraw-Hill, 2007.

———. *George Washington's Great Gamble: And the Sea Battle That Won the American Revolution.* New York: McGraw-Hill, 2010.

Nelson, Paul David, *William Alexander, Lord Stirling.* Tuscaloosa: University of Alabama Press, 1987.

Neuenschwander, John A. *The Middle Colonies and the Coming of the American Revolution.* Port Washington and London: Kennikat Press, 1973.

Nickerson, Hoffman. *The Turning Point of the Revolution; or Burgoyne in America.* Boston and New York: Houghton Mifflin, 1928.

O'Beirne, Thomas Lewis. *A Candid and Impartial Narrative of the Transactions of the Fleet, Under the Command of Lord Howe, from the Arrival of the Toulon Squadron on the Coast of America to the Time of His Lordship's Departure for England. With Observations by an Officer Then Serving in the Fleet.* London: Printed for J. Almon, 1779.

———. *Narrative of the Fleet Under Lord Howe.* New York: New York Times/Arno Press, 1969.

O'Shaughnessy, Andrew Jackson. *The Men Who Lost America: British Leadership, the American Revolution, and the Fate of the Empire.* New Haven, CT: Yale University Press, 2013.

Papas, Philip. *The Ever Loyal Island: Staten Island and the American Revolution.* New York: New York University Press, 2007.

———. *Renegade Revolutionary: The Life of General Charles Lee.* New York: New York University Press, 2014.

Partridge, Bellamy. *Sir Billy Howe.* New York: Longmans, Green and Co., 1932.

Pennypacker, Morton. *George Washington's Spies on Long Island and in New York.* Brooklyn: Long Island Historical Society, 1939.

Peterson, Harold L. *The Book of the Continental Soldier.* Harrisburg, PA: Stackpole Books, 1968.

Peterson, Merrill D. *Thomas Jefferson and the New Nation.* New York: Oxford University Press, 1970.

Rakove, Jack. *Revolutionaries: A New History of the Invention of America.* New York: Houghton Mifflin Harcourt, 2010.

Rael, Patrick. *Black Identity and Black Protest in the Antebellum North.* Chapel Hill: University of North Carolina Press, 2002.

Ralfe, James. *The Naval Biography of Great Britain: Consisting of Historical Memoirs of Those Officers of the British Navy Who Distinguished Themselves During the Reign of His Majesty George III.* 4 vols. London: Whitmore and Fenn, 1828.

Randall, Willard Sterne. *Benedict Arnold.* New York: William Morrow, 1990.

Rappleye, Charles. *Robert Morris: Financier of the American Revolution.* New York: Simon & Schuster, 2010.

Roberts, Michael. *Splendid Isolation.* Reading, UK: University of Reading, 1970.

Rodger, N. A. M. *The Insatiable Earl: A Life of John Montagu, 4th Earl of Sandwich.* New York: W. W. Norton, 1993.

Rogers, Susan Fox. *My Reach: A Hudson River Memoir.* Ithaca, NY: Cornell University Press, 2011.

Royster, Charles. *A Revolutionary People at War: The Continental Army and American Character, 1775–1783.* Chapel Hill: University of North Carolina Press, 1979.

Ryan, Dennis P., ed. *A Salute to Courage: The American Revolution as Seen Through Wartime Writings of Officers of the Continental Army and Navy.* New York: Columbia University Press, 1979.

Sargent, Winthrop. *The Life and Career of Major John André of the British Army in America.* New York: W. Abbatt, 1902.

Schecter, Barnet. *The Battle for New York: The City at the Heart of the American Revolution.* New York: Penguin, 2002.

Scheer, George F., and Hugh F. Rankin. *Rebels and Redcoats: The American Revolution Through the Eyes of Those Who Fought and Lived It.* New York: Da Capo Press, 1957.

Selby, John E. *Revolution in Virginia, 1775–1783.* Charlottesville: University of Virginia Press, 2007.

Shonnard, Frederic, and W. W. Spooner. *History of Westchester County, New York, from Its Earliest Settlement to the Year 1900.* New York: New York History Co., 1900.

Skemp, Sheila L. *William Franklin: Son of a Patriot, Servant of a King.* New York: Oxford University Press, 1990.

Smith, Paul. *Loyalists and Redcoats: A Study in British Revolutionary Policy.* Chapel Hill: University of North Carolina Press, 1964.

Spector, Margaret M. *The American Department of the British Government, 1768–1782.* New York: Columbia University Press, 1940.

Spinney, David. *Rodney.* London: Allen & Unwin, 1969.

Stark, James H. *The Loyalists of Massachusetts.* Boston: Augustus M. Kelley, 1910.

Stahr, Walter. *John Jay: Founding Father.* New York: Hambledon and London, 2005.

Stephenson, O. W. "The Supply of Gunpowder in 1776." *American Historical Review* 30 (January 1925).

Stille, Charles J. *Major General Wayne and the Pennsylvania Line in the Continental Army.* Philadelphia: J. B. Lippincott, 1893.

Stevenson, Charles G., and Irene Wilson. *The Battle of Long Island.* Brooklyn: Brooklyn Bicentennial Commission, 1975.

Syrett, David. *Admiral Lord Howe: A Biography.* Annapolis: Naval Institute Press, 2006.

———. *The Royal Navy in American Waters, 1775–1783.* Aldershot, Hants, UK: Scolar Press, 1989.

Thomas, Peter D. G. *Lord North.* London: Allen Lane, 1976.

Tiedemann, Joseph S., Eugene R. Fingerhut, and Robert W. Venables, eds. *The Other Loyalists: Ordinary People, Royalism, and the Revolution in the Middle Colonies, 1763–1787.* Albany: State University of New York Press, 2009.

———. *The Other New York: The American Revolution Beyond New York City, 1763–1787.* Albany: State University of New York Press, 2005.

Tornquist, Karl G. *The Naval Campaigns of Count de Grasse During the American Revolution, 1781–1783.* Translated by Amandus Johnson. Philadelphia: Swedish Colony Society, 1942.

Upton, I. F. S. *The Loyal Whig: William Smith of New York and Quebec.* Toronto: University of Toronto Press, 1969.

Valentine, Alan. *Lord George Germain.* New York: Oxford University Press, 1962.

———. *Lord North.* 2 vols. Norman: University of Oklahoma Press, 1967.

Wade, Herbert T., and Robert A. Lively. *This Glorious Cause: The Adventures of Two Company Officers in Washington's Army.* Princeton, NJ: Princeton University Press, 1958.

Wallace, William M. *Traitorous Hero: The Life and Fortunes of Benedict Arnold.* New York: Harper, 1954.

Ward, Christopher. *The War of the Revolution.* 2 vols. New York: Macmillan, 1952.

Watson, Steven. *The Reign of George III, 1760–1815*. Oxford: Oxford University Press, 1960.

Weigley, Russell F. *The Partisan War: The South Carolina Campaign of 1780–1782*. Columbia: University of South Carolina Press, 1970.

Wilson, Ellen Gibson. The *Loyal Blacks*. New York: Capricorn, 1976.

Whiteley, W. H. "The British Navy and the Siege of Quebec, 1775–1776." *Canadian Historical Review* 61, no. 1 (1980).

Wildman, Shute. *The Political Life of William Wildman, Viscount Barrington*. London: Printed for Payne and Foss, 1815.

Willcox, William B. "Admiral Rodney Warns of Invasion, 1776–1777." *American Neptune* 4 (July 1944).

———. *Portrait of a General: Sir Henry Clinton in the War for Independence*. New York: Alfred A. Knopf, 1964.

Young, Philip. *Revolutionary Ladies*. New York: Alfred A. Knopf, 1977.

Illustration Credits

1. *Major General Nathanael Greene*
    Artist: James Trenchard
    1786
    Library of Congress, Prints and Photographs Division, LC-USZ62- 45507

2. *His most excellent majesty George the third, by the grace of god, of the United Kingdom of Great Britain & Ireland, king, defender of the faith &c, &c, &c*
    Artist: William Skelton
    1810
    Library of Congress, Prints and Photographs Division, LC-DIG-pga-04155

3. *General John Burgoyne, 1722–1792*
    1944
    Library of Congress, Prints and Photographs Division, LC-USZ62-45781

4. *Treason of Arnold*
    Artist: Charles F. Blauvelt
    1874
    Library of Congress, Prints and Photographs Division, LC-DIG-ppmsca-30575

5. *Lieutenant General Henry Clinton, 1730–1795*
    Library of Congress, Prints and Photographs Division, LC-USZ62-53580

6. *George Washington*
    Artist: James Peale
    Engraver: John Sartain
    1840
    Library of Congress, Prints and Photographs Division, LC-USZ62-113388

7. *Richard Lord Viscount Howe, rear admiral of the white and commander in chief of the fleet in N. America*
    1780
    Library of Congress, Prints and Photographs Division, LC-USZ62-45254

8. *Marie Joseph Paul Yves Roch Gilbert du Motier, Marquis de Lafayette, 1757–1834. At the Battle of the Brandywine, binding up the wound in his leg*
    Library of Congress, Prints and Photographs Division, LC-USZ62-55024

9. *Count de Grasse, the French admiral, resigning his sword to Admiral Rodney, after being defeated by that gallant commander in the West Indies, on April 12th, 1782*
    Library of Congress, Prints and Photographs Division, LC-USZ62-45213

10. *Charles Gravier comte de Vergennes—conseiller d'Etat ordinaire, ministre et secretaire d'Etat et chef du conseil royal des finances*
    Artists: Vincenzio Vangelisti and Antoine-François Callet
    Between 1774 and 1789
    Library of Congress, Prints and Publications Division, LC-USZ62-45183

11. *"Evacuation Day" and Washington's triumphal entry in New York City, Nov. 25, 183*
    Artists: Edmund P. Restein and Ludwig Restein
    1879
    Library of Congress, Prints and Photographs Division, LC-USZ62-3915

Index